MW01101048

CONTENTS

TRAVEL & LEISURE

New York

by Julie L. Belcove

Macmillan • USA

Schuster, Inc.

MACMILLAN is a registered trademark of Macmillan, Inc.

ISBN 0-02-860691-4
ISSN 1088-4831

Editor: Margaret Bowen
Map Editor: Doug Stallings
Design by Amy Peppler Adam—designLab, Seattle
Digital Cartography by Ortelius Design
Illustrations on pages 89, 115, 122, 123, 125, 126, 131, 136,
140, 145, 150, 156, 157, 158, 162, 164, 167, and 172 by
Ray Skibinski.

SPECIAL SALES
Bulk purchases (10+ copies) of Frommer's and selected
Macmillan travel guides are available to corporations,
organizations, institutions, and charities at special discounts,
and can be customized to suit individual needs. For more
information write to Special Sales, Macmillan General
Reference, 1633 Broadway, New York, NY 10019.

Manufactured in Singapore

LIST OF MAPS

About the Author

A resident of New York City since 1993, **Julie L. Belcove** is Associate Editor of *W* magazine. She is also the author of *Frommer's Chicago*.

Acknowledgments

I wish to express my gratitude to Gabriel Dorman, a most able research assistant without whom this book would not have been completed. My appreciation goes to Herbert Bailey Livesey for his previous edition. Thanks are also due to my understanding friends and peerless family: Merle and Fred Belcove, Ira Belcove, and Amy, Mark, and Rachel Bernstein.

An Additional Note

Please be advised that travel information is subject to change at any time—and this is especially true of prices. We therefore suggest that you write or call ahead for confirmation when making your travel plans. The author, editor, and publisher cannot be held responsible for the experiences of readers while traveling. Your safety is important to us, however, so we encourage you to stay alert and be aware of your surroundings. Keep a close eye on cameras, purses, and wallets, all favorite targets of thieves and pickpockets.

NEW YORK . . .
RAINBOW ON THE
HUDSON

NEW YORK. NO OTHER CITY PROVOKES SUCH ADORA-
tion and abhorrence, often at the same time,
in the same individual. Few words applied to it can be
dismissed as hyperbole. It is a place of exhilarating,
numbing, horrifying, glorious excess.

Once you plunge into the street canyons, warring
stimuli battle for attention. The noise of endless construction and millions of lurching vehicles is trapped
between the rearing phalanxes of stone and steel and
glass. In winter, clouds of steam billow from manholes
as if from an inferno just below. Rivers of people press
forward, set on apparently urgent tasks. Traffic jerks and
clogs along congested arteries. The senses stagger under this continual bombardment.

Yet, believe it or not, New York has its quiet places
too. Side streets end in shaded cul-de-sacs, and more
than 50 museums muffle the clamor beyond their thick
walls. The city also boasts nearly 37,000 acres of parks,
the most important of which is Central Park, in the
heart of Manhattan. Two Monacos could be contained
within its borders, with room left over.

New York covers nearly 300 square miles and has a
population of more than 7.3 million—some 2.6 million, or almost one in three, born in another country.
New arrivals tend to gather together and take care of
one another, entering the vocations of those who pre-
cede them. Hence the high proportions of former Is-
raelis who own limousine companies, Koreans who are
greengrocers, Indians who run service stations, Greeks
who have coffee shops.

The reputation New Yorkers have earned for rudeness and pugnacity is not without foundation. Yet beneath their often brusque exterior lies an enviable openness to new experiences and relationships. There is no fad, art form, lifestyle, or ideology that they will not sample, or at least tolerate. Outside of working hours—and, in a 24-hour city, that means any time—they can be seen jogging, cycling, flipping Frisbees, roller- or ice-skating, dancing in nightclubs, demonstrating at the United Nations, taking the sun on the Hudson piers, or watching it set from Riverside Park. Of all the surprises of a first visit to this city, one of the most agreeable can be New Yorkers themselves.

> **There are two million interesting people in New York—and only 78 in Los Angeles.**
>
> —*Neil Simon*

City of Villages

Water-girt New York is comprised of 5 distinct divisions called boroughs, only one of which—The Bronx—is situated on the North American continent. The island of Manhattan is, of course, the central borough. Brooklyn (largest in population) and Queens (largest in area) take up the western tip of Long Island, which itself stretches 125 miles east into the Atlantic Ocean. Staten Island, to the south of its sisters, snuggles up to New Jersey.

When approached from the east through the outlying industrial dross, the famous Manhattan skyline appears diminutive. At the southern tip of the island, the twin pillars of the World Trade Center dominate the concrete spires and glass slabs of the Financial District.

Downtown Skyline

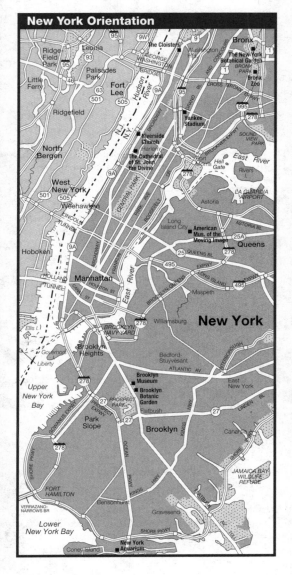

New York Orientation

The profile then dips to the lower heights of converted warehouses (loft buildings) and tenements, lifting gradually once more to Midtown and the peaks of the instantly recognizable Empire State and Chrysler buildings. After another 2 miles, the skyline dips again, nearly meeting the rising ground that continues for another

6 miles, terminating at the lip of the inky tidal course known as the Spuyten Duyvil.

New York's Neighborhoods
Manhattan

Manhattan is 12 miles long from north to south and about 3 miles across at its widest point. If you can count and know your east from your west, you can find your way easily around most of the island. Remember that streets run east and west and are numbered consecutively. Avenues run north and south. Streets and avenues usually bisect one another at right angles. Unfortunately, this doesn't apply to neighborhoods in Lower Manhattan—like Wall Street, Chinatown, SoHo, TriBeCa, and the Village—since they sprang up before engineers devised this grid scheme; the maps in the back of this guide will help when you explore these areas. In Manhattan, the roll of history and fashion flows northward, for development started with a Dutch settlement at the southern tip and spread in the only direction available.

Financial District

The southern end of Manhattan has long shuddered beneath the thrusting monoliths of international commerce. The world eavesdrops on every whisper at the Stock Exchange, and conglomerates eye one another from their steel and concrete towers. A few public buildings survive from the late Colonial and early Federalist periods—fragments of history among the modern towers of concrete and glass. The area offers captivating vistas of New York's rivers and harbor as well as the Statue of Liberty and Ellis Island. There's also nautical history and shopping at South Street Seaport (see "Walk 1" in "Sights and Attractions").

Until recently, there were few hotels and first-class restaurants in this area. That's changing, with 3 large hotels now open and several good-to-excellent new restaurants. The city is even attempting to make the Wall Street environs an attractive residential neighborhood.

Chinatown

Chinatown is no longer confined to the 8 square blocks bordered by The Bowery and Mulberry, Worth, and Canal streets. In recent years, it has all but swallowed up Little Italy, to the north. The core of the neighborhood is gratifyingly exotic, the air heavy with dialects and enticing aromas. In the shops along Mott Street, Canal Street, and East Broadway you'll find unusual foodstuffs, herbal medicines, and collectibles that you'd think only a trip to Hong Kong or Shanghai could net.

Restaurants close earlier than you might think, and it can be desolate after about 9pm. If you visit during the day or in the early evening, be prepared to fight your way through crowds on the sidewalks.

Little Italy

Bounded on the west by Lafayette Street, and on the north and south by Houston and Canal streets, the neighborhood is shrinking, but still vigorous.

Sicilian and Neapolitan immigrants settled in this area in 1880 to 1925, and this warren of narrow streets and stunted tenements retains the flavor of the Old Country. Gray-haired women, dressed in black, clutch string bags as they move from fish store to bakery while men play bocce or sip espresso in murky coffeehouses. Authentic restaurants abound. The **Festa di San Gennaro** in September booms with brass bands and sizzles with booth after booth of sausage and calzone. (See "Calendar of Events" in "Basics.")

Lower East Side

Immigrants of every race and nationality have made this shabby tenement district east of The Bowery and north of Canal Street their first stopover, but its identity for many decades was Eastern European Jewish. Millions of indigent Slavs, Poles, Russians, and Lithuanians poured into these mean streets from 1870. They lived in 5-story buildings without plumbing, 2 or 3 families to an apartment, creating a population density surpassing that of Calcutta. They were pushcart peddlers, or they labored in the sweatshops of the garment trade. Yiddish was the prevailing tongue, and at one time the population supported 500 synagogues.

African-Americans and Hispanics now dominate, but a taste of that former era—and some remarkable shopping bargains—can be had along Orchard Street. On Sunday, the 3 blocks between Delancey Street and East Houston Street are the liveliest on the Lower East Side, so jammed with shoppers, residents, and merchants that cars are banned. Designer items can be found at prices 20% to 50% below retail. In addition, look for discount kitchenware, lighting, and home furnishing stores at the southern end of the Bowery.

Parts of the neighborhood can be quite desolate, especially at night. But if you keep your wits about you, you'll discover an emerging scene of cutting-edge clubs and hipper-than-thou bars, led by the venerable (CBGB's) as well as the trendy (Bowery Bar).

SoHo

SoHo, "South of Houston Street," is bounded by Houston Street, Canal Street, Sullivan Street, and Broadway.

Three decades ago, SoHo was a dreary industrial district with pot-holed streets of worn Belgian blocks. In the early 1960s, artists of the New York School, seeking ever-larger work space, discovered the lofts and moved in on the cheap—and illegally, according to zoning laws. By 1970, municipal authorities no longer could ignore the fact that their ordinances were being violated, and simply changed them. SoHo went from cultural workplace to artistic community to general free-for-all in just a few years. Rents have skyrocketed, leaving struggling artists to find more affordable space and yuppies to fight over the best properties.

Those one-time warehouses now house art galleries, restaurants, gourmet food emporiums, and even a branch of the Guggenheim Museum. Eclectic boutiques sell yuppie fashions and home furnishings, prints, crafts, and antiques.

Admire the cast-iron architecture for which the neighborhood is known. These factory buildings are noted for their gargoyles, Corinthian columns, and sculptural detail that reflect Venetian, Romanesque, and French Second Empire influences.

TriBeCa

Just south of Soho is the TRIangle BElow CAnal Street, roughly bounded by West Broadway to the east, the Hudson River to the west, and Canal Street in the north.

Many artists, displaced by SoHo landlords and speculators who saw the profits to be realized in sales to nonartists with regular incomes, moved a few blocks south and west to TriBeCa. Inevitably, the SoHo phenomenon has begun to assert itself, with bars, restaurants, and funky nightclubs. It has some successful art galleries too, but doesn't yet challenge SoHo's superiority in that regard.

Greenwich Village

Washington Square is the focal point of the neighborhood, which is usually delineated by Houston Street, 14th Street, 4th Avenue, and the Hudson River (see

"Walk 2" in "Sights and Attractions"). New York University occupies buildings north, east, and south of Washington Square.

After a period as an upper–middle-class suburb, the Village became an artist's enclave. Henry James, Winslow Homer, Edgar Allan Poe and, later, Edna St. Vincent Millay, Eugene O'Neill, and Edward Hopper were among the luminaries who lived here, and the Village became America's Left Bank. The artists and writers are largely working elsewhere today (starving creative types can't afford to live here anymore). The Village still is, however, the spiritual center of the city's gay and lesbian community, especially around Sheridan Square and Christopher Street. Today, elegant brownstones and carriage-house mews alternate with slovenly commercial streets. The West Village is one of the most expensive residential districts in Manhattan. Restaurants here and in SoHo blanket the entire field of price and achievement.

East Village

The funky fringe of the city's arts and nightlife scene, this area extends from Broadway to First Avenue and beyond to Avenues A, B, C, and D. The northern border is 14th Street and the southern is Houston. Diversity is the East Village's defining characteristic; street life here is rather scruffy and chaotic. The hippies of the 1960s have been replaced by anachists, drug dealers, and yuppies who can't yet afford uptown rents. Gentrification notwithstanding, the East Village remains the city's last bastion of bohemianism.

Exploring here is not for the weak of heart. The action centers around St. Mark's Place, which has become a hyperkinetic street bazaar. Cheap-chic restaurants abound, as well as more authentic ethnic eateries, including the Second Avenue Deli, assorted Ukrainian diners, and a whole stretch known as Little India along East 6th Street.

Chelsea

Chelsea runs from 14th Street to 23rd Street, and 7th Avenue to the Hudson River.

Spotty gentrification has taken place of late; the gay and lesbian community has been migrating from Greenwich Village over the last few years. The area is brimming with antique stores, a sports and entertainment complex at the piers (see "Staying Active"), music pubs, and nightclubs chic enough to entice uptowners into the long taxi ride. The West 20s, along

Sixth Avenue, contains the Flower Market and a number of popular weekend flea markets between 24th and 27th streets. Below 23rd Street, mass-market discounters like Filene's Basement and Barnes & Noble have moved in to create a bustling new shopping area. Art galleries and studios continue to open along Tenth Avenue in West Chelsea.

Flatiron District

Bounded by 7th Avenue and Broadway from 23rd to 14th streets, this former light industry area has changed its face radically in recent years. The renaissance of this most recent of reemergent neighborhoods in lower Manhattan can be credited in large measure to the book publishers and modeling and advertising agencies that began moving down here from Madison Avenue in the 1970s. More space and lower rents were the appeal, and the movement alerted savvy entrepreneurs, who have opened a plethora of shops, restaurants and nightspots. Among the attractions are the four-times-a-week farmer's market in revamped Union Square, the **Flatiron Building,** and such hot eateries as **Flowers** and the **Union Square Café** (see "Dining").

Garment Center

Between breakfast and dinner, rag traders and garment workers pour through the streets of this scruffy district along 7th Avenue between 34th and 40th streets, dodging handcarts, gulping coffee from paper containers, grabbing lapels, rushing to appointments, making deals. The fashions they produce sometimes rival the best of Paris and Milan—or end up in your local Wal-Mart. It's not a neighborhood for tourists and is deserted at night.

Gramercy Park & Murray Hill

East of Park Avenue and south of 43rd Street are the contiguous neighborhoods of Gramercy Park and Murray Hill, where pockets of 19thC elegance persist. Quiet and relatively small hotels provide alternatives to the flashy behemoths farther north, and restaurants and nightspots offer fair value without sacrificing elbow room.

Gramercy Park is a small community forever battling the dreary commercial encroachments nibbling at its edges. These few square blocks evoke 19thC residential elegance as no other area in Manhattan. The focal point is the rectangular park from which the district takes its name. The park is enclosed by a high fence, and only people living in the surrounding houses have keys to the gate. President Theodore Roosevelt lived nearby. Gramercy Park is part of an official Historic District, a designation that has been awarded by the city's Landmarks Preservation Commission.

Midtown West

This area, from 42nd Street to 59th Street and Fifth Avenue to the Hudson River, is perhaps most notable for its theaters, hotels, and office buildings. Most of the city's major hotels, theaters, shops, and world-class restaurants are within this and Midtown East's elastic boundaries.

The concentration of corporate headquarters, foreign consulates, and publishing and advertising firms brings in streams of businesspeople and diplomats. The crowds are thick, and rooms and meals are costly.

Some of the most exciting attractions are the **Museum of Modern Art,** the **Empire State Building,** and **Rockefeller Center.** And, of course, the lights are bright in the fabled Broadway theater district.

THEATRE DISTRICT   Broadway is either the city's longest avenue or a synonym for the theatrical district through which it passes on its diagonal slash through midtown. Times Square is essentially the intersection of that famous street and 7th Avenue.

Within the area bounded by 40th Street, 55th Street, 6th Avenue, and 8th Avenue are many large movie houses and most of the major theaters. It's a crowded, noisy, hectic neighborhood. On New Year's Eve, this area is packed shoulder-to-shoulder with revelers, more than 100,000 strong.

Times Square is undergoing a major facelift, with Disney and MTV entertainment complexes set to open soon right on 42nd Street. However, between 7th and 8th avenues, 42nd Street remains seedy. Avoid it, and the northerly stretch of 8th Avenue it joins, but don't be deterred from seeing a show on the streets nearby.

The biggest changes are happening on 57th Street, where the Walt Disney Store, the Harley-Davidson Cafe, the Jekyll & Hyde Club, the Motown Cafe, and Steven Spielberg's upcoming Dive! restaurant have joined Planet Hollywood, the Hard Rock Cafe, and others to bring a touch of mass appeal to this once-exclusive stretch of boutiques and galleries. Lots of locals are grumbling about the changes, but these places clearly have their fans—visitors line up down the block to get into them.

Midtown East

This area, from 42nd Street to 59th Street and Fifth Avenue to the East River, contains a disproportionate share of the attractions for which New York is known, including the **United Nations Headquarters, St. Patrick's Cathedral, Grand Central Terminal,** and those exemplars of the International Style in architecture, **Lever House** and the **Seagram Building.** Shoppers are inexorably drawn toward the fabled luxury emporia of 5th Avenue and 57th Street.

TURTLE BAY   Diplomats, writers, and assorted celebrities make their homes in this neighborhood bordering the East River at midtown. The district, bounded by 3rd Avenue and 53rd and 43rd streets, was home to stockyards and tenements crowded with immigrants until after World War I. The development of the Turtle Bay Gardens residential complex, now an official landmark, began the ascent back to the respectability it enjoyed in the post-Revolution period. Its best-known occupant is the **United Nations,** built on land donated by John D. Rockefeller, Jr.

Upper East Side

From 5th Avenue to the East River and from 59th Street to 92nd Street, this chic precinct harbors most of the city's major museums, as well as resident millionaires, and the most exclusive shops. Tree-shaded cross streets near 5th Avenue are lined with attractive town houses, the owners of which have succeeded in fending off the blandishments of developers. Near the river are the luxury enclaves of **Beekman Place** and **Sutton Place.** On the low-numbered avenues (1st, 2nd, 3rd), young professionals yet to make their first millions live in densely populated apartment towers. Closer to the park, beautiful people swirl in a fickle flow from this month's bistro to the bar-of-the-moment and meet each other in lines for the latest movie.

YORKVILLE   Germans were among the earliest large immigrant groups of the 19thC, and many settled in this Upper East Side district centering on 86th Street. They assimilated speedily and for the most part had dispersed by the 1930s. Traces of their occupation remain, with a *bierstube* or two, several bakery-coffee houses, and some dark-paneled restaurants specializing in wienerschnitzel and sauerbraten. Prodigals return for the Steuben Day parade in mid-September.

Upper West Side

Of all the recently resurgent neighborhoods, the Upper West Side most resists easy classification. It lacks the handy ethnic, social, or cultural identity of other districts. It's not as sleek as the Upper East Side, and it has large concentrations of low-income families; it has become a mecca for professionals, writers, and others who find the area and its people less superficial than across town. Chic boutiques stand beside seedy bodegas, and working-men's bars adjoin boisterous singles' hangouts. Wealthy residents tend to reside on Central Park West or Riverside Drive, while the blocks in between can fester.

The **Lincoln Center for the Performing Arts** and the **American Museum of Natural History** are the centerpieces. Important sights and institutions include the **American Museum of Natural History,** the **New York Historical Society,** the **Cathedral Church of St. John the Divine, Columbia University, General Grant National Memorial, Riverside Park,** and the city's grandest boulevard, Riverside Drive. To food-crazed New Yorkers, however, the destinations that require repeated ritualistic pilgrimages are the food shops **Zabar's, Fairway,** and **Citarella** (see "Food and Kitchenware" in "Shopping").

Harlem

Harlem stretches from river to river, from 96th to 165th Street, immediately to the north of the Upper East and Upper West sides. Spanish Harlem, called El Barrio by its Hispanic residents, is the subdivision from 5th Avenue to the East River and north to 125th Street. Remnants of Italian Harlem are found in the vicinity of the intersection of 116th Street and 2nd Avenue.

Despite its substandard housing, poverty, and attendant ills, Harlem boasts a number of important cultural institutions, especially the 4 specialized museums of **Audubon Terrace,** the **Museo del Barrio,** the **Schomburg Center for Research in Black Culture,** the restored **Apollo Theater,** and the **Studio Museum.** Architectural restorations of note include the Victorian cottage row of Sylvan Terrace near the **Morris-Jumel Mansion** and the 1890s' St. Nicholas Historic District, which is popularly known as Strivers' Row. The safest ways to see these are by taxi, chauffeured car, or as part of conducted tours such as those offered by Harlem, Your Way! (☎ 212/690-1687).

At the turn of the century, Harlem was a semirural district. Shortly before World War I, African Americans from the harshly segregationist South began migrating to the tenements that had begun encroaching on area farmland and summer homes. With them came jazz, and a number of lively music halls and nightclubs flourished. During the 1920s and early 1930s, whites from downtown engaged in the social ritual of dancing to jazz and drinking bathtub gin at such places as the Cotton Club (in which blacks worked and entertained but could not be patrons).

The Bronx

The only borough on the mainland, the Bronx was one of New York's first affluent suburbs; wealthy Manhattanites migrated north during the late 19thC to build majestic mansions with sprawling lawns. These days, the Bronx works hard to fight pervasive, negative stereotypes, owing to the crippling poverty and infrastructural decay found in several neighborhoods of the borough's southern part. Spend a full, enjoyable day at the **Bronx Zoo** and **New York Botanical Garden,** with a side trip to the **Van Cortlandt Mansion and Museum.** Up near Fordham University is imposing **Yankee Stadium,** the "house that [Babe] Ruth built."

Brooklyn

Had it resisted annexation in 1898, Brooklyn would now be the 4th largest city in the United States. It is still self-contained, with its own civic and cultural centers, concert halls, downtown shopping district, beaches, colleges, and residential neighborhoods both elite and prosaic. Among its inducements are the **Brooklyn Museum, New York Aquarium, Brooklyn Heights,** and the promenade that overlooks an extraordinary panorama of the Manhattan skyline from the **Statue of Liberty** to the **Empire State Building.**

Brooklyn Heights

Brooklyn Heights is bounded by the East River, Fulton Street, Court Street, and Atlantic Avenue. In 1646, a handful of Dutch families decided to give official status to their settlement on the bluffs overlooking the juncture of the Hudson and East rivers and the larger village at the toe of Manhattan Island. They called their new home *Breuckelen* (broken land). The establishment of a regular steam ferry service in 1820 transformed the rural community into a suburb. Terraced row houses and mansions competed for harbor views; a substantial number persisted into the 20thC, but by the 1950s, Brooklyn Heights was in decline.

A plan to ram a highway through the neighbohood was narrowly averted, and the resulting community spirit signaled its renaissance. It's designated a historic district, and is the most desirable residential enclave in the borough.

Queens

Queens has become the primary home of New York's immigrant population during the last part of the 20thC. Largely residential, the borough is a veritable United Nations, with scores of neighborhood ethnic delegations: Flushing is overwhelmingly Chinese and Korean; Astoria is predominantly Greek. Perhaps not surprisingly, you'll find some of the city's best, and cheapest, restaurants here. Queens has both La Guardia and JFK airports, making it New York's transportation hub. Sports fans take the subway to the **Aqueduct Racetrack** for thoroughbred racing, to **Shea Stadium** for Mets baseball games, and, in late August, to the **USTA National Tennis Center** for the U.S. Open. (See "Spectator Sports A to Z" in "Staying Active.")

Staten Island

Despite the 1964 completion of the **Verrazano Narrows Bridge,** which connects Staten Island with Brooklyn, this borough remains somewhat isolated from the others (in 1990, residents even held a referendum recommending secession from the city). Those who take the time to look around, however, will discover golf courses, beaches, country clubs, even a wildlife refuge. Among the pockets of bucolic solitude Richmondtown Restoration, a village of Colonial and 19thC homes and shops; Snug Harbor Cultural Center, a living museum of buildings in every 19thC style; and the **Jacques Marchais Museum of Tibetan Art,** which has a Buddhist altar on its grounds. And of course, the **Staten Island Ferry**, still a true New York bargain at 50¢ per round trip, provides stunning views of lower Manhattan and Lady Liberty.

DINING

SCOTT TUROW, THE AUTHOR OF *PRESUMED INNOCENT*, once said, "New York is the only city where one week the hot new restaurant will have people standing in the cold waiting to get in and 3 months later will be closed." When it comes to food, New Yorkers can be notoriously fickle and demanding. The restaurant-of-the-moment as we go to print easily could have shuttered its doors by the time this guide hits the shelves. I have tried to focus on restaurants that have proved their consistency and staying power, but it's always wise to call ahead.

What kind of food should you sample in the Big Apple? Any and every kind. Manhattan has an estimated 15,000 restaurants—so satisfying a craving for, say, a juicy steak is no problem. That said, be daring. The city has eateries serving the cooking of most every ethnic group imaginable: Russian, Polish, Swiss, German, Hungarian, Korean, Thai, Indonesian, Indian, Afghan, Spanish, Greek, Caribbean, and Armenian, to name just a few. Chinese, Italian, and Mexican establishments abound (you can even find kosher Chinese). Some of the world's finest French restaurants, both nouvelle and haute, are located here. Several excellent kitchens now prepare what is referred to as New American cooking, in which accomplished chefs borrow from distinctive regional styles, such as Southern and Southwestern. Many of the most creative chefs in town, including Jean-Georges Vongerichten of Vong and JoJo, are developing a global, or fusion, cuisine, melding elements of Asian cooking with those of France and other cultures.

In recent years, New York restaurants have responded to patrons' new-found health concerns. Sauces are lighter and have less oil; vegetarian dishes are widely available, and meats are leaner. At the same time, nouvelle has given way to heartier cooking, or comfort food. Roast chicken and mashed potatoes are ubiquitous. Mashed potatoes, in fact, may be the most popular side dish going these days.

I list many of the best and most expensive restaurants and also a range of more affordable options. Some tips for the money-conscious: avoid top-ranked restaurants for dinner—go for lunch (or brunch) instead, when prices can drop as much as 40%. Prix fixe meals are almost always a bargain; and pretheater dinners, served in the early evening, are another way to savor the ambiance and cuisine of a great restaurant without getting indigestion from the bill. Budget options are plentiful. Stroll the streets of Chinatown, Little Italy, Greenwich Village, or the Upper West Side, and you'll stumble across restaurants with low prices and tasty fare.

I've also included a number of newer restaurants that appear strong enough to beat the odds against survival in a very tough business. The usual caveats still apply: even the hardiest performers stumble, through changes in management, departures of key personnel, or simple off days. Loyalists continue to exchange blows over the relative virtues of Sparks and The Palm, Le Bernardin and Le Cirque, all recommended here. No amount of arbitration will resolve the disputes.

What to Expect

New York waiters have an undeserved reputation for churlishness. Service can be lackadaisical, and individuals are sometimes sullen or patronizing, but in roughly the same proportion as in any large city. Inexperience and ineptitude are more often the complaints, for the field has a shortage of formally trained employees. Struggling MAWs—models-actors-whatevers—take their place. (That may be the next Tom Hanks or Winona Ryder grating your parmesan.)

Advance reservations are essential for "high-end" restaurants. Some places ask for a telephone number so that reservations can be confirmed on the day of the anticipated meal, some ask that the patron call back to confirm reservations by a certain hour. Despite such precautions, so many customers do not honor their reservations that restaurants are forced to overbook. Some restaurants book two complete sittings in a lunch period that comfortably accommodates only one. These practices can result in knots of people waiting at the door or in the bar, their appointed times ticking away.

You should also be aware that New York recently passed a strict no-smoking law, which all but eliminates smoking in most restaurants. There are exceptions— smoking is permitted in restaurants with less than 35 seats, and at those with separate, ventilated areas. Smoking is also allowed at an establishment's bar, as long as the bar is more than 6 feet away from the eating area. If a mid-meal puff is what you're after, you may be hard pressed to find an accommodating restaurant. Call ahead to check the restaurant's policy.

Cocktails, Wines & Other Drinks

Liquor consumption in America is at a 3-decade low. The hard-drinking business lunch is a thing of the past, but enjoying a predinner cocktail is not unusual.

Some drinks are favored for particular meals or foods—the Bloody Mary for brunch, and the margarita before Mexican or Latin meals. A glass of white wine, perhaps with a dash of cassis (kir) or soda water (spritzer), or mineral water with lime is often preferred to the harder liquors, especially at lunch. Dark liquors, such as bourbon and Scotch have become less popular. Although wines are still appropriate for most cuisines, beer is often preferred with Middle-European, Chinese, Mexican, and Indian meals.

Pretension or pragmatism or a little of both, no doubt, made New Yorkers long reluctant to embrace the wines of California. In truth, European wines were substantially cheaper than the Cabernets and Zinfandels of the West, until recently, when currency fluctuations changed that. Now more than 70% of all wines consumed in the United States are from California. Labels to look for are Robert Mondavi, Sterling, Cakebread Cellars, Rutherford Hill, Kendall-Jackson, Duckhorn, Silver Oak Cellars, Sonoma-Cutrer, Jordan Vineyard, and Frog's Leap, among many others. Among the prominent reds are Cabernet Sauvignon, Petite Sirah, Pinot Noir and Zinfandel; favored whites are Chardonnay, Chenin Blanc, Johannisberg Riesling, and Sauvignon Blanc. Weather is a factor in California wines, but its influence is less pronounced than in Europe.

New York State is a distant second in production, accounting for only 10% of domestic consumption. Its Finger Lakes and Hudson Valley vineyards are best known for sparkling wines, but a number of vintners create worthy blends of offbeat varietals, and wineries recently established on eastern Long Island are doing well. Look for Bridgehampton, Clinton, Benmarl, and Bully Hill.

Beers are often served at glacial temperatures, and imported brands are sold everywhere, in greatest profusion at pub-style restaurants. And following what has become a national trend, microbreweries have sprung up all over town. Tap water is excellent, but at the trendier restaurants you'll see a bottle of sparkling water on almost every table.

Prices

In this chapter, restaurants are divided into 5 price categories. These price ranges include appetizer, main course, and dessert for 1 person for dinner. They do not include beverage, tax, or tip. The following abbreviations are used for credit cards: AE = American Express; CB = Carte Blanche; DC = Diners Club; DISC = Discover; MC = MasterCard; V = Visa.

Price Chart	
$	= Less than $20
$$	= $20–$30
$$$	= $31–$40
$$$$	= $41–$50
$$$$$	= More than $50

Critic's Choice

At press time, two of New York's finest were conspicuous in their absence. Bouley, in Tribeca, closed in June of 1996 to move to a new space in the neighborhood; Chef/owner David Bouley plans to reopen in the fall of 1997. Similarly, the Russian Tea Room shut down for extensive renovations, but should be open by spring 1997—so check before you go. Superlatives are tough when it comes to dining in New York. But everyone has favorites, and here are some of mine. For an intimate, romantic restaurant, try **Café des Artistes** or **Sign of the Dove.** The trendiest spots in town change spontaneously, but chances are that **Gramercy Tavern, Match,** and **Tribeca Grill** will have beautiful people

continues

gathered at the tables. If you've come to gawk at the rich and powerful, reserve a table at the **Four Seasons, 21 Club,** or **Le Bernardin.** Ladies who lunch, on the other hand, prefer **Le Cirque** and **Mortimer's.** Folks looking for exquisite cuisine, pure and simple, can't go wrong at **Lutèce, Lespinasse,** or **Montrachet.**

For ethnic cuisine, try **Monsoon** or **Nha Trang** for Vietnamese, **Yama** for sushi, **Pamir** for Afghan, **Dawat** for Indian, and **Chin Chin** for Chinese. **Sarabeth's** and **Sylvia's** are two local favorites for brunch, and John's generally gets the nod as the best pizzeria in town. The **Second Avenue Deli** is sure to provide you with an authentic New York experience. And if you have your tots in tow, the popular spots include **Hard Rock Café, Serendipity 3,** and **EJ's Luncheonette.**

Restaurants by Neighborhood

Lower Manhattan (Below Canal St.)

Alison on Dominick Street. **$$$$**
Bridge Cafe. **$$**
Chanterelle. **$$$$$**
Golden Unicorn. **$$**
Hudson River Club. **$$$$$**
★ Montrachet. **$$$$**
Nha Trang. **$**
Nice. **$$**
★ Nobu. **$$$$$**
Odeon. **$$**
Thailand. **$$**
Tribeca Grill. **$$$**
Windows on the World. **$$$$**

SoHo/Greenwich Village (Canal St.–13th St.)

L'École. **$$**
Gotham Bar and Grill. **$$$$**
Home. **$$**
Jane Street Seafood Café. **$$**
John's Pizzeria. **$**
Louisiana. **$$$**
Lucky Cheng's. **$$**
Match. **$$$**
Miracle Grill. **$$**
Monte's. **$$**
Il Mulino. **$$$**
One if by Land, Two if by Sea. **$$$$$**
Second Avenue Deli. **$**
T Salon. **$$**
Time Café/Fez. **$$**

Chelsea/Garment District (W. 14th St.– W. 40th St.)

Eighteenth & Eighth. **$$**
Flowers. **$$$**
Lola. **$$$**
Periyali. **$$$**
Woo Chon. **$$$**

Gramercy Park/Murray Hill (E. 14th St.– E. 42nd St.)

Aja. **$$$$**
Cafe Beulah. **$$$**
Coffee Shop/World Room. **$$**
C.T. **$$$$$**
★ Gramercy Tavern. **$$$$$**
Mesa Grill. **$$$$**
Park Bistro. **$$$**
★ Sonia Rose. **$$$**
★★ Union Square Cafe. **$$$**
Yama. **$$**

Midtown East (E. 43rd St.–E. 59th St.)

Akbar. **$$$**
Bice. **$$$$**
★ Chin Chin. **$$$**
Dawat. **$$$**
★ Four Seasons. **$$$$$**
Hatsuhana. **$$**
★ Lespinasse. **$$$$$**
★★ Lutèce. **$$$$$**
★ March. **$$$$$**
★ Monkey Bar. **$$$$**
Oyster Bar and Restaurant. **$$$**
The Palm. **$$$**
Rosa Mexicano. **$$$**
Smith & Wollensky. **$$$$**
Solera. **$$$$**
Sparks Steak House. **$$$$**
Take-Sushi. **$$$$**
★★ Vong. **$$$$**
Zarela. **$$**

Midtown West (W. 43rd St.–W. 59th St.)

Aquavit. **$$$$$**
★ Le Bernardin. **$$$$$**
Broadway Grill. **$$**
Bryant Park Grill. **$$$**
Cabana Carioca. **$$**
Carnegie Delicatessen. **$$**
China Grill. **$$$$**
Cité. **$$$$**
La Côte Basque. **$$$$$**
★ 44 (Forty-Four). **$$$$**
★ Palio. **$$$$$**
Pétrossian. **$$$$**
★ Rainbow Room. **$$$$$**
★ Remi. **$$$$**
La Réserve. **$$$$**
The Sea Grill. **$$$$**
Siam Inn. **$$**
Tout va Bien. **$$$**
Trattoria Dell'Arte. **$$$$**
21 (Twenty-One) Club. **$$$$$**
Un Deux Trois. **$$$**
Virgil's Real BBQ. **$$**
Zen Palate. **$$**

Upper East Side (E. 60th St.–E. 96th St.)

★ Arcadia. **$$$$$**
Arizona 206 and Cafe. **$$$$**
★ Aureole. **$$$$$**
Café Crocodile. **$$**
★ Le Cirque. **$$$$$**
Contrapunto. **$$**
★ Daniel. **$$$$$**
Elaine's. **$$$**
JoJo. **$$$$**
mad.61. **$$$$**
Mortimer's. **$$$$**
Nino's. **$$$**
Pamir. **$$**
Serendipity 3. **$$/$$$**
Sign of the Dove. **$$$$$**

Upper West Side (W. 60th St.–W. 96th St.)

★ Café des Artistes. **$$$$$**
Café Luxembourg. **$$$**
Fishin Eddie. **$$**
Iridium. **$$$**
Isabella's. **$$$**
★ Lenge. **$$$**
Mad Fish. **$$$$**
Merchant's. **$$**
★ Monsoon. **$**
The Saloon. **$$**
The Shark Bar. **$$**
★ Shun Lee. **$$$**
Tavern on the Green. **$$$**
Vince & Eddie's. **$$$**

Upper Manhattan

Sylvia's. **$**

Brooklyn

Patsy's Pizzeria. **$**
Peter Luger. **$$$$$**
River Café. **$$$$**

Restaurants by Cuisine

Afghan

Pamir. **$$**

American

★ Arcadia. **$$$$$**
★ Aureole. **$$$$$**
Eighteenth & Eighth. **$$**
★ Gramercy Tavern. **$$$$$**
Home. **$$**

Merchant's. **$$**
Serendipity 3. **$$/$$$**
T Salon. **$$**
21 (Twenty-One). **$$$$$**

American/International
Cite. **$$$$$**
One if by Land, Two if by Sea.
$$$$$
Tavern on the Green. **$$$**

Asian
★★ Vong. **$$$$**
Zen Palate. **$$**

Asian Fusion
Aja. **$$$$**
China Grill. **$$$$**
Lucky Cheng's. **$$**
Match. **$$$**

Barbecue
Virgil's Real BBQ. **$$**

Brazilian
Cabana Carioca. **$$**
Coffee Shop/World Room.
$$

Caribbean
Lola. **$$$**

Chinese
★ Chin Chin. **$$$**
Golden Unicorn. **$$**
Nice. **$$**
★ Shun Lee. **$$$**

Creole/Cajun
Louisiana. **$$$**

Eclectic American
Bridge Café. **$$**
Broadway Grill. **$$**
Bryant Park Grill. **$$$**
Fishin Eddie. **$$**
Flowers. **$$$**
★ 44 (Forty-four). **$$$$**
Gotham Bar and Grill. **$$$$$**
Hudson River Club. **$$$$$**
Iridium. **$$$**
Isabella's. **$$$**
★ March. **$$$$$**
Odeon. **$$**
River Café. **$$$$**
The Saloon. **$$**
Sign of the Dove. **$$$$$**

Time Café/Fez. **$$**
Tribeca Grill. **$$$**
Vince & Eddie's. **$$$**

French
Alison on Dominick Street.
$$$$
Chanterelle. **$$$$$**
La Côte Basque. **$$$$$**
★ Daniel. **$$$$$**
L'Ecole. **$$**
JoJo. **$$$$**
★★ Lutèce. **$$$$$**
★ Montrachet. **$$$$**
Park Bistro. **$$$**
La Réserve. **$$$$**
★ Sonia Rose. **$$$**
Tout va Bien. **$$$**
Un Deux Trois. **$$$**

French/Asian
★ Lespinasse. **$$$$$**

French/Italian
Le Cirque. **$$$$$**
★★ Union Square Café.
$$$

French/Latin Fusion
C.T. **$$$$$**

French/Mediterranean
Café Crocodile. **$$**

Greek/Mediterranean
Nino's. **$$$**
Periyali. **$$$**

Indian
Akbar. **$$$**
Dawat. **$$$**

International
★ Café des Artistes. **$$$$$**
Café Luxembourg. **$$$**
★ Four Seasons. **$$$$$**
★ Monkey Bar. **$$$$**
Mortimer's. **$$$$**
Pétrossian. **$$$$**
★ Rainbow Room. **$$$$$**
Windows on the World.
$$$$

Italian
Bice. **$$$$**
Contrapunto. **$$**
Elaine's. **$$$**

mad.61. **$$$$**
Monte's. **$$**
Il Mulino. **$$$**
★ Palio. **$$$$$**
★ Remi. **$$$$**
Trattoria Dell'Arte. **$$$$**

Japanese
Hatsuhana. **$$**
★ Lenge. **$$$**
★ Nobu. **$$$$$**
Take-Sushi. **$$$$**
Yama. **$$**

Jewish
Carnegie Delicatessen. **$$**
Second Avenue Deli. **$**

Korean
Woo Chon. **$$$**

Mexican
Rosa Mexicano. **$$$**
Zarela. **$$**

Pizza
John's Pizzeria. **$**
Patsy's Pizzeria. **$**

Scandinavian
Aquavit. **$$$$$**

Seafood
★ Le Bernardin. **$$$$$**
Jane Street Seafood Café. **$$**

Mad Fish. **$$$$**
Oyster Bar and Restaurant.
$$$
Sea Grill. **$$$$**

Southern/Soul Food
Café Beulah. **$$$**
Shark Bar. **$$**
Sylvia's. **$**

Southwestern
Arizona 206 and Café.
$$$$
Mesa Grill. **$$$$**
Miracle Grill. **$$**

Spanish
Solera. **$$$$**

Steakhouse
The Palm. **$$$$**
Peter Luger. **$$$$$**
Smith & Wollensky.
$$$$
Sparks Steak House.
$$$$

Thai
Siam Inn. **$$**
Thailand. **$$**

Vietnamese
★ Monsoon. **$**
Nha Trang. **$**

New York's Restaurants A to Z

Aja
937 Broadway (at 22nd St.).
☎ 212/473-8388. AE, MC, V.
Reservations recommended.
Closed: Sat lunch, Sun. Subway:
N, R, 4, 5, 6 to 23rd St. ASIAN
FUSION. **$$$$**.
At Aja, dense tropical plants
arch over diners like a rain
forest canopy; dark woods, low
lighting, and a pressed-tin
ceiling convey an exotic feel.
Chef Gary Robins puts a flashy
spin on a cuisine that is equal
parts Thai, Chinese, Indian,
and Japanese: Steamed lobster
is spiked with a zesty penang
curry; the beef tenderloin is
offset by a chutney made with

roasted red chilies. The bar,
furnished with comfy sofas
and eclectic antiques, opens
onto the street when the
weather gets warm—a place to
see and be seen for Flatiron-
District regulars.

Akbar
475 Park Ave. (57th St.). ☎ 212/
838-1717. AE, CB, MC, V.
Reservations advised. Wheelchair
accessible. Closed: Sat lunch;
Sun lunch. Subway: 4, 5, 6 to
59th St.; N, R to Lexington Ave.
INDIAN. **$$$**.
Considering its high-rent
location, Akbar's use of space is
uncommonly generous. The

Midtown Dining

same can be said of the prices, especially for the so-called business lunch, offered instead of the midday buffet that is standard at other Indian restaurants. The Northern mughlai cooking is more refined than its Southern Indian counterpart. Crimson tandoori chicken, fish tikka, biriyani, prawn kabob, and fiery lamb vindaloo are all satisfying, and several vegetarian dishes of note are on the menu. Service is bored but attentive; recorded sitar music plinks unobtrusively away. Most men wear jackets and ties, but neither is required. A second branch (256 E. 49th St. ☎ 212/755-9100) is within easy walking distance.

Alison on Dominick Street

38 Dominick St. (bet. Varick and Hudson sts.). ☎ 212/727-1188. AE, DC, MC, V. Reservations recommended. Open for dinner daily. Subway: 1,9 to Canal St. FRENCH. **$$$$**.

This soothingly romantic restaurant, in an unlikely location on the industrial edge of Soho, is an oasis of subtle sophistication amid the downtown buzz. The oversized banquettes in the strategically designed room make each table feel like it's in its own private universe. The seasonal menu is just as pleasing: It includes such sophisticated comfort fare as a creamless asparagus soup with fresh herbs, lobster, and sorrel mushrooms; roasted quail salad with onion confit and herbs; and Muscovy duck in plum red wine sauce. The service is gracious and attentive.

Aquavit

13 W. 54th St. (bet. 5th and 6th aves.). ☎ 212/807-7311. AE, CB, MC, V. Reservations advised. Jacket and tie suggested. Closed: Sat lunch; Sun. Subway: E, F to 5th Ave./53rd St. SCANDINAVIAN. **$$$$$** dining room; **$$$** cafe.

This bright and saucy place has filled a vacancy with the only authentic Scandinavian cuisine in Manhattan. It's located behind the Museum of Modern Art and below an imposing Beaux Arts building, once owned by Nelson Rockefeller and now housing a private bank. Aquavit, the Scandinavian firewater, is served ice-cold, poured to the brim of stemmed glasses. The usual chaser is beer. At lunch-time only, those intricate open-faced sandwiches (smørrebrød) are available, evoking fond memories of Copenhagen's Tivoli. Snacks and light meals include gravlax with mustard sauce and dill, a smörgåsbord plate of herring, bleak roe, liver pâté and *vasterbotten* cheese, and salmon terrine. Downstairs, complete dinners might include monkfish with saffron, snow grouse or loin of venison. The menu changes frequently. Fixed price lunches in the upstairs cafe are a relative bargain for this level of quality.

★ Arcadia

21 E. 62nd St. (bet. Madison and 5th aves.). ☎ 212/223-2900. AE, MC, V. Reservations required. Closed: Sun. Subway: N, R to 5th Ave./60th St. AMERICAN. **$$$$$**.

Anne Rosenzweig ascended rapidly into the pantheon of celebrity chefs at this, her compact and innovative Upper East Side showcase. The menu is avowedly New American—with such delectables as a warm portobello mushroom and goat cheese salad, and a caramelized loin of tuna with cucumber ragout and papaya/corn fritters. At dinner, Arcadia offers a $29.95 fixed-price 3-course meal for a pretheater 6pm seating. In warm weather, the front opens, allowing 4 sidewalk tables. In the relatively larger room in back, many a table is arranged so that a party of two sits side by side rather than facing one another, a design I find less than conducive to good conversation. But perhaps many patrons prefer people-watching to talking.

Arizona 206 and Cafe

206 E. 60th St. (near 3rd Ave.). ☎ 212/838-0440. AE, DC, MC, V. Reservations advised. Open daily. Subway: 4, 5, 6 to 59th St.; N, R to Lexington Ave. SOUTHWESTERN. **$$$** cafe; **$$$$** restaurant.

When it arrived on the scene, the then-exotic Arizona 206 single-handedly created the lust for New Southwestern cooking. The inevitable copy-cats never did manage to duplicate the panache of this one. The handsome main rooms are straight out of picture-book Santa Fe. The great regional cuisine fires the palate without (necessarily) scorching the gullet. Essential ingredients of this cooking—cactus pears, poblano chilies, and such—are foreign to the shores of the Hudson, which partly explains the high prices in the main rooms. So, following a minitrend in the restaurant industry, Arizona 206 added a no-frills annex, offering fewer, less complex dishes at tariffs reduced by one-third to one-half. Not a bit of taste is lost. For proof, try the chicken quesadilla or the marinated shrimp salad. Both sections are open daily for lunch and dinner. Blooming-dale's is just a traffic light away.

★ Aureole

34 E. 61st St. (near Madison Ave.). ☎ 212/319-1660. AE, CB, MC, V. Reservations advised. Jacket required. Closed: Sat lunch; Sun. Subway: N, R to 5th Ave./60th St. AMERICAN. **$$$$$**.

One of the most eagerly anticipated restaurants when it opened, Aureole is nestled in 2 stories of a town house on the Upper East Side. The downstairs looks out on a garden; upstairs is an airy, more private loft. Conservative and understated, the dining rooms are outfitted with banquettes and wall reliefs of assorted animals—deer, swans, geese. Huge baskets of flowers provide the color. Service is amiable, and not the least bit pompous. As for Charles Palmer's food, self-described as "progressive American," it hits all the right notes. Appearing one night were yellowfin tuna carpaccio on a medley of mushrooms, partridge dumplings, sole wrapped in crisp-cooked potato and garnished with baby clams, and fresh-snipped thyme twigs. Desserts are "killers." The daunting chocolate plate, for one, has a dollop of chocolate mousse, a glob of chocolate Bavarian cream, rolled wands of striated white and dark chocolate, and a chocolate basket with a chocolate lid. No chocolate freak can resist it.

★ Le Bernardin

155 W. 51st St. (near 7th Ave.). ☎ 212/489-1515. AE, DC, MC, V. Reservations required. Closed: Sun. Subway: 1, 9 to 50th St.; N, R to 49th St. FRENCH SEAFOOD. **$$$$$**.

The grandfather of the original chef-proprietor was a fisherman, and his father was a fisherman who also ran a bistro. Continuing the evolution, Gilbert Le Coze changed the way chefs prepare fish. Fresh and simple. When Le Coze died in 1994, he left his kitchen in the very capable hands of Eric Ripert, who successfully defended Le Bernardin's coveted 4 stars in *The New York Times*. Provided the patron is not a fish-hater, the meal will delight. The event moves from raw fish, such as tuna tartare in a potato nest, to lightly cooked items, such as a "pizza" of broiled shrimp. The main courses roam from roast skate or monkfish to seared salmon to poach halibut. You'll feel like swimming by the time you leave. The room is large and somewhat clubby, but with plenty of fresh flowers to add warmth. The staff is friendly (when encouraged to be) and very professional. It will be no surprise that such munificence comes at a price—$42 for prix fixe lunch, $68 for dinner, each menu containing numerous $10 and $15 supplemental charges. Save a little by ordering wine by the glass—there are 2 reds and 2 whites available daily, evenly divided between French and California vintages. And if need be, dine on bread for the other 2 meals of the day so as not to miss this experience.

Bice

7 E. 54th St. (bet. 5th and Madison aves.). ☎ 212/ 688-1999. AE, CB, MC, V. Reservations advised. Open daily. Subway: E, F to 5th Ave. ITALIAN. **$$$$**.

One of the better Italian kitchens in New York is at Bice, a favorite with the business crowd both for the cuisine and for the professional service. The menu changes daily but is rather long

nonetheless. Appetizers that pop up repeatedly include goat cheese salad, smoked tuna carpaccio, and lobster salad. Popular entrees are the veal-and-spinach ravioli with mushroom sauce, the pappardelle with mozzarella and tomato sauce, and the risotto with game ragoût. The veal chop milanese is also a winner. Banquettes in the attractive dining room, up a few steps from the bar area, are a bit close together, making for conversations that sometimes carry from one party to another.

The Bridge Café

279 Water St. (Dover St.). ☎ 212/227-3344. AE, CB, MC, V. Reservations advised. Wheelchair accessible. Closed: Sat lunch. Subway: 4, 5, 6 to Brooklyn Bridge/City Hall. ECLECTIC AMERICAN. **$$**.

Wavy floors, a stamped tin ceiling painted brown, and a well-used bar-counter attest to the age of this venerable seamen's watering hole. It is believed that the core structure went up in 1801, and it looks much as it must have a century ago. An imaginative menu at fair tariffs brings a loyal clientele of aware New Yorkers from the lower Manhattan and Brooklyn communities. The blackboard of the day's fare changes daily, according to market availability. Among the seasonal staples, chili, calamari, tortellini, and omelets are dependable. Irish coffee with real whipped cream is sufficient reason to stop by after a chilly day at the nearby **South Street Seaport,** as is Sunday brunch.

Broadway Grill

1605 Broadway (48th St.). ☎ 212/315-6161. AE, DC, MC, V. Reservations advised.

Wheelchair accessible. Closed: Sat lunch; Sun. Subway: 1, 9 to 50th St. ECLECTIC AMERICAN. **$$**.

Founded by David Leiderman of David's Cookies fame, this restaurant is a welcome addition to the cheesy Times Square dining scene, despite its being located in the rather tacky Crowne Plaza Manhattan. The food is your basic, uncomplicated American sort—Caesar salad, crab cakes, grilled chicken, and baby lamb chops. The kids will be happy with burgers or thin-crusted pizza. Everyone will be tempted by the desserts.

Bryant Park Grill

25 W. 40th St. (in Bryant Park, bet. 5th and 6th aves.). ☎ 212/840-6500. AE, DC, MC, V. Reservations recommended. Open daily. Subway: B, D, F, Q to 42nd St.; 7 to 5th Ave. ECLECTIC AMERICAN. **$$$**.

Thanks to a sprucing-up by the city, the once trash-ridden Bryant Park is now a verdant retreat amid midtown's skyscrapers. Bryant Park Grill occupies a glass-encased space behind the New York Public Library. The restaurant has 3 parts. At the Grill, offerings range from salmon tartare with spring vegetables to pasta with broccoli rabe, fava beans, and wild mush-rooms. The Terrace, on the roof of the Grill, specializes in cold seafood dishes. The Cafe is a less-expensive sandwich and salad eatery with outdoor tables. Beware: The service can be slow, and the din in the wide-open dining area deafening. The food is by no means exceptional, but the restaurant's airy charm is a refreshing alternative in a neighborhood overwhelmed by fast food, theme-park cafes and stodgy culinary institutions.

Cabana Carioca

123 W. 45th St. (near 6th Ave.). ☎ 212/581-8088. AE, CB, MC, V. Reservations advised. Wheelchair accessible. Open daily. Subway: B, D, F, Q to 42nd St. BRAZILIAN. **$$**.

When the bills of the city's best-known restaurants start to make you lose your appetite, consider the ethnic restaurants. This one is on a midtown block handy to the Broadway theaters. Brazilian food has not caught the attention of the larger populace, so a full dinner for two here is still very reasonable. Inside, the place looks as if it were once a hut on the banks of the Amazon River, blaring with bright colors and gaudy folk paintings. The tropical drinks (try an inhibition-loosening caipirinha) are a fitting way to contemplate the raucous scene. No one need remain an outsider for long. The luncheon buffets are an uncommon bargain, but if the national dish, feijoada, is on hand, don't hesitate. A boggling portion of the black stew of beef, pork, and sausage is easy enough to share for 2, or even 3, people. Or, take the safer route of shrimp paulista. The best soup is caldo verde.

Café Beulah

39 E. 19th St. (bet. Broadway and Park Ave. S.) ☎ 212/777-9700. AE, DC, MC, V. Reservations recommended. Closed: Sat lunch. Subway: L, N, R, 4, 5, 6 to 14th St./Union Square. SOUTHERN/SOUL FOOD. **$$$**.

Café Beulah has taken the Flatiron District by storm with sophiscated, inventive versions of traditional Southern favorites, like deviled crab cakes and baked ham. Start with the Carolina she-crab soup, or perhaps a plate of chicken wings, which have the zip of Tabasco and cayenne. Whatever you do, don't miss the biscuits and the sautéed collard greens. This down-home comfort food is prepared with a much lighter touch than you'd expect, and it's all served in a homey, convivial setting.

Café Crocodile

354 E. 74th St. (bet. 1st and 2nd aves.). ☎ 212/249-6619. AE, MC, V. Reservations required. Closed: Sun. Subway: 6 to 77th St. FRENCH/MEDITERRA-NEAN. **$$**.

An intimate bistro in an Upper East Side town house with bare wood floors and close tables. Regulars come for the fairly priced all-points-Mediterranean cuisine. That rubric reaches across Tuscany and Morocco, and from the pillars of Hercules to the Aegean. What comes out of the kitchen of the French chef is as variable and unpredictable as it probably sounds—a watery couscous one night, an exceptional seafood sausage the next, a pallid paella, a memorable pasta. The odds for a decent meal at a decent price are good.

★ Café des Artistes

1 W. 67th St. (Central Park W.). ☎ 212/877-3500. AE, CB, MC, V. Reservations required. Jacket required. Wheelchair accessible. Open daily. Subway: 1, 9 to 66th St. INTERNATIONAL. **$$$$$**.

Perhaps the most romantic restaurant in New York, Café des Artistes completes a perfect evening at Lincoln Center. A nostalgic 1920s' glow defines the decor, with murals of voluptuous nudes by Howard Chandler Christy, banks of plants, and ornate mirrors. Several daily specials supplement the already ambitious menu. Among

recent memorable offerings are a grilled swordfish paillard with mustard sauce, roast duck with brandied pear compote, pot-au-feu, and cassoulet. The very popular weekend brunch has featured curried seafood stew, and a meal-in-itself pâté and charcuterie platter. One could wish for a trace more warmth from the service staff, but there is little else to fault.

Café Luxembourg

200 W. 70th St. (near Amsterdam Ave.). ☎ 212/873-7411. AE, CB, MC, V. Reservations advised. Wheelchair accessible. Closed: Mon–Sat lunch. Subway: 1, 2, 3, 9 to 72nd St. INTERNATIONAL. **$$$**.

This Upper West Side spot, the younger offshoot of TriBeCa's Odeon, replicates the blend of funk and professionalism that made that estimable *boîte* a solid success for so many years. The Deco-Moderne setting of marble and mirrors, jazzy window treatments, and colorful tiles is filled from late afternoon to early morning with an ecumenical spectrum of social types: elderly neighborhood couples, flamboyant singles, young executives, and conceptual artists. Some members of the staff could use booster shots in humility. The nightly precurtain dinner costs roughly half the price of a meal ordered after 6:30pm, which is no small matter, given the high prices.

Carnegie Delicatessen

854 7th Ave. (55th St.). ☎ 212/757-2245. No credit cards. No reservations. Wheelchair accessible. Open daily. Subway: N, R to 57th St.; B, D, E to Seventh Ave. JEWISH. **$$**.

The co-owner of this prototypical Jewish "deli" was a minor media star, abetted by

Woody Allen, who chose the Carnegie as a set for one of his films. That fact is duly noted on the menu. The waiters are, by turns, rude, chatty, and amusingly cynical. Eating (it can't be called dining) at the Carnegie means sitting elbow to elbow at tables crammed together in rows, with requisite bowls of free pickles placed at intervals among them. Matzo ball soup and cheesecake are winners. Be forewarned: When the Carnegie describes its sandwiches as gargantuan, it is not hyperbole. A construction of turkey and beef brisket is 6 inches high, with nearly a pound of each meat inside. The prices may seem similarly excessive. The line often spills out onto the sidewalk, but it moves quickly. Closed only from 4 to 6:30am.

Chanterelle

2 Harrison St. (bet. Hudson and Greenwich sts.). ☎ 212/966-6960. AE, CB, DC, DISC, MC, V. Reservations required. Closed: Mon lunch and Sun. Subway: 1, 9 to Franklin St. FRENCH. **$$$$$**.

Chanterelle is simply splendid, with grand columns, monumental floral arrangements, and prices to match. The justly celebrated contemporary French cuisine includes such appetizers as zucchini blossoms filled with chicken and black truffles, and entrees like crisp soft-shell crabs with corn coulis, grilled seafood sausage or sweetbreads with caramelized leeks and orange. The signature dessert is the crisp chocolate soufflé cake—too heavenly to pass up. Service is impeccable; the waiters are extremely knowledgeable about each dish and the sommelier is happy to make suggestions from the outstanding wine list.

China Grill

60 W. 53rd St. (near 6th Ave.). ☎ 212/333-7788. AE, CB, MC, V. Reservations advised. Wheelchair accessible. Closed: Sat and Sun lunch. Subway: B, D, F, Q to 47th-50th sts./ Rockefeller Center. ASIAN FUSION. **$$$$**.

Much of the 1st floor of CBS headquarters, which is tagged "Black Rock" for its dark granite facing, is set aside for a restaurant. The cavernous block-to-block space has no carpets or drapes to absorb sound, and the buzz of 400 diners soon builds to a roar, helped by a stereo system thumping out rock music. The type of Californian cuisine often called Chinois is served in this arena, the marriage of Eastern and Western ingredients and techniques symbolized by the open kitchen in the corridor between the 2 dining rooms. On one side, Asians cook with huge woks, on the other, Occidentals use skillets. What they produce can be stunning. No one believes the crispy spinach, the leaves of the humble vegetable flash-fried in peanut and sesame oil to the texture of ancient paper. Confucius chicken salad comes in a much larger helping, a fitting prelude to the tasty grilled, dry-aged Szechuan beef, tossed in scented oil and cilantro. Since all dishes are served Chinese-style (to share), 2 people can ease the bite of the bill by ordering only 1 appetizer, 1 main course, and 1 dessert.

★ Chin Chin

216 E. 49th St. (bet. 2nd and 3rd aves.). ☎ 212/888-4555. AE, DC, MC, V. Reservations required. Closed: Sat lunch; Sun lunch. Subway: E, F to Lexington/ 3rd Ave.. CHINESE. **$$$**.

With the low arched ceiling, cream walls, and polished wood wainscoting, the main room suggests the first-class lounge of a Kowloon ferry. The effect is heightened by rows of sepia photographs of several generations of the extended family of Wally and Jimmy Chin, the owners. Chin Chin does duck well, especially in the famous Peking and meaty tea-smoked versions. For adventurous to timid eaters, the menu zips from shredded jellyfish and "thousand-year-old" eggs with pickled shallots to spring rolls and barbecued spare ribs. All are in monster portions, cunningly presented, and appetizers aren't really necessary. Seasonal crab dishes are typically superior. The author and Chinese food expert Kurt Vonnegut, Jr. is a regular. The packed crowd can grow loud, so plan an intimate dinner elsewhere.

★ Le Cirque

58 E. 65th St. (near Madison Ave.). ☎ 212/794-9292. AE, DC. Reservations required. Closed: Sun; 1 week in July. Subway: 6 to 68th St. FRENCH/ITALIAN. **$$$$$**.

Some of the ladies who lunch here are principally concerned with maintaining their X-ray figures; others are key players in the mightiest circles of finance, politics, and Hollywood. The excellent cuisine does not, however, distract from the mutual ogling and exchanges of insider gossip that charge the atmosphere. The arena is a lovely, flower-bedecked room ringed by banquettes, the tables scant inches apart (the better to eavesdrop). Mere mortals can attend, providing they dress well and have made

reservations 2 weeks ahead and confirmed them the day before. Sirio Maccioni orchestrates. He is one of those personages known by his first name, a transplanted Italian who rules his domain with unquestioned, if velvety, authority. Chef Sylvain Portay is French, and the menu reflects both influences. In a show of currently fashionable menu rustication, the otherwise plebeian pot-au-feu is brought to new heights of perfection. The chocolate desserts are staggering, and some diners no doubt will find the bill equally so. Consider a fixed-priced lunch at $35.75 or a pretheater dinner for $38 (Mon–Fri seating at 6pm).

Cité

120 W. 51st St. (near 7th Ave.). ☎ 212/956-7100. AE, MC, V. Reservations advised. Main room closed Sat and Sun lunch; grill open daily. Subway: N, R to 49th St. AMERICAN/INTERNATIONAL. **$$$$**.

This extravaganza in close proximity to the theater district was a hit from the day it opened its doors. When business faltered, the restaurant came up with a clever offer: Wine Dinner. Served after 8pm, the dinner includes 3 courses and 4 (high quality) wines, all for $49.50. The menu includes onion soup, shrimp cocktail, and mesclun salad, among the appetizers; roasted duck, baby rack of lamb, and swordfish steak, among the main courses; and desserts such as crème brûlée and cheesecake. Nothing ground-breaking, but good food. The main room is a dual-level Art Deco phantasmagoria with giant chandeliers and crimson velvet banquettes. The adjoining grill, which serves

American bistro food, is quieter and less conspicuously decorated.

Coffee Shop/World Room

29 Union Square W. (at 16th St.).
☎ 212/243-7969. AE.
Reservations accepted for six or more. Open daily. Subway: L, N, R, 4, 5, 6 to 14th St./Union Sq.
AMERICAN/BRAZILIAN. **$$**.
A unassuming, peeled-paint facade and retro neon sign hide this too-hip meeting spot for the trendy, the beautiful, and the casually famous. The waitstaff are, for the most part, well-meaning models between jobs. Dishes are studiously low-fat and, like the Bahian seafood paella, have a definitive Brazilian slant. The Coffee Shop comes alive at night, when the cappucino bar is packed three-deep with posers eager to make the scene. The adjacent World Room is less chaotic, and serves fabulous brick oven pizzas.

Contrapunto

200 E. 60th St. (3rd Ave.).
☎ 212/751-8616. AE, DC, MC, V. No reservations. Open daily.
Subway: 4, 5, 6 to 59th St.; N, R to Lexington Ave. ITALIAN. **$$**.
The minimalist quasi-Milanese setting is on the 2nd floor overlooking lively 3rd Avenue, next door and upstairs from Arizona 206, under the same ownership. Very bright track lighting, wooden chairs, a perky espresso machine, and glass tops over white tablecloths give the place a cheerful, if unelaborate, ambiance. The heart of the menu is the fresh pasta, teamed with all manner of goodies: fettucine, for example, with portobello, pancetta bacon, sun-dried and cherry tomatoes, basil oil, garlic, and

pecorino. Other pastas come with seafood or with sweet sausage and cannellini beans or with spinach and ricotta cheese. Mushrooms of the season are grilled, peppered, sprinkled with minced garlic and parsley, drizzled with oil—a delicious starter. Italian-style gelati are made right here, in such flavors as praline, grapefruit and white chocolate. The prices are reasonable, particularly for this neighborhood, so expect a wait.

La Côte Basque

60 W. 55th St. (bet. 5th and 6th aves.). ☎ 212/688-6525.
AE, CB, MC, V. Reservations advised. Jacket and tie required. Wheelchair accessible. Closed: Sun. Subway: E, F to 5th Ave./53rd St. FRENCH. **$$$$$**.
Henry Soulé introduced serious haute cuisine to New York. La Côte Basque was one of the maestro's creations, and he died while working here in 1966. Not long after, it looked as if the restaurant might expire as well, but it was resuscitated by chef-proprietor Jean-Jacques Rachou in the early 1980s. Soulé would be proud of his successor, for Rachou is not afraid to create such familiar fare as cassoulet and tarragon chicken, in generous portions. The cozy room even retains its red banquettes and the original Lamotte murals of the Basque coast. Its resultant popularity with the privileged over-40 set causes traffic jams in the vestibule, especially at lunchtime. The flavors of some dishes prove somewhat wan and the French-only menu is an affectation in New York. The staff, however, is gracious, the customers genteel and/or celebrated, and the prices, though high,

are not unreasonable. The lunch menu is up to 40% cheaper than dinner.

C.T.

111 E. 22nd St. (bet. Park Ave. S. and Lexington Ave.). ☎ 212/ 995-8500. AE, CB, DC, DISC, MC, V. Reservations required well in advance. Closed: Sun. Subway: 6, N, R to 23rd St. FRENCH/LATIN FUSION. **$$$$$**

Chef Claude Troisgros presides over the kitchen at C.T. with self-assurance, and foodies all over the city have taken notice. His creations lend a Latin accent to traditional French recipes: Seared foie gras appears with jicama, and the breast of duck is dressed with a puree of passionfruit. Try the tasting menus (available at both lunch and dinner) and leave yourself in Claude's capable hands. Try to get a table in the dramatic columned downstairs area for optimum people-watching.

★ Daniel

At the Surrey Suite Hotel, 20 E.76th St. (bet. 5th and Madison aves.). ☎ 212/288-0033. AE, DC, DISC, MC, V. Reservations required one month in advance. Jacket and tie required. Closed: Mon lunch, Sat lunch, Sun. Subway: 6 to 77th St. FRENCH. **$$$$$**

The fanfare hasn't waned since Chef Daniel Boulud (formerly of Le Cirque) stepped out on his own 3 years ago and opened this elegant four-star restaurant, and for good reason: It's nearly perfect. Exquisite preparations of classic French are presented with a flourish in a room that *New York* magazine called "so buoyant that any occasion becomes a celebration." But it's the food that grabs your attention, from the first taste

of the cold lobster bisque or high-rise mesculan salad to the bottom of the chocolate souffle. And the service is top-notch: A whole army of waitstaff caters to your every need, but doesn't overwhelm. Don't miss it if you can manage the tab.

Dawat

210 E. 58th St. (bet. 2nd and 3rd aves.). ☎ 212/355-7555. AE, CB, MC, V. Reservations advised. Wheelchair accessible. Closed: Sun lunch. Subway: 4, 5, 6 to 59th St.; N, R to Lexington Ave. INDIAN. **$$$**

In a city with a burgeoning number of restaurants of Indian and other subcontinental persuasions, Dawat surpasses the genre. Go for lunch to get a bargain in the process. The 3 special noon meals cost less than a couple of hamburger platters at far less distinguished eateries. The "light" fish lunch for one, arrives in bowls and little copper pans—one with curried tilefish, another with gingered cauliflower, a third with rice and vegetables, plus salad, mango chutney, yogurt, and a superb nan bread. At dinner, a similar spread, with drinks, wine, and dessert, can race toward the **$$$$$** price category. Service is, if anything, too attentive. Decor is restrained, with carved heads spotlighted on salmon-pink walls.

L'École

462 Broadway (Grand St.). ☎ 212/219-3300. AE, CB, MC, V. Reservations required. Wheelchair accessible. Closed: Sun. Subway: 6 to Spring St. FRENCH. **$$**

On the seedy southeast edge of SoHo, an airy, light-filled, ground-floor space catches the eyes of passersby. It is a vision of understated elegance, with

French country chairs, spinning overhead fans, and a small wine bar. Despite appearances, it is a classroom for students in the respected French Culinary Institute. The ambitious menu changes monthly. Expect glitches in service and presentation, but the overall performance is admirable. Besides, the fixed-price lunches and dinners are considerably less expensive than at other establishments with similarly satistfying food. The wine card features several bottles a day, at retail prices, not the usual 100% or 200% markup. Go to give the kids a chance to show what they've learned. In a few years, you'll have to pay a lot more for their services.

Eighteenth & Eighth

159 8th Ave. ☎ 212/242-5000. MC, V. Reservations not accepted. Open daily. Subway: 1, 9 to 18th St. AMERICAN. **$$**. It's easy to find this place: Follow the line to the corner of 18th Street and 8th Avenue—there's always a wait for a table in this stylish Chelsea hangout. It's consistently packed, even though true to the upscale-diner ambience, the tables are pushed close together. The wide-ranging menu concentrates on reliable food—the pastas, salads, and meat loaf are particularly good. Breakfast and brunch are yummy and worth a visit.

Elaine's

1703 2nd Ave. (near E. 88th St.). ☎ 212/534-8114. AE, CB, MC, V. Reservations required. Wheelchair accessible. Closed: Sat and Sun lunch. Subway: 4, 5, 6 to 86th St. ITALIAN. **$$$**. Luminaries of the literary, entertainment, and political worlds, make this saloon-restaurant their own. If the

Wood man isn't in, chances are someone famous will be. The proprietress takes care of them, saving their favorite tables and shooing away paparazzi and gapers. The listless food cannot possibly be the draw, which may account for the fact that no one shows up before 10pm.

Fishin Eddie

73 W. 71st St. (Columbus Ave.). ☎ 212/874-3474. AE, CB, MC, V. Reservations advised. Closed: Lunch daily. Subway: B, C to 72nd St. ECLECTIC AMERICAN. **$$**. Another, younger version of **Vince & Eddie's**, it, too, was virtually an instant success. The formula is the same— unfussy preparations of simple ingredients at moderate prices. Fishin Eddie is a little more conspicuously decorated, with a deliberately casual selection of Shaker chairs and wood tables left bare or with blue-and-white oilcloths. A peaked glass skylight covers most of the large back room, visually alleviating the rather cramped seating. The emphasis is on seafood, even among the inevitable pastas. Grilled salmon, swordfish, tuna, red snapper, and others are served with ratatouille and polenta cakes. Platters for two include the fish stew cioppino and a heap of airily crisp fritto misto.

Flowers

21 W. 17th St. (bet. 5th and 6th aves.). ☎ 212/691-8888. AE, CB, DC, MC, V. Reservations recommended. Open daily. Subway: L, N, R, 4, 5, 6 to 14th St./Union Sq.; F to 14th St. ECLECTIC AMERICAN. **$$$**. The Flatiron District has witnessed an explosion of new restaurants in the past few years. One standout amid the gaggle is Flowers, a homey, rustic place with fine-print

Uptown Dining

Arcadia **15**
Arizona 206 and Cafe **19**
Aureole **17**
Café Crocodile **25**
Café des Artistes **10**
Café Luxembourg **7**
Le Cirque **21**
Contrapunto **18**
Daniel **26**
Elaine's **29**
Fishin Eddie **6**
Iridium **14**
Isabella's **4**
JoJo **22**
Lenge **8**
mad.61 **16**
Mad Fish **3**
Merchant's **1**
Monsoon **2**
Mortimer's **27**
Nino's **24**
Pamir **28**
The Saloon **13**
Serendipity 3 **20**
Shark Bar **5**
Shun Lee **12**
Sign of the Dove **23**
Sylvia's **30**
Tavern on the Green **11**
Vince & Eddie's **9**

wallpaper and huge displays of fresh-cut blooms. Service can be glacially slow, so while away the time by spying on New York sports stars and other assorted celebs. Chef Mark

Salonsky changes the menu frequently, but don't pass up the Moroccan roasted lamb with orzo. In warmer weather, head for the rooftop garden, which has a raw bar, a juice

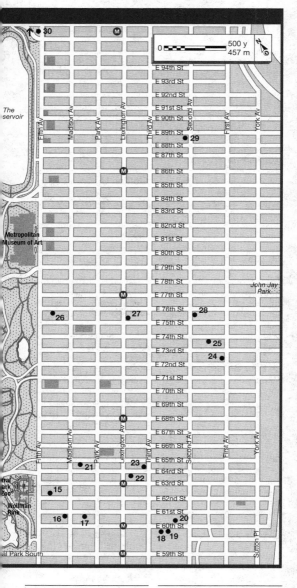

bar, and a refreshing menu of salads.

H 44 (Forty-Four)

44 W. 44th St. (bet. 5th and 6th aves.). ☎ 212/869-4400. AE, CB, MC, V. Reservations advised. Open daily. Subway: B, D, F, Q to 42nd St.; 7 to 5th Ave. ECLECTIC AMERICAN. **$$$$.**

Occupying the lobby of Manhattan's hippest hotel, the

Royalton, 44 feeds the city's auteurs of fashion. But 44 surprisingly has more than atmosphere (though it has that in spades). For starters, the asparagus salad and the chilled sweet corn soup are both very good, and the tomato-mango salad is refreshing and light. Of the main courses, the red snapper, served with a tomato gazpacho, stands out. The roasted organic chicken and the wood-grilled veal chop are also delicious. The $36.50 pretheater dinner offers many more options than most competitors. Now back to the atmosphere for a moment: As if the big names who frequent the place, such as Calvin Klein and Sandra Bernhard, didn't create enough of a stir, management has hung tassles from angled mirrors over the velvet banquettes. The lighting is dim and flattering, and Pellegrino is the beverage of choice.

★ Four Seasons

99 E. 52nd St. (Park Ave.).
☎ 212/754-9494. AE, CB, MC, V. Reservations required. Jacket required. Wheelchair accessible. Closed: Sun. Subway: 6 to 51st St.; E, F to Lexington/3rd Ave. and 53rd St. INTERNATIONAL. **$$$$$**.
Lunch is the main event here, and the Grill Room is the arena. Business tycoons seal deals over dessert. Unknowns are hustled up and out of sight into the Grill Room Siberia, a small room with a portrait of James Beard to compensate for being away from the action. At dinner, the locus shifts to the Pool Room, with its floral bounty and marble-bound pool. It is a vaulted space 3 stories high, at the base of the Seagram Building. Officially designated a landmark space, it

is the first restaurant in New York to be so honored. The food, usually of the highest quality, is almost worth the prices. The scope is broad enough to qualify for the catch-all "continental" label, with chocolate cake the preferred dessert. Fixed-price pre-theater dinners are a way to sample these delights at lower cost.

Golden Unicorn

18 E. Broadway (Catherine St.).
☎ 212/941-0911. AE, CB, MC, V. Reservations advised. Jacket required. Wheelchair accessible. Open daily. Subway: 4, 5, 6 to Brooklyn Bridge/City Hall; J, M, Z to Chambers St. CHINESE. **$$**.
A flashy building just east of Chatham Square heralds the presence of a much-noted Hong Kong restaurant. It feels like a snowed-in airport lounge, but it doesn't take long to be summoned forth and sent aloft in the 2 elevators. After all, the restaurant can seat 600 people up there. (Diners expressing a willingness to share a table with strangers will get the nod faster.) Splendid dim sum spark the din, especially at lunch. Solemn young women in white tuxedo jackets rattle by pushing trolleys laden with goodies, pausing at each table and explaining what is on offer with varying levels of fluency in English. Be patient, because more than 50 types of dim sum are available. Full Cantonese meals are also available, and patrons exclaim over the inventive seafood specialties, in particular. To make the most of it all, go with a gang of 4 or more dedicated eaters. An uptown branch is in the Waldorf-Astoria (see "Accommodations").

Gotham Bar and Grill

12 E. 12th St. (5th Ave. and University Place). ☎ 212/620-4020. AE, CB, MC, V. Reservations required. Closed: Sat and Sun lunch. Subway: L, N, R, 4, 5, 6 to 14th St./Union Sq. ECLECTIC AMERICAN. **$$$$**.

Despite the folksy name, little is self-effacing about this monument to contemporary American cooking. It is large, bustling, and, abetted by New Age music, inevitably loud at peak dining hours. Gotham's trademark is its presentation—food piled into pyramids in imminent danger of collapse. Portale's kitchen is a more than competent one, serving up cuisine with some invention: warm skate salad, duck terrine, goat cheese ravioli, veal carpaccio, and, of course, pasta with almost anything. The service, unfortunately, may be the slowest I have encountered in an (otherwise) fine restaurant.

★ Gramercy Tavern

42 E. 20th St. (bet. Broadway and Park Ave. S.). ☎ 212/477-0777. AE, MC, V. Reservations required. Closed: Sat lunch, Sun lunch. Tavern open Mon–Sat from noon. Subway: 6, N, R to 23rd St. AMERICAN. **$$$$$**.

Before Gramercy Tavern even opened a few years ago, it had already been hailed as the best restaurant in New York. Owner Danny Meyer, who also owns Union Square Cafe, has established another hit just three blocks away. Book way in advance for a table in the comfortable yet luxurious dining room; the tavern room around the bar serves excellent lighter fare that's also lighter on the wallet. What else is there to say but that the food is fantastic? Such hearty yet intricate peasant fare as white bean and roasted garlic soup or rabbit sauteed with rosemary and olives never ceases to surprise and delight. There's a prix-fixe dinner and tasting menu—even a special one in spring celebrating morels.

Hatsuhana

17 E. 48th St. (bet. 5th and Madison aves.). ☎ 212/355-3345. AE, CB, MC, V. Reservations advised. Wheelchair accessible. Closed: Sat lunch; Sun. Subway: B, D, F, Q to 47th–50th sts./Rockefeller Center. JAPANESE. **$$**.

Hatsuhana remains a heavy favorite of sushi and sashimi enthusiasts. It is authentic. Close quarters make conversation easy. A full meal is light enough to precede 2 hours in a theater seat. Young Japanese adroitly slice fish so fresh it's still quivering, wrap it in sheets of kelp, top it with salmon eggs, and arrange it artistically on lacquered trays of vinegared rice, all within inches of the diners at the 2 long, narrow pine counters. Most customers eat at the sushi-sashimi bars, where they can see their food being prepared. But tables also are available. This location and the other, slightly younger branch (237 Park Ave.; ☎ 212/661-3400) by now are looking a little ragged from heavy use, in this case a sign of continued popularity rather than of neglect.

Home

20 Cornelia St. (bet. Bleecker and W. 4th sts.). ☎ 212/243-9579. Reservations advised. Open daily. Subway: A, B, C, D, E, F, Q to W. 4th St. AMERICAN. **$$**.

There's no place like Home for creative yet simple American fare at relatively inexpensive prices. The endearing setting, on the ground floor of a brownstone, may be too cozy for some—keep your party to 4 or less—but there's also a charming all-weather garden in back. Start with blue cheese fondue with rosemary caramelized shallots and walnut bread toasts, followed by grilled guinea hen with a salad of patty-pan squash and watercress topped with grilled peach sauce. And you must save room for the rich, creamy chocolate pudding: I wish my mom could have made it this way.

Hudson River Club

4 World Financial Center, 250 Vesey St. (West St.). ☎ 212/786-1500. AE, DC, MC, V. Reservations required. Wheelchair accessible. Closed: Sat lunch; Sun dinner. Subway: E to World Trade Center; 1, 9, R to Cortlandt St. ECLECTIC AMERICAN. **$$$$$**.

This is one of those Wall Street–area restaurants where no one eats without an expense account. It gets away with the sky-high prices because of its location in the World Financial Center and the view of the marina, the river, Ellis Island, and the Statue of Liberty that goes with it. Not that the food isn't very good. Fittingly, the kitchen specializes in American cuisine with a focus on the Hudson River region. Many dishes, such as the rabbit pot pie and the veal shank, are braised. Even many of the wines are from regional vineyards. Desserts are uncomplicated American classics: a brownie with ice cream, a brown sugar and peach pot pie, a berry shortcake. Seating is comfortable, and tables are set well apart, ideal for high-level business lunches or romantic

dinners. For a less costly meal, order the prix-fixe lunch for $19.95 or the pretheater dinner, with seating between 5:30 and 6pm, for $42.

Iridium

44 W. 63rd St. (bet. Broadway and Columbus Ave.). ☎ 212/582-2121. AE, CB, MC, V. Reservations advised. Wheelchair accessible. Open daily. Subway: 1, 9 to 66th St./Lincoln Center. ECLECTIC AMERICAN. **$$$**.

Less than 50 yards from **Lincoln Center** is Iridium, a chic addition to the Upper West Side. The look is Salvador Dali, with bulging copper fixtures and surreal slopes and curves throughout the crowded space. The bar and lounge at the entrance is always wall-to-wall people, mostly attractive and in their 20s and 30s. It's a scene. Tables in the dining room are close but not uncomfortably so. For starters, the simple salads—one with goat cheese, another an eggless Caesar—are best. The shrimp wontons, served with a miso hoisin vinaigrette, also are tasty. The main courses range from comfort food like the chicken pot pie and grilled angus sirloin to contemporary dishes, such as tuna wrapped in Japanese scallion. Jazz combos play downstairs nightly.

Isabella's

359 Columbus Ave. (77th St.). ☎ 212/724-2100. AE, CB, MC, V. Reservations advised (no reservations Sun brunch). Open daily. Subway: B, C to 81st St./Museum of Natural History. ECLECTIC AMERICAN. **$$$**.

Several dining possibilities reside behind the American Museum of Natural History, but this prototypical Columbus Avenue bistro is the most well-known and by far the most packed. The French doors all around the corner location open in warm weather, when 18 tables are set out on the sidewalk. Inside are 2 levels with marble floors and raffia safari chairs pulled up to tables with vases of fresh flowers. The scene is more happening than the food. At midday, working women and ladies of a certain age lunch on sandwiches and salads. Dinner brings couples and such modish victuals as fried calamari with 2 sauces, grilled portobello mushroom salad, baby lamb with rosemary, and roast Cornish hen with garlic-mashed potatoes.

Jane Street Seafood Café

575 Hudson St. (bet. Bank and 11th sts.). ☎ 212/242-0003. AE, CB, MC, V. Reservations advised. Open daily, dinner only. Subway: A, C, E, L to 14th St. SEAFOOD. **$$**.

A hint of spare and salty New England in the northwest corner of Greenwich Village. The ceiling is low and tables are bare wood. Wear comfortable clothes and arrive in a patient mood, since you will encounter a wait. Eventually, though, you will settle in to a meal composed of produce fresh from the market. Everyone raves about the bread, the coleslaw, and the chowder, but those are merely starters. Little that follows will disappoint. Steamed lobster, for one example, is done as well as it can be.

John's Pizzeria

278 Bleecker St. (bet. Cornelia St. and 7th Ave.). ☎ 212/243-1680. No credit cards. Reservations recommended for parties of 10 or more. Open daily. Subway: 1, 9 to Sheridan Square; A, B, C, D, E, F to West 4th St. PIZZA. **$**.

John's has been the Muhammad Ali of New York pizza for decades—contenders come and go, but no one's been able to unseat the champ. "No slices" is the rule at John's—only whole pies for take-out or on-the-spot consumption. John's pies, with thin crusts and just the right amount of sauce, cheese, and toppings, avoid the greasy overkill perpetrated by so many these days. I heartily recommend the fresh Italian sausage and onion pie; it's so good I never order anything else. There are lines well down the block every evening to get into the original restaurant (the characterless annex next door should be avoided), which has brusque, no-frills service and a Sinatra-laden jukebox. Go early to avoid waiting.

JoJo

160 E. 64th St. (near Lexington Ave.). ☎ 212/223-5656. AE, CB, MC, V. Reservations advised. Closed: Sun. Subway: 6 to 68th St. FRENCH. **$$$$**. Chef-proprietor Jean-Georges Vongerichten (known to his chums as JoJo) created both this upscale bistro and the innovative Vong. The restaurant is primarily French, with an emphasis on fish and seafood. Crammed in the ground floor of an Upper East Side town house, JoJo has a cubbyhole front bar and wool crimson banquettes in the main room. Menus are in nonhyperbolic English so plain that selection can be difficult. From the kitchen, come ragouts and terrines that take humble bistro dishes to new heights. Salmon arrives with a tiny rosemary tree and an underlying sauce of black beans, corn, and scallions; lobster is poached, in

sauternes and orange juice. But I found the menu limited, and my duck was almost raw. The truly triumphant course of my meal was the dessert: a chocolate cake with hot, oozing chocolate inside, accompanied by vanilla ice cream. Exceptional.

★ Lenge

200 Columbus Ave. (69th St.). ☎ 212/799-9188. AE, CB, MC, V. No reservations. Open daily. Subway: B, C to 72nd St. JAPANESE. **$$$**.

For fans of raw fish, Lenge is one of the best, drawing its loyal clientele from across the city. The decor is low-key, with simple tables and chairs lined up in front of picture windows that look out to busy Columbus Avenue. In a back room, patrons can remove their shoes and sit Japanese-style. All the standard brands of sushi are represented here, best topped off with a potent dose of sake.

★ Lespinasse

2 E. 55th St. (in the St. Regis Hotel, at 5th Ave.). ☎ 212/ 339-6719. AE, CB, DC, DISC, JCB, MC, V. Reservations required. Jacket and tie required. Closed: Sun lunch and dinner. Subway: E, F to 5th Ave./53rd St. FRENCH ASIAN. **$$$$$**.

The conversation is hushed, the service impeccable, and the banquettes luxuriously plush in this ornate, old-world hotel dining room. The ambience borders on stuffy, but the focus is on the virtuosic food, awarded a rare four stars by the *New York Times*. Chef Gray Kunz invigorates classic French dishes with unexpected Asian flourishes. The menu changes seasonally, but may include an exquisite foie gras with peppered-pineapple

confit or seared loin of rabbit in a silky rosemary-mustard sauce. Though tasting menus won't lower the stratospheric bill, they're a delectable introduction to Kunz's mastery.

Lola

30 W. 22nd St. (near 6th Ave.). ☎ 212/675-6700. AE, CB, MC, V. Reservations advised. Wheelchair accessible. Closed: Sat lunch. Subway: F to 23rd St. CARIBBEAN. **$$$**.

Despite the thoroughly obnoxious staff and a decibel level that reaches that of an overworked steel mill, Lola remains a very popular Chelsea eatery. The tumult is rounded out by spirited combos playing jazz, reggae, calypso, or, at Sunday brunch, gospel music. So go in a party mood and expect your reservations to be ignored. When you finally get a table, more likely than not you'll enjoy the flavorful Southern food with elements of Caribbean and Creole cooking. The fried chicken is excellent, with tender meat beneath the crisp crust, prepared with a hint of vinegar and a nosegay of spices. Rum drinks such as Planter's Punch prevail, but many patrons choose the Lola, a frozen slush of brandy, triple sec, lemonade, and grenadine. Lola herself has departed, by the way, but it is interesting to note that the present head chef, the sous chef, and the pastry chef are all women, something that is rare in a profession still largely dominated by men.

Louisiana

622 Broadway (Houston St.). ☎ 212/460-9633. AE, MC, V. Reservations required weekends; advised weekdays. Open daily for dinner. Subway: B, D, F, Q to Broadway/Lafayette St. CREOLE/ CAJUN. **$$$**.

Formerly K-Paul, owned and run by New Orleans restaurateur Paul Prudhomme, Louisiana maintains the Cajun cuisine that thrust bayou cooking into the national consciousness. Now that the fad has faded, Louisiana has lowered its prices and has given the restaurant a casual, fun feel, with live Dixie or blues nightly, Cajun dance lessons every Sunday night, and peanut shells on the floor. Come for the Cajun "popcorn" (batter-fried crawfish), the gumbo, the crawfish etoufée, or the fried catfish with hush puppies. Louisiana even serves up a crawfish boil (sucking heads is a must) in-season.

Lucky Cheng's

24 1st Ave. (bet. 1st and 2nd sts.). ☎ 212/473-0516. AE, DC, DISC, MC, V. Reservations advised. Open for dinner daily. Subway: F to 2nd Ave. ASIAN FUSION. **$$**.
The food's not bad, but your meal is secondary—you come here for the scene. The waitstaff are all dressed in drag, though sometimes it's hard to tell. Don't tell your dining companions, and see how long it takes them to figure it out. The menu has a good but not great selection of Cal-Asian dishes. A mixed crowd keeps this funky East Village joint busy, and quite noisy.

★★ Lutèce

249 E. 50th St. (near 2nd Ave.). ☎ 212/752-2225. AE, CB, MC, V. Reservations required. Jacket required. Wheelchair accessible. Closed: Sat and Mon lunch; Sun. Subway: 6 to 51st St.; E, F to Lexington/3rd Ave. and 53rd St. FRENCH. **$$$$$**.
Lutèce was long the standard against which any American restaurant that aspired to French cuisine was measured, and even today hardly half a dozen establishments in New York approach its mark. While to dine here is very nearly an honor—reservations usually must be secured at least 3 weeks in advance—no one is made to feel less than an eagerly anticipated guest. The captains contrive to be attentive but not unctuous, friendly but not familiar, helpful but never patronizing. This exquisite balance, which carries from reception to appetizer to entree to coffee, is orchestrated by chef-proprietor André Soltner and his wife Simone, who functions as maîtresse d'. They have been here more than 30 years, and he is one of the few men in America whom the great chefs of France acknowledge as their equal. He emerges from the cramped, narrow kitchen periodically, geniality personified in his unsoiled whites, circulating among his patrons to make suggestions and answer questions. One might quibble that the famous Garden Room is a trifle too unassuming for such a grand reputation, and that some waiters are too avuncular and offhanded, especially with customers for whom this is a once-in-a-blue-moon event. Those grumbles aside, you almost cannot go wrong ordering. The cellar is a library of great vintages of Bordeaux and Burgundy, usually at breathtaking prices. A secondary list of serviceable wines offers rational substitutes, and white wine is served by the glass.

mad.61

10 E. 61st St. (in Barney's, at Madison Ave.). ☎ 212/833-2200. AE, DC, MC, V.

Downtown Dining

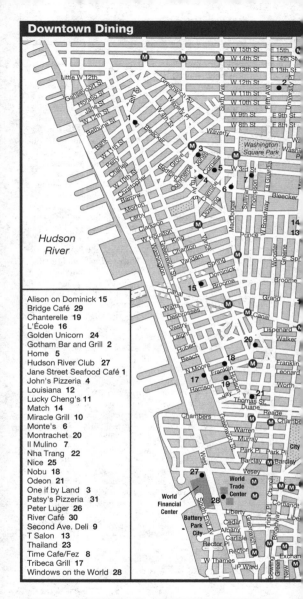

Alison on Dominick **15**
Bridge Café **29**
Chanterelle **19**
L'École **16**
Golden Unicorn **24**
Gotham Bar and Grill **2**
Home **5**
Hudson River Club **27**
Jane Street Seafood Café **1**
John's Pizzeria **4**
Louisiana **12**
Lucky Cheng's **11**
Match **14**
Miracle Grill **10**
Monte's **6**
Montrachet **20**
Il Mulino **7**
Nha Trang **22**
Nice **25**
Nobu **18**
Odeon **21**
One if by Land **3**
Patsy's Pizzeria **31**
Peter Luger **26**
River Café **30**
Second Ave. Deli **9**
T Salon **13**
Thailand **23**
Time Cafe/Fez **8**
Tribeca Grill **17**
Windows on the World **28**

Reservations Recommended.
Closed: Sun dinner. Subway: N, R
to 5th Ave. CONTEMPORARY
ITALIAN. **$$$$**.
Located in the basement
of Barneys uptown

department store, mad.61 is
where the sleek meet to eat.
The centerpiece of this
beige-and-charcoal Art
Deco dining room is a mosaic-
tiled reflecting pool; it's a

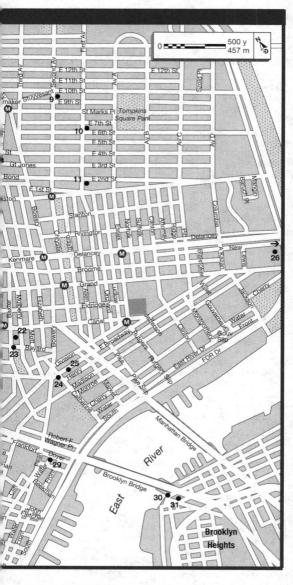

popular spot for stargazers and gossip hounds, so the lunch scene can be frenetic. Pino Luongo, of Coco Pazzo fame, designed the menu, which features

delightful pizzas, pastas, and risottos. The bread is so heavenly that you may not care if the food ever arrives. An espresso bar and a charcuterie-style

market are on hand for
those who prefer to grab
their chic on the run.

Mad Fish

2182 Broadway (bet. 76th and
77th sts.). ☎ 212/787-0202.
AE, DC, DISC, MC, V.
Reservations recommended.
Open for dinner nightly. Subway:
1, 9 to 79th St. SEAFOOD.
$$$$
One of the trendiest places on
the Upper West Side (at least
for the moment), Mad Fish
occupies a comfortable,
attractive space, complete with
an extensive raw bar. Service
can be a little scattered with
crowds like these, but it's
always pleasant and well-
intentioned. The kitchen
focuses on what's fresh each
day, so the menu changes
constantly, but the lobster
risotto is a standout, and a
barbecued bluefish is also
nicely done. The wine list is
notable, with some nice
affordable choices. Whatever
you do, save room for your
own small chocolate cake.
Each one comes to you still
warm from the oven, with a
decadent, creamy chocolate
center.

★ March

405 E. 58th St. (bet. 1st Ave. and
Sutton Place). ☎ 212/754-6272.
AE, DC, MC, V. Reservations
required. Jacket and tie
requested. Closed: lunch and
Sun. Subway: 4,5,6 to 59th St.;
N,R to Lexington Ave. ECLECTIC
AMERICAN. **$$$$$**
Understated elegance is the
keynote here, from the
intimate town house setting
and refined service to Wayne
Nish's subtly innovative
New American cuisine, both
creative and comfortably classic
at the same time. Schooled in
both Eastern and Western
styles of cooking, Nish

combines techniques and
flavors deftly, in inspired
marriages that please rather
than shock the palate. The
seasonal menu might include
such wonders as sesame-crusted
seared rare tuna in a caramel
soy; New Zealand clams in
broth and sake; and grilled
breast of Long Island duck with
Turkish figs and tamarind sauce.
Nish's partner, host Joseph
Scalice, has compiled an award-
winning wine list that's a
perfect accompaniment to the
menu. There are always 2
multi-course tasting menus
available, with specially selected
wines to match.

Match

160 Mercer St. (bet. Prince and
Houston sts.). ☎ 212/343-0020.
AE, CB, MC, V. Reservations
advised. Wheelchair accessible.
Open daily. Subway: R to Prince
St. ECLECTIC/ASIAN. **$$$**
This SoHo spot is the
restaurant of the moment (but,
remember, in New York
moments can be fleeting). One
suspects all the supermodels,
actors, and fashion designers
have been flocking here for
the casually hip atmosphere
because the food, while more
than edible, is not exactly
earth-shattering. The menu of
sushi and Asian-inspired fare
includes a shrimp and glass
noodle summer roll, chicken
sate with peanut lime sauce,
barbecued steak frites, and
spicy duck pizza with shiitake
mushrooms. The desserts—
chocolat brûlée, apple pie, and
such—are mighty tempting.
Another location opened on
the Upper East Side at 33 E.
60th St. (between Park and
Madison avenues), ☎ 212/
906-9173.

Merchant's

521 Columbus Ave. (85th St.).
☎ 212/721-3689. AE, CB,

MC, V. No reservations. Wheelchair accessible. Open daily. Subway: B, C to 86th St. AMERICAN. **$$**.

The Upper West Side's young singles are packed in at the bar every night after work. In the summer, they take tables on the sidewalk. After some mingling, a drink or two, and maybe some nachos, they sit down to surprisingly tasty food. The grilled portobello mushroom salad is tasty and enough for a meal. The menu has plenty of salads, sandwiches, chicken dishes, and the like. Another location is at 112 7th Ave. (between 16th and 17th sts.), ☎ 212/366-7267.

Mesa Grill

102 5th Ave. (bet. 15th and 16th sts.). ☎ 212/807-7400. AE, DC, DISC, MC, V. Reservations recommended. Open daily for lunch and dinner. Subway: L, N, R, 4, 5, 6 to 14th St./Union Sq. SOUTHWESTERN. **$$$$**.

Columns soar up to the mezzanine level in the large, colorful dining room at Mesa Grill. Beautiful people squeeze into the cowboy banquettes (a little too close together for privacy) and crowd into the Art Deco bar. It's too loud for romance, but if you're in the mood to celebrate, the margaritas are terrific and Chef Bobby Flay's menu lives up to the hype, with innovative entrees such as cascabel chile-crusted rabbit, a spicy maple-glazed veal chop, and grilled pork chops adobo with apple chutney. Everything is nicely presented.

Miracle Grill

112 1st Ave. (at 7th St.). ☎ 212/254-2353. AE, MC, V. Reservations accepted for 6 or more in winter. Open daily. Subway: 6 to Astor Place. SOUTHWESTERN. **$$**.

The decor may be minimalist, but the creative, red-hot food is out of this world. Miracle Grill serves up southwestern entrees that rival Arizona 206 or Mesa Grill (see above)—but at prices that won't strain your pocketbook. Try the manly ribeye, spiced up with chipotle butter and a garlic-stuffed potato, washed down with one of the grill's sublime margaritas. Weekend brunch is best enjoyed out back in the lovely, spacious garden. An eminently affordable hit, so be prepared to wait for a table.

★ Monkey Bar

60 E. 54th St. (bet. Park and Madison aves.). ☎ 212/838-2600. AE, CB, MC, V. Reservations required. Jacket required. Wheelchair accessible. Closed: Sat, Sun lunch. Subway: E, F to 5th Ave./53rd St. INTERNATIONAL. **$$$$**.

The reopening of the famed Monkey Bar in the fall of 1994 couldn't have been more welcome. The 1990s' version of the restaurant, off the lobby of the jewel-box Elysée Hotel, evokes the glamor of the 1930s, the era of its first incarnation. Ella Fitzgerald recordings are playing in the dining room, and it's not hard to imagine Tallulah Bankhead and Joe DiMaggio gathered around the piano. Tiny sculpted monkeys perch on the railings in the main room, where the crowd is vibrant but not noisy. The food lives up to its surroundings. Appetizers include an eggless Caesar salad, a warm goat-cheese salad, and ricotta ravioli. Among the best entrees are the grilled yellowfin tuna and the roast amish chicken. The Monkey Bar also makes some of the best french-fried onions around; if they're not on the menu, just ask and the kitchen probably will be happy to whip up a batch for you. The servers are well-schooled and polite, but not stuffy; several even have a sense of humor.

★ Monsoon

435 Amsterdam Ave. (81st St.). ☎ 212/580-8686. AE, DC, MC, V. Reservations advised. Open daily. Subway: 1, 9 to 79th St. VIETNAMESE. **$**.

Top-notch, authentic Vietnamese cooking keeps New Yorkers standing in line at Monsoon—even a year after its opening. Don't worry, the line moves quickly, and the prices are very reasonable. The bo sate (barbecued beef in peanut sauce) is exceptional, and curry buffs favor the curry tom. The menu has a long list of vegetarian and noodle dishes, plus seafood, chicken, and pork. Lunch specials are less than $7. Service is no-nonsense.

Monte's

97 MacDougal St. (bet. Bleecker and W. 3rd sts.). ☎ 212/228-9194. AE, CB, MC, V. Reservations advised. Closed: Tues. Subway: A, B, C, D, E, F, Q to W. 4th St./Washington Sq. ITALIAN. **$$**.

Looking for a charming Greenwich Village Italian restaurant where hand-holding is encouraged? Try Monte's. It's not new; it's not trendy. It's low pressure, with traditional northern Italian fare. A few steps down from the sidewalk, the entrance opens into a dimly lit dining room, filled mainly with white-clothed tables for two, but the occasional larger party, frequently European, energizes the place. The kitchen offers a broad selection of delicious pastas, veal, chicken, and fish. Service is friendly and efficient, and if

you have to wait, the maitre d' will chat you up.

★ Montrachet

239 W. Broadway (bet. Walker and White sts.). ☎ 212/219-2777. AE. Reservations required. Closed: Mon–Thurs lunch; Sat lunch; Sun. Subway: 1, 9 to Franklin St. FRENCH. **$$$$**.

For years, this TriBeCa outpost was known nearly as much for its low-key minimalism as for its often superb food. The walls were neutral, empty of embellishments. There were no flowers on the tables. The staff was dressed in black from chin to toe. Ownership finally took note of the loud hints by hanging abstract art, installing mirrors, and giving the staff less glum outfits to wear. What appears on the plate remains excellent, as always. Chris Gesualdi took over as chef in 1994 and the food is familiar, not dull. To begin, try the endive salad with pears, walnuts, and Roquefort. Then move on to the roasted chicken with potato puree and garlic sauce or the truffle-crusted salmon. Finish off with the banana and chocolate gratin. If the prices seem steep, the restaurant offers fixed-price meals, beginning at about $30. But if you're feeling truly indulgent, consider the weekday tasting menu of 5 abbreviated courses for $65.

Mortimer's

1057 Lexington Ave. (75th St.), ☎ 212/517-6400. AE, CB, MC, V. Reservations advised. Jacket required. Wheelchair accessible. Open daily. Subway: 6 to 77th St. INTERNATIONAL. **$$$$**.

The ingredients of success cannot be isolated; otherwise everyone would achieve it. What wizardry transforms a restaurant with indifferent food at middling-high prices in unremarkable surroundings into a de facto semiprivate club for power-hitters, trendsetters, and their eager followers? Mortimer's has crossed over into the status of an institution. To witness the phenomenon at flood stage, drop in after 11pm. A parade of lovelies and their attendants, some of them celebrated, fill the big bar and modest dining room. If they choose to eat, it is from a conventional Continental menu featuring such items as gravlax and paillard of chicken. Considering the floor show, prices are reasonable.

Il Mulino

86 W. 3rd St. (Bleecker St.). ☎ 212/673-3783. AE, CB, MC, V. Reservations advised. Jacket required. Closed: Sat lunch; Sun; July. Subway: A, B, C, D, E, F, Q to W. 4th St./ Washington Sq. ITALIAN. **$$$**
Italian restaurants in the Village used to mean checkered tablecloths, melted candles in old Chianti bottles, and watery sauces on overdone spaghetti. Il Mulino is a good deal more ambitious, and its efforts have paid off. Limousines and expensive foreign sedans line drab West 3rd Street on weekend nights, and often reservations for Saturday evening must be made 3 weeks ahead. Except for those nights, the welcome is gra-cious and the service is deft. A dish of nibbles arrives with cock-tails and the menu. Have the prosciutto with ripe figs, and the soft-shell crabs when they're available. Otherwise, you won't go wrong with any of the various pasta offerings, the fish or shellfish, all in hefty helpings. Go for lunch to avoid the crowds.

Nha Trang

87 Baxter St. (between Bayard and Canal Sts.). ☎ 212/ 233-5948. No credit cards. No reservations. Closed by 10pm nightly. Subway: 6, N, R, Z, J, or M to Canal St. or the B, D, Q to Grand St. VIETNAMESE. **$**.
There's not even a hint of decor in this downtown dive, and you'll usually have to brave a pretty long wait to get a table. But never mind. This is the best Vietnamese food in the city, hands down. Try the sugarcane shrimp to start, before moving on to heavenly pork chops or calamari deftly sautéed with chilis and onions. If you're not sure what to order, just tell your waiter how adventurous you feel, and put yourself in his hands.

Nice

35 E. Broadway (near Catherine St.). ☎ 212/406-9776. AE. Reservations advised. Wheelchair accessible. Open daily. Subway: 4, 5, 6 to Brooklyn Bridge/City Hall; J, M, Z to Chambers St. CHINESE. **$$**.
The giant Golden Unicorn, across the street, siphons off hundreds of seekers of dim sum. But if the wait there begins to seem like Friday night in an emergency ward, pop over here for a friendlier welcome and even lower prices. Women with only a slight command of English trundle carts of those tasty nibbles around the room; point at what looks intriguing. The variety isn't as great as at its larger rival, but the quality is equal. Each item is totaled up on a card, so point and eat until full. In all probability, you'll be sharing a large table with other diners, nearly all of them Chinese.

Nino's

1354 1st Ave. (72nd St.).
☎ 212/988-0002. AE, CB,
MC, V. Reservations advised.
Wheelchair accessible. Closed:
Sat lunch; Sun lunch. Subway:
6 to 68th St./Hunter College.
MEDITERRANEAN. **$$$**.
Fair prices and gratifying
creations keep the regulars
coming back. The lovely yet
informal presentations are part
of the story, as with crispy
striped bass fillets bedded on
kale, with a flourish of grapes,
or grilled mahi-mahi, lying
atop a mash of polenta framed
with haricots verts. The rooms
are attractive and somewhat
noisy, the staff ingratiating, if
sometimes distracted. Most of
the main courses are less than
$20, and decent wines can be
ordered by the glass.

★ Nobu

105 Hudson St. (at Franklin St.)
☎ 212/219-0500. AE, DC, MC,
V. Reservations required. Closed:
Sat lunch, Sun. Subway: 1, 9 to
Franklin St. JAPANESE. **$$$$$**.
After he brought jaded L.A. to
its knees with Matsuhisa, chef
Nobu Matsuhisa came east to
perform the same amazing feat
in New York—and he did.
Winner of the James Beard
Award for Best New Rest-
aurant for 1995, Nobu is the
toast of the town. And no
wonder: Raw fish has never
met a chef like Matsuhisa
before. Traditional preparations
with Latin American and
Wolfgang-Puckish California
twists result in sushi swathed in
crunchy cucumbers, monkfish
liver pate crowned with Beluga
caviar, soft-shell crab rolls, and
other flavor combinations and
textures that delight. The
artfully capricious room more
than lives up to the cuisine;
note the bar stools made of
giant chopsticks. But a repu-
tation, and a location, like

this doesn't come without a
price: Be prepared for attitude.

Odeon

145 W. Broadway (Thomas St.).
☎ 212/233-0507. AE, CB,
MC, V. Reservations advised.
Open: Sun–Fri noon–3pm,
7pm–2:30am; Sat 7pm–2:30am.
Subway: 1, 9 to Franklin St.
ECLECTIC AMERICAN. **$$**.
This eatery is an Art Moderne
cafeteria of World War II
vintage, left pretty much as it
was, with a speckled marble
floor and chrome tubular
chairs with leatherette
upholstery. Some customers
wear studded leather and
green hair, others Wall Street
pinstripes. Most, however, are
the jeans-and-tweeds sorts of
the TriBeCa-SoHo commu-
nity, who come for semi-
nouvelle dishes of brook trout
with mint and almonds,
gingered roast duck, chilled
black bean soup, or whatever
the chef has devised that night.
Steak au poivre and roast
chicken with mashed potatoes
are comforting counterpoints
to the jazzier entries. Full
dinners are served until
12:30am, light suppers until
2:30am, and the clientele
grows more entertainingly
bizarre as the night wears on.

One if by Land,
Two if by Sea

17 Barrow St. (bet. W. 4th St. and
7th Ave.). ☎ 212/228-0822.
Reservations recommended.
Jacket and tie requested. Open
for dinner daily. Subway: 1, 9 to
Christopher St. AMERICAN/
INTERNATIONAL. **$$$$$**.
This historic West Village
carriage house, once owned
by Aaron Burr, is home to
one of the city's most romantic
restaurants. The fireplace
crackles, white lights twinkle,
flowers perfume the air, and
a pianist plays as you dine on

classics like rack of lamb, perfectly prepared farm-raised Maine salmon (flown in that day), and the signature dish, an extraordinary Beef Wellington. Accompany your meal with a selection from the fabulous (if pricey) wine list, and finish it all off with a soufflé. The staff makes every day seem like a special occasion; you'll feel like they're here just for you.

Oyster Bar and Restaurant

Grand Central Terminal (42nd St. and Vanderbilt Ave.). ☎ 212/490-6650. AE, DC, MC, V. Reservations advised. Closed: Sat–Sun. Subway: 4, 5, 6, 7, S to 42nd St./Grand Central. SEAFOOD. **$$$**

Reclaimed from oblivion in the late 1970s, this venerable 1913 fishhouse is better than ever. The cavernous vaulted space is sheathed in beige tiles, its high arches echoed by pinlights. When seasons and shipments overlap, the menu is crammed with more than 120 items, changed daily according to availability. Up to a dozen types of oysters are usually on hand, along with chowders, pan roasts, stews, lobsters, and crabs. Lake sturgeon, salmon, and trout are smoked on the premises. Nearly everything is super-fresh, not too surprising in a place with this high volume. The simplest prepar-ations are best. Service is speedy, without any flourishes. Since the Oyster Bar does not close between lunch and dinner, unhurried pretheater meals are possible. To avoid the lunchtime cacophony of the main room, ask for a table in the adjoining "Saloon."

★ Palio

Equitable Center, 151 W. 51st St. (near 7th Ave.). ☎ 212/245-4850. AE, CB, MC, V. Reservations advised. Jacket and tie required. Wheelchair accessible. Closed: Sat lunch; Sun. Subway: 1, 9 to 50th St. ITALIAN. **$$$$$**

Vivid expressionist murals by Sandro Chia surround the striking horseshoe marble bar inside the entrance. Snacks called sfiziosi are available here all the time; just right as an appetite-assuager before the curtain rises. To the right is an elevator that carries the sleek crowd to the restaurant proper, 1 floor up. Wide aisles permit easy passage for diners and waiters, an amenity to be cherished, given the cost of floor space in Manhattan. Despite the room to man-euver, service can get a trifle confused at times, perhaps because most of the staff is more comfortable with Italian than English. Food is of the nuova cucina variety, often brought out at excessively long intervals and a little too light for those accustomed to heartier Italian fare. Nonethe-less, Palio continues to be an excellent choice for business meals by day and dressy couples at night.

The Palm

837 2nd Ave. (near E. 45th St.). ☎ 212/687-2953. AE, CB, MC, V. Reservations advised for parties of 4 or more. Closed: Sat lunch; Sun. Subway: 4, 5, 6, 7, S to 42nd St./Grand Central. STEAKHOUSE. **$$$$**

Beef is the reason for The Palm, and for its annex across the street, Palm Too (☎ 212/697-5198). Admirers of precisely seared slabs of unadorned prime cow-flesh are a manly lot, it would appear, impatient with the fancy rituals of those frou-frou French places. Giant steaks or lobsters are what they want, and they get them here, with loaves of hashed brown potatoes, preceded by shrimp and followed by cheesecake, all of them in stupefying portions. (Split portions to keep the total cost down.) Sawdust covers the floor, and faded cartoons line the walls and ceiling. The bored and/or sullen waiter recites the menu, for none is written, and there isn't all that much to remember. Those inclined to dining in such places insist that The Palm is one of the three best steak-houses in New York and are willing to pay for the privilege.

Pamir

1437 2nd Ave. (near 75th St.). ☎ 212/734-3791. MC, V. Reservations advised. Wheelchair accessible. Open daily, dinner only. Subway: 6 to 77th St. AFGHAN. **$$**.

Another way to shave expenses with ethnic food? Try Afghan, and try it here, for it is packed with satisfied wallet-watchers every night. It conjures up a central Asian club with its red ceiling, flickering candles, and Oriental rugs on walls and floor. Staff members are eager to please, explaining every dish. Kabobs are favorites, and lamb dishes are pervasive. The heady scents of cilantro and cardamom drift lightly through the air. A newer branch with the same name is at 1065 1st Ave. (☎ 212/694-9158), but opinion is mixed on whether its food matches that of the original.

Park Bistro

414 Park Ave. S. (near 29th St.). ☎ 212/689-1360. AE, CB, MC, V. Reservations advised. Open daily. Subway: 6 to 28th St. FRENCH. **$$$**.

One of the last districts to undergo gentrification is lower Park Avenue, and this still-hot

bistro has made the most of it. Among the often-changed items have been sautéed skate wing in vinegar sauce with cabbage, terrine of rabbit, roasted monkfish with fennel and tomato coulis. As usual, lunch is the time to keep costs within reason. The same owners opened another, similar place nearby to sop up the spillover. Les Halles (411 Park Ave. S.; ☎ 212/679-4111) looks as if it were transplanted from the old Parisian market district.

Patsy's Pizzeria

19 Old Fulton St., Brooklyn. ☎ 212/718/858-4300. No credit cards. No reservations. Open daily. Subway: 2,3 to Clark St. PIZZA. **$**.

Many people prefer John's in the Village (see above), but some die-hards swear by Patsy's pies. Thin, lighter-than-air crusts topped with fresh tomatoes and basil, homemade mozzarella, and your choice of traditional toppings (nothing nouvelle here), baked to per-fection in one of the oldest brick ovens in town. Patsy makes his way around the room, making sure everybody's fat and happy. In the warm months, the pizzeria makes the most of its enviable location—on the waterfront, just under the Brooklyn Bridge—by expanding out onto the sidewalk, where the Manhattan skyline looms just across the East River. Nowhere else do views this fabulous come this cheap. Patsy's also has a New Jersey outpost in the bedroom community of Hoboken.

Periyali

35 W. 20th (bet. 5th and 6th aves.). ☎ 212/463-7890. AE, CB, DC, MC, V. Reservations recommended. Closed: Sat lunch and Sun. Subway: F, N, R to 23rd

St. GREEK /MEDITERRANEAN.
$$$.

This stylish Greek gem has a low, fabric-draped ceiling, stone walls, and tiled floors straight out of an upscale taverna. Such seafood dishes as the charcoal-grilled octopus are simply prepared but exceptional, and the lamb (kebobs or chops) is similarly winning. Start with a plate of paradosiaka orektika, or traditional Greek appetizers, and you'll feel like you're dining just steps from the Aegean.

Peter Luger

178 Broadway (at Driggs Ave.), Brooklyn. ☎ 212/718/387-7400. No credit cards. Reservations required. Open daily. Subway: J, M, Z to Marcy St. STEAK.
$$$$$.

There's nothing nouvelle about this steakhouse extraordinaire. Don't expect much beyond a cramped beer hall atmosphere and don't even bother asking for a menu. You come here for steak, and there's no doubt: It's New York's best, aged on the premises and cooked to perfection. If your appetite is gargantuan, start with a jumbo shrimp cocktail and ask for crisp German fried potatoes on the side.

Pétrossian

182 W. 58th St. (7th Ave.). ☎ 212/245-2214. AE, CB, MC, V. Reservations advised. Jacket and tie required. Open daily. Subway: B, D, E to 7th Ave.; N, R to 57th St. INTERNATIONAL.
$$$$.

The famed Parisian firm of Pétrossian provides sustenance for those who can't get through the week without periodic infusions of foie gras and caviar. To showcase the products in the New World, Pétrossian opened this upmarket restaurant/takeout-boutique in an appropriately grand Beaux Arts building. Immediately inside the entrance are glass cases filled with such essential edibles as duck and goose terrines, truffles, smoked silver eel, and Scottish trout. A right turn leads into the restaurant, a snug Art Deco setting with marble floors and nudes etched on the mirrors behind the angled bar. Deft waiters bring présentoirs heaped with caviar, or impeccably arranged plates of the several Pétrossian Teasers, such as roulades of smoked sturgeon with wild mushrooms or bouquets of shrimp with smoked cod roe. Main courses are half nouvelle, half classical French. The vodka is Russian, of course, and the house champagnes are available by the glass. The prix-fixe luncheons and weekend brunches are still bargains.

★ Rainbow Room

30 Rockefeller Plaza, 65th Floor (bet. 49th and 50th sts.). ☎ 212/ 632-5000. AE, DC, MC, V. Reservations required. Closed Mon. Subway: B, D, F, Q to 47th-50th sts./Rockefeller Center. INTERNATIONAL..
$$$$$.

This is the New York of a 1940s' movie-set idyll, complete with velvet drapes, black-tie waiters, and smooching patrons. The menu features just as many "standards" as a lounge act in the neighboring cabaret: such dishes as lobster thermidor, oysters Rockefeller, and baked Alaska may sound old hat, but here they still taste fresh. The revolving dance floor (with accompanying orchestra) cries out for a post-dinner spin; in short, the magical romanticism is nearly unparalleled. If you can't manage the sky-high prices, try the Promenade, a more informal and affordable cafe with similarly stunning views. The Rainbow Room is actually one venue in a 2-floor complex of restaurants, banquet rooms, and supper clubs. See "Cabarets & Supper Clubs" in "New York After Dark" for more information.

★ Remi

145 W. 53rd St. (bet. 6th and 7th aves.). ☎ 212/581-4247. AE, CB, MC, V. Reservations advised. Wheelchair accessible. Closed: Sat, Sun lunch. Subway: E, F to 5th Ave./53rd St. ITALIAN. **$$$$**.
A very stylish, spacious dining room with bleached wood floors, wide windows, and a blue-and-white nautical theme give Remi an upbeat sensibility. One reason for the jovial mindset is the food. Those patrons who tend to feel restrained in establishments with richer food feel more free to partake here. Dieters appre-ciate the grilled fresh vege-tables with garlic, and the simple tuna and salmon dishes. Diners with a looser inter-pretation of healthy eating can indulge in the boneless quail wrapped in bacon, and the daily risotto dish, and the potato gnocchi with braised veal.

La Réserve

4 W. 49th St. (near 5th Ave.). ☎ 212/247-2993. AE, CB, MC, V. Reservations advised. Closed: Sat lunch; Sun. Subway: B, D, F, Q to 47th-50th sts./Rockefeller Center. FRENCH. **$$$$**.
Venetian glass chandeliers illuminate La Réserve's 2 large rooms, which are hung with large murals of game preserves. The decor is richly elegant but not ostentatious. The china is Limoges, and the balloon-shaped goblets allow the proper savoring of a Château

Laffitte. The food is haute, with an up-to-date concern for presentation. Mediocrity is not permitted, nor is novelty for novelty's sake. Tables are closely placed, but not oppressively so, and service is efficient, if not warm. The pretheater dinner, which must be ordered between 5:30 and 6:45pm, is a less expensive way to sample the kitchen's wares, but beware of slow service. Although it can take several weeks to reserve a table at others of this class, 2 to 3 days' notice is usually sufficient here.

River Café

1 Water St., Brooklyn, NY. ☎ 718/522-5200. AE, DC, MC, V. Reservations required. Open daily. Subway: A to High St./Brooklyn Bridge; 2, 3 to Clark St. ECLECTIC AMERICAN. **$$$$**.
The breathtaking views of the Manhattan skyline from this remodeled barge beneath the Brooklyn Bridge more than compensate for the frequent changes of the guard behind the stoves. One celebrity chef after another. first came to wide attention for his work here before moving on. Now Rick Laakkonen is at the kitchen's helm. The French influence is undeniable, but the sensibility is more Amer-ican, perhaps inspired by the Statue of Liberty visible through the portholes. Ingre-dients include yellowfin tuna, rainbow trout, salmon, rabbit, and jumbo quail. The most atmospheric time to be there is at dusk, when lights are kept low. A piano is played, and tables are set out on the terrace in summer. Sunday brunch is popular.

Rosa Mexicano

1063 1st Ave. (58th St.). ☎ 212/753-7407. AE, CB, MC, V. Reservations advised. Open daily.

Subway: 4, 5, 6 to 59th St.; N, R to Lexington Ave. MEXICAN.

$$$.

The management here feels compelled to specify on the menu that "you may not find some of the Americanized dishes associated with Mexican food." Authenticity aside, these dishes are just plain tasty. In a city of rubbery, shop-bought tortillas, Rosa Mexicano makes its own, fresh daily. In contrast to the usually vapid yuppie margaritas, the bar here concocts them with fresh lime juice and premium tequila. Duck comes in a creamy green pumpkinseed sauce with a hint of serrano; raw bay scallops are marinated in lemon juice, chili, and coriander. Specials often feature recipes from one or more of Mexico's regional cuisines, such as Yucatán's shredded peppery pork, slow-baked in banana leaves. The wine list is adequate, but this food cries for real Mexican beer—Corona or Dos Equis.

The Saloon

2010 Broadway (64th St.).
☎ 212/874-1500. AE, CB, MC, V. Reservations advised. Open daily. Subway: 1, 9 to 66th St./Lincoln Center. ECLECTIC AMERICAN. **$$**.

Directly across Broadway from Lincoln Center, The Saloon's vast, open dining room is both a neighborhood favorite and a spot well-trafficked by patrons from other parts of the city on their way to or from a performance. The menu is extensive, borrowing from Chinese, Mexican, and Italian cooking. It has complex salads, pastas, sandwiches, pizzas, seafood, even heart-healthy choices. One of The Saloon's biggest draws is its good-size sidewalk cafe, with the front row of seating facing out for unabashed people-watching on

the order of its prime Parisian counterparts.

The Sea Grill

19 W. 49th St. (near 5th Ave.).
☎ 212/246-9201. AE, CB, MC, V. Reservations advised. Jacket required. Wheelchair accessible. Open daily. Subway: B, D, F, Q to 47th-50th sts./ Rockefeller Center. SEAFOOD. **$$$$**.

When the skating rink at the foot of the GE Building in Rockefeller Center was overhauled, it was the management's intent to upgrade the eating places that bordered the popular arena. That's not saying much, given the feeble performances of a succession of previous occupants. The fact that The Sea Grill turned out to be better than required is a pleasant surprise. The decor is neither flashy nor dowdy, with comfortable leather chairs allowing views of skaters (in winter) twirling outside, and cooks flashing knives and spatulas over the open grill. It is an atmosphere in which both businesspeople and adult tourists feel at ease. The menu leans toward regional American dishes, an elastic rubric that incorporates grilled fish, chowders, oysters Rockefeller, charred pompano and chicken, and the San Francisco invention, cioppino (seafood stew). Most of it is competent, if rather ordinary. The companion restaurant across the rink is the American Festival Café (20 W. 50th St.; ☎ 212/246-6699). With its broader menu and lower prices, it may be a better choice for families.

Second Avenue Deli

156 2nd Ave. (corner of 10th St.).
☎ 212/677-0606. AE. Reservations recommended for

large parties. Subway: 6 to Astor Place; N, R to 8th St.; L to 3rd Ave. JEWISH. **$**.

Carnegie shmarnegie—who needs a $10 corned-beef sandwich? At Second Avenue, you get Jewish soul food—kasha, knishes, and soups that regulars swear will cure the common cold. The capital chopped liver, pastrami, and corned beef are on par with any in the city—and cheaper too. You get more authentic Borscht Belt banter from the fast-talking waiters than you'd find at Second Avenue's much-lauded but more expensive Midtown rivals, the Stage and Carnegie delicatessens.

Serendipity 3

225 E. 60th St. (bet. 3rd and 2nd aves.). ☎ 212/838-3531. Reservations advised. AE, DC, DISC, MC, V. Open daily. Subway: 4, 5, 6 to 59th St.; N,R to Lexington Ave. AMERICAN. **$$** or **$$$**.

Little children's eyes will light up when they see the bowls of signature frozen hot chocolate and other luscious dessert concoctions at Serendipity. The wild black-and-white menu also includes foot-long hot dogs, juicy burgers, sandwiches, and salads. You'll be pleased with the super-friendly waitstaff, but there's often a line to get in this whimsical ice cream parlor/restaurant/toy museum, which is just around the corner from Bloomingdale's.

The Shark Bar

307 Amsterdam Ave. (bet. 74th and 75th sts.). ☎ 212/874-8500. AE, CB, MC, V. Reservations advised (not accepted Fri-Sat for parties of less than 5). Open daily. Subway: 1, 2, 3, 9 to 72nd St. SOUTHERN. **$$**.

Short of the renowned Sylvia's (see below), the city has no more accomplished purveyor of Southern soul food than this lively West Side haunt. A mixed crowd of yuppies and boomers, both black and white, testifies to this, drawn by the reasonable prices and party-time atmosphere. Steps up from the packed front bar is a dining room a-chatter with people digging into crawfish cocktails, seafood gumbo, blackened catfish, black-eyed peas, honey-dipped fried chicken, and sweet potato pie. Service is affable but often overworked, especially at the popular Saturday gospel brunches. Tuesday evenings feature live music at 11pm. Dinner is served until after midnight.

★ Shun Lee

43 W. 65th St. (near Broadway). ☎ 212/595-8895. AE, CB, MC, V. Reservations advised. Jacket and tie recommended. Wheelchair accessible. Open daily. Subway: 1, 9 to 66th St./Lincoln Center. CHINESE. **$$$**.

One of a small group of restaurants that brought high style to Chinese restaurants back in the 1970s, Shun Lee was a happy improvement upon the quiche-and-burger emporia that long dominated the Lincoln Center area. The black-and-white decor is enlivened at the entrance and in the lounge by papier mâché dragons and monkeys with glowing red eyes. Spicy Szechuan and Hunan cuisines are the specialty. Among the resulting winners are pan-fried pork dumplings, crispy Hunan sea bass, and sliced duckling with young ginger root. When a full meal might rest too heavily on the stomach during a night at the opera, the fare at the adjoining Shun Lee Café ☎ 212/769-3888) is just the ticket—and at a much lower price. The Café is open for dinner only from Monday to Friday, for lunch and dinner on Saturday and Sunday.

Siam Inn

916 8th Ave. (bet. 54th and 55th sts.). ☎ 489-5237. AE, DC, MC, V. No reservations. Subway: 1, 9, A, B, C, D to 59th St./Columbus Circle. THAI. **$$**

Siam Inn looks like just another pleasant, generic Asian restaurant, the kind of place you'd duck into only if you were hungry and it was right in front of you. But its unremarkable appearance belies the skill of its kitchen: This is one of Manhattan's best Thai restaurants. Appetizers—soups, satays, Thai spring rolls, and flaky, greaseless curry puffs—are outstanding here. Among the main courses, I'm especially partial to the rich masaman curry. But every dish is good, and splendidly presented. Another branch, Siam Inn Too, is just 3 blocks down on 8th Avenue.

Sign of the Dove

1110 3rd Ave. (at 65th St.). ☎ 212/861-8080. Reservations required. AE, DC, DISC, MC, V. Closed: Mon lunch. Subway: 6 to 68th St. ECLECTIC AMERICAN. **$$$$$**.

This elegant restaurant, all soft lighting and aromatic floral bouquets, is as romantic as dining gets. The service is flawless, and the tables are spaced far enough apart to ensure a sense of intimacy wherever you sit. Chef Andrew D'Amico's innovative menu includes a delicious wild mushroom strudel appetizer, as well as a superb roast duck served with carmelized beets

and figs. All the seafood dishes are excellent, and the venison practically melts in your mouth. A lighter menu is served in the happening cafe/bar; the calamari is crisp and quite good.

Smith & Wollensky

797 3rd Ave. (at 49th St.). ☎ 212/753-1530. AE, MC, V. Reservations recommended. Closed Sat lunch, Sun lunch. Subway: 6 to 51st St.; E, F to Lexington/3rd Ave. STEAK. **$$$$**.

A throwback to the days when deals were negotiated over gargantuan sirloins in smoke-filled rooms, Smith & Wollensky is a steakhouse in the darkened wood, brass rail, forest-green walls tradition. The waitstaff is old-school and friendly, and the dependable menu holds no surprises: steaks, chops, seafood, and the occasional salad. Wollensky's Grill serves many of the same dishes at slightly lesser prices.

Solera

216 E. 53rd St. (bet. 2nd and 3rd aves.). ☎ 212/644-1166. AE, CB, MC, V. Reservations advised. Wheelchair accessible. Closed: Sat lunch; Sun. Subway: 4, 5, 6 to 59th St.; N, R to Lexington Ave. SPANISH. **$$$** tapas bar; **$$$$** dining room.

The brief enthusiasm for Spanish tapas never really caught fire in this city, but several restaurants still serve them. Solera serves the appetizer-sized tapas at the long bar just inside the front door. A changing blackboard menu lists about 12 tapas each night, often including the sturdy potato-and-egg omelet called a tortilla, and fried squid rings or white beans tossed in vinaigrette with strips of sweet peppers and salami. Two or three choices shared by a couple constitute a light, relatively inexpensive meal. In the dining rooms in back and upstairs, such regional specialties as paella, salt-cod salad, and monkfish medallions with black olive purée are carefully prepared by the American chef.

Sonia Rose
132 Lexington Ave. (bet. 28th and 29th sts.) ☎ 212/545-1777. AE, DC, MC, V. Reservations required. Closed: Sat lunch, Sun lunch, Mon lunch. FRENCH. **$$$**.

This undiscovered treasure serves eclectic French cuisine that's lovingly prepared. Each night, there's a different $36 prix-fixe menu, from which you'll have 7 or 8 choices for appetizer, entree, and dessert. The dishes are superior and make fabulous use of herbs. If you can, try the sautéed monkfish, served with a punchy tomato, garlic, and crabmeat sauce. It's such an intimate spot, with only 11 tables and wonderfully attentive service, you'll want to keep this place a secret.

Sparks Steak House
210 E. 46th St. (near 3rd Ave.). ☎ 212/687-4855. AE, DC, MC, V. Reservations required. Closed Sat lunch; Sun. Subway: 4, 5, 6, 7, S to 42nd St./Grand Central. STEAK. **$$$$**.

One of the best of the classic Manhattan steakhouses, Sparks's huge chops and lobsters are as succulent and overpriced as any in town. If anything, it has pulled ahead of most of its competition. What makes it even more notable is that few restaurants of any category can match its inventory of fine wines. Wine buffs can test the virtues and vintages of dozens of California labels, plus those of France, Italy, and Spain. Between sips, dig into sublimely simple sirloins and filet mignons or any of a half dozen types of fish, all cooked precisely to order. "Steak fromage" is about as fancied as things get. Service in the masculine room, with its dark wainscoting and landscapes in gilded frames, is solemn and correct, with covered plates and debris rolled silently away on trolleys.

Sylvia's
328 Lenox Ave. (Malcolm X Blvd., bet. 126th and 127th sts.). ☎ 212/996-0660 or 996-2669. AE. Reservations required for Sunday brunch. Open daily. Subway: 2, 3 to 125th St. SOUTHERN/SOUL FOOD. **$**.

One of the grand old institutions of Harlem, Sylvia's has been the royal court of Gotham's southern cookery for more than 30 years. It looks like just another family-style restaurant, but Sylvia's is a place to celebrate African-American culture— community leaders and celebrities often convene here to shoot the breeze and eat some of the real deal. Mainstays include fried chicken; a string of side dishes like collards, black-eyed peas, and some seriously beatific candied yams; sweet iced tea; and of course, "Sylvia's World Famous Talked About Bar-B-Que Ribs Special"—meaty and tender, covered in a sauce that's sweet on top with a slow, spicy burn underneath. Sunday brunch is a venerable tradition here, featuring the heavenly sounds of the tuxedo-clad Gospel Brothers.

T Salon
142 Mercer St. (at Prince). ☎ 212/925-3700. AE, CB, MC, V. Reservations advised.

Wheelchair accessible. Open daily. Subway: N, R to Prince St. AMERICAN. **$$**.

Adjoining the Guggenheim Museum's SoHo branch is the T Salon, a cafe specializing in tea, that drink renowned for its soothing and comforting qualities. Afternoon tea here, with finger sandwiches and sweets, is a good alternative to a rushed pretheater dinner. It's also a pleasant experience in itself. Although the regular menu is not remarkable, it is fine for a light lunch or dinner, and the T Salon also has a juice bar and an impressive selection of rare port and wine. The cozy atmosphere makes it an appealing place to congregate with friends for a chat.

Take-Sushi

71 Vanderbilt Ave. (near 46th St.), ☎ 212/867-5120. AE, CB, MC, V. Reservations required. Closed: Sat lunch; Sun. Subway: 4, 5, 6, 7, S to 42nd St./Grand Central. JAPANESE. **$$$$**.

Sushi and sashimi—raw fish with and without rice—neophytes are welcome at this friendly, growing, family-owned chain. The kimonoed waitresses and the chefs themselves go out of their way to instruct gently on the niceties of this specialized sort of eating. They might urge that you begin with the unadorned, buttery-soft "fatty tuna," or that you eat the yellowtail rolled with rice in seaweed sheets with your fingers, not chopsticks. The result is a far more gratifying evening of culinary theater than you will find at one of those places where the eating of uncooked fish is regarded as a mystic ritual.

Tavern on the Green

Central Park W. (67th St.). ☎ 212/873-3200. AE, DC, MC, V. Reservations advised.

Open daily. Subway: 1, 9 to 66th St./Lincoln Center. AMERICAN/INTERNATIONAL. **$$$**.

Tavern on the Green is one of those places that must be mentioned simply because it is there and everybody knows about it. Once a barn for the sheep that wandered in the adjacent meadow, it has been a restaurant since 1934. Warren LeRoy has turned it into a visual stunner, crammed with carved plaster, etched mirrors, and a profusion of brass, crystal, and copper ornamentation. The trees outside are strung with thousands of pinlights, seen from blocks away. Some describe the experience as "festive"; others call it noisy, disorganized, and pretentiously cute. The food—the usual pasta, fish, steak, etc.—can be good, but predicting which dishes will work traditionally has been hard. A new executive chef, Patrick Clark, is said to have brought some consistency. Service is erratic. Nonetheless, out-of-towners and many New Yorkers love it. Maybe you'll agree. To find out, try the relatively inexpensive pretheater dinner. Or eat elsewhere and come for the good jazz in the Chestnut Room or the dancing in the garden in summertime.

Thailand

106 Bayard St. (Baxter St.). ☎ 212/349-3132. AE. Reservations advised. Wheelchair accessible. Closed: Mon. Subway: N, R, 6 to Canal St. THAI. **$$**.

It might seem sacrilegious to venture into Thai food while you are in Chinatown, since a year of uninterrupted consumption would not exhaust the Szechuan, Mandarin, Cantonese, and Hunan cuisines to be sampled in its perhaps 200 restaurants. But this admittedly seedy little place across from Columbus Park deserves consideration, with prices as low as any in the neighborhood. The menu is bewilderingly comprehensive, with nearly 100 listed items. A party of four can take advantage of the variety.

Time Cafe/Fez

380 Lafayette St. (at Great Jones St.). ☎ 212/533-7000. AE, MC, V. Reservatons recommended on weekends. Open daily. Subway: 6 to Astor Place or Bleecker St. ECLECTIC AMERICAN. **$$**.

Plunge into the fashionably hip scene at this laid-back bistro. If possible, dine outside in summer and people-watch to your heart's content. The menu leans toward the wholesome and the organic; tangy goat cheese and a zesty vinaigrette enliven that run-of-the-mill cafe staple, the grilled chicken salad. In back is Fez, a smoky, elegant lounge with a regular schedule of live music and poetry readings. The atmosphere at Fez evokes a 1950s' jazz club; sit back, order a gimlet or a martini, and don't miss the Thursday night Mingus Big-Band show.

Tout va Bien

311 W. 51st St. (bet. 8th and 9th aves.). ☎ 212/265-0190. AE, MC ,V. Reservations recommended for dinner. Open daily. Subway: 1, 9 or C, E to 50th St. FRENCH. **$$$**.

A good choice for a pre-theater dinner, Tout va Bien has been around for decades, serving classic French bistro food. The atmosphere is charming, authentic, and anything but pretentious, and the prices are surprisingly reasonable for traditional favorites like garlicky escargot, filet of sole, steak with pommes frites, and more.

It would be a sin to top off your meal with anything other than the crème brûlée.

Trattoria Dell'Arte

900 7th Ave. (57th St.). ☎ 212/245-9800. AE, CB, MC, V. Reservations advised. Wheelchair accessible. Open daily. Subway: N, R to 57th St. ITALIAN. **$$$$**.

Some people are pained by the decor, which features outsized representations of body parts—a nose, lips, an ear, a breast—and Renaissance drawings of the same. If you're apt to find that offensive, don't go, but you'll miss super pizzas and pastas and a most tantalizing antipasto bar. (Single diners can sit at the marble counter around that delectable array, pointing and eating until buttons pop.) Most members of the staff haven't been any closer to Rome than Little Italy, but they're a cheerful and efficient lot. The Italian touch is evident in the weekend brunch with polenta pancakes and fruit focaccia. Some of the main courses fall short, but all in all, it's a good spot for a meal or snack pre- or post-performance at Carnegie Hall, directly across the street.

Tribeca Grill

375 Greenwich St. (Franklin St.). ☎ 212/941-3900. Reservations advised. Closed: Sat lunch. Subway: 1, 9 to Franklin St. ECLECTIC AMERICAN. **$$$**.

Occupying the first 2 floors of the Tribeca Film Center, the Tribeca Grill remains a trendy eatery 5 years after opening. The degree to which co-owner Robert DeNiro—and a roster of celebrity investors—has affected that popularity is debatable. Hard to label, the food tastes of many cultures; much of it is grilled or sautéed.

Chef Don Pintabona also does a roast chicken and a veal with whipped potatoes. The wine list numbers 140, many of them under $40. Bobby's partner, Drew Nieporent (the man who put the laudable Montrachet on the map) has given the cavernous space an industrial feel with lots of exposed brick and a heavy mahogany bar salvaged from the near-legendary Maxwell's Plum before the wrecking ball hit. Large semiabstract figurative canvases by DeNiro's late father hang on the walls. Brokers in shirtsleeves and artists in T-shirts and jeans mingle merrily, with lots of hugging and laughing going on, and the gatekeepers display no favoritism.

21 (Twenty-One) Club

21 W. 52nd St. (near 5th Ave.). ☎ 212/582-7200. AE, CB, MC, V. Reservations advised. Jacket and tie required. Wheelchair accessible. Closed Sat (in summer); Sun. Subway: B, D, F, Q to 47th-50th sts./Rockefeller Center. AMERICAN. **$$$$$**

Once a Prohibition-era speakeasy, 21 went on to become a sanctuary for the power elite. Celebrities are often on view, but the well-groomed and garbed regulars who frequent the place are more often senior partners in important law firms or executives of multinational corporations. It is not a club in the sense of excluding the general public, but strangers are granted no more than distant courtesy. The ambiance, too, is of a gentlemen's club, with lots of dark paneling and leather chairs. Under new management, the food has been up and down, but currently appears to be on the ascendancy. Prices are high,

however, and many people settle for a manly martini in the colorful bar and go elsewhere to eat.

Un Deux Trois

123 W. 44th St. (near Times Sq.). ☎ 212/354-4148. AE, CB, MC, V. Reservations advised for large parties. Closed: Sat and Sun lunch. Subway: N, R, S, 1, 2, 3, 7, 9 to 42nd St./Times Sq. FRENCH. **$$$**

This restaurant's allegiance to the brasserie archetype is not slavish, but with its vast room, paper tablecloths, and hearty rather than delicate victuals, it makes its point. Not a destination restaurant, Un Deux Trois is a welcome eatery in the theater district, where the dining options generally serve bad food at inflated prices. At lunch, its clients run to business sorts, but at nightfall, a theater crowd takes over—the place virtually empties out at 7:53pm. No one raves about the food, but the simple menu fare—roast chicken, steak au poivre—are usually preferable to the daily specials.

★★ Union Square Café

21 E. 16th St. (near 5th Ave.). ☎ 212/243-4020. AE, DC, MC, V. Reservations required. Open daily. Subway: L, N, R, 4, 5, 6 to 14th St./Union Sq. FRENCH/ ITALIAN/AMERICAN. **$$$**

One of the best overall dining experiences in New York, from the welcome by a host, who appears so delighted to see you that you hardly notice he is steering you to the worst table in the house, to the equally bubbly servers to, of course, the food, the very model of pan-oceanic eclecticism, with myriad flavors that explode in the mouth at every bite. Not even the check, totaling about half what uptown emporia charge for comparable eats, will sour the meal. Now more about the food: There's Maine crabmeat tortelli with roast tomato-oregano butter for starters, then crispy lemon-pepper duck with peach-fig chutney. A touch of whimsy is evident in such side dishes as hot garlic potato chips and mashed potatoes with frizzled leeks. Seated under big expressionistic murals of floating nudes, the crowd seems more interested in enjoying itself than in seeing and being seen.

Vince & Eddie's

70 W. 68th St. (bet. Columbus Ave. and Central Park W.). ☎ 212/721-0068. AE, CB, MC, V. Reservations advised. Open daily. Subway: 1, 9 to 66th St./Lincoln Center. ECLECTIC AMERICAN. **$$$**.

Winters, a fire crackles in the raised fireplace; summers, the back opens to a small terrace. In between, this mightily successful eatery strives to resemble a Kansas farmhouse. Its close quarters contain mismatched chairs and oil-cloths on the tables, antique picture frames and old tools on the walls. The food fits the setting—hearty soups and stews, roast chickens, fried oysters, memorable lamb shank with mashed potatoes. Weekend brunches get a Continental touch, with baked mussels, seafood crepes, and fried calamari among the selections. Popular in the evenings and on weekends, it is often easiest to gain entrance at lunchtime. A little more polish might be asked of the service staff, but they work with earnestness.

Virgil's Real BBQ

152 W. 44th St. (bet. 6th and 7th aves.) ☎ 212/921-9494.

AE, MC, V. Reservations recommended. Open daily. BARBECUE. **$$**.

Smack in the thick of Times Square, this 2-floor restaurant can get quite crowded. Portions are huge; the pork BBQ, sandwiches, and po'boys are excellent—and the chicken is fabulous whether it's pulled, fried, or roasted. The biscuits served with maple butter are everything you've envisioned a biscuit to be. Side dishes include corn bread, mashed potatoes with mushroom gravy, and macaroni and cheese that's gritty with cheese. When you're done you'll get a hot towel to clean up with. There's also an extensive beer list.

★★ Vong

200 E. 54th St. (3rd Ave.). ☎ 212/486-9592. AE, CB, MC, V. Reservations advised. Subway: 6 to 51st St.; E, F to Lexington/3rd Ave. and 53rd St. ASIAN. **$$$$**.

The atmosphere may pay homage to colonial Southeast Asia, with bamboo detailing, private booths, and romantic lighting, but the cuisine of the innovative chef Jean-Georges Vongerichten is anything but old-fashioned. Vongerichten, who also created JoJo, blends Asian elements with those of traditional French cooking. My favorite is an appetizer, the crab spring rolls. Some of the other concoctions are lobster with Thai herbs, duck breast with a spicy sesame sauce, and roasted chicken with lemon grass and sweet rice steamed in a banana leaf. The desserts, such as pepper ice cream, may push the limits of some diners' taste buds, but Vong also offers some more mainstream items, such as crème brûlée.

Windows on the World

1 World Trade Center. ☎ 212/
938-1111. AE, CB, MC, V.
Subway: C, E to World Trade
Center; N, R, 1, 9 to Cortlandt St.
Subway: C, E to World Trade
Center; N, R, 1, 9 to Cortlandt St.
INTERNATIONAL. The Cellar in the
Sky: **$$$$$**; reservations
required; dinner only, closed Sun.
The Hors d'Oeuvrerie: **$$$**; no
reservations. The Restaurant:
$$$$; reservations required;
closed Sun dinner.

Three different eating places fall
under the Windows on the
World umbrella, all of them in
the north tower on the 107th
floor. Enduring the wait at
the reception desk of The
Restaurant can be a chore, but
persevere, for the stunning
urban vista justifies the
temporary aggravation. As is
usual in rooftop restaurants,
competence on the plate proves
elusive, but the fixed-price
dinner at least eases the fiscal
bite. The premise of The Hors
d'Oeuvrerie is to make entire
meals of appetizers, a gimmick
that was overdue. The starter
dishes of different countries—
Chinese dim sum, Italian
antipasti, Spanish tapas—are
featured on a rotating monthly
basis. Jazz performers are on
duty from 4:30pm until closing.
The Cellar in the Sky has no
views but attempts to compen-
sate with ambitious 7-course
meals enhanced by 5 different
wines. It has only 1 sitting each
evening (dinner only) for a
maximum of 36 diners. Avoid
the hectic Sunday buffet and
brunch.

Woo Chon

8-10 W. 36th St. (5th Ave.).
☎ 212/695-0676. AE, CB,
MC, V Reservations advised.
Wheelchair accessible. Open daily
24 hrs. Subway: B, D, F, N, Q, R
to 34th St.; 6 to 33rd St.
KOREAN. **$$$**.

A glance at the signs up and
down this seedy street west of
5th Avenue confirms that this
is Little Korea, tiny compared
to Chinatown, but growing.
Right in the middle is this
shining example of how good
an ethnic restaurant can be
without pandering to the
uninitiated. The long menu
includes sushi, sashimi, and
other Japanese dishes, but the
star attractions are the several
barbecued items. Immediately
upon seating, one waiter pours
glasses of hot tea and another
brings small bowls of kim
chee, pickled cabbage, or tur-
nips marinated in a juice of
vinegar, garlic, red pepper,
and other spices—it can be
anything from mild to potent
and peppery. They merely
keep you occupied until the
meal arrives. Lunch specials
are uncommon bargains.
Typical are the compart-
mentalized red-and-
black lacquered bento
trays that come with
barbecued short ribs, tem-
pura shrimp with dipping
sauce, a green vegetable,
mixed salad and rice, with
a bowl of miso soup on the
side. All this can be had
for less than $10. The staff
is helpful to the limits of
their respective commands
of English.

Yama

122 E. 17th St. (at Irving Pl.).
☎ 212/475-0969. AE, MC,
V. Reservations not taken.
Closed: Sun. Subway: 4, 5, 6, N,
R to Union Square. JAPANESE.
$$.

Hidden away in a Gramercy
Park basement is the best sushi
deal in town. How do they do
it? The secret is size: Yama
serves up fresh sushi and
sashimi artfully cut into pieces
practically as big as your fist.
Ever since the Zagat Survey

pegged Yama as one of the city's 50 best restaurants, the line for a table in this bright, crowded, noisy dining room has extended down the block. Go early and be prepared to wait—but for sushi this good at easy-on-the-wallet prices, you'll be glad you did.

Zarela

953 2nd Ave. (bet. 50th and 51st sts.). ☎ 212/644-6740. AE, DC. Reservations advised. Open daily. Subway: 6 to 51st St.; E, F to Lexington/3rd Ave. and 53rd St. MEXICAN. **$$**.

Fans call it the best Mexican in the city. Loyalists of Rosa Mexicano (see above) beg to differ. But who cares? This is a perpetual fiesta in progress, full of tumult and people enjoying themselves to the sounds of live music. Ceilings are hung with piñatas and loops of colorful paper cutouts; a staircase wall has cubbyholes loaded with south-of-the border folk art. Plates are plain and white, flatware is stainless steel, the young patrons are casually attired. Among the most ordered dishes are fajitas, chilaquiles, and escabeche de pollo oriental. Spices are kept on the mild side, with few fire-breathers.

Zen Palate

663 9th Ave. (46th St.). ☎ 212/582-1669. AE, CB, MC, V. Reservations advised for dinner. Open daily. Subway: C, E to 50th St. ASIAN. **$$**.

Muted cherry woodwork, ocher walls, terra-cotta floors, and horticultural prints of squash and bok choy set the gentle mood. Friendly servers illuminate the innovative menu items, in which shredded gluten, tofu, and other veggies stand in for chicken, squid, and duck. Apart from the no-alcohol, vegetarian stance, the recipes are not dogmatic. The kitchen borrows from China, Japan, Thailand, and Indonesia, with curries and pastas as well as moo shu rolls and scallion pancakes. Even dedicated carnivores find Zen the perfect pre-theater repast, with no danger of nodding off halfway through the first act because of overindulgence in wine or beef.

Good Fast Food

It isn't necessary to resort to the ubiquitous representatives of the franchised food chains for a quick snack or an inexpensive meal. Here are some more gastronomically acceptable alternatives.

Atomic Wings

1644 3rd Ave. (92nd St.). ☎ 212/410-3800.

Spicy chicken wings, that is, the ultimate bar snack.

Benny's Burritos

113 Greenwich Ave. (Jane St.). ☎ 212/633-9210.

Greenwich Village's numero uno tortilla joint. These Tex Mex burritos are about the length and thickness of a man's forearm, with many tempting choices.

Broome Street Bar

363 W. Broadway (Broome St.). ☎ 212/925-2086.

Salads, sandwiches, and pub grub in SoHo.

Dallas BBQ

1265 3rd Ave. ☎ 212/772-9393; 21 University

Place ☎ 212/674-4450;
and other locations.
Generous margaritas and
copious portions of Texas-style
barbecued fare compensate for
the noise and the slap-dash
service.

★ Diane's Uptown
249 Columbus Ave. (bet. 71st
and 72nd sts.). ☎ 212/
799-6750.
I have yet to find a better
burger and fries in the city.
Thick, juicy, no unnecessary
complications. Diane's also has
salads, sandwiches, turkey
burgers, omelets, and, best of
all, marvelous ice cream
creations from the Ben and
Jerry's next door.

Dosanko
135 E. 45th St. ☎ 212/
697-2967; 423 Madison Ave.
☎ 212/688-8575; 329 5th Ave.
☎ 212/686-9359, and other
locations.
No-decor Japanese noodle
shops featuring cheap, filling
soup and fried chicken.

★ EJ's Luncheonette
433 Amsterdam Ave. (bet.
80th and 81st sts.).
☎ 212/873-3444.
A cut above the corner diner,
with chili, salads, burgers, and
waffles—and open daily from
early morning to 11pm or
midnight.

Fine and Shapiro
138 W. 72nd St. (near Broadway).
☎ 212/877-2874.
One of the better Jewish delis.

1st Wok
1374 3rd Ave. (78th St.).
☎ 212/861-2600.

One of a growing Szechuan
chain.

Great Jones
54 Great Jones St. (near
Broadway). ☎ 212/674-9304.
Low-cost Cajun.

Hamburger Harry's
157 Chambers St. (near W.
Broadway). ☎ 212/267-4446.
Imaginative variations on the
classic.

Jackson Hole
517 Columbus Ave. (85th St.)
☎ 212/362-5177; 1270
Madison Ave. (91st St.) ☎ 212/
427-2820; and other locations.
Huge burgers, sandwiches,
salads.

Papaya King
179 E. 86th St. (3rd Ave.).
☎ 212/369-0648.
Maybe the tastiest hot dogs
in town—two plus a cup
of papaya juice for less than a
Big Mac. Not to be confused
with others with similar
names.

Tortilla Flats
767 Washington St. (W. 12th St.).
☎ 212/243-1053.
Tex-Mex in the West Village.

Veselka Coffee Shop
144 2nd Ave. (9th St.).
☎ 212/228-9682.
Honest renditions of Polish
and Ukrainian dishes; located
in the East Village.

Wylie's Rib
891 1st Ave. (50th St.).
☎ 212/751-0700.
Decent Southern barbecue and
chili, served with onion loaves
as big as bricks.

Open Late
Whether looking for a light post-theater supper or some
post-partying junk food, you might try one of these
establishments, all open well past midnight.

Brasserie
100 E. 53rd St. (near Park Ave.).
☎ 212/751-4840.
Sort of French, but best
known for staying open 24
hours.

Carnegie Delicatessen
854 7th Ave. (near 55th St.).
☎ 212/757-2245.
Open until 4am. See write-up
above.

Corner Bistro
331 W. 4th St. (Jane St.).
☎ 212/242-9502.
Greenwich Village chili,
burgers, and brew.

Empire Diner
210 10th Ave. (22nd St.)
☎ 212/243-2736.
Retro-glitz, often packed
with club-goers. Open 24
hours.

Hard Rock Café
221 W. 57th St. (near Broadway).
☎ 212/459-9320.
Always jammed, always loud—
a favorite for teens. Open until
4am.

Odeon
145 W. Broadway (Thomas St.).
☎ 212/233-0507.
TriBeCa haunt. Open until
2:30am. See write-up above.

P.J. Clarke's
915 3rd Ave. (55th St.).
☎ 212/759-1650.
Tavern food, lively mixed
crowd. Open until 4am.

Stage Deli
834 7th Ave. (near 54th St.).
☎ 212/245-7850.
An alternative to the Carnegie
Deli. Open until 2am.

Wilson's
201 W. 79th St. (Amsterdam Ave.)
☎ 212/769-0100.
Comfortable pub-eatery, great
for after an evening at Lincoln
Center. Open until 4am.

Wollensky's Grill
205 E. 49th St. (bet. 2nd and 3rd
aves.). ☎ 212/753-0444.
A cheaper offshoot of Smith
& Wollensky's steakhouse.
Open until 2am. See write-up
above.

Sunday Brunch

Many people go out for Sunday brunch in New York.
And almost every restaurant serves it. Frequently
offered in a fixed-price menu that includes a glass of
champagne or a Bloody Mary, brunch can be an every-
thing-but-the-kitchen-sink buffet or a limited-menu
table service. The more expensive restaurants accept
reservations, but the real Manhattan method calls for
going to an informal neighborhood favorite—and
waiting. Most are open from 10 or 11am to 3 or 4pm.
This list just scratches the surface.

Café des Artistes
1 W. 67th St. (Central Park W.).
☎ 212/877-3500.
Romantic setting, very
popular. See write-up above.

Darbar
44 W. 56th St. (near 6th Ave.).
☎ 212/432-7227.

Bargain northern Indian
buffet.

Lola
30 W. 22nd St. (near 6th Ave.).
☎ 212/675-6700.
The gospel brunch is very
loud and very popular at this

Southern/Caribbean/Creole eatery. See write-up above.

La Metairie

189 W. 10th St. (W. 4th St.). ☎ 212/989-0343. Somewhat pricey Village French. Another branch uptown at 1442 3rd Avenue (near 82nd St.).

Phoebe's

380 Columbus Ave. (78th St.). ☎ 212/724-5145. Cozy Upper West Side hangout with a fireplace and sofas in one room and windowseats with pillows in the other. Brunch is about $10, with a choice of eggs, French toast, salads, and such.

Pig Heaven

1540 2nd Ave. (near 80th St.). ☎ 212/744-4887. Gimmicky Chinese, but enjoyable.

Le Regence

37 E. 64th St. (near Madison Ave.). ☎ 212/606-4647.

The lovely, so-French dining room of the Hotel Plaza Athénée.

El Rio Grande

160 E. 38th St. (3rd Ave.). ☎ 212/867-0922. Large Tex-Mex joint in Murray Hill frequented by young singles.

Sarabeth's Kitchen

423 Amsterdam Ave. (near 80th St.). ☎ 212/496-6280; 1295 Madison Ave. (near 93rd St.) ☎ 212/410-7335. With locations on both the Upper East and Upper West Sides, Sarabeth's is always crowded. The reason is clear: delectable waffles, French toast, omelets, etc.

20 Mott Street

20 Mott St. (near Pell St.). ☎ 212/964-0380. Superb, inexpensive dim sum. Packed on weekends.

Cafe Craze

Coffee culture is firmly entrenched in the Big Apple; a once fairly standard "cup of Joe to go" has become a "double-decaf latte with skim." A sampling of New York's java hangouts:

Big Cup

228 8th Ave. (bet. 21st and 22nd sts.). ☎ 212/206-0059. A modern, breezy cafe that caters to a jovial Chelsea crowd. Go on a "theme" night (bingo, etc.).

Café Lalo

201 W. 83rd (bet. Amsterdam and Broadway). ☎ 212/496-6031. A smallish space packed with folks clamoring for the sinful cakes and tortes. An afternoon visit is more tranquil.

Caffe Rafaella

134 7th Ave. S. (bet. Charles and W. 10th sts.). ☎ 212/929-7247. Camping out is de rigeur for the patrons at this easygoing salad-and-sandwich spot. Settle into a battered armchair to write a letter or linger over a good book.

Eureka Joe's

168 5th Ave. (at 22nd St.). ☎ 212/741-7500. Stylish and homey, with roomy easy chairs and slouchy sofas for interminable lounging. No

meals per se, but a nice selection of baked goods.

French Roast Cafe

456 6th Ave. (at 11th St.).
☎ 212/533-2233.
A "scene" for NYU students and late-night clubbers. Open 24 hours. Salads, hot appetizers, and other comfort foods are on the menu.

Starbucks

13 Astor Place. ☎ 212/982-3563.
This Seattle-based coffee chain is becoming as ubiquitous as McDonalds. The Astor Place location is one of the city's largest, glass-walled, and airy.

Tea & Sympathy

108 Greenwich Ave. (at 13th St.).
☎ 212/807-8329.
Not a coffee bar per se, this tatty, welcoming nook serves such Brit comfort food as scones, bangers and mash, and shepherd's pie. The tea is sturdy, there's a stable of gregarious regulars, and the laid-back waitstaff won't rush you out.

ACCOMMODATIONS

NO ONE NEIGHBORHOOD IN NEW YORK HOUSES ALL of its finest hotels. Many leisure travelers enjoy staying along affluent Central Park South or on the Upper East Side, both of which are near the major art museums, and the most glamorous shopping.

Business travelers often prefer accommodations near the business centers, typically Midtown (42nd to 55th streets) where the greatest number of hotels are concentrated, or near Wall Street. Most of the accommodations in Midtown East are within walking distance of Grand Central Station or the United Nations. Midtown West, on the other hand, encompasses the theater district, which to some visitors is a glorious, pulsating thrill but to others, a gritty, seedy tangle to be avoided. While congested and noisy during the day, Midtown can get quiet, even desolate on side streets, at night. As for Wall Street, the towers of power are steps away from a few major hotels, but restaurants and nightlife are limited. Still, Chinatown, Little Italy, and SoHo are reasonably close.

Two neighborhoods less often considered for accommodations are the Upper West Side and Murray Hill (roughly 33rd to 42nd streets between Park and 3rd avenues). The former puts visitors near Central Park, Lincoln Center, and the Museum of Natural History, plus innumerable restaurants. The latter is a quiet (for Manhattan, anyway) East Side area just south of Midtown and near the Empire State Building. It's pretty and centrally located, but it can also be on the dull side.

Regardless of where you stay, I strongly advise making reservations at least a month in advance. New York can be a difficult place to find a room at the last minute. The busiest season is Labor Day through New Year's, when many hotels are booked solid every night. The dead of winter and summer are slower, and most hotels offer an array of enticing discount packages then. Throughout the year, hotels regularly provide corporate rate discounts of 10% off the rack rate (just ask for them). Many also have senior citizen rates, and virtually all eagerly slash prices for weekend stays—by as much as 40%. Don't be shy about asking for a deal; hotels work with a range of rates and are usually willing to offer some reduction. Children under 16 often can stay in their parent's room for no extra charge.

Almost all high-end properties have concierges, 24-hour room service, and minibars (beware—a Coke can set you back $3). Fitness centers are ubiquitous, but some are full-service health clubs with swimming pools and aerobics classes, while others are converted guest rooms with a couple of StairMasters and LifeCycles. The hotels seeking a corporate clientele typically have data ports, enabling guests to hook up fax machines or computers. Many also have fax machines available in the rooms, and practically all have business centers that provide services ranging from secretaries to photocopying and interpreting.

Most hotels are at least partially accessible to people using wheelchairs. Inquire when reserving. Dogs and other pets are usually prohibited or discouraged. Garage parking is costly. Most hotels charge you each time the car is used.

Prices

Keep in mind that these categories represent hotels' rack rates, or the highest price charged. Corporate or weekend discounts can bring the tariffs down by 10% to 40%. The rates below do not include taxes, which total about 21%. The hotels below accept American Express, Visa and other major credit cards unless noted.

Price Chart

$ = Less than $130
$$ = $130–$180
$$$ = $181–$240
$$$$ = $241–$325
$$$$$ = More than $325

Hotels by Neighborhood

Lower Manhattan (Below 14th St.)

★ Larchmont. **$**
Marriott Financial Center. **$$$**
Millenium Hilton. **$$$**
New York Vista. **$$$**

Gramercy Park/Murray Hill (E. 14th St.– E. 42nd St.)

Doral Court. **$$$**
Doral Park Avenue. **$$$**
Doral Tuscany. **$$$$**

Gramercy Park. **$$**
Inn at Irving Place. **$$$$**
Morgans. **$$$**
Quality Hotel Fifth Avenue. **$$**

*Lower West Side/
Garment District (W.
14th St.–W. 42nd St.)*
Pennsylvania. **$$**

*Midtown East (E. 43rd
St.–E. 59th St.)*
Beekman Tower. **$$$**
Beverly. **$$**
The Box Tree. **$$$–$$$$**
Drake Swissôtel. **$$$**
★ Elysee. **$$$**
Fitzpatrick Manhattan. **$$$**
★★ Four Seasons. **$$$$$**
Grand Hyatt New York.
    $$$$
Helmsley Middletowne. **$$**
★ Inter-Continental. **$$$$**
Lexington. **$**
Loew's New York. **$$$**
New York Helmsley. **$$$**
New York Palace. **$$$$**
Omni Berkshire Place.
    $$$$$
★★ Peninsula. **$$$$**
★ Plaza. **$$$**
Roger Smith. **$$$**
★★ St. Regis. **$$$$$**
Tudor. **$$$**
UN Plaza-Park Hyatt. **$$$$**
Waldorf Astoria. **$$$$**

*Midtown West (W. 43rd
St.–W. 59th St.)*
Algonquin. **$$$**
Crowne Plaza Manhattan. **$$**
Dorset. **$$**

Doubletree Guest Suites. **$$$**
Essex House. **$$$$**
Howard Johnson Plaza. **$$**
Millenium Hilton. **$$$**
Mansfield. **$$**
Marriott Marquis. **$$$**
★ Michelangelo. **$$$$**
Milford Plaza. **$**
New York Hilton. **$$$**
Novotel. **$$$**
★ Paramount. **$$**
Park Lane. **$$$**
Le Parker Meridien. **$$$$**
Ramada Inn. **$**
Ramada Renaissance. **$$$$**
★ Ritz-Carlton. **$$$$**
★★ Royalton. **$$$$**
St. Moritz. **$$**
Salisbury. **$$**
Travelodge Midtown. **$$**
Warwick. **$$$**
Wyndham. **$$**

*Upper East Side (E.
60th St.–E. 96th St.)*
★ Carlyle. **$$$$$**
Lowell. **$$$$$**
The Mark. **$$$$$**
Mayfair. **$$$**
★★ Pierre. **$$$$$**
Plaza Athénée. **$$$$**
★ Regency. **$$$$**
★ Stanhope. **$$$$$**
Wales. **$$**
Westbury. **$$$$**

*Upper West Side (W.
60th St.–W. 96th St.)*
Inn New York City. **$$$**
Mayflower Hotel on the Park.
    $$
Radisson Empire. **$$**

Critic's Choice

For the most self-indulgent, this-must-be-how-royalty-lives pampering, book your stay at the **St. Regis.** If you're looking for an urban spa, try its neighbor, the **Peninsula.** Being so densely packed, New York is stingy with its views, but if a vista is what you're after, try the Central Park South stretch of the **Plaza,** the **Park Lane,** the **Ritz–Carlton,** and the **Essex House,** or, for the impression that the world is at your feet, the soaring **Four Seasons.**

The 2 hotels that best capture the traditional wealth and luxury that many associate with New York are the **Pierre** and the **Carlyle.** But to others, Manhattan is about actors, high fashion, super-models, and celebrity photographers. Then one place stands out: the **Royalton.** If you can't afford its tariffs but want to approximate the experience, make a reservation at the **Paramount.**

If you're coming on a family vacation and would like to save the cost of an additional room for the kids, the **Doubletree Guest Suites** offers 2-room suites for about what most hotels charge for a standard double. Art lovers who'll be spending a good deal of time at the Metropolitan, the Guggenheim, the Whitney, and the Frick, all on the Upper East Side, probably would appreciate the charming **Stanhope** or the **Westbury.** And for you adventurers whose true calling is acquisition (i.e., shopping), your mecca is in the vicinity of 57th Street or Madison Avenue. I favor the **Four Seasons.**

Countless couples come to New York for a romantic weekend, and this category's a toughy, but if money's no object, I'd have to go with the **St. Regis.** But for a top-secret hideaway, where you'd have to be really unlucky to run into someone you know, select one of four suites at the **Inn New York City.**

New York's Hotels A to Z

Algonquin

59 W. 44th St. (near 5th Ave.), New York, NY 10036. ☎ 212/840-6800; 800/548-0345; fax: 212/944-1419. 165 rooms. Subway: B, D, F, Q to 42nd St.; 7 to 5th Ave. **$$$**.

Back in the 1920s and 1930s, the storied writers and humorists Dorothy Parker, George S. Kaufman, Robert Benchley, and others traded quips and aphorisms around the Algonquin's famed Round Table. Some members of the intelligentsia and theater world still frequent this turn-of-the-century hotel, now part of the Westin chain. The rooms are smallish and could use some freshening, but the traditional furnishings and tile bathrooms are adequate. The lobby takes on the shabby chic feel of an English club, with lots of dark wood and numerous sitting areas of sofas and wing chairs. The *New York Times* is delivered daily, and a Continental breakfast is included in the rate. Caution: While an evening at the Oak Room cabaret is a treat, dining at the hotel is not.

Beekman Tower

3 Mitchell Place (corner of 1st Ave. and 49th St.), New York, NY

10017. ☎ 212/355-7300; 800/637-8483; fax: 212/753-9366. 171 rooms and suites. Bus: M15, M27. Subway: 6 to 51st St. **$$$**. Flagship of a local chain of 9 suite hotels, this 1928 Art Deco structure has been the beneficiary of a recent top-to-bottom renovation. The tranquil lobby is expertly done in trappings of the original period, and the Zephyr Grill, with similar detailing, is a decided improvement over its predecessors. On the 26th floor is the Top of the Tower cocktail lounge, which takes full advantage of the excellent views and has background piano music Tuesday to Saturday to enhance the mood. While the claim of "all suites" is a slight exaggeration, all have kitchenettes equipped with microwaves. Some also have terraces overlooking the East River. A complete fitness center is on the premises.

Standard rates approach the high end, but special weekend, extended stay, and summer discounts bring them down to moderate levels. In addition, most of the suites have sofas that can be converted into beds, saving the additional charges many hotels impose for roll-away cots for children. For a list of other hotels in the group, see "Manhattan East Suite Hotels" on page 96.

The Box Tree

250 E. 49th St. (3rd Ave.), New York, NY 10017. ☎ 212/758-8320; fax: 212/308-3999. 13 rooms and suites. Subway: 6 to 51st St. **$$$–$$$$**. There is no hotel remotely comparable to The Box Tree within the city limits. Known primarily for its restaurant, these adjoining brownstones also contain lodgings wrapped

in an over-the-top voluptuousness that few people unrelated to the Bourbons could imagine. All the rooms are singular in their trappings, some of them formal suites, some double rooms with sitting areas. A favorite of mine is the room named for King Boris III of Bulgaria (the owner's homeland), its mirrored walls and gilt and silk as regal as a Versailles salon. Louis XVI might have swept in here to elude Marie Antoinette. Bathrooms, although small, are lavished with lapis lazuli and pink marble. And while the outlay for all this sounds steep at first blush, it might help to know that room rates include Continental breakfast and a $100 credit toward dinner in either of the 2 restaurants.

★ Carlyle

35 E. 76th St. (Madison Ave.), New York, NY 10021. ☎ 212/744-1600; 800/227-5737; fax: 212/717-4682. 500 rooms. Subway: 6 to 77th St. **$$$$$**. Step out of your Jacuzzi and into a terry robe before dressing and heading downstairs to hear Bobby Short sing at the piano. Yes, the Carlyle is so terribly civilized, it's almost a parody of the Upper East Side itself. All the rooms are outfitted with fax machines, VCRs, CD players, and even umbrellas. The decor is tasteful and traditional, with soothing colors such as ecru and pale blue. The Carlyle is the rare hotel that does not carpet over its beautiful hardwood floors, selecting large area rugs instead. Special services include dog walkers (pets are permitted at an extra charge), limousines ready at the curb, an exercise room, and morning newspaper.

Come for afternoon tea, or evening cocktails at Bemelmans' Bar, the clubby home of murals by the author and illustrator of the Madeleine books. It is scotch-and-soda country, with piano music from 5:30pm. The Carlyle claims to have more Steinways in its guest rooms than any other hotel in the city.

Crowne Plaza Manhattan

1605 Broadway (49th St.), New York, NY 10019. ☎ 212/977-4000; 800/243-6969; fax: 212/333-7393. 770 rooms. Subway: 1, 9 to 50th St.; N, R to 49th St. **$$**.

Place this gaudy newcomer in the jukebox subspecies of postmodernist architecture. The designer giddily admits he wanted the pink-and-burgundy exterior to look like a Wurlitzer, complete with huge bands of multicolored lights racing around the sides. Certainly no one can claim it's an intrusion on its Times Square neighborhood. Among its attractions are the largest indoor pool of any Manhattan hotel, an extensive health club, a business center, and 3 restaurants. The executive floors have many of the perks standard at the luxury hotels, such as robes and a concierge.

Doral Court

130 E. 39th St. (Lexington Ave.), New York, NY 10016. ☎ 212/686-1100; 800/223-6725; fax: 212/889-0287. 199 rooms. Subway: 4, 5, 6, 7, Shuttle to Grand Central. **$$$**.

One of a trio of ingratiating Doral hotels in upper Murray Hill, the Doral Court boasts atypical amenities for most hotels in its class—namely VCRs, bathrobes, and the morning paper. King-sized beds, generous dimensions, walk-in closets, and separate dressing alcoves are the norm. Downstairs, the Courtyard Café is favored by neighborhood executives, who enjoy the enclosed patio setting in warm weather. Rates are at the low end of the expensive range and are cut by 40% on weekends, when free parking is included. Half the rooms come with exercise bikes, and the full-service Doral Fitness Center on nearby Park Ave., providing everything but sneakers, is available to guests of the 3 Doral hotels in the immediate vicinity.

Doral Park Avenue

70 Park Ave. (38th St.), New York, NY 10016. ☎ 212/687-7050; 800/223-6725; fax: 212/808-9029. 188 rooms. Subway: 4, 5, 6, 7, Shuttle to Grand Central. **$$$**.

Murray Hill doesn't have the gloss and hum of the Midtown core, but those who live and stay here see that trait as a virtue. This serene stopping-place makes the most of its setting. Reasonable needs are skillfully met, without fuss or show, although the restaurant and room service close down early. Bedrooms are comfortably furnished, tasteful but not lavish, and the bathrooms are marble. The *New York Times* arrives at your door each morning. Two restaurants and a summer sidewalk cafe are on the premises. Guests can use the Doral Fitness Center 1 block away.

Doral Tuscany

120 E. 39th St. (near Park Ave.), New York, NY 10016. ☎ 212/686-1600; 800/223-6725; fax: 212/779-7822. 121 rooms. Subway: 4, 5, 6, 7, Shuttle to Grand Central. **$$$$**.

This, the third of the trio of admirable Murray Hill Dorals, charms in many small details—at the entrance, a large thermometer-barometer; in the bedroom, a vanity area with an extra sink; in the marble bathroom, a telephone and a 3-nozzle massaging showerhead; outside the window, another thermometer. Even Exercycles are available, on request. Overnight shoe-shines are complimentary, as are the morning papers. The residential neighborhood offers a quiet environment, but the Tuscany is not inconvenient to the action. The Adirondack Grill is a good restaurant, particularly for Murray Hill. The staff is friendly and reassuring. Conventioneers and tour groups are never in evidence, and the hotel is less likely to be booked up on short notice.

Dorset

30 W. 54th St. (near 6th Ave.), New York, NY 10019. ☎ 212/247-7300; 800/227-2348; fax: 212/581-0153. 400 rooms. Subway: B, D, F, Q to 47th–50th St./Rockefeller Center. **$$**.
The dark paneled lobby has worn red carpeting but is welcoming in a quirky way. The rooms are similarly middle-of-the-road: clean and neat, but nothing beautiful or luxurious. Personalities from the nearby television network headquarters often lunch at the streetside bar-cafe. The hotel does not charge for children under 14 sharing their parents' room. If your stay in New York will be an extended one, you might want to inquire about the monthly rates.

Drake Swissôtel

440 Park Ave. (56th St.), New York, NY 10022. ☎ 212/421-0900; 800/372-5369; fax: 212/371-4190. 622 rooms. Subway: 4, 5, 6, N, R to 59th St./Lexington Ave. **$$$**.

It can confidently be observed that the Swiss know how to run hotels. Swissôtel's acquisition of the Drake has brought renewed luxury and crispness to the operation, currently undergoing a $38-million renovation. The refurbishing is said to include a facelift for all the rooms; a new fitness center; and a new business center, where guests will have 2 complimentary hours' use of meeting rooms. In keeping with the hotel's positioning as a business-oriented property, all the rooms have fax machines, and guests receive a morning paper. Rooms are spacious, owing to the hotel's origins as an apartment building. Some have terraces or wood-burning fireplaces. The prime East Side venue is a bonus, as is the free morning transport to the Financial District.

★ Elysée

60 E. 54th St. (Madison Ave.), New York, NY 10022. ☎ 212/753-1066; 800/535-9733; fax: 212/980-9278. 99 rooms. Subway: E, F to 5th Ave. **$$$**.
This quietly elegant boutique hotel rivals its competitors for luxury and conveniences but beats them out when it comes to value. Amazingly, the rates include Continental breakfast, all-day tea and cookies, and evening wine and hors d'oeuvres. Also complimentary is the use of a nearby health club, which even provides sneakers and workout wear. Graceful and distinctive, the lobby welcomes its visitors with fragrant fresh flowers and a starburst marble floor. The rooms are somewhat more subdued, with muted colors and a country French decor. All the rooms have VCRs. Brass fixtures accent the marble bathrooms, which contain

robes and phones. Off the
lobby is the smashing Monkey
Bar, a restaurant recently
restored to the splendor it first
enjoyed as a supper club in the
1930s. The staff balances
warmth with discretion, a
quality appreciated by the
many artists and celebrities
who have stayed here, from
Marlon Brando to Tennessee
Williams, who died in the
Elysée in 1983.

Essex House

160 Central Park S. (bet. 6th Ave.
and 7th aves.), New York, NY
10019. ☎ 212/247-0300; 800/
645-5687; fax: 212/315-1839.
595 rooms. Subway: B, Q, N, R
to 57th St. **$$$$**.
The Art Deco exterior and
lobby of the Essex House
harken to its 1931 construction, but the remainder of the
hotel speaks more to its 1991
$75-million renovation,
which enlarged the guest
rooms and brought the hotel
into the new era with such
modern necessities as a health
spa, a business center, and
almost 40 wheelchair-
accessible rooms. The U.S.
flagship of the Nikko hotel
group, the Essex House leaves
little to be desired. Rooms are
elegantly furnished in the
Chippendale or Louis XVI
style, and the marble
bathrooms are large. Every
room has a fax machine, a
VCR, and terry robes, and the
hotel offers complimentary
shoe-shines and *New York Times*
delivery. For an additional $10
or so, you can upgrade to a
park-view room—a true
bargain compared to what the
Plaza charges. Both the
luxurious 14-table Les
Célébrités restaurant and the
more casual Café Botánica
have gathered plaudits from
reviewers and devoted
gourmands. The former is

decorated with paintings
by such personages
as Peggy Lee, Gene Hackman,
James Dean, Tennessee
Williams, and other famous
hobbyists, explaining the
name.

Fitzpatrick Manhattan

687 Lexington Ave. (bet. 56th and
57th sts.), New York, NY 10022.
☎ 212/355-0100; 800/367-
7701; fax: 212/308-5166. 92
rooms. Subway: 4, 5, 6, N, R to
59th St./Lexington Ave. **$$$**.
The first North American
venture of an Irish hotelier is
this resuscitated oldster built in
1926 and abandoned for much
of the 1980s. A top-hatted
bellhop bows guests into a
bright blue and (of course)
emerald green lobby. Off to
the right are the bar and
Fitzer's restaurant, where the
featured dish, naturally, is Irish
lamb stew. The configurations
of the rooms and suites in the
upper 16 floors are largely
unchanged from the years as
the Dover Hotel. They are
of good size, the bathrooms
newly fitted with black mar-
ble and white tile. Every tub
is a whirlpool bath, no less
standard equipment than is
the trouser press.

★★ Four Seasons

57 E. 57th St. (bet. Madison and
Park avenues), New York, NY
10022. ☎ 212/758-7000; fax:
212/758-5711. 367 rooms.
Subway: 4, 5, 6, N, R to 59th St./
Lexington Ave. **$$$$$**.
I. M. Pei designed it. Need I
say more? Every time I enter
the limestone lobby, with its
soaring 33-foot ceiling, I am
overcome with a feeling of
serenity. Opened in mid-1993,
the Four Seasons' 52 floors
make it the tallest hotel in
New York and enable it to
boast of unobstructed park and
city views in half its rooms.

(The best views, incidentally, begin on the 24th floor and are in the no. 1, 11, and 12 tiers.) Awash in creamy English sycamore, the rooms are large and thoughtfully arranged, with the beds facing the wide picture windows. At bedside are controls for the motorized window treatments, allowing sunrises (or sunsets) to be appreciated without getting out of bed. The marble bathrooms are shrines to luxury, with tubs that fill in 60 seconds, separate glass showers that can be preset for temperature and water pressure, phones, TVs, and terry robes. Downstairs is a fitness center offering spa services and individual TVs with headphones, a business center, and Fifty Seven Fifty Seven, an excellent restaurant that is the spot for many a power breakfast. Harkening to the suave sophistication of a past decade, the bar serves 14 types of martinis.

Grand Hyatt New York

Park Ave. at Grand Central Terminal, New York, NY 10017. ☎ 212/883-1234; 800/233-1234; fax: 212/697-3772. 1,407 rooms. Subway: 4, 5, 6, 7, Shuttle to Grand Central. **$$$$**.
Perhaps the only property Donald Trump ever bought without naming it after himself, the Grand Hyatt nonetheless scores on the glitz scale. Dominating the 4-story atrium lobby is a noisy, tiered waterfall. The rooms are not nearly as showy; in fact, they're rather bland but are scheduled for a full facelift in early 1996. An additional $15 will buy the Hyatt Business Plan, which provides a fax machine in the room plus complimentary coffee, Continental breakfast, and newspaper, and free access for local and 800-number

phone calls (the hotel also has a business center). For about $25 extra, guests can stay on the Regency Club floors, which offer such goodies as breakfast, afternoon pastries, and evening hors d'oeurves. The Grand Hyatt does not have a fitness center, but for $10 guests can use the facilities, including an indoor pool, at the nearby Vertical Club. The Grand Hyatt has 3 restaurants and an espresso bar in the lobby.

Helmsley Middletowne

148 E. 48th St. (near Lexington Ave.), New York, NY 10017. ☎ 212/755-3000; 800/321-2323; fax: 212/832-0291. 192 rooms. Subway: 6 to 51st St. **$$**.
Don't be fooled by the Helmsley name. The Middletowne is not some big Manhattan spectacle. On the contrary, the lobby is so tiny that visitors often ask where the main lobby is while standing in the middle of it. In place of amenities that some travelers have come to expect—a restaurant, a bar, a fitness center—the Middletowne offers homier accommodations. Many of the rooms have fully operable kitchens, and some have fireplaces, terraces, or charming details like arched entryways. Rates might be negotiable for longer stays.

Inn at Irving Place

56 Irving Place (bet. 17th and 18th sts.), New York, NY 10003. ☎ 212/533-4600. Fax: 212/533-4611. 5 rooms, 7 suites. Subway: 4, 5, 6, N, R, L to 14th St./Union Square. **$$$$**.
This warm, New England-style inn, just south of quiet Gramercy Park, is a romantic getaway for grown-ups (children under 13 are not

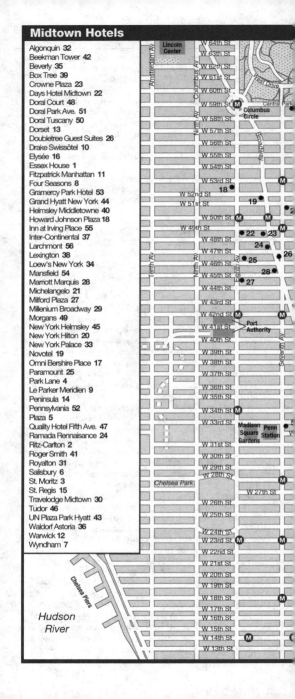

Midtown Hotels

Algonquin **32**
Beekman Tower **42**
Beverly **35**
Box Tree **39**
Crowne Plaza **23**
Days Hotel Midtown **22**
Doral Court **48**
Doral Park Ave. **51**
Doral Tuscany **50**
Dorset **13**
Doubletree Guest Suites **26**
Drake Swissôtel **10**
Elysée **16**
Essex House **1**
Fitzpatrick Manhattan **11**
Four Seasons **12**
Gramercy Park Hotel **53**
Grand Hyatt New York **44**
Helmsley Middletowne **40**
Howard Johnson Plaza **18**
Inn at Irving Place **55**
Inter-Continental **37**
Larchmont **56**
Lexington **38**
Loew's New York **34**
Mansfield **54**
Marriott Marquis **28**
Michelangelo **21**
Milford Plaza **27**
Millenium Broadway **29**
Morgans **49**
New York Helmsley **45**
New York Hilton **20**
New York Palace **33**
Novotel **19**
Omni Bershire Place **17**
Paramount **25**
Park Lane **4**
Le Parker Meridien **9**
Peninsula **14**
Pennsylvania **52**
Plaza **5**
Quality Hotel Fifth Ave. **47**
Ramada Rennaisance **24**
Ritz-Carlton **2**
Roger Smith **41**
Royalton **31**
Salisbury **6**
St. Moritz **3**
St. Regis **15**
Travelodge Midtown **30**
Tudor **46**
UN Plaza Park Hyatt **43**
Waldorf Astoria **36**
Warwick **12**
Wyndham **7**

allowed). The Inn at Irving Place occupies two 19thC Greek Revival townhouses; period antiques, fine linens, and needlepoint rugs decorate the sumptuous rooms. Guests have access to fax machines and laptop computers—but you'll be so smitten with the inn's urban charm that I guarantee business will be the last thing on your mind.

Inn New York City

266 W. 71st St. (bet. Amsterdam and West End aves.), New York, NY 10023. ☎ 212/580-1900; fax: 212/580-4437. 4 suites. Subway: 1, 2, 3, 9 to 72nd St. **$$$**.

There is no sign out front, and not because it's trying to be chic (à la the Royalton or the Paramount). With only 4 apartment suites and a loyal and growing clientele that reserves them far in advance, the Inn sees no point in encouraging passersby to drop in, even for a look. But what an eyeful they would get! Four floors of a brownstone on a quiet side street have been remodeled painstakingly and furnished by their energetic on-premises hosts. All are equipped as completely as any home, with VCR, telephone answering machine, CD player, intercom security, clothes washer and dryer, robes, board games, and kitchens with pots, crockery, and stocked refrigerator (yes, that's a quiche in there with the wine and soft drinks). A self-serve breakfast is laid out, including, but not limited to, bagels, muffins, freshly ground coffee, tea, juice, and milk. The Inn imposes a 2-night minimum stay, except for the Spa Suite, for which an extra $100 will buy you a 1-night booking.

★ Inter-Continental

111 E. 48th St. (Lexington Ave.), New York, NY 10017. ☎ 212/755-5900; 800/332-4246; fax: 212/644-0079. 692 rooms. Subway: 6 to 51st St. **$$$$**.

Simply put, this is how a hotel ought to look. From the lobby's leather furniture in groupings conducive to conversation to the imposing arrangements of fresh flowers, the Inter-Continental bespeaks elegance. The hotel's trademark is the lobby's brass birdcage with several colorful varieties of live birds. The rooms, though perhaps not as large as the spacious public areas and halls suggest, are quiet and well-appointed with rich wood furnishings. The beige marble bathrooms have graceful pedestal sinks. The fully equipped fitness center includes treadmills, stair machines, and cycles—with mini-TVs for entertainment—plus sauna and steam rooms and massage. The Inter-Continental is more than an oasis; it's convenient to the Theater District, Midtown offices and shopping, among other things.

★ Larchmont

27 W. 11th St.(bet. 5th and 6th aves.), New York, NY 10011. ☎ 212/989-9333; fax 212/989-9496. 50 rooms, none with bath. Subway: F to 14th St., L to 6th Ave. **$**.

One of Manhattan's newer and most affordable hotels, on a lovely, tree-lined Greenwich Village block. Housed in a 19thC brownstone that was a luxury-apartment building early in the century, the Larchmont is a European-style hotel (bathrooms are down the hall). The cheery, if somewhat cramped, rooms have rattan furniture, ceiling fans, and washbasins.

Continental breakfast is served in the backyard solarium. If you don't mind the (very clean) shared baths, the hotel, and the location—just a few blocks north of Washington Square—simply can't be beat.

Loew's New York

569 Lexington Ave. (51st St.), New York, NY 10022. ☎ 212/752-7000; 800/223-0888; fax: 212/758-6311. 729 rooms. Subway: 6, E, F to 51st St./Lexington Ave. **$$$**.

All the usual comforts are to be found in this large, international-breed hotel. Once inside, you might be in any of its counterparts in Lisbon, London, or Rio, which is intentional, as Loew's is courting the international traveler. Tour groups also seem to be attracted to the place, and at times the lobby can be quite a mob scene. Loew's offers a well-equipped fitness center and weekend packages ranging from extra indulgences like theater tickets, dinner, or free parking, to the "no-frills" variety, which squeezes costs down to the moderate level.

The Lowell

28 E. 63rd St. (near Madison Ave.), New York, NY 10021. ☎ 212/838-1400; fax: 212/319-4230. 65 rooms. Subway: N, R to 5th Ave.; B, Q to Lexington Ave. **$$$$$**.

A jewel box of a hotel on the Upper East Side, the Lowell is so intimate it feels like a private pied-à-terre. Erected as a residential hotel in the 1920s, the Lowell has maintained its Art Deco rose-and-cream-tiled exterior. Inside, the ambiance is more French Empire, with a dramatic black marbled lobby. In a city of sealed glass and steam heat, all of the casement windows open, 33 of the units have wood-burning fireplaces

and 10 have private terraces (the Garden Suite has 2). Most rooms also have kitchenettes. Real books line the shelves, and live plants and cut flowers freshen the rooms. No 2 rooms, most of which are suites, are exactly alike, although antique furniture, down comforters and marble bathrooms set the tone. Each room comes with a VCR, 2 robes, and an umbrella. The Lowell recently installed a new gym. Management promotes highly personal attention and is discreet almost to a fault about its more celebrated clients—one reason they keep coming back.

Mansfield

12 W. 44th St. (bet. 5th and 6th aves.), New York, NY 10019. ☎ 212/944-6050; fax: 212/764-4477. 102 rooms, 27 suites. Subway: B, D, F, Q to 42nd St. **$$**.

If Midtown is where you want to be, head for the Mansfield. Just blocks from the theater district, it's the latest in a series of hotel makeovers undertaken by the Gotham Hotel Group, which lists among its previous successes the Wales, Franklin, and Shoreham hotels. Many details (stained-glass ceilings, iron grillwork, marble columns) from the original turn-of-the-century structure have been preserved. Rooms have striking, ebony-stained wood floors, streamlined furniture, and granite bathtubs; in-room VCRs and CD players send guests scurrying to the hotel's extensive audio/video library. A light but tasty continental breakfast is included in the price.

The Mark

25 E. 77th St. (Madison Ave.), New York, NY 10021. ☎ 212/744-4300; 800/843-6275; fax: 212/744-2749. 180 rooms. Subway: 6 to 77th St. **$$$$$**.

Across the street from that
dowager empress, the Carlyle,
is the Mark, a more recent
addition to the Upper East
Side. One-third of the units
here are suites, and those on
the top 3 floors—14 to 16—
garner the raves. The 14th
floor boasts terraces. Details
include meticulously crafted
moldings, custom-designed
fabrics, and Italianate
furnishings. All rooms have
CD players and VCRs (more
than 200 cassettes are available
for rent). The marble
bathrooms are oversized, with
separate shower and tub, and
terry robes. The Mark has a
new fitness center and a
restaurant, Mark's.

Marriott Financial Center

85 West St. (Albany St.), New
York, NY 10006. ☎ 212/
385-4900; 800/228-9290; fax:
212/227-8136. 504 rooms.
Subway: 1, 9 to Cortland St.;
C, E to World Trade Center. **$$$**.
Only the second major hotel
erected in the Financial
District in this century (see the
New York Vista below), this
addition to the pervasive chain
does its job surprisingly well.
The lobby, with a brass-
banistered staircase and an
Oriental screen, makes a good
impression, but the rooms are
over-stimulating. The
conflicting carpet, bedspread,
and upholstery patterns, each
busier than the next, made me
dizzy. Within walking distance
are the World Financial Center,
South Street Seaport, Wall
Street, and the ferries to the
Statue of Liberty and Ellis
Island. Rates are deeply
discounted on weekends,
when the business-day
neighborhood is pretty dead
and the 2 restaurants and
microbrewery pub come
in handy.

Marriott Marquis

1535 Broadway (45th St.),
New York, NY 10036. ☎ 212/
398-1900; 800/228-9290; fax:
212/980-6175. 1,874 rooms.
1, 2, 3, 9, N, R, to 42nd St./
Times Square. **$$$**.
Cavernous. Garish. It took me
more than 5 minutes just to
find the 8th floor lobby, and
even then I felt as if I had
walked into an upscale train
station. The Marriott is a
convention hotel, as evidenced
by the halls and lobbies awash
at all hours with frolicking
conventioneers. To its credit,
the Marriott makes an effort to
be attractive, with live plants
growing along the balconied
perimeter of the atrium lobby.
The room decor is uninspired
at best, with matching pastel
paintings and chairs. But the
rooms are very clean, and
many have good city views.
The Marriott also has its
convenient location going
for it, and its size alone
makes it difficult for this
guide to ignore.

Mayfair

610 Park Ave. (65th St.), New
York, NY 10021. ☎ 212/
288-0800; 800/223-0542; fax:
212/737-0538. 201 rooms.
Subway: 6 to 68th St.; B, Q to
Lexington Ave. **$$$**.
Best known as the home of
Le Cirque, that altar of ladies-
who-lunch, the Mayfair
attracts a very chic, interna-
tional clientele. The initial
impression of the Mayfair is
one of such beauty and luxury,
with the exquisite floral
arrangements and salmon
walls and white-gloved
elevator operators, that the
guest rooms can disappoint.
The room furnishings overall
are uninspired, and the desk
chair, for example, is
uncomfortable. Suites

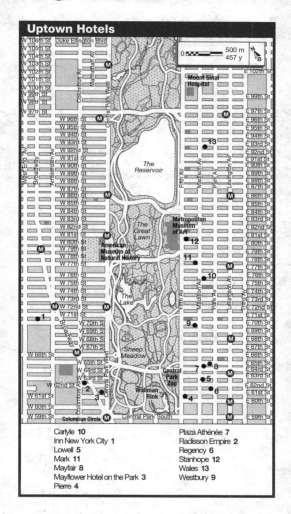

Uptown Hotels

Carlyle **10**	Plaza Athénée **7**
Inn New York City **1**	Radisson Empire **2**
Lowell **5**	Regency **6**
Mark **11**	Stanhope **12**
Mayfair **8**	Wales **13**
Mayflower Hotel on the Park **3**	Westbury **9**
Pierre **4**	

comprise the majority of units, and 30 of them have working fireplaces, a great treat on a winter visit. The Mayfair does know how to spoil its guests, whether by maintaining a "pillow bank" of myriad styles and fills—and noting preferences so that a repeat guest need never ask again—or by serving complimentary chicken

soup to guests fighting colds. Local calls, newspapers (in several languages), and shoe-shines are all complimentary. The fitness center has a practice putting green. Evidently the Mayfair thinks it has found the way to its guests' hearts: The hotel will happily deliver a putting machine directly to your room.

Mayflower Hotel on the Park

15 Central Park West (61st St.), New York, NY 10023. ☎ 212/265-0060; 800/223-4164 (US and Canada) or 0-800/891-256 (UK); fax: 212/265-5098. 577 rooms. Subway: 1, 9, A, B, C, D to 59th St./Columbus Circle. **$$**.

I suspect the Mayflower has seen better days. With its spectacular location right on the park, 2 blocks north of Columbus Circle, the Mayflower begs for a little attention. The hotel, built in 1925, has been in the process of modernizing its bathrooms and has installed an exercise room, but even so, the Mayflower today is just this side of seedy. The furniture is bland, the bedspreads faded, and, at least in the yet-to-be-renovated tile bathrooms, the bathtubs need to be reglazed, and everything could use a thorough scrubbing. The Mayflower does have those fabulous park views, though, and it offers suites with pantries for about what you'd pay for a standard double at the more upscale hotels.

★ Michelangelo

152 W. 51st St. (7th Ave.), New York, NY 10019. ☎ 212/765-1900; 800/338-1338; fax: 212/541-6604. 178 rooms. Subway: 1, 9 to 50th St.; N, R to 49th St. **$$$$**.

Formerly the Parc Fifty One, the Michelangelo is a study in refinement. Everything here is highly polished, from the coral and taupe marble in the coolly elegant lobby to the rich wood armoires in the bedrooms to the service provided by the full staff. Yet, the Michelangelo remains something of a secret in this city that prides itself on being in the know. The standard rooms are oversized, and, more importantly, come stocked with Bacci chocolate and Pellegrino water. The large marble bathrooms have 55 gallon tubs, TVs, robes, and little stools in front of the vanities. The Michelangelo serves a complimentary breakfast, and the intimate lounge off the lobby, with its overstuffed green sofas and baby grand piano, is one of my favorites in the city. Courtesy limos leave each morning for Wall Street. And when the Sunday *New York Times* is delivered, it comes with white gloves so the ink won't smear on the guest's hands. Now we couldn't have that, could we?

Millenium Broadway

145 W. 44th St. (bet. Broadway and 6th Ave.), New York, NY 10036. ☎ 212/768-4400; 800/622-5569; fax: 212/768-0847. 629 rooms. Subway: 1, 2, 3, 9, N, R to 42nd St./Times Square; B, D, F, Q to 42nd St. **$$$**.

Expanses of veined black marble and wall-sized paintings contribute to one of the most stunning interiors in New York. The on-premises presence of the restored 1902 Hudson Theatre underlines a certain showbiz pizzazz. The smallish rooms, in sleek black and gray with leather furniture, present a more contemporary attitude than most hotels in the city. With 52 floors, the Millenium (formerly the Macklowe) also offers some very nice views. The hotel has a high-tech interactive TV service, MackTel, that enables guests to order theater or airline tickets or to make restaurant reservations without leaving the room, and one old-fashioned comfort—windows that open.

Millenium Hilton

55 Church St. (Fulton St.),
New York, NY 10007. ☎ 212/
693-2001; 800/445-8667; fax:
212/571-2317. 561 rooms.
Subway: 1, 9 to Cortlandt St.; C,
E to World Trade Center. **$$$**
Built in 1992, the Millenium
markets itself to the business
traveler with an array of
amenities, including fax
machines in every guest room,
voice mail that can be activated
prior to arrival, the *New York
Times* delivered daily, 2 rest-
aurants, and a business center
offering complimentary use of
computers and, for a rental fee,
mobile phones, pagers, and
VCRs. The rooms, typically
decorated in soft beiges or
peaches, are comfortable if not
fancy. The maple and teak
furniture is modern but not
sterile in feel. The bathrooms
are marble and are outfitted
with phones, robes, and
slippers. Since the hotel is 58
stories high, many of the rooms
have excellent views of the
city, the river, and the Statue
of Liberty, to name a few. The
hotel has a 40-foot indoor
pool with a wall-window
overlooking St. Paul's Chapel.

Morgans

237 Madison Ave. (near 37th St.),
New York, NY 10016. ☎ 212/
686-0300; 800/334-3408; fax:
212/779-8352. 154 rooms.
Subway: 6 to 33rd St. **$$$**.
Call it a "boutique hotel." The
owners do. It is youthful,
unusual, and trendy enough
for Mick Jagger, Billy Joel, and
executives of the fashion and
design industries. To highlight
this in-the-know status that
also infuses its sister hotels
the Paramount and the
Royalton—Morgans posts no
identifying sign outside and
never will. Guests are whisked
into rooms of almost Oriental

simplicity decked in chic
black, white, and gray tones.
Built-in storage walls are of
gray-stained bird's-eye maple,
the low beds covered with pin-
striped duvets. Rooms have
refrigerators, and Morgans was
one of the first hotels in the
city with stereo cassette decks
as well as VCRs in its rooms.
(The front desk can provide
videocassettes from its library.)

New York Helmsley

212 E. 42nd St. (3rd Ave.),
New York, NY 10017. ☎ 212/
490-8900; 800/221-4982; fax:
212/986-4792. 788 rooms.
Subway: 4, 5, 6, 7, Shuttle to
Grand Central. **$$$**.
One of the chain assembled
by Harry Helmsley and long
ruled with an iron hand by his
wife, Leona, the New York
Helmsley is geared to the
corporate crowd with the
assumption that business
travelers have little time for
ceremony. Some of the
furniture is chipped, and
outdated blue and Mylar
wallpaper covers the bath-
rooms. The hotel has made an
effort to be wheelchair
accessible, as all doorways are
wide enough, and the front
desk has a low counter. The
hotel has a restaurant and a
bar but no fitness center;
instead, it sells $20 day-passes
to the New York Health &
Racquet Club. When the hotel
empties of its suits on
weekends, discounted rates
bring in a different crowd
equally appreciative of the
convenient Midtown subway:
tourists coming for some
museum-hopping and
Broadway shows.

New York Hilton

1335 6th Ave. (53rd St.),
New York, NY 10019. ☎ 212/
586-7000; 800/445-8967;

fax: 212/315-1374. 2,131 rooms.
Subway: B, D, F, Q to 50th St./
Rockefeller Center. **$$$**.
Your basic convention hotel
nightmare. Big, brassy, and
bustling, this vertical town
within the city is a mob scene
whenever a convention is in
town, which is to say, just
about always. The staff is
harried, and I sensed that the
hotel has a tendency to
overbook the way airlines do,
sending the overflow to other
hotels in the city. The Hilton
has everything, from shops to
secretarial services to a week's
worth of bars and restaurants
and live entertainment. Only
the claustrophobic singles are
to be avoided. Comforting
features include closed-circuit
movies and heated bathroom
floors. Half-day rates are
available for lie-downs and
wash-ups between shopping
excursions and theater
matinees.

New York Palace

455 Madison Ave. (50th St.),
New York, NY 10022. ☎ 212/
888-7000; 800/221-4982; fax:
212/303-6000. 773 rooms.
Subway: 6 to 51st St.; E, F to 5th
Ave. **$$$$**.
Preservation of worthwhile
buildings has a checkered
history in New York. More
often than not, commerce has
triumphed over heritage. Not
so in the case of the Palace.
Bent upon erecting a princely
flagship for his real-estate
empire, Harry Helmsley was
persuaded not only to spare
the proud Villard Houses from
demolition, but to restore
them to their 1886 opulence.
The Franco-Italianate interiors
were lovingly scrubbed and
mended, revealing marble
inlays, Tiffany glass, frescoes,
rich paneling, gold-leaf
ceilings, and intricately carved
wood friezes. In the adjoining

modern tower, guest rooms are
spacious and continue the
theme with huge Baroque
headboards, soft velvets, and
tasteful Louis XV reproduc-
tions. The concierge can
arrange for translators in nearly
40 languages. Not many hotels
in town can match this
experience.

New York Vista

3 World Trade Center, New York,
NY 10048. ☎ 212/938-9100;
800/258-2505; fax: 212/321-
2237. 820 rooms. Subway: 1, 9
to Cortlandt St.; C, E to World
Trade Center. **$$$**.
Since no one had built a major
hotel in lower Manhattan since
1836, the New York Vista filled
a glaring need. But just having
completed a $70 million reno-
vation in March 1995, the
Vista still seems to be lacking
something. It has vast public
spaces, but they aren't arranged
in any logical or inviting way.
Guests have free access to an
indoor pool and jogging track,
but the hotel charges $10 for
use of its exercise equipment
and the racquetball courts.
For an additional $40 or so,
Vista Club rooms on the
20th and 21st floors enjoy
complimentary breakfasts with
morning newspapers, fax
machines, bathrobes, and a
private lounge with free
hors d'oeuvres and a con-
cierge. Upper floors have
good views of the harbor,
and windows open. The 3
restaurants are cuts above most
of the Financial District
competition. Still, the rates
may seem a little higher than
can be fully justified.

Novotel

226 W. 52nd St. (Broadway),
New York, NY 10019. ☎ 212/
315-0100; 800/221-3158; fax:
212/765-5369. 470 rooms.
Subway: 1, 9 to 50th St.; B, D, E
to 7th Ave. **$$$**.

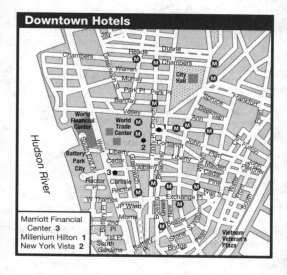

Downtown Hotels

Marriott Financial Center **3**
Millenium Hilton **1**
New York Vista **2**

This European-owned tower assaults the eye with its orange-and-green exterior, built above a grim, 4-story commercial building. The riotously gaudy lobby, 1 giant lounge, is on the 7th floor. Rooms are awash in pastels and Formica furniture. None of this aesthetic criticism is meant to suggest that the Novotel is not comfortable, for the usual services and facilities of its class—including a fitness center, a restaurant with live entertainment, and some nice views—are at hand. It is also quieter than might be expected, and the staff is very friendly. Visitors intent upon a week of theater-going are within a few blocks of all the major houses.

Omni Berkshire Place

21 E. 52nd St. (Madison Ave.), New York, NY 10022. ☎ 212/688-1405; 800/790-1900 or 800/578-0600; fax: 212/355-7646. 420 rooms. Subway: E, F to 5th Ave. **$$$$$**. During the week, it is essentially a posh executive

stopover; on the weekends, couples escaping to Manhattan find themselves treated to breakfast in bed, chocolates and wine at their bedside, and bowls of fresh flowers, all at about 30% less than the price of the same rooms Monday to Thursday. Harmonious tints of green, peach, and beige accompany tasteful seating arrangements and decorative accessories. The lobby soothes with print fabrics, potted palms and ivy—a handsome setting for an above-par afternoon tea.

★ Paramount

235 W. 46th St. (8th Ave.), New York, NY 10036. ☎ 212/764-5500; 800/225-7474; fax: 212/354-5237. 610 rooms. Subway: C, E to 50th St. **$$**. European designer Philippe Starck was commissioned to overhaul the dowdy old Century Paramount. It is apparent upon entering that Starck did not take into account the tastes of the American heartland, not with all that gray marble and loopy

furniture. To the right is an outpost of the gourmet deli Dean & Deluca; to the left, The Whiskey Bar, an essential stop for fashionable nightbirds. The bedrooms are small, but all the off-the-wall features, like the stainless steel conical sinks, work to prevent a constricted feeling. Headboards are big gilt picture frames, some with enlargements of Renaissance paintings. The international clientele is mostly young, good-looking, and denimed, and many are in the fashion and entertainment trades. Guests have access to a video library of more than 500 titles and a business center that rents pagers and cellular telephones. The neighborhood is great if you love the theater, but skip the late-night sojourns to gritty 8th Avenue around the corner. In place of a sign outside the Paramount, look for the row of lollipop-shaped trees, and doormen with model-like looks dressed in black suits and T-shirts.

Park Lane

36 Central Park S. (near 5th Ave.), New York, NY 10019. ☎ 212/371-4000; 800/221-4982; fax: 212/319-9065. 640 rooms. Subway: N, R to 5th Ave. **$$$**.
Much used to be made of the fact that Harry and Leona Helmsley, owners of a group of New York hotels, chose to live in this one. Classical music plays in the lobby, which is wall-to-wall, floor-to-ceiling, sand-colored marble. The guest rooms are very large for this city, with picture windows unveiling grand Central Park from the pond up to the Metropolitan Museum. Phone, robes, and stools make the bathroom a convenient place to primp. Privileges at the New York Health & Racquet

Club are available to guests for about $20 a day.

Le Parker Meridien

118 W. 57th St. (6th Ave.), New York, NY 10019. ☎ 212/245-5000; 800/543-4300; fax: 212/708-7477. 700 rooms. Subway: B, Q to 57th St. **$$$$**.
Although it reminds me more of Miami Beach than Paris, the pink-columned, 3-story atrium that runs from 56th to 57th Street clearly announces the entrance of a luxury hotel. The French theme is more apparent in the Bar Montparnasse and Le Restaurant. But in the end, Le Parker Meridien speaks more of New York. To satisfy Americans' craze for fitness, the health club, which also sells memberships, offers an extensive array of equipment and a schedule of daily classes that includes step, body sculpting, yoga, exercise for $2^{1}/_{2}$ to 5-year-olds, and aquatic workouts in the 42nd floor pool. The hotel also has squash and racquetball courts and a jogging track. Mildly Art Deco, the renovated guest rooms are tasteful in beige and black, but the bathrooms are unremarkable. The *New York Times* is delivered in the morning, and shoe-shines are complimentary. For an additional $15 or $20, you can obtain a room with a park view, available above the 25th floor.

★★ Peninsula

700 5th Ave. (55th St.), New York, NY 10022. ☎ 212/247-2200; 800/223-5652; fax: 212/903-3949. 242 rooms. Subway: E, F to 5th Ave. **$$$$**.
Quite simply, the Peninsula has few rivals. Built in 1905 as a twin to the St. Regis directly across 5th Avenue, the Peninsula

suffered through periods of deterioration but, since being sold to the Hong Kong Peninsula group, has regained its past splendor, evident in the abundant fresh flowers and in the grand staircase sweeping down the lobby in the glow of a glittering chandelier. The hotel's 3-level spa is easily the finest hotel fitness center in the city. Fully equipped with top-quality equipment, the spa also houses a beautiful indoor pool, a whirlpool, a sauna, a steam room, and aerobics rooms. The locker rooms are stocked with robes, flip-flops, and stacks of towels. The beauty services available—in treatment rooms with heated tables—include an impressive range of facials, body treatments, waxing, and massage, plus hair styling and manicures. Your room is likely to be equally compelling. Most are of a good size, with traditional furniture, some of it antique, and modern conveniences, such as fax machines and bedside and desk command-center phones that control lighting, TV, and temperature. Most of the rooms have standing-room-only balconies, and virtually all are light and cheerful. Bathrooms are marble and come with oversized tubs, bidets, robes, and slippers. The Peninsula has 4 restaurants and bars, most notably the Gotham Lounge, known for its high tea and cocktails.

Pennsylvania

401 7th Ave. (33rd St.), New York, NY 10001. ☎ 212/736-5000; 800/223-8585; fax: 212/502-8712. 1,700 rooms. Subway: 1, 2, 3, 9 to 34th St./Penn Station. **$$**.
Large, anonymous, unremarkable, this giant spent a reported $6 million for renovations in anticipation of the 1992 Democratic National Convention, which took place in Madison Square Garden, across the street. Another few million might have made a real difference. Look upon it as an alternative to more desirable stops, or when business or pleasure require ready access to The Garden, Penn Station, or the Garment Center. Tariffs are moderate by local standards, and the rooms are comfortable enough. For a bit more money, the Concierge Floor offers better rooms and suites and a private lounge.

★★ Pierre

2 E. 61st St. (5th Ave.), New York, NY 10021. ☎ 212/838-8000; 800/332-3442 (US) or 800/268-6282 (Canada); fax: 212/940-8109. 206 rooms. Subway: N, R to 5th Ave. **$$$$$**.
Monarchs and presidents select the Pierre, a part of the distinguished Four Seasons chain. It has to be one of the safest addresses in town. Unfortunately, it's also one of the most popular, so much so that most of the park-facing rooms are co-ops. The guest rooms have something of a Sister Parish feel, with, for example, striped wallpaper, plaid bedskirts that match the window drapes, and floral chairs. Black marble covers the floors of the bathrooms, which have large pedestal sinks and white-eyelet shower curtains. Other pleasing touches are the terry robes, the magnifying shaving mirrors, and the bathroom phones. The staff members make notes of preferences in flowers and other idiosyncrasies and try to remember names. An elevator attendant is on duty 24 hours. Cafe Pierre, adjacent to the circular-muraled Rotunda, is a favorite for breakfast and high tea. Reserve for your visit as far ahead as possible.

Incidentally, even the Pierre has substantial discounts on weekends.

★ The Plaza

768 5th Ave. (59th St.), New York, NY 10019. ☎ 212/546-5495; 800/759-3000; fax: 212/ 759-3167. 815 rooms. Subway: N, R to 5th Ave. **$$$**.

The Plaza continues to serve as Hollywood shorthand for Manhattan glamor. Although too big and too glitzy—it is, after all, owned by Donald Trump—to stand among the most elite hostelries, the Plaza remains a living symbol of between-the-wars opulence. Among the Plaza's numerous restaurants, the central Palm Court is abuzz for afternoon tea and Sunday brunch, and the atmospheric Oak Bar is so popular it requires a maitre d' to control the crowds. Surprisingly, the guest rooms live up to the lobby's drama, with high ceilings, thick walls, and rich colors. Nonworking fireplaces with ornate mantles are the centerpieces of many rooms, and Oriental rugs, canopy beds, and terry robes further communicate images of luxury. You'll pay a couple hundred bucks more to overlook the park, while most of the Plaza's Central Park South neighbors charge about $50 for the privilege.

Plaza Athénée

37 E. 64th St. (near Madison Ave.), New York, NY 10021. ☎ 212/734-9100; 800/ 447-8800; fax: 212/772-0958. 153 rooms. Subway: N, R to 5th Ave. **$$$$**.

Literally no expense was spared to transform what was the lackluster Hotel Alrae into a paragon of the Continental standard of superb innkeeping. The aged, tiered structure was stripped to the shell and rebuilt, from plumbing and wiring to the lavish use of Brazilian mahogany in the public rooms, and pastel silk wall-coverings in the spacious suites. The overhaul cost $50 million, and operating expenses are as dazzling a testament to intent—the monthly florist bill is said to exceed $100,000. Now it matches up favorably with the neighborhood's other gems. Only a curmudgeon could find serious fault, apart from some smallish rooms. There is superb dining in the elegant fin de siècle setting of Le Regence.

Quality Hotel Fifth Avenue

3 E. 40th St. (near 5th Ave.), New York, NY 10016. ☎ 212/ 447-1500; 800/668-4200; fax: 212/213-0972. 186 rooms. Subway: 4, 5, 6, 7, Shuttle to Grand Central. **$$**.

Formerly known as the Journey's End, the Quality Hotel is owned by a Canadian economy chain. Frills are few, but public and private rooms in the 29-story sliver of a building are clean and uncluttered. And rates go as low as $95 on weekends. Most rooms have queen-sized beds, and many also have sofa-beds. An Italian restaurant is just off the lobby. Arrangements can be made for use of a nearby health club.

Radisson Empire

44 W. 63rd St. (Broadway), New York, NY 10023. ☎ 212/ 265-7400; 800/333-3333; fax: 212/315-0349. 372 rooms. Subway: 1, 9 to 66 St./Lincoln Center. **$$**.

You'd never guess by walking in the lobby—with its 1710 French tapestry and

The Plaza

Renaissance decor—that the Radisson chain had bought the Empire. The guest rooms, though, don't lie quite as well. There the bedspreads and drapes are of that hideous floral variety and the furniture doesn't have much personality. The only other caveat is that some rooms and/or baths are of cramped or odd dimensions. Some of the Empire's pluses are the stereo tuners, CD players, VCRs, and audio tape-decks in all its rooms, and the free use of the adjacent health club. Guests can order room service or check out on a special channel on the remote-control TV, and messages are conveyed via electronic voice mail. Perhaps the best perk, at least for culture-seekers, is the address, with Lincoln Center across the street and Carnegie Hall and Broadway theaters within easy walking distance. The Empire is also just a block west of Central Park. I recommend Iridium, a very hip jazz club

and restaurant with a Daliesque decor, right on the corner.

Ramada Renaissance

2 Times Square (47th St.), New York, NY 10036. ☎ 212/765-7676; fax: 212/765-1962. 305 rooms. Subway: 1, 2, 3, 7, 9, N, R, Shuttle to 42nd St./Times Square. **$$$$**.

This Ramada has made a determined effort to make it into the ranks of the upscale hotels. Despite having to contend with the likes of Times Square (yes, it's been cleaned up, but it's hardly Central Park South), the Renaissance makes a good presentation. The rooms are highlighted by wood furniture and marble bathrooms with phones and cotton robes. But the area in which the Renaissance is trying to distinguish itself is service, assigning a butler to every floor to supervise the housekeeping staff, arrange limousines and theater tickets, have shirts pressed, bring umbrellas and coffee, make wake-up calls, unpack luggage—just about anything legal. A waterfall introduces the restaurant, which has banks of windows framing an unobstructed panorama of The Great White Way. A seat there on New Year's Eve? Last price quoted: $1,000. By 1999, that might look like a bargain.

★ Regency

540 Park Ave. (61st St.), New York, NY 10021. ☎ 212/759-4100; 800/223-0888; fax: 212/826-5674. 400 rooms. Subway: 4, 5, 6, N, R to 59 St./Lexington Ave. **$$$$**.

The Regency is the ideal place for those compulsive capitalists who roll out of bed and hit the floor running. The downstairs 540 Park restaurant is the place to conduct business breakfasts. Waiters make photocopies betwixt serving eggs and pouring coffee. Guests can keep in fighting trim in the lower lobby fitness center. As for comforts, the pretty marble bathrooms have TVs and phones. The bedrooms, in soft, happy colors like peach and green, have throw pillows on the beds and marble-topped end tables in a decor that might be called Corporate Louis XVI. Afternoon tea is served in the bar-lounge. The Regency is more upper-crust than trendy, as evidenced by the preponderance of facelifted guests.

★ Ritz-Carlton

112 Central Park S. (near 6th Ave.), New York, NY 10019. ☎ 212/757-1900; 800/241-3333; fax: 212/757-9620. 214 rooms. Subway: B, Q to 57th St. **$$$$**.

Vying for a top ranking among New York hotels is the Ritz-Carlton. Its ideal location is only one of the many things that make the hotel special. Beginning with the softly lit, intimate lobby, the Ritz-Carlton evokes a European ambiance. The highly polished marble is in gray and salmon tones, and the furniture is gold-leafed and ornate. In the generously sized rooms, the decor is just a touch too formal, which reinforces the sense of luxury the chain works so hard to achieve. For a spectacular view of the park, expect to pay an additional $100 to $150. The fitness center is small but sufficient, and the business center offers cellular phone rentals. Fantino, the 1st-floor restaurant, serves Northern Italian cuisine and has macrobiotic options, but it's the bar, or, more precisely, the bartender, who may be the biggest single attraction. A classic New York bartender, Norman keeps up a nightly barrage of jokes and patter in pure Brooklynese. Fortunately, he also knows when to leave patrons alone.

Roger Smith

501 Lexington Ave. (47th St.), New York, NY 10017. ☎ 212/755-1400; 800/445-0277; fax: 212/319-9130. 130 rooms. Subway: 4, 5, 6, 7, Shuttle to Grand Central. **$$$**.

What happens when a serious artist inherits an urban hotel? Sound like a bad sitcom? Actually, it's the Roger Smith, a little hotel with a wacky personality. The Roger Smith has what you might call character, from the bronze nude sculptures announcing the front door to the colorful murals in Lily's, the restaurant and bar. James Knowles, the owner, created those works, but he also is dedicated to promoting the works of other artists, rotating the lobby displays monthly and converting the gift shop into a gallery for young unknowns. Although no 2 rooms are alike, most are decorated in a homey, early-American style. I found the rooms a little dark and depressing, but the staff is very warm and friendly. Prices include Continental breakfast, an unusual practice in New York that effectively lowers the room rate.

★★ Royalton

44 W. 44th St. (bet. 5th and 6th aves.), New York, NY 10036. ☎ 212/869-4400; 800/ 635-9013; fax: 212/869-8965. 205 rooms. Subway: B, D, F, Q to 42nd St. **$$$$**.
Incomparably hip, the Royalton is the home away from home for actors, models, fashion designers, photographers, and other assorted celebrities. Not a shock, considering one of the principles is Ian Schrager, who helped usher in the big disco-era with Studio 54 and the Palladium. French interior designer Philippe Starck, who created a shiny blue-black mine tunnel of a lobby, its couches and chairs wrapped in bone-white cotton. At one end is the arresting eatery, 44, where the food, though very good, takes a back seat to the people-watching. The bedrooms are dramatic, with low beds pushed deep into the walls and wall-to-wall banquettes replacing dull chair and ottoman combos. The slate bathrooms, punctuated with stainless steel, conical sinks rising out of glass counters, and 5-foot tubs or glass showers, are equally spectacular. The Royalton also understands luxury, outfitting 40 rooms with working fireplaces, placing down comforters, fresh flowers, VCRs, CD players, and the morning *New York Times* in all the rooms, and offering to arrange sessions with a celebrity trainer in the hotel's fitness room. No doubt some visitors would find the Royalton's secret-society attitude intimidating: No sign announces the entrance. Even the front desk, a crucial destination in any hotel, is concealed within the long stretch of wall that glides from 44th to 43rd Street.

St. Moritz

50 Central Park S. (6th Ave.), New York, NY 10019. ☎ 212/ 755-5800; 800/221-4774; fax: 212/751-2952. 680 rooms. Subway: B, Q to 57th St. **$$**.
Occupying one of the city's prime locations, the St. Moritz is like that one neighbor who doesn't keep up his lawn. The hotel, sadly, has fallen into a state of shlockdom. The shabby lobby has a separate check-in for airline crews at the front desk and a glass counter selling tchotchkes. The rooms are on the small side and look as though they haven't been updated in a decade or two. But the park views, as you might expect, are amazing. The other main attraction is Rumplemayers restaurant, with outdoor cafe seating under umbrellas and intriguing ice-cream concoctions.

★★ St. Regis

2 E. 55th St. (5th Ave.), New York, NY 10022. ☎ 212/753-4500; 800/759-7550; fax: 212/ 787-0447. 362 rooms. Subway: E, F to 5th Ave. **$$$$$**.
John Jacob Astor was right when he decided to name his grand new hotel for the patron saint of hospitality. Today, more than 90 years and many millions of dollars of renovations later, the St. Regis

remains a model of luxury living. Every floor has its own British-trained butler, who serves tea or coffee upon arrival and is at guests' disposal for just about any service, from pressing clothes to packing them and from running out to buy pantyhose to drawing a bath. The butlers reportedly brush their teeth 14 times a day to ensure fresh breath when discreetly serving their guests. In the enlarged bedchambers, furnishings are Louis XV and XVI reproductions, but the hi-tech telephones are programmed in 6 languages to control lights, room temperatures, TVs, and radios. The marble bathrooms are delightfully large, with separate tub and shower, a phone beside the enclosed toilet, and very fluffy robes. The extras are almost endless, from the fruit platter replenished daily and the afternoon cookies or sweets to the complimentary mineral water and newspaper of choice to the free local and credit-card calls. Lespinasse has drawn raves for its French cuisine with Asian flourishes, and the Astor Court is a must for high tea to the strains of a harp. The King Cole Bar, over which hangs the marvelous 1906 Maxfield Parrish mural, is a terribly civilized choice for a cocktail. The executive center enjoys every plausible amenity, and the fitness center is well-equipped. Every staff member speaks at least 2 languages. It will come as no surprise that all this comes with the highest room rates in New York.

★ Stanhope

995 5th Ave. (81st St.), New York, NY 10028. ☎ 212/288-5800; 800/828-1123; fax: 212/ 517-0088. 141 rooms. Bus: M1, M2, M3, M4. Subway: 4, 5, 6 to 86th St. **$$$$$**.

The Stanhope may have discovered that perfect combination of charm and elegance that eludes so many luxury hotels. The lobby is small but well appointed with Baccarat crystal chandeliers, 18thC furniture, and an intriguing wood and marble floor. Room furnishings are similarly pleasant, with interesting touches such as marble-topped desks and chests. Real plants and fresh flowers provide warmth, and, if you're lucky, a view of the park provides inspiration. Tariffs, of course, are on the high side, but travelers in a position to pay them are accorded such conveniences as robes and slippers, phones in the bathrooms, and complimentary car service to Midtown. The restaurant operation has earned the admiration of local food critics, as has tea in the salon, but my recommendation is an iced tea or other cold beverage at The Terrace, the Stanhope's popular sidewalk cafe, together with leisurely 5th Avenue people-watching.

Tudor

304 E. 42nd St. (bet. 1st and 2nd aves.), New York, NY 10017. ☎ 212/986-8800; 800/879-8836; fax: 212/986-1758. 317 rooms. Bus: M15, M106. Subway: 4, 5, 6, 7, Shuttle to Grand Central. **$$$**.

Erected in 1931, the Tudor's fortunes waxed and waned until it degenerated into a warehouse for backpackers and economy tour groups. The Sarova Hotel Group, which has a dozen properties in London and Kenya, acquired it and closed it down for more than

2 years to affect a complete overhaul, stripping down to bare brick and concrete before reopening in 1992. Now the Tudor is desirable again, a solid choice for businesspeople who plan quick in-and-out visits to the city. The hotel does not skimp on the gadgets and comforts, such as trouser presses and bathroom speakers for TV sound. Rooms in the south tower are larger and quieter than those in the north, and some enjoy terraces, wet bars, and/or Jacuzzis. Guests have access to a fitness center and a business center. Cecil's Grill, a British-style carvery, has a rather limited menu. High tea and a light menu are served in the Regency Lounge.

UN Plaza-Park Hyatt

1 United Nations Plaza (44th St. at 1st Ave.), New York, NY 10017. ☎ 212/758-1234; fax: 212/702-5051. 427 rooms. Bus: M15, M106. Subway: 4, 5, 6, 7, Shuttle to Grand Central. **$$$$**. An underappreciated hotel, the UN Plaza-Park Hyatt offers more than most of its competitors with similar prices. Its glassy, angular "International Style" of architecture is appropriate to its ownership by the eponymous world organization. Guest rooms begin on the 28th floor, so the views over the East River or west into Midtown are arresting. They can also be enjoyed from the huge indoor swimming pool and the rather small but fully-equipped exercise room. On the 39th floor is a tennis court, the only such facility in a Manhattan hotel (open 6:30am–10pm). Personal trainers and swimming and tennis lessons are available. Felicitous extras include

baskets of fruit on arrival, overnight shoe-shines, delivery of the *New York Times,* and courtesy shuttle van during the day to Wall Street, the World Trade Center, and the garment district, and at night to the theater district. The hotel also has a business center. Members of the staff speak an estimated 42 languages.

Waldorf Astoria

301 Park Ave. (49th St.), New York, NY 10022. ☎ 212/872-4534; 800/WALDORF; fax: 212/758-9209. 1,410 rooms. Subway: 6 to 51st St. **$$$$**. The original Waldorf, a name long synonymous with luxury, gave way to the Empire State Building. This replacement threw open its doors in 1931, its public rooms a paean to the Art Deco fashion of that period. A costly facelift has restored the classic lobby and anterooms to their former glory. All the amenities that might be expected are here, and the rooms and suites of the Towers section are superior or equal to anything of their like in the city. In effect a hotel within the hotel, The Towers, with its own reception desk and concierge (entrance on 50th St.), has completed its own $30 million renovation, including refinished hardwood floors, original oil paintings, and period European furnishings. Guest rooms in the main building feature glass furniture and large marble bathrooms. Black-lacquered doors are striking against pale yellow-striped wallpaper in the wide hallways. If you need further evidence of the luxe life, check out the exclusive Sulka boutique in-house, or the rare bookstore, or the legions of well-heeled New Yorkers traipsing through

the lobby on the way to a charity benefit in the Grand Ballroom.

Warwick

65 W. 54th St. (6th Ave.), New York, NY 10019. ☎ 212/247-2700; 800/223-4099; fax: 212/957-8915. 419 rooms. Subway: B, D, E to 7th Ave. **$$$**.

Overshadowed by the mammoth Hilton across the street, this medium-sized hotel has the same proximity to the major television headquarters and Broadway theaters but at lower tariffs and in a more agreeable atmosphere. Many bedrooms are larger than the New York norm, rivaling most hotels' junior suites. Seniors receive 25% discounts off standard room rates, and weekend discounts are deep. Be sure, however, to make a specific request for the lower rates. That said, the Warwick ranks with most midtown stopovers in its price category, and is superior to most.

Westbury

15 E. 69th St. (Madison Ave.), New York, NY 10021. ☎ 212/535-2000; 800/225-5843; fax: 212/772-0958. 237 rooms. Subway: 6 to 68 St./Hunter College. **$$$$**.

This cousin of the Plaza Athénée can hold its own in the luxury hotel class. Converted from a 1920s' apartment house, this fashionable retreat endeavors to retain a residential quality—that is, if one normally lives with crystal chandeliers, 17thC tapestries, and lavish displays of fresh flowers. Such lobbies

often give an inaccurate foretaste of the rooms upstairs. Not here. This one features bedrooms with English needlepoint rugs and, in the style of your eccentric old aunt, mahogany furniture, yards of chintz, and lots of striped wallpaper. Even the smallest single rooms are cozy, not cramped, and are equipped with CD players, speaker-phones, and useful work desks. The staff is warm and helpful. A health club with sauna, steam room, whirlpool, and the usual equipment is open to guests only. The revamped Polo restaurant, dedicated to procuring foods locally, is excellent.

Wyndham

42 W. 58th St. (near 5th Ave.), New York, NY 10019. ☎ 212/753-3500. 202 rooms. Subway: B, Q to 57th St. **$$**.

In one of the most desirable locations in town is a sweet, if slightly musty, inn. The owner-managers live on the premises, and many of their guests are theater folk settling in for long runs on Broadway. These rooms weren't designed by computer imaging. Old furniture (but not what you'd call antique) combines with floral wallpaper and lace curtains to give the rooms a sort of fading gentility. The bar and restaurant are good enough; there is no room service, though. A buzz-in front door gives the place some added security. At these low prices, reservations must be made 4 to 6 weeks in advance.

Some Budget Recommendations

The hotels listed below are a selection of some of New York's moderately priced hotels. If you have difficulty finding a room in one of these, there is no shortage of alternatives. If the following accommodations don't meet your expectations, remember that many of the more upscale hotels listed in the previous section offer discounted rates, and you may be able to get a lot more hotel for not much more money.

Beverly

125 E. 50th St. (Lexington Ave.), New York, NY 10022. ☎ 212/753-2700; 800/223-0945. **$$**. Located in Midtown East, near Grand Central Terminal, this hotel offers reasonable prices that include Continental breakfast weekdays. The rooms are fine, with floors that creak in a charming manner.

Days Hotel Midtown

790 8th Ave. (49th St.), New York, NY 10019. ☎ 212/581-7000; 800/223-0888; fax: 212/974-0291. **$**. Midtown theater district. Relatively modest family rates, swimming pool. Good value.

Doubletree Guest Suites

1568 Broadway (47th St.), New York, NY 10036. ☎ 212/719-1600; fax 921-5212. **$$$**. Comfortable suites for the price of a double, with sofa-beds and microwaves, are to be found at this hotel rising above Times Square. Bright and clean, with a fitness center, and a play room for kids. A great value, particularly for families requiring some elbow room.

Gramercy Park

2 Lexington Ave. (21st St.), New York, NY 10010. ☎ 212/475-4320; 800/221-4083; fax: 212/505-0535. **$$**. Near Gramercy Park, away from the main traffic arteries. Popular with budget-minded Europeans, this peaceful hotel has a relatively quiet situation, plus access to an attractive private park nearby.

Howard Johnson Plaza

851 8th Ave. (near 52nd St.), New York, NY 10019. ☎ 212/581-4100; 800/223-0888; fax 974-7502. **$$**. Near theaters and Midtown, with easy car-access and moderate rates. Muzak in the lobby. Rooms are okay.

Lexington

48th St. and Lexington Ave., New York, NY 10017. ☎ 212/755-4400; 800/223-0888; fax: 212/751-4091. **$**. Near Grand Central Station and the United Nations, catering heavily to airline crews. The place is generally clean, but peeling paint and such point to the need for some updating. Attractive weekend and seasonal discounts. Sung Dynasty on the main floor is a good option for Chinese food.

Milford Plaza

270 W. 45th St. (8th Ave.), New York, NY 10036. ☎ 212/869-3600; 800/221-2690; fax 944-8357. **$**. Located on a tacky stretch of 8th Avenue on the edge of the theater district, the Milford calls itself the "Lullabuy of Broadway." Well, it's a little off-key, with mostly small rooms furnished circa 1974, complete with turquoise curtains. Tour groups mill about in the dingy lobby. I found a staff member literally asleep at his desk. But the rates are relatively low.

Salisbury

123 W. 57th St. (bet. 6th and 7th aves.), New York, NY 10019.

☎ 212/246-1300; 800/
223-0680. **$$**.
Across from Carnegie Hall.
Many refurbished rooms with
big new beds, some with
serving pantries, all with
microwaves. No nonsense.
Continental breakfast included.

Travelodge Midtown
132 W. 45th St. (near Ave. of the
Americas), New York, NY 10036.
☎ 212/921-7600; 800/242-
8935; fax: 212/719-0171. **$$**.
A good theater district location
and modest rates (that include
continental breakfast) make

this a decent economy choice.
The elevator may be the
slowest in Manhattan, but the
rooms are clean.

Wales
1295 Madison Ave. (92nd St.),
New York, NY 10028. ☎ 212/
876-6000; 800/428-5252; fax:
212/860-7000. **$$**.
On the Upper East Side, near
the Guggenheim Museum in a
pretty residential neighbor-
hood. Many rooms and suites
have an Edwardian flair. The
plant-filled lobby is cozy. Ask
to see the room first.

Manhattan East Suite Hotels

Businesspeople and families willing to forgo some mi-
nor services can obtain studios or 1- to 3-bedroom suites
at the price of standard doubles in a glossier hotel. All
have refrigerators, most have kitchens, and some have
terraces. Prices are per suite, not per person, so chil-
dren can be accommodated on convertible sofas
without extra cost. Since all suites have kitchenettes,
further economies are possible with meals and snacks.

From outside New York State, reservations can be
made for any of the following Manhattan East hotels
at ☎ 800/637-8483. Local numbers are given below.
The following are moderately expensive, but potential
savings, as noted, can be substantial. Seasonal and week-
end discounts and special long-stay rates are available.

Southgate Tower 371 7th Ave. (31st St.),
☎ 212/563-1800. Health club and restaurant.

Dumont Plaza 150 E. 34th St. (Lexington
Ave.), ☎ 212/481-7600.

Shelburne Murray Hill 303 Lexington Ave.
(37th St.), ☎ 212/689-5200.

Eastgate Tower 222 E. 39th St. (near 2nd Ave.),
☎ 212/687-8000. Bar, garage, cafe.

Beekman Tower 49th St. and 1st Ave., ☎ 212/
355-7300. Rooftop bar, restaurant, (see also the
expanded entry above).

Plaza Fifty 155 E. 50th St. (3rd Ave.), ☎ 212/
751-5710.

Lyden House 320 E. 53rd St. (near 2nd Ave.),
☎ 212/888-6070. Garage.

Lyden Gardens 215 E. 64th St. (near 3rd Ave.), ☎ 212/355-1230.

Surrey 20 E. 76th St. (Madison Ave.), ☎ 212/288-3700.

Bed-and-Breakfasts

The impersonality and often breathtaking expense of a stay in New York have inspired efforts to get around those twin liabilities. One answer is the bed-and-breakfast movement. Although it isn't comparable to those of the usual American version, the attempt is laudable. The agencies named below are essentially referral services, matching up clients with hosts. They represent hundreds of lodgings.

The variety is considerable, from SoHo lofts to East Side town houses to spare rooms in high-rise apartments. In some, the owners are present, to provide welcome, advice, and breakfast. In others, they are not, but leave stocked refrigerators and numbers where they can be reached. With that diversity, and the frequent modifications of rosters, quality is unpredictable. Maid service, for example, is rarely provided, meaning you must make your own bed and tidy up. But prices are as much as 60% less than standard hotel rates, and the opportunity to live as New Yorkers is appealing to those who don't require conventional hotel services. An advance deposit must be paid, usually equal to at least half of the 1st night's fee. Some, not all, agencies accept credit cards. A minimum stay is required, usually at least 2 nights. Several days' or weeks' notice of cancellation is required for refund of deposits. Be clear about requirements when making reservations. Hosts often do not allow smoking or young children. The field is still volatile, and no guarantees can be made about accommodation, or even the continued existence of the referral services listed below.

Abode Bed and Breakfast P.O. Box 20022, New York, NY 10028, ☎ 212/472-2000.

Bed-and-Breakfast Network of New York 134 W. 32nd St., Suite 602, New York, NY 10001, ☎ 212/645-8134.

New World Bed & Breakfast 150 5th Ave., Suite 711, New York, NY 10011, ☎ 212/675-5600 or 800/443-3800.

Urban Ventures 306 W. 38th St., New York, NY 10018, ☎ 212/594-5650.

SIGHTS AND ATTRACTIONS

Introduction

New York is a city of sheer diversity—at every level. Its world-renowned theaters, museums, and cultural attractions provide visitors and residents an endless choice of experiences. For a balanced picture of what the city has to offer, I'll try to steer you to some of the more idiosyncratic sights, as well as the star attractions.

Keep in mind that some sights, particularly the Statue of Liberty and the Empire State Building, can build up long lines, so try hitting those places in the morning. Also don't count on speeding through Midtown traffic in a taxi at rush hour or during lunchtime—a slow crawl is often all you'll manage. At these times, it's faster (and cheaper) to take the subway or walk. If you're having trouble cramming everything into your schedule, note that many museums have evening hours.

Because many of the institutions in this chapter receive public funding, they cannot require admission fees and instead request donations of suggested amounts. Paying the full amounts can make touring prohibitively expensive, so be brave and insist on paying less. Most attractions discount admission prices for senior citizens (generally over 62 or 65) and for students and children.

Some of the attractions might have changed their exhibitions, hours, or admission prices by the time this book hits the shelves—so call to confirm.

In the alphabetical listings that follow, you'll find several **Oases**—free resting places—where you can escape the crowds.

For First-Time Visitors

Here are some of the highlights—a few time-tested New York landmarks—you won't want to miss:

American Museum of Natural History

Bronx Zoo

Central Park

Greenwich Village

Guggenheim Museum

Metropolitan Museum of Art

Museum of Modern Art

Observation deck of Empire State Building
or World Trade Center

SoHo

Statue of Liberty and Ellis Island

Orientation Tours

As in all cities, tour guides come with varying degrees
of knowledge and personalities. Too often, their "spiels"
are tangled nests of opinion, half-digested facts, irrel-
evancies, and failed attempts at humor. Some guides
compound their deficiencies by imagining that they are
the show. My advice is to enjoy the views, use the tour
to get the lay of the land, and filter the guide's declara-
tions through a fine net of skepticism.

Circle Line, Pier 83, end of W. 43rd St.; ☎ 212/
563-3200. Three-hour boat cruises around Manhattan,
Apr–Nov, and 2-hour nighttime cruises of the harbor.

Gray Line Tours, 900 8th Ave. (near 53rd St.);
☎ 212/397-2600. Twenty-six tours of 2 hours to a full
day, some conducted in foreign languages.

Island Helicopter, Heliport at end of E. 34th St.;
☎ 212/683-4575. Daily flights, all year, minimum of 2
passengers.

Liberty Helicopter Tours, Hudson River, end of
W. 30th St.; ☎ 212/465-8905. Four flight plans, with
a minimum of 3 passengers.

New York Apple Tours, 203 E. 94th St.; ☎ 212/
348-5300. Forty-nine stops, do-it-yourself bus tours
with pickups every 15–60 minutes.

Special-Interest Tours

Adventures on a Shoestring, 300 W. 53rd St.;
☎ 212/265-2663 . Walking tours with diverse themes;
participants are often New Yorkers. Call to reserve and
to learn starting points, which are changed from tour
to tour.

Harlem, Your Way! Tours Unlimited, 129 W. 130th St.; ☎ 212/690-1687. Various tours of Harlem, a district in upper Manhattan that has historically been inhabited by African-Americans.

Harlem Spirituals, 1697 Broadway; ☎ 212/757-0425. Four different itineraries through Harlem, in 5 languages.

Seaport Liberty Cruises, Pier 16, South Street Seaport; ☎ 212/425-3737. One-hour cruises of the harbor on a 19thC paddle wheeler and a steamboat. In summer, additional cocktail and music cruises.

Spirit of New York, Pier 62, W. 23rd St.; ☎ 212/742-7278. Lunch, brunch, dinner, and late-night party cruises, lasting 2–3 hours.

Best Bets for Kids

The "Cue" section in the back of the weekly magazine *New York* lists current activities for children, and the *New York Times* has a "For Children" page in its Friday editions. The following are some of the most family-friendly attractions—see "Sights and Attractions A to Z" for their hours and full descriptions.

Central Park is a child's paradise with its zoo, carousel, playgrounds, lakeside boat rentals, skating rinks, and special activities like puppet theaters and model-boat sailing. For a morning of outdoor storytelling, go to **Hans Christian Andersen Memorial** (near 5th Ave. and 72nd St.), where stories are read (May–Sept, Sat at 11am) to children, some of whom sit in the bronze lap of the master.

Young children will have fun with the interactive exhibits at the **Children's Museum of Manhattan. The New York Aquarium** fascinates both young children and their older siblings—not to mention their parents. The **Bronx Zoo** and the **American Museum of Natural History,** particularly the colossal dinosaur display, are equally fascinating. Older children (10 and over) will be able to appreciate **Ellis Island.** Most also will get a thrill from going aboard the antique ships at the **South Street Seaport Museum.**

A number of game shows and variety specials originate in New York. Children between the ages of 6 and 18 must be accompanied by an adult. Tickets are free, and sources are: American Broadcasting Company, 1330 6th Ave. (☎ 212/456-1000); Columbia Broadcasting System, 51 W. 52nd St. (☎ 212/582-0220); National Broadcasting Company, 30 Rockefeller Plaza,

(☎ 212/664-3055); and the New York Convention and Visitors Bureau, 2 Columbus Circle (☎ 212/397-8222).

Special Events

If your kids are into Christmas and Hanukkah decorations, the luxury shops and large department stores are ablaze with holiday lights and window-dressing from late November to late December, and 5th Avenue in Midtown is a glorious spectacle. The centerpiece is the 70-foot tree with myriad winking lights looming above the skating rink at the foot of the **GE Building;** the **Channel Gardens** that lead into **Rockefeller Center** from 5th Avenue are transformed; shop windows and interior displays of invariable delight are those of **Lord & Taylor** (38th St.), **Saks Fifth Avenue** (50th St.), and **FAO Schwarz** (58th St.). Down at **South Street Seaport,** carolers arrange themselves into a living Christmas tree while they sing.

Among the special events for children each year is the **Big Apple Circus**—New York's very own 1-ring circus in a tent, modeled after the intimate European troupes that have no other equivalent in the United States. Clowns cavort, aerialists execute the fabled triple somersault, elephants dance, and jugglers and acrobats twirl and tumble. Prices are low at this not-for-profit enterprise, with performances most likely in summer and the Christmas season. **Radio City Music Hall** (6th Ave. and 50th St.; ☎ 212/632-4041) holds Christmas and Easter Shows (featuring the precision-dancing Rockettes) that are geared toward families, as are such special appearances as Walt Disney's World on Ice.

Special Moments

I hope that each of you will find your own special moments in New York, but here are some places to start: During the warm months, go to the Metropolitan Museum's rooftop sculpture garden (take the elevator)—you'll find a stupendous view of Central Park. You can order a glass of wine or a soda if you like and you're free to walk around and soak up the view.

On a weekday (when everyone's at work) take a stroll through Zabar's gourmet food shop on the Upper West Side; graze over the assortment of cheeses, baked goods, and delicacies, and smell the delicious coffee being ground. Another idea: Go to the New York Public Library on 5th Avenue (enter on 42nd St.); wander through its wood-paneled precincts, gaze at the paintings, peek into the Main Reading Room and get a taste of a New York City landmark. Something else? Walk around the jogging path of the Central Park Reservoir—alternating views of one-of-a-kind Manhattan will frame its tranquil blue waters.

Mostly, though, don't feel pressured to schedule every second of every day. Stop and stand back from the intensity of it all and just look around you. If you absorb one one-hundreth of the whirl of life, you'll be ahead of the game.

Sights & Attractions by Category

Bridges
Brooklyn Bridge
George Washington Bridge
Verrazano Narrows Bridge

Churches & Synagogues
Cathedral Church of St. John
   the Divine
Central Synagogue
Church of the Ascension
Church of the Transfiguration
Grace Church
Riverside Church
St. Bartholomew's Church
St. Mark's-in-the-Bowery
St. Patrick's Cathedral
St. Paul's Chapel
Temple Emanu-El
Trinity Church

Colleges & Universities
Columbia University
Cooper Union
New York University
Yeshiva University

Exhibition Halls
Forbes Magazine Galleries
Jacob K. Javits Convention
   Center
Seventh Regiment Armory

Historic Buildings
Abigail Adams Smith
   Museum
Bouwerie Lane Theatre
Castle Clinton National
   Monument
City Hall
Dakota Apartments

Dyckman House
★ Ellis Island
Federal Hall National
   Memorial
Gracie Mansion
Grand Central Terminal
Merchant's House Museum
Morris-Jumel Mansion
New York Stock Exchange
Theodore Roosevelt
   Birthplace
Van Cortlandt Mansion and
   Museum
Villard Houses

Libraries
American Bible Society
★ New York Public Library
Pierpont Morgan Library

Monuments
Cleopatra's Needle
General Grant National
   Memorial
Hall of Fame for Great
   Americans
★ Statue of Liberty

Art Museums
American Academy and
   Institute of Arts and
   Letters
American Craft Museum
Americas Society
Asia Society
Audubon Terrace
★ The Cloisters
Cooper-Hewitt National
   Design Museum
★ Frick Collection
Guggenheim Museum

International Center of
Photography
★★ Metropolitan Museum
of Art
El Museo del Barrio
Museum of American Folk Art
Museum of American
Illustration
★ Museum of Modern Art
National Academy of Design
New Museum of Contempo-
rary Art
Queens Museum of Art
Studio Museum in Harlem
Whitney Museum of
American Art

History or Cultural Museums

American Museum of the
Moving Image
American Museum of Natural
History
American Numismatic
Society
Brooklyn Museum
China Institute
Fraunces Tavern Museum
French Institute/Alliance
Française
Goethe House
Hispanic Society of America
Jacques Marchais Museum of
Tibetan Art
Japan Society
Jewish Museum
Museum of the City of New
York
National Museum of the
American Indian
New York City Fire
Museum
New York Historical Society
Police Academy Museum
South Street Seaport
Spanish Institute
Ukrainian Museum

Science or Technology Museums

Children's Museum of
Manhattan
Hayden Planetarium
Intrepid Sea-Air-Space
Museum

Museum of Television and
Radio

Music & Sports Halls

Carnegie Hall
Chelsea Piers
Lincoln Center
Madison Square Garden

Parks & Gardens

Battery Park
Bowling Green
★ Brooklyn Botanic
Garden
Bryant Park
Carl Schurz Park
Central Park
Fort Tryon Park
Greenacre Park
New York Botanical Garden

"Oases"

Paley Park
Prospect Park
Riverside Park
Union Square
Washington Square
★ Wave Hill

Skyscrapers

Chrysler Building
Citicorp Center
★★ Empire State
Building
Equitable Center
Ford Foundation Building
Flatiron Building
GE Building
Lever House
Lipstick Building
Metropolitan Life Building
News Building
Rockefeller Center
Seagram Building
Sony Building
Trump Tower
United Nations
Woolworth Building
World Financial Center
World Trade Center

Zoos & Aquarium

★ Bronx Zoo
Central Park Zoo
New York Aquarium
Staten Island Zoo

Sights & Attractions by Neighborhood

*Lower Manhattan/
Financial District
(below Worth St.)*
Battery Park
Bowling Green
Castle Clinton National
    Monument
City Hall
★ Ellis Island
Federal Hall National
    Memorial
Fraunces Tavern Museum
National Museum of the
    American Indian
New York Stock Exchange
St. Paul's Chapel
South Street Seaport
★ Statue of Liberty
Trinity Church
Woolworth Building
World Financial Center
World Trade Center

*Little Italy/Chinatown/
TriBeCa/SoHo (below
Houston St., above
Worth St., west of
Bowery)*
Brooklyn Bridge
New Museum of
    Contemporary Art
New York City Fire Museum

*East Village/Lower East
Side (below 14th St.,
above Canal St.; east
of Bowery)*
Bouwerie Lane Theatre
The Bowery
Cooper Union
Merchant's House Museum
St. Mark's-in-the-Bowery
Ukrainian Museum

*Greenwich Village
(below 14th St., west
of 4th Ave., above
Houston St.)*
Church of the Ascension
Forbes Magazine Galleries

Grace Church
New York University
Washington Square

*Gramercy Park/Murray
Hill (E. 14th St.–
E. 42nd St.)*
Church of the Transfiguration
★★ Empire State Building
Flatiron Building
Pierpont Morgan Library
Police Academy Museum
Theodore Roosevelt
    Birthplace
Union Square

*Lower West Side/
Garment Center (W.
14th St.–W. 42nd St.)*
Chelsea Piers
Jacob K. Javits Convention
    Center
Madison Square Garden

*Midtown East (E. 43rd
St.–E. 59th St.)*
Bryant Park
Chrysler Building
Citicorp Center
Ford Foundation Building
Grand Central Terminal
Greenacre Park
Japan Society
Lever House
Lipstick Building
Metropolitan Life Building
News Building
Paley Park
St. Bartholomew's Church
St. Patrick's Cathedral
Seagram Building
Seventh Regiment Armory
Sony Building
Spanish Institute
Trump Tower
United Nations
Villard Houses

*Midtown West (W. 43rd
St.–W. 59th St.)*
American Craft Museum
Carnegie Hall

GE Building
Equitable Center
Intrepid Sea-Air-Space
 Museum
★ Museum of Modern Art
Museum of Television and
 Radio
★ New York Public Library
Rockefeller Center
Theater District

Upper East Side (E. 60th St.–E. 96th St.)

Abigail Adams Smith
 Museum
Americas Society
Asia Society
Carl Schurz Park
Central Park
Central Synagogue
China Institute
Cleopatra's Needle
Cooper-Hewitt National
 Design Museum
French Institute/Alliance
 Française
★ Frick Collection
Goethe House
Gracie Mansion
Guggenheim Museum
International Center of
 Photography
Jewish Museum
★★ Metropolitan Museum
 of Art
Museum of American
 Illustration
National Academy of Design
Temple Emanu-El
Whitney Museum of American
 Art

Upper West Side (W. 60th St.–W. 96th St.)

American Bible Society
American Museum of Natural
 History
Central Park
Children's Museum of
 Manhattan
Dakota Apartments
Hayden Planetarium
Lincoln Center
Museum of American
 Folk Art

New York Historical
 Society
Pomander Walk
Riverside Park

Upper Manhattan (97th St.–155th St.)

American Academy and
 Institute of Arts and
 Letters
American Numismatic
 Society
Audubon Terrace
Cathedral Church of St. John
 the Divine
Columbia University
General Grant National
 Memorial
El Museo del Barrio

Harlem

Hispanic Society of America
Morris-Jumel Mansion
Museum of the City of
 New York
Riverside Church
Studio Museum in Harlem

Inwood/Washington Heights (156th St.–220th St.)

★ The Cloisters
Dyckman House
Fort Tryon Park
George Washington Bridge
Yeshiva University

Bronx

★ Bronx Zoo
Hall of Fame for Great
 Americans
New York Botanical Garden
Van Cortlandt Mansion and
 Museum
★ Wave Hill

Brooklyn

★ Brooklyn Botanic Garden
Brooklyn Heights
Brooklyn Museum
Coney Island
New York Aquarium
Prospect Park

Staten Island

Jacques Marchais Museum of
    Tibetan Art
Staten Island Zoo
Verrazano Narrows Bridge

Queens

American Museum of the
    Moving Image
Queens Museum of
    Art

Sights and Attractions A to Z

Abigail Adams Smith Museum

421 E. 61st St. (1st Ave.). ☎ 212/838-6878. Open Mon–Fri noon–
4pm; Sun 1–5pm. Closed Sat, Aug. $3 adults; free for children under
12. Subway: 4, 5, 6 to 59th St.; N, R to Lexington Ave.

An unexpected retreat amid the feverish pace of the
East Side, this 1799 carriage house sits on a slope
behind stone retaining walls, a fetching remnant of
the Federalist era. The estate it served was owned by
William Stephens Smith, but the titular tenant was his
wife, the daughter of the eventual second President of
the United States. She didn't stay long. After dismem-
berment of the property, it became a residence in 1826.

The house remained in private hands until its purchase in 1924 by the Colonial Dames of America. That
organization still has its headquarters here and maintains several exhibition rooms.

American Academy and Institute of Arts and Letters
(See Audubon Terrace)

American Bible Society

1865 Broadway (61st St.). ☎ 212/406-1200. Open Mon–Fri 9am–
5pm. Closed Sat, Sun. Free. Subway: 1 to Columbus Circle.

More than 38,000 volumes are on permanent display,
including scraps of the Dead Sea Scrolls, pages from
the 15thC Gutenberg Bible, and braille editions once
owned by Helen Keller.

American Craft Museum

40 W. 53rd St. (6th Ave.). ☎ 212/956-3535. Open Wed–Sun 10am–
5pm; Tues 10am–8pm. Closed Mon. $5 adults; $2.50 seniors and
students; free for children under 12. Wheelchair accessible. Subway:
E, F to 5th Ave.

Wit, panache, and impeccable workmanship mark the
ever-changing displays of antique and contemporary
works, the latter often blurring the line that once
separated crafts from pure art. The handsome 3-level
building is down the street from the **Museum of
Modern Art.** The library is at the American Craft
Council, 72 Spring St.

American Museum of the Moving Image

3601 35th Ave. (36th St.), Astoria (Queens). ☎ 718/784-0077.
Open Tues–Fri noon–4pm; Sat, Sun noon–6pm. Closed Mon.

$5 adults; $4 seniors; $2 students and children. Subway: R or G train to Steinway St.

Filmmaking in America began not in the Hollywood Hills but in and around New York City. Much of it took place here in Astoria, continuing from the earliest days of the silents to the first talkies. The Marx Brothers, Gary Cooper, and Claudette Colbert were only a few of the stars who appeared before the cameras of the Astoria studios. The old sound stages have been refurbished, and a 3-floor studio building has been set aside for this fascinating museum.

Movies, television shows, and videos are the featured attractions but are by no means the extent of the 70,000-item collection. Memorabilia and artifacts are as ephemeral as old fan magazines, tin lunch boxes with inept portraits of actors, Disney toys, posters, costumes, and Cher dolls; as nostalgic as bulky models of 1940s' TV receivers, and complete stage sets. The museum casts a wide net, including an amusing send-up by artist Red Grooms of extravagantly ornate old-time movie palaces, and a hi-tech theater capable of screening both ancient nitrate prints and the latest 70-millimeter spectacles.

American Museum of Natural History

Central Park W. (79th St.). ☎ 212/769-5100. Open Sun–Thurs 10am–5:45pm; Fri, Sat 10am–8:45pm Suggested admission: $7 adults; $5 seniors and students; $4 children. Combined museum and Imax theater: $10 adults; $7 seniors and students; $5.50 children. Wheelchair accessible. Subway: C or B to 81st St.; 1, 9 to 79th St.

One of the hottest tickets in town, thanks to the dinosaurs exhibit, this museum has been newly recast to catch up with science's most recent discoveries on extinct creatures. Generations of schoolchildren have *oohed* and *aahed* at its realistic animal dioramas and models of Indian villages, while adults often are drawn to the halls highlighting the crafts, costumes, jewelry, masks, and artifacts of the peoples of Africa, Asia, Mexico, and precolonial North America. The collections, begun in 1874, include 34 million items, from a 94-foot (29m) model of a blue whale to the fabled Star of India.

Children are certain to take grisly delight in the assembled shrunken heads and blowpipes of the Amazon rain forest, in the Hall of South American Peoples. On the 4th floor are the famous reassembled dinosaur skeletons, another children's favorite. The awesome Tyrannosaurus Rex, which figures in so many Grade B fantasy movies, is the star.

Nature Max, the museum's mega-large Imax movie screen, alternates showings of 2 films, such as *Destiny in*

Space and *Titanica,* which dives miles below the ocean in a narrative about the ill-fated ocean liner. The films are generally about 40 minutes long, and kids especially, but not exclusively, love them. (Call the general number for times.)

Hayden Planetarium. Central Park W. (81st St.). ☎ 212/769-5920. Open Sun–Thurs 10am–5:45pm; Fri–Sat 10am–11:30pm (laser shows at 7, 8:30, and 10pm for $9). Special shows Mon–Fri 1:30pm and 3:30pm; Sat, Sun 1pm, 2pm, 3pm and 4pm. Extra shows during holiday weeks and July–Sept. Admission included in American Museum of Natural History, which has an entrance on the 1st floor. Subway: C or B to 81st St.; 1, 9 to 79th St.

Since 1935, the Hayden Planetarium has projected the movements of constellations, planets, and meteor showers onto its domed ceiling. Seasonal shows focus on the "Star of Wonder," nebulae and stellar formations, and the theoretical end of the world through astronomical accident. Music and commentary supplement the 1-hour presentations, and on Friday and Saturday nights, lasers move the shows even more into the realm of sci-fi entertainment.

Saturday mornings are set aside for programs designed for preschoolers and children aged 7 to 12, who might be just as enthralled by the regular shows. Just observing the 2-ton projector in action is worth the admission.

American Numismatic Society (See Audubon Terrace)

Americas Society

680 Park Ave. (68th St.). ☎ 212/249-8950. Open Tues–Sun noon–6pm. Closed Mon. $2 suggested donation in the gallery. Wheelchair accessible. Subway: 6 to 68th St.

The architectural firm of McKim, Mead & White was responsible for many notable buildings of the late 19th and early 20thC in New York, and a substantial number of them still exist. Perhaps because the third and most famous partner, Stanford White (see Who's Who, in "Portraits"), died at the hands of a jealous husband in 1906, this 1909 structure is a neo-Georgian departure from the Italianate preferences of their earlier projects.

After a period as home for the Soviet Delegation to the United Nations, one of the Rockefellers bought the building and gave it to the Center for Inter-American Relations, which is now known as the Americas Society. The gallery exhibits feature arts and crafts of every country and age of the Western Hemisphere, but the emphasis is on Latin America.

Asia Society

725 Park Ave. (E. 70th St.). ☎ 212/288-6400. Open Tues–Wed, Fri–Sat 11am–6pm; Thurs 11am–8pm; Sun noon–5pm. Closed Mon. $3 adults; $1 seniors and students; free after 6pm Thurs. Subway: 6 to 68th St.

A striking addition to a bland stretch of Park Avenue, the 1981 headquarters of the Asia Society echoes imperial palaces of India, with its facing of alternately polished and textured red granite. The gallery floors house one of the many benefactions of the Rockefeller family: in this case, the collection of Nepalese and Chinese artifacts assembled by John D. III. These artifacts are not the extent of the holdings, however, and exhibitions rotate 3 to 4 times a year. The society also sponsors films, author lectures, and dance recitals, among other events.

Audubon Terrace

Broadway at 155th St. Subway 1 to 157th St.; A, B to 155th St.

Gathered around a neoclassical plaza in a northwest precinct of Harlem is a remarkable complex of 3 museums and associated societies. While they are not all individually of great importance, as a group they rival all but a handful of the city's cultural repositories. Only their location has denied them the recognition they deserve. Unfortunately, it recently lost its centerpiece, the Museum of the American Indian (see National Museum of the American Indian below).

Ornithologist John James Audubon owned this property at the crest of the slope above the Hudson River and intermittently lived here from 1825 until his death in 1851. A speculator purchased it, convinced that the steady northward thrust of the city would eventually make him rich. When it became clear that growth had stabilized at a point 5 miles south, the tract changed hands. A master plan was drawn up in 1908, and the present buildings were completed by 1926.

American Academy and Institute of Arts and Letters. ☎ 212/368-5900. Open Tues–Sun 1–4pm. Closed Mon. Telephone first to confirm hours and exhibitions. Admission free.

Primarily an association of celebrated artists and intellectuals, not unlike its French counterpart, this institution mounts exhibitions on a range of subjects, from ancient manuscripts to architectural themes, 3 times a year.

American Numismatic Society. ☎ 212/234-3130. Open Tues–Sat 9am–4:30pm; Sun 1–4pm. Closed Mon. Ring bell for entry. Admission free.

The 1st floor is given over to a large display of coins, medals, and banknotes, the 2nd floor to a specialist library.

Hispanic Society of America. ☎ 212/926-2234. Open Tues–Sat 10am–4:30pm; Sun 1–4pm. Closed Mon. Admission free.

An equestrian bronze of 11thC Spanish hero El Cid marks the entrance—a fitting choice for a museum that concerns itself with Iberian rather than Latin American culture and history. Of conventional interest are the canvases and drawings of El Greco, Velázquez, and Goya. But the Spain of the Catholic kings is upstaged by that of the earlier Moors, with tiled chambers and relics of exquisite workmanship.

Battery Park

Battery Pl. and State St. (foot of Broadway). Subway 1, 9 to South Ferry; 4, 5 to Bowling Green.

Named for a rank of cannon that defended the old town from uncertain foes—presumably British—after the Revolution, the present 21 acres of Battery Park occupy the west rim of the extreme south tip of Manhattan.

Among the attractions are the Verrazano Memorial, commemorating the Italian explorer who first saw New York Bay in 1524, and the **Castle Clinton National Monument,** once on an islet but later joined by land-fill to what is now the park. The ferries taking passengers to the **Statue of Liberty** and **Ellis Island** depart from piers at the edge of the park, and the ferry to Staten Island is nearby.

Bouwerie Lane Theatre

330 Bowery (Bond St.). ☎ 212/677-0060. Open for theatrical performances. Subway: 6 to Bleecker St.

Vaguely resembling a set of stacked Greek temples, at least in its 5 floors of cast-iron columns with Ionic and Corinthian capitals, the building was commissioned by a bank in 1874. It was converted into an off-Broadway theater in 1963, and is now the home of the Jean Cocteau Repertory Company, with such productions as *Waiting for Godot* and *Tartuffe*.

Bowling Green

Battery Pl. (foot of Broadway). Subway: 4, 5 to Bowling Green.

This oval green once hosted early Colonial bowlers, under the eyes of a statue of George III. It was the city's first park, leased in 1733 at a rent of 1 peppercorn per year. True to revolutionary tradition, the monument to the king was pulled down in 1776; the fence that still

Downtown Sights

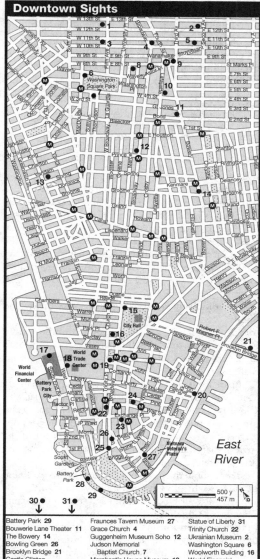

Battery Park 29
Bouwerie Lane Theater 11
The Bowery 14
Bowling Green 26
Brooklyn Bridge 21
Castle Clinton
    National Monument 28
Church of the Ascension 3
City Hall 15
Cooper Union 9
Ellis Island 30
Federal Hall National
    Memorial 24
Forbes Magazine
    Galleries 1

Fraunces Tavern Museum 27
Grace Church 4
Guggenheim Museum Soho 12
Judson Memorial
    Baptist Church 7
Merchant's House Museum 10
National Museum of
    the American Indian 25
New York City Fire Museum 13
New York Stock Exchange 23
New York University 8
St. Mark's-in-
    the-Bowery 5
St. Paul's Chapel 19
South Street Seaport 20

Statue of Liberty 31
Trinity Church 22
Ukrainian Museum 2
Washington Square 6
Woolworth Building 16
World Financial
    Center 17
World Trade Center 18

encloses the green dates from then. For a long time, it was the only lingering element of even minor historical or visual interest, but the green and its benches have been restored, and a fountain and circular pool have been added.

★ Bronx Zoo

Southern Blvd. (185th St.), Bronx. ☎ 718/367-1010. Open Mon–Fri 10am–5pm; Sat, Sun, holidays 10am–5:30pm (4:30pm in winter). Most outdoor exhibits, and all rides, closed in winter (roughly Nov–Apr). $6.75 adults; $3 seniors, students, and children; free for everyone Wed. Modest extra charges for a few special attractions, including tractor train, aerial tram, and monorail. Guided tour free by appointment; ☎ 718/220-5141. Wheelchair accessible. Subway: 2 to Pelham Pkwy.

Along with the **New York Botanical Garden,** the Bronx Zoo is one of the best reasons to venture over the Harlem River. Known as the New York Zoological Park when it was inaugurated in 1899, it is now the largest urban zoo in the United States, with more than 4,000 animals of 800 species, deployed in imaginative settings carved out of the hills and meadows of 265 acres.

In addition to free walking tours on Saturday and Sunday (☎ 212/220-5141), and the Zoo Shuttle tractor tram, the Skyfari aerial tram glides over the African Plains section, and the Bengali Express monorail meanders about Wild Asia, where tigers and elephants roam freely.

Apart from a few necessary structures, animals are at liberty in much of the park, in simulated habitats. Cleverly camouflaged moats keep them apart and protect the public. The Skyfari aerial tram carries observers above the remarkably convincing veldt of the African Plains, and you can look down on moving lion prides, antelope, and deer.

Throughout the park are specimens no longer found in the wild. In the Children's Zoo, young and gentle animals are available for petting and feeding. Watching animals eat is inexplicably fascinating to most people. In their respective habitats, sea lions dine at 3pm daily, the penguins at 11am and 3:45pm, and on Monday and Thursday at 2pm, the crocodiles, who take longer to digest.

★ Brooklyn Botanic Garden

1000 Washington Ave. (Eastern Pkwy.), Brooklyn. ☎ 718/622-4433. Open Apr–Sept, Tues–Fri 8am–6pm; Sat and Sun, public holidays 10am–6pm. Oct–Mar, Tues–Fri 8am–4:30pm; Sat and Sun, public holidays 10am–4:30pm. Closed Mon. Admission free on Tues.; at other times, $3. Wheelchair accessible. Subway 2 or 3 to Eastern Pkwy./Brooklyn Museum.

Although much smaller than the **New York Botanical Garden** (see below), a visit to the Brooklyn Botanic Garden is nonetheless worthwhile, especially in concert with a visit to the neighboring **Brooklyn Museum.** Specialized gardens include one with fragrances for the blind, another exclusively of roses, one of herbs, 3 authentic Japanese settings supplemented by a superb bonsai display, and an ebullient horticultural tribute to Shakespeare, incorporating 80 plant species mentioned in his plays.

The restrained Victorian conservatory was designed by the McKim, Mead & White firm in 1918, and was restored in 1989 and incorporated into the new Steinhardt Conservatory.

Brooklyn Bridge
On Park Row. Subway: 4, 5, 6 to Brooklyn Bridge/City Hall; A, C, To High St./Brooklyn Bridge in Brooklyn.

Perhaps the most spectacular engineering achievement of its time, the bridge's 1,595-foot (486m) span has inspired paeans by painters and poets, awed by its enduring grace. John Roebling conceived it in 1857, but construction did not begin until 1869. Critics were skeptical of its feasibility, the need for a bridge across a river well-served by ferry lines, and the projected expense. In the manner of public projects, those costs routinely multiplied, eventually totaling the then-stunning sum of nearly $16 million. Since construction paralleled the reign of one of New York's most corrupt political regimes, it is assumed that the notorious Boss Tweed and his cronies diverted undetermined portions of the budgeted funds.

Roebling died in the 1st year of construction, contracting tetanus after his foot was crushed by a docking ferry. His son Washington took over. While rising from an underwater chamber, he suffered an attack of the bends and was permanently disabled. Although confined to a wheelchair, he oversaw the project to its conclusion, employing his wife Emily as a go-between. Take a stroll on the elevated walkway for incomparable vistas of East River traffic and the lower Manhattan skyline.

Brooklyn Museum
200 Eastern Pkwy. (Washington Ave.), Brooklyn. ☎ 718/638-5000. Open Wed–Sun 10am–5pm. Closed Mon and Tues. $4 adults; $2 students; $1.50 seniors; free for children under 12. Wheelchair accessible. Subway: 2, 3 to Eastern Pkwy.-Brooklyn Museum.

Despite a history of fiscal uncertainty, this fine institution has launched a massive expansion project that probably won't be completed until the year 2030. This ambitious undertaking will double the size of what is already one of the largest museums in the United States. It has long been the keystone of the borough's cultural and recreational complex, which includes the adjacent **Brooklyn Botanic Garden, Prospect Park,** and zoo, and the Brooklyn Public Library.

Inside are 5 floors of arts and antiquities spanning centuries and continents from Egypt to Oceania. Exhibits are grouped essentially along geographical or societal lines. The pride of the museum is the collection of relics of Dynastic and Coptic Egypt on the 3rd floor, with sarcophagi mingling with alabaster figurines and an ebony sphinx. More than 500 objects dating from 1350 B.C. and the reign of Akhenaton and Nefertiti through Cleopatra VII are on display. Of particular interest are the Assyrian reliefs in the Kevorkian Gallery, just beyond the elevator vestibule. The wall sculptures, some from the Palace of Ashurnasirpal II, depict winged deities and griffin-headed genies. With them are ceremonial vessels, partly animal-shaped, and engraved silver bowls. Don't miss the wrapped 2,600-year-old human mummy.

Bryant Park
6th Ave. and 42nd St. Subway: B, D, F, Q to 42nd St.

Most Midtown blocks have had different functions over the last 150 years of development, but few as profound as this site. In the early 19thC, it was a potter's field. Two decades later, a fortresslike reservoir was completed. In 1858, it was designated a park, dedicated to poet and journalist William Cullen Bryant (1794–1878).

At the turn of the century, the reservoir was drained and filled and the **New York Public Library** and park extension took its place. The lush 4-acre lawn covers the new underground stacks for the library. The half-price music-and-dance booth on 42nd Street remains.

In the back, the Bryant Park Grill, an upscale bistro with more than a little of the ambiance of Paris has become an immediate success. Now that drug dealers have been forced out, the park is a popular place for picnic lunches. Concerts of live and recorded music have been introduced, as has a summer film series (kind of like a drive-in without the car).

Carnegie Hall

Carl Schurz Park
East End Ave., bet. 84th and 90th streets. Subway: 4, 5, 6 to 86th St.
Schurz was a German-born immigrant who became a
U.S. senator. The park in his name is at the east end of
86th Street, which is the central artery of the formerly
German community known as **Yorkville.** The official
residence of the mayor, **Gracie Mansion,** is at the north
edge of the green.

Carnegie Hall
154 W. 57th St. (7th Ave.). ☎ 212/247-7459. Guided tours Mon,
Tues, Thurs at 11:30am, 2pm and 3pm. ☎ 212/247-7800 for tour
information. $6 adults; $5 seniors and students; $4 children.
Wheelchair accessible. Subway: N, R to 57th St.
New Yorkers feared that the 1891 hall would be
demolished along with the old Metropolitan Opera
House after the completion of **Lincoln Center.** Pres-
ervationists scored a too-infrequent victory, however,
and raised funds to renovate the interior, and, in a second stage, the exterior. The acoustics are still superb
and the concert schedule is full.

Castle Clinton National Monument
Battery Park (foot of Broadway). ☎ 212/344-7220. Open 9am–5pm.
Free admission. Subway: 1, 9 to South Ferry.
Built as a fort before the war of 1812, this circular sandstone structure was transformed into an entertainment center, hosting concerts, fireworks, balloon
ascensions, and recitals during the early 19thC. In
1855 it became an immigrant processing center. **Ellis
Island** took over that function in 1892, and the
city converted the fort into a public aquarium, a role it
held until 1941.

Since 1975 it has been a federal landmark run by the National Park Service. Inside, booths sell tickets for the ferries to the **Statue of Liberty** and **Ellis Island.** The boats leave from docks on the promenade to the west of the Castle.

Cathedral Church of St. John the Divine
1047 Amsterdam Ave. (112th St.). ☎ 212/316-7540 for information, 212/662-2133 for tickets for special events Open 7am–5pm. Admission free. Subway: 1, 9 to 110th St.

Work on the Episcopal cathedral began in 1892. By the year 2000, the church hopes to have the 2 towers completed. That will still leave the transepts and other additions to be undertaken—perhaps somewhere around 2050? Even now, the interior space is second in size only to St. Peter's in Rome. The measured pace of construction is a result of the determination to use methods that reach back to the Middle Ages.

Religious and secular works have been donated to the cathedral over the last 100 years. A recent inventory revealed the surprising scope of the collection, which includes 13th through 16thC tapestries and paintings of the Italian renaissance. They are on view on a circulating basis in the museum (Mon–Sat 11am–4pm; Sun noon–5pm; tours Mon–Sat 11am, 2pm; Sun 12:30pm). A visit to this impressive monument is easily combined with one to **Columbia University.**

Central Park
Between Central Park W. and 5th Ave., from Central Park S. (59th St.) to Central Park N. (110th St.). ☎ 212/360-8111; 212/360-3456 for recorded information. Subway: B, D, A, C, 1 or 9 to 59th St./ Columbus Circle; N, R to 5th Ave.

In 1844, most of Manhattan north of 50th Street was a wasteland, supporting only squatters. Poet William Cullen Bryant prodded City Hall into acquiring 840 acres between what were to become 5th and 8th avenues and 59th and 110th streets. Frederick Law Olmsted and Calvert Vaux submitted the park's winning landscaping scheme in 1857.

Its execution required 20 years, but the results are cherished by every New Yorker, whether cyclist, jogger, stroller, lover, picnicker, or baseball player. It has lakes, bridges, ponds, glades, hillocks, meadows, fountains, zoos, boat houses, playgrounds, bandstands, bridle paths, sculptures, terraces, a skating rink, and an outdoor theater for summer Shakespeare. In a real sense, it is New York's greatest single achievement. (See "Walk 3" on page 179.)

Central Park Zoo. 5th Ave. and 64th St. ☎ 212/439-6500. Open daily 11am–5pm. $2.50 adults; $1.25 seniors; 50¢ children. Wheelchair accessible.

Relatively small and often crowded, the zoo is a handy alternative for those without the time or inclination to travel to the far larger **Bronx Zoo.** Midafternoon feeding time for the seals is a major draw, but the red pandas, monkeys, penguins, and polar bears (including Gus, the one with obsessive-compulsive disorder) are nearly as diverting.

Central Synagogue

123 E. 55th St. (Lexington Ave.). ☎ 212/838-5122. Visiting Hours: Mon–Thurs noon–2pm. Services: Fri 5:45pm, Sat 10:30am. Subway: 6 to 51st St.; E, F to Lexington Ave./53rd St.

Sephardic Jews have carried the memory of Spain at the time of their expulsion, which was in the same year Columbus discovered America. This synagogue, one of the oldest in continuous use in the city, reflects that period and the subsequent dispersal of the Sephardim throughout Arab Africa and the Middle East. Designed by Henry Fernbach, one of the first successful Jewish architects in New York, the exterior is in a Moorish style, with horseshoe-shaped windows and two bulbous cupolas. It was completed in 1872.

Chelsea Piers (See "Staying Active")

Children's Museum of Manhattan

212 W. 83rd St. (bet. Amsterdam and Broadway). ☎ 212/721-1234. Open Fri–Sun 10am–5pm; Mon, Wed, Thurs 1:30pm–5:30pm; closed Tues. $5 adults and children; $2.50 seniors; free for children under 2. Wheelchair accessible. Subway: 1, 9 to 86th St.

Endeavoring to merge instruction and play, this 4-story museum employs interactive exhibits full of sound, light, and color. The Brainatarium, to take one example, is a 20-foot-high domed theater, a kind of cerebral planetarium that glories in the wonders of the human mind, with a short film and a rap song describing its functions.

Behind the main building is the Sussman Environmental Center. This Urban Tree House, as it is also known, tries to teach children about environmental issues through serious play, rather than overt instruction. Judging by the way young visitors eagerly run from the water-cycle display to the composting corner (with its 4,000 earthworms), the approach works.

China Institute

125 E. 65th St. (Park Ave.). ☎ 212/744-8181. Open Mon–Sat 10am–5pm. $5 suggested donation. Subway: B, Q to Lexington Ave.

Chrysler Building

Ferocious carved dogs at the entrance, exhibitions of art from the mother country (usually held in spring and late fall), and cooking and language classes help satisfy (and arouse) curiosity about things Chinese.

The China Institute has, however, had a longer life and different sponsorship than might be expected. The parent institute was created in 1926 to aid Chinese-Americans and foster cultural relations with the West. In 1945, a grand East Side house was donated by publisher Henry Luce to serve as its headquarters.

Chrysler Building

405 Lexington Ave. (42nd St.). ☎ 212/682-3070. Open Mon–Fri 9am–5pm. Closed Sat, Sun. Subway: S, 4, 5, 6, 7 to 42nd St./Grand Central.

For a flicker of time after its completion in 1930, the Chrysler Building was the highest structure in the world at 1,048 feet (319m), the first to surpass the Eiffel Tower. But that was a period of intense speculative competition, and the **Empire State Building** soon stole the title. More than 65 years later, however, the Chrysler is still in the top 10, and it remains one of the most satisfying aesthetic results of the skyscraper mania. Art Deco arches of stainless steel surmount the tower, flaring in the sun and illuminated at night, the base for a slender spire that thrusts 123 feet (37m) into the clouds. Abstract representations of automobile parts inform friezes and other decorative details, in deference to the first owner's business. There is no observation floor, but step inside for a look at the cubist assemblages of grained marble and chrome in the lobby.

Church of the Ascension

36 5th Ave. (10th St.). ☎ 212/254-8620. Open Mon–Sat noon–2pm, 5–7pm. Subway: N, R to 8th St.

The first church on lower 5th Ave. (when upper 5th was still farmland), it was also the first to be executed in

Midtown East Sights

Central Synagogue **4**
Chrysler Building **20**
Church of the Transfiguration **24**
Citicorp Center **10**
Flatiron Building **25**
Ford Foundation Building **22**
Grand Central Terminal **19**
Greenacre Park **12**
IBM Garden Plaza **2**

Japan Society **16**
Lever House **8**
Lipstick Building **11**
Metropolitan Life Building **18**
Museum of Television and
Radio **6**
News Building **21**
Paley Park **7**
Pierpont Morgan Library **23**

Police Academy Museum **28**
Queensboro Bridge **5**
St. Bartholomew's Church **15**
St. Patrick's Cathedral **13**
Seagram Building **9**
Sony Building **3**
Theodore Roosevelt Birthplace **26**
Trump Tower **1**
Union Square **27**
United Nations **17**
Villard Houses **14**

the Gothic Revival mode then sweeping through Europe. Brownstone was used for the facing, a material that was to become a favorite of the well-to-do for their row houses. In 1889, McKim, Mead & White remodeled parts of the interior and the parish house, hiring Louis Comfort Tiffany for the design of some of the stained glass and John LaFarge for the altar mural.

Church of the Transfiguration
1 E. 29th St. (5th Ave.). ☎ 212/684-6770. Open 8am–6pm. Subway: N, R to 28th St.

It is said that when an actor asked to be married, he was firmly dispatched to this "Little Church Around the Corner," an institution presumably not as fastidious as others about the dubious professions and social status of its parishioners. Another story claims the referral was of friends seeking a funeral for a deceased thespian. Either way, the church, built around 1850, has a long association with show folk.

Citicorp Center
153 E. 53rd St. (Lexington Ave.). ☎ 212/559-4259. Open 8am–midnight. Subway: E, F to Lexington Ave./53rd St.

Posterity has yet to render its verdict on this building. Its distinctive sloping roofline moves it into the postmodernist category of skyscraper design, away from the rectangular glass boxes of the Bauhaus and Mies van der Rohe school. The 1978 building incorporated into its design the modest but striking St. Peter's Lutheran Church. Office floors begin at 127 feet (39m), clearing the church steeple and providing a public atrium embracing 22 shops and restaurants.

City Hall
City Hall Park (Broadway and Murray St.). ☎ 212/566-5200. Open Mon–Fri 10am–4pm. Closed Sat, Sun. Admission free. Subway: 4, 5, 6 to Brooklyn Bridge/City Hall/Centre St.

Both dwarfed and enhanced by the taller buildings that enclose it on 3 sides, the third and present City Hall (1811) is a Georgian-Federal-Renaissance gem that even the Sun King might have accepted (at least as a summer cottage's guest house). (See "Walk 1," page 170.)

Cleopatra's Needle, Central Park
One of only 4 obelisks outside Egypt, it was erected in **Central Park** in 1881, behind the **Metropolitan Museum of Art.** The red granite spire is covered with hieroglyphics from the time of Thutmose III (c.1600 B.C.). Regrettably, the change in climate and air pollution have worn them down.

Midtown West Sights

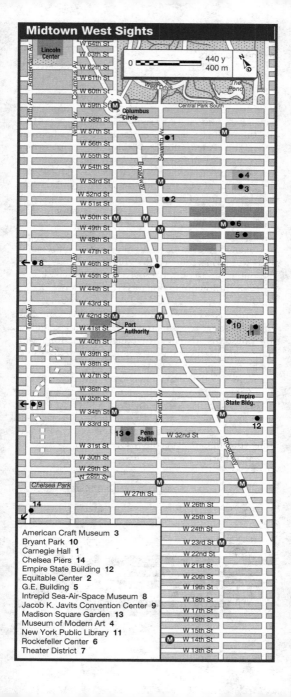

American Craft Museum **3**
Bryant Park **10**
Carnegie Hall **1**
Chelsea Piers **14**
Empire State Building **12**
Equitable Center **2**
G.E. Building **5**
Intrepid Sea-Air-Space Museum **8**
Jacob K. Javits Convention Center **9**
Madison Square Garden **13**
Museum of Modern Art **4**
New York Public Library **11**
Rockefeller Center **6**
Theater District **7**

★ The Cloisters

Fort Tryon Park. ☎ 212/923-3700. Open Mar–Oct 9:30am–5:15pm;
Nov–Feb 9:30am–4:45pm. Closed Mon, some holidays. $7 adults;
$3.50 seniors and students; free for children under 12. Ticket includes
same-day admission to Metropolitan Museum of Art. Wheelchair
accessible. Subway: A to 190th St. or Bus 4 up Madison Ave.

Save The Cloisters for a day when the freneticism of
the Big Apple becomes overbearing. This far-uptown
unit of the **Metropolitan Museum of Art** is a won-
drous sanctuary in **Fort Tryon Park,** overlooking the
Hudson River from the northern heights of the island.
On the summit of a high hill banked by woodland and
meadows, parts of several European monasteries and
chapels blend with fragrant, landscaped gardens in a
unified edifice of blissful serenity. George Grey Barnard,
who gathered vast amounts of superb medieval sculpture, stained glass, woodwork, and jewelry on his many
visits to Europe, founded the collection. It opened to
the public in 1914 and moved to its present home
in 1938, following a donation by the Rockefeller
family.

Scholarly consensus ranks the 16thC Unicorn
Tapestries, a set of 7 superbly executed panels, among
the finest in existence. In concept, detailing, and
craftsmanship, they appear peerless. The remarkable
renderings of plants and flowers make it possible to iden-
tify many of the live specimens seen downstairs in the
Trie Cloister. Beyond such surface delights, however,
is the telling of a tale with deep symbolic under-
currents. Christ is portrayed as a Unicorn, Gabriel as a
hunter with a horn, Satan as a snake; pagan beliefs are
mingled with Christian convictions; fruits and blossoms
represent purity, lust, or fertility.

The Cloisters

Low Library,
Columbia University

Columbia University
Broadway at 116th St. ☎ 212/280-1754. Campus open 24 hrs.
Subway: 1 to 116th St./Columbia University. Subway: 1, 9 to 116th St.

Established in 1754 as King's College, Columbia is one
of the wealthiest universities in the United States.

Columbia College for men finally went coed in the
1980s; women now represent almost half the undergraduate population. The university is renowned for its
schools of business administration, law, medicine, and
journalism, and it also supports schools of education,
dentistry, library science, social work, and public health.
Founding father Alexander Hamilton graduated from
here, and Dwight Eisenhower was the university's president for a time after World War II, before he moved on
to a somewhat higher office.

McKim, Mead & White lent their skills to the original layout of the campus and two of the first buildings.
Fortunately, the university opened up the design to
permit larger pedestrian plazas, which in turn added
greater drama to the most prominent building, Low
Library. Its style is neoclassical, with a surmounting
dome and a portico with 10 columns and coffered ceiling. The elevated site makes the most of the building's
monumentality.

The Terrace Restaurant Atop Butler Hall (☎ 212/
666-9490) is open to the public (it is not affiliated with
the university). The food and service are quite good,
and it affords excellent views of lower Manhattan.

Coney Island
Brooklyn. Free admission. Subway: B, D, F, M, N, Q to Stillwell Ave./
Coney Island.

For generations of working-class New Yorkers, Coney
Island was Riviera-on-the-subway, a wide strip of
powdery sand on the Atlantic Ocean that granted

relief from the steaming streets and tenements of the city. Although it has fallen on hard times—the shattered and burned-out housing inland occupied primarily by pensioners and the poor—Coney Island continues to draw hundreds of thousands of people every hot summer weekend.

The beach has been cleaned up and sand added to make it wider. Urbanites and tourists alike crowd around the original Nathan's Famous, which serves up thousands of hot dogs and fried clams daily. Teenagers squeal through roller-coaster dips on the 1927 Cyclone at Astroland, the amusement park adjacent to the beach. Families gape at the sharks and dolphins of the **New York Aquarium.** Thousands of Soviet immigrants have made nearby Brighton Beach a virtual Little Odessa.

Cooper-Hewitt National Design Museum

2 E. 91st St. (5th Ave.). ☎ 212/860-6868. Open Tues 10am–9pm; Wed–Sat 10am–5pm; Sun noon–5pm. Closed Mon. $3 adults; $1.50 seniors and students; free for children under 12. Free Tues 5–9pm. Subway: 4, 5, 6 to 86th St.

When Scottish-born Andrew Carnegie built this 64-room version of an English manor house, in 1901, he left himself a green buffer all around and transplanted mature trees from upstate. In this neighborhood of pricey 5th Avenue real estate, only a business associate such as Henry C. Frick could indulge himself in a similar fashion (see the **Frick Collection**).

If pressed, an art historian might describe the Carnegie house as Georgian, but it really defies classification. Within are the decorative art acquisitions of industrialist Peter Cooper (founder of **Cooper Union**) and his granddaughters Eleanor, Amy, and Sarah Hewitt.

A branch of the Smithsonian Institution, the Cooper-Hewitt Museum's mission is to explore the historical development of design and how it affects our daily lives. Its nearly 250,000 objects span 14 centuries. Design buffs will delight in wallpapers and leather wall-coverings, gilded furniture, Iranian glassware and Greek pottery, antique locks and keys, candlesticks and doorknockers, hatboxes and copper food-molds. Some recent exhibits have varied from package design to men's vests to 1950s' wallpaper. The museum is undergoing renovations slated to be complete by September 1996, so call ahead to confirm exhibitions.

Cooper Union

Cooper Union

Cooper Sq. ☎ 212/353-4100. Open 8am–10pm. Subway: 6 to Astor Pl.

Peter Cooper became a millionaire through participation in the key 19thC industries of railroads and iron-making. In the benevolent manner of his fellows, he founded this college for the training of artists, architects, and engineers and built the somber pile (1859) that still houses part of the institution. In a bold move, Cooper made provision for a free-tuition curriculum for talented persons of any race, sex, creed, or economic status, at a time when such notions were deemed dangerous to the natural order of things. That policy persists, and has profited tens of thousands of Americans who might not otherwise have had the chance of higher education. The Great Hall within hosted many celebrated 19thC speakers, among them suffragette Susan B. Anthony, abolitionist Henry Ward Beecher, Mark Twain, and, in a rare New York appearance, Abraham Lincoln.

Dakota Apartments

1 W. 72nd St. (Central Park W.). Subway: B, C to 72nd St.

Until 1884, members of New York's establishment would not have considered living in anything but a private house. This luxury 10-floor apartment building changed their minds, even though it was so far uptown that wags said it was in Dakota territory. Its capacious rooms, high ceilings, thick-walled, quiet, and offbeat Bavarian fortress exterior ensure its continued cachet with celebrities and other privileged folk. John Lennon, who lived here, was murdered outside the entrance in 1980. (Strawberry Fields, Yoko Ono's memorial to him, is in Central Park just across the street.)

The Dakota

Dyckman House
4881 Broadway (204th St.). ☎ 212/304-9422. Open Tues–Sun 11am–4pm. Closed Mon. Subway: 1 to 217th St., A to 207th St.; or Bus M100 to 204th St. and Broadway.

The original owner of the property was Jan Dyckman, who came to New Amsterdam in 1661 and swiftly assembled the substantial estate he was to pass on to his descendants. The existing house, though, was not erected until 1783. The estate was once thick with fruit trees and was tilled by tenant farmers well into the 19thC. Brick and flagstone form portions of the lower sections of the house, with weatherboarding rising to a low gambrel roof. Some of the furnishings are authentic not only to the period but to the original family.

Although it is a long subway ride north to the Inwood district, the tranquil setting smooths nerve ends frayed by the clamor of midtown.

★ Ellis Island
New York Harbor. ☎ 212/269-5755. Open daily in winter 9:30am–5pm; summer 9:30am–5:30pm. Ferry: $7 adults; $5 seniors: $3 children aged 3 to 17. Circle Line ferry from Battery Park or Liberty State Park in Jersey City.

These echoing, gloomy halls must have seemed forbidding to the 12 million immigrants who passed through this bureaucratic purgatory between 1892 and 1954. Most were processed in a day, but some were held for weeks or months before being permitted entry to the tantalizing city in sight across the bay.

The National Park Service completed restoration of the principal buildings—of more than 30 on the island—in 1990, at a cost of $156 million. Chandeliers were rehung in the Great Hall of the Beaux Arts Main Building, and its 4 copper domes were laboriously cleaned to their original condition. Rubble was cleared, and the grime of decades of neglect was scoured away.

Graffiti left by the immigrants has been preserved, however. The Registry Room is easily the most impressive, with a tiled, domed, 2-story ceiling and three of those chandeliers.

Public interest in the reopening continues to be very high. The phrase "huddled masses yearning to breath free," has renewed meaning for anyone embarking on this excursion. Plan on a total of at least 3 hours—5, if also visiting the **Statue of Liberty.**

For even a remote chance of avoiding crowds, arrive by 9am to catch the first ferry, and don't make firm lunch plans. Despite the wait, a visit here often proves an emotional experience for immigrants or their descendants—i.e., virtually every American. The ticket booth for both the Statue of Liberty and Ellis Island is inside **Castle Clinton National Monument.**

★★ Empire State Building

350 5th Ave. (34th St.). ☎ 212/736-3100. Observatory floors open 9:30am–midnight. Last ticket sold at 11:30pm. $4 adults; $2.75 seniors; $2 children. Check visibility notice before buying tickets. Wheelchair accessible. Subway: B, D, F, N, R to 34th St.

From its inception, the Empire State Building has attracted superlatives—in achievement and in tragedy. Designated a national historic landmark, it is now the 7th highest building in the world, and it remains the foremost symbol of New York. It does, after all, stand 1,472 feet (449m) high, including TV mast. By comparison, the Eiffel Tower is 984 feet (299m).

King Kong swatted at biplanes from his perch in the 1931 movie classic, a plane crashed into the 79th floor in 1945, and at least 17 people have flung themselves to

Empire State Building

their deaths off parapets and down elevator shafts. The distinctive stepped cap was sketched in during one of the later design stages. Without the rounded cap, the original 86 stories were only 2 feet (61cm) higher than the **Chrysler Building.** With it, architects added another 200 feet (61m) and a second public observatory. Perhaps even more remarkable than its height is the fact that the Empire State Building came in under schedule and under budget.

Twice a month, maintenance crews wash 6,500 windows. For reasons best known to the participants, an annual race is run up the 1,575 steps to the 86th floor. The facing is limestone, fashioned in modified Art Deco. The observatory on the 86th floor has both a glass-enclosed area and an outdoor promenade around 4 sides of the building; while the smaller one on the 102nd floor is fully enclosed.

Equitable Center
787 7th Ave. (bet. 51st and 52nd sts.). Open Mon–Sat 9am–6pm. Subway: N, R to 49th St.

A continuation of the postmodernist trend in skyscraper architecture that began with the **Sony Building,** the center incorporates the Equitable Tower and the Paine Webber Building. While attractive enough by those standards, with its arches and cream-and-brown exterior, it is more notable for what it contains than the visage it presents to the street. Within its walls are several good-to-excellent restaurants, including Le Bernardin, described in "Dining." The nearly 4–story mural in the lobby off 7th Avenue is by Roy Lichtenstein, and down one corridor is a panoramic vision of America executed by Thomas Hart Benton.

Federal Hall National Memorial
26 Wall St. (Nassau St.). ☎ 212/825-6991. Open Mon–Fri 9am–5pm. Closed Sat, Sun. Admission free. Tours by appointment. Subway: 4, 5 to Wall St.

Federal Hall

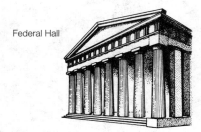

Paradigm of the early 19thC enthusiasm for the Greeks, Federal Hall is not the building in which Washington took his oath of office in 1789, as is inferred by many. The statue of George Washington, outside, stands where the first president did indeed make those vows, but the building behind was not completed until 1842. It housed government offices from then until 1939, when it was converted to its present use as a museum. Inside are artifacts of the Revolutionary War period. All in all, it is the finest example of Greek Revival in Manhattan. Free concerts are occasionally given at the Hall.

Flatiron Building
175 5th Ave. (23rd St.). Subway: N, R to 23rd St.

Here are 2 reasons to seek out the Flatiron Building: its disputed claim to be the first true skyscraper, and its odd triangular shape (dictated by its plot at the confluence of 5th Ave. and Broadway). In the earliest tall buildings, made possible by the invention of the electric elevator, metal cages supported floors while masonry facings bore their own weight. In the decade before the Flatiron, new techniques allowed riveted steel frames to bear both floors and facing. Architects employed that sort of steel skeleton here, in 1901, building it 286 feet (87m) high and only 6 feet (2m) wide at its narrow end.

To calm the conservative citizenry, a rusticated limestone facade imitated a stacked Italianate palace. Nevertheless, many were convinced that the building would collapse in the high winds characteristic of the area. It didn't. A thorough steam cleaning has made it gleam as it has not in over 50 years. You can enter the lobby during business hours, but there is no compelling reason to do so.

Flatiron Building

Forbes Magazine Galleries

62 5th Ave. (12th St.). ☎ 212/206-5548. Open Tues, Wed, Fri, Sat 10am–4pm; Thurs guided group tours (must reserve in advance). Admission free. Subway: 4, 5, 6 or N, R to 14th St./Union Square.

The late Malcolm Forbes was America's favorite millionaire. Many saw the immensely successful publisher as an ebullient man who enjoyed every dollar of his vast wealth, from his motorcycling tours and hot-air ballooning to his sumptuous yachts and lavish parties.

Forbes was also an inveterate collector, most noticeably of bejeweled Fabergé Eggs. He possessed 12 of only 54 ever made. They are on view here, along with flotillas of model warships and ocean liners, legions of toy soldiers (more than 12,000), and a gallery of presidential papers and memorabilia.

Ford Foundation Building

320 E. 43rd St. (2nd Ave.). ☎ 212/573-5000. Open Mon–Fri 9am– 5pm. Closed Sat, Sun. Admission free. Subway: S, 4, 5, 6, 7 to 42nd St./Grand Central.

Atriums have become a cliché; as pervasive as sunken plazas in contemporary New York commercial architecture—sops to planning boards and environmental groups. The resulting spaces are often bleak and inhuman. The Ford Foundation presented a gift to the city, however, not a burden, with its 1967 headquarters,recently cited in an award by the American Instituteof Architects as a "timeless classic" and "one of thepostwar era's most elegantly conceived and detailed buildings." The interior contains a third of an acre of mature trees and shrubs, with a clear pool of recycled rainwater at its center. Passersby are welcome to step inside for a moment's respite.

Fort Tryon Park

Subway: A to 190th St.

While **The Cloisters** museum is the prime motive for taking the long subway ride to this tranquil pastoral sanctuary close to the northern tip of Manhattan, other attractions here are hills, woodlands, meadows, a small but fascinating botanical garden, a children's playground with wading pool, and staggering vistas of the Hudson River from the site of the namesake fortification.

Fraunces Tavern Museum

54 Pearl St. (Broad St.). ☎ 212/425-1778. Open Mon–Fri 10:45am– 4:45pm; Sat noon–4pm; closed Sun. $2.50 adults; $1 seniors and students. Subway: J, M, Z to Broad St.

A 20thC approximation of the tavern in which George Washington bade farewell to his troops, it was

Fraunces Tavern

constructed on the site of the original, incorporating parts of the remaining walls.

Downstairs is now a restaurant; upstairs is a collection of Revolutionary musketry and mementoes, and 2 period rooms.

French Institute/Alliance Française
22 E. 60th St., (Madison Ave.). ☎ 212/355-6100. Open Mon–Thurs 10am–8pm; Fri 10am–6pm; Sat (Sept–June) 10am–1:30pm. (Special events are frequently held after hours.) Closed Sun. Admission free. Subway: 4, 5, 6 to 59th St.; N, R, to Lexington Ave.

In a spectrum of activities to gladden the heart of every Francophile, the institute offers language and cooking classes, wine tastings, films, concerts, recitals, lectures— all of which relate to the mother country. Students and homesick expatriates can find French magazines, newspapers, videos, and CD-ROMs in the library, and perhaps a new friend in the small cafe.

★ Frick Collection
1 E. 70th St. (5th Ave.). ☎ 212/288-0700. Open Tues–Sat 10am– 6pm; Sun 1–6pm. Closed Mon, major holidays. $5 adults; $3 seniors and students; children under 10 not admitted; children ages 10–16 must be with an adult. Wheelchair accessible. Subway: 6 to 68th St.

From the 1890s onward, the part of 5th Avenue facing lower Central Park has been a millionaires' row. Now the privileged live in duplex penthouses, for not even the very wealthy can afford to maintain the palatial residences built by their predecessors. Most of those mansions have been demolished, a few converted for institutional use. All this makes the Frick Collection even more special, for the house is much the way that the first and only owner left it—filled with paintings, furniture, clocks, and Persian carpets.

Carnegie and industrialist Henry C. Frick were business associates who parted company over policy disputes. Frick chose to build his house only 20 blocks south of his former friend's 64-room residence. There is no more gracious oasis in the city than the interior court with its splashing fountain and flowering plants. The house was opened to the public in 1935.

Among the treasures on display are works by Rembrandt, Velázquez, Goya, and Vermeer. Chamber music concerts take place on occasional Sundays. Inquire at the entrance desk for detailed information.

GE Building (formerly RCA Building)

30 Rockefeller Plaza (bet. 5th Ave. and 6th Ave. and 49th and 50th sts.). Subway: B, D, F, Q to 47-50th St./Rockefeller Center.

Long known as the RCA Building, the new owners, General Electric, have imposed this name. As fast as Manhattan real estate changes hands, chances are this centerpiece of **Rockefeller Center** will again be sold. The 70-story skyscraper (850 feet, or 259m), was completed in the depression years. Its 1st-floor murals are in the heroic Social Realist mode. Unfortunately, the observation deck is now closed.

General Grant National Memorial

Riverside Drive (W. 122nd St.). ☎ 212/666-1640. Open Wed–Sun 9am–5pm. Closed Mon, Tues. Admission free. Subway: 1, 9 to 125th St.

Popularly known as Grant's Tomb, it is no accident that the official designation honors the Civil War service of Ulysses S. Grant rather than his scandal-ridden tenure as the 18th U.S. President. The mausoleum is fashioned after the style of a 4thC Greek tomb, and was financed by private contributions rather than by Congress. After its completion in 1897, both Grant and his wife were interred within, behind impressive bronze doors.

The exuberant free-form mosaic benches that surround the somber structure on 3 sides are the work of Chilean artist Pedro Silva. They are entirely inappropriate to the site, but are a lot more fun than the monument itself.

George Washington Bridge

Dreamers of the 19thC insisted that the broad Hudson River could be spanned, but it took the capitalistic euphoria of the late 1920s to bring together the necessary funds and determination to make it a reality. The bridge was completed in 1931, within months of the **Empire State, Chrysler,** and **GE (Formerly RCA) buildings,** and, like them, was defiant of the economic desolation of the Great Depression. For a time, the 3,500 feet (1,067m) between its main towers made it the world's longest suspension bridge.

Goethe House

1014 5th Ave. (82nd St.). ☎ 212/439-8700. Open Wed, Fri, Sat noon–5pm; Tues, Thurs noon–7pm. Closed Sun, Mon. Subway: 4, 5, 6 to 86th St.

Films, lectures, art exhibitions, and research materials fill this cultural repository, one of dozens that are sponsored by Germany around the world.

Grace Church

802 Broadway (10th St.). ☎ 212/254-2000. Open Mon–Fri 9am–5:45pm; Sat noon–4pm; Sun for services. Subway: N, R to 8th St.

Although a practicing engineer, James Renwick took advantage of the mid-19thC tolerance for professional generalism to design this fine Episcopal church. Its success led to commissions for **St. Patrick's Cathedral** and the Smithsonian Institution in Washington, all in the Gothic Revival style then in favor. The lovely English garden to the north, in front of the rectory, is a later Renwick accomplishment and a favorite spot for a few moments' meditation.

Gracie Mansion

East End Ave. (E. 88th St.). Tours Wed at 10 and 11am, 1 and 2pm, Mar–Nov, by appointment only (write to: Tour Program, Gracie Mansion, East End Ave., NY 10128; or call ☎ 212/570-4751). Group tours are offered on Mon, Tues, Thurs, and Fri. $3 adults, $2 seniors. Subway: 4, 5, 6 to 86th St.

Now the residence of the mayor of New York City, the mansion is named after Archibald Gracie, the merchant and shipowner who built it in 1799. Prominent details are the encompassing veranda and lattice railings at porch and roof levels. It is hard to believe that the house once served as a public lavatory in **Carl Schurz Park,** in which it is still located.

Gracie Mansion

Tours of Gracie Mansion are difficult to arrange and tourists without reservations are fenced off at some distance, so the best way to view the house is from the deck of a Circle Line tour boat (see "Useful Numbers & Addresses" in "Basics").

Grand Central Terminal
Park Ave. and 42nd St. Open 6am–2am. Subway: S, 4, 5, 6, 7 to 42nd St./Grand Central.

An attempt to level the terminal to make way for yet another speculative office tower was thwarted in the late 1970s, thanks in large part to the efforts of the late Jacqueline Kennedy Onassis. Grand Central was therefore saved from the fate of Penn Station, over on the West Side. The conservationist effort was worthwhile.

Inside, a vast vaulted space 125 feet (38m) wide, and more than twice as long, arcs over rush-hour throngs. Line paintings depict the celestial constellations against the pale blue ceiling, and light streams through high arched windows. Musicians of varying persuasions and aptitudes often perform in the great hall, some with official sanction. Take it all in from the open bar inside the Vanderbilt Avenue entrance, or wend down to the Oyster Bar and Restaurant (see "Dining"), one of the top seafood eateries in the city, between the main and lower levels. On New Year's Eve, the terminal time-travels back to the big-band era when it opens to the public for an evening of swing dancing.

Grant's Tomb
(See General Grant National Memorial)

Greenacre Park
51st St. (2nd Ave.). Subway: 6 to 51st St.

Private benefactors have contributed a number of public "pocket" parks that bestow touches of grace and greenery upon otherwise congested neighborhoods. This example is somewhat ostentatious, its open space cluttered up with a semisculptural arrangement of rough-hewn sentinels, but it is an agreeable retreat from the exhaust fumes and noise.

Guggenheim Museum
1071 5th Ave. (88th St.). ☎ 212/423-3500, TDD 212/423-3607. Open Sun–Wed 10am–6pm; Fri–Sat 10am–8pm. Closed Thurs. $8 adults; $5 seniors and students; free for children under 12 (must be accompanied by adult to enter); pay what you wish Fri 6–8pm. Wheelchair accessible; wheelchairs available. Subway: 4, 5, 6 to 86th St.

Frank Lloyd Wright detested New York—he suggested that it be razed and begun again. The Solomon

Upper East Side Sights

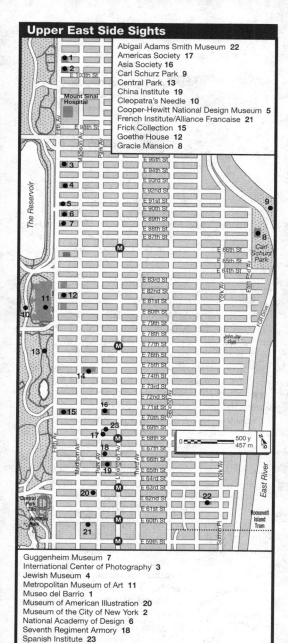

Abigail Adams Smith Museum 22
Americas Society 17
Asia Society 16
Carl Schurz Park 9
Central Park 13
China Institute 19
Cleopatra's Needle 10
Cooper-Hewitt National Design Museum 5
French Institute/Alliance Francaise 21
Frick Collection 15
Goethe House 12
Gracie Mansion 8

Mount Sinai Hospital

E 103rd St
E 98th St
E 95th St
E 94th St
E 93rd St
E 92nd St
E 91st St
E 90th St
E 89th St
E 88th St
E 87th St
E 86th St
E 85th St
E 84th St
E 83rd St
E 82nd St
E 81st St
E 80th St
E 79th St
E 78th St
E 77th St
E 76th St
E 75th St
E 74th St
E 73rd St
E 72nd St
E 71st St
E 70th St
E 69th St
E 68th St
E 67th St
E 66th St
E 65th St
E 64rd St
E 63rd St
E 62nd St
E 61st St
E 60th St
E 59th St

The Reservoir

Fifth AV
Madison AV
Park AV
Lexington AV
Third AV
Second AV
York AV
East End AV
FDR Drive

Carl Schurz Park
John Jay Park
East River
Roosevelt Island Tram
Sutton PL

Central Park Zoo
Wollman Rink

0   500 y
     457 m

Guggenheim Museum 7
International Center of Photography 3
Jewish Museum 4
Metropolitan Museum of Art 11
Museo del Barrio 1
Museum of American Illustration 20
Museum of the City of New York 2
National Academy of Design 6
Seventh Regiment Armory 18
Spanish Institute 23
Whitney Museum of American Art 14

Guggenheim Museum

R. Guggenheim Museum, which opened in 1959, was his only completed commission in the city.

To say that the result was controversial falls well short of the truth. Along a boulevard characterized by conservative apartment houses and neoclassical public buildings, the exterior of the Guggenheim resembles a flower pot teetering on the edge of a coffee table. The circular central gallery with its spiral stripe of glass is smaller at the base than at the top and squats off-center on a floating horizontal slab.

Vigorous debate ensued over the interior design of the core structure. Logic insists that the best way to view a museum's exhibits is to begin at the top and work down, not exhausting yourself with thoughts of missing rooms and finding elevators. Wright was a logical architect. Take the elevator to the top and slowly descend along the spiral ramp, past bays of paintings and sculptures.

Many viewers, though, including an influential group of artists whose works are on display here, felt that the ramp made it uncomfortable to consider a painting for more than a moment or two, that it hurried patrons along and made pictures appear lopsided. The furor was stoked anew when the entire museum was closed for more than 2 years to permit construction of a 9-floor limestone annex and a rooftop sculpture garden, as well as a complete overhaul of the original building, including floor-by-floor access to the annex. After the usual delays, it reopened in 1992.

Architectural arguments aside, the collections and loan exhibitions concentrate on the masters of modern art Picasso, Cézanne, Mondrian, Braque, Klee, Chagall, Kandinsky—and Establishment exponents of the New York School of abstract expressionism and their successors. Younger experimental artists provide spice.

On Friday and Saturday evenings, the museum often has live jazz music.

Guggenheim Museum SoHo
575 Broadway (Prince St.). ☎ 212/423-3500. Open Sun, Wed–Fri 11am–6pm; Sat 11am–8pm. Closed Mon, Tues. Subway: B, D, F, Q to Broadway/Lafayette St.; N, R to Prince St.

The Guggenheim Museum uses this space in a 19thC landmark building for special exhibitions. Downstairs is T Salon, a very cool tea salon and restaurant (see "Dining").

Hall of Fame for Great Americans
Bronx Community College, 181st St., Bronx. ☎ 718/289-5162. Open daily 10am–5pm. Admission free. Subway: 4 to Burnside Ave.

This neglected national monument was designed by Stanford White and dedicated in 1901, when the land it stood on was part of the new uptown campus of **New York University.** To attract the prestige it so coveted, the university decided to invent a memorial to Americans who had made substantial contributions to the arts, sciences, statesmanship, and pedagogy.

White conceived a semicircular neoclassical loggia, to curve around his Gould Memorial Library, with busts of national heroes such as Lincoln, Benjamin Franklin, Thomas Edison, Booker T. Washington, Thomas Paine, and Alexander Graham Bell. A total of 98 are on display. To be considered for inclusion, candidates must have been dead for at least 25 years. The campus is now Bronx Community College, part of the City University of New York.

Hayden Planetarium
(See American Museum of Natural History)

Hispanic Society of America
(See Audubon Terrace)

Historical Society (See New York Historical Society)

International Center of Photography
1130 5th Ave. (94th St.). ☎ 212/860-1777. Open Tues noon–8pm; Wed–Fri noon–5pm; Sat, Sun 11am–6pm. Closed Mon. $4 adults; $2.50 seniors and students. Subway: 6 to 96th St.

One of New York's younger (1974) museums occupies a 1914 Georgian-Federal house. As the only museum in the city devoted solely to photography, its expanding collection focuses on such 20thC luminaries as Henri Cartier-Bresson, Weegee, and Robert Capa. As many as 15 special-theme and 1-person shows every year supplement the permanent installations. The center has a midtown branch (1133 6th Ave.; ☎ 212/768-4682).

Intrepid Sea-Air-Space Museum

Pier 86 Hudson River, end of W. 46th St. ☎ 212/245-0072. Open Wed–Sun 10am–5pm: Closed Mon, Tues. $10 adults; $7.50 seniors and students; $5 children. Wheelchair accessible. Bus: Crosstown 42nd St. or 49th St.

The *Intrepid* is an aircraft carrier that first saw active service in the Pacific in World War II, with subsequent duty off Vietnam and as a recovery ship for space vehicles. Now decommissioned and permanently moored in the Hudson, it displays weaponry, warplanes, and space hardware. The carrier holds more than 3 dozen aircraft, among them one of the first to ever land on an aircraft carrier.

Most of the exhibits are under cover, so while the flight deck is bone-chillingly windswept much of the year, *Intrepid* can be visited in winter.

Jacob K. Javits Convention Center

655 W. 34th St. (12th Ave.). ☎ 212/216-2000.

The city sorely needed a center for extra-large meetings and expositions, and this contemporary crystal palace facing the Hudson was the solution. Designed by the noted I. M. Pei firm, its 2 main halls are the size of 15 football fields, and the lobby is high enough to shelter the Statue of Liberty. It is the venue of choice for such events as conventions and auto shows. The only deficiency is its somewhat isolated location and the resultant difficulty in finding transport.

Jacques Marchais Museum of Tibetan Art

338 Lighthouse Ave., Staten Island. ☎ 718/987-3500 or 718/987-3478. Open Apr–Nov Wed–Sun 1–5pm; Dec–Mar by appointment. Closed Mon, Tues. $3 adults; $2.50 seniors; $1 children under 12. Staten Island Ferry from Manhattan. Near Richmondtown Restoration. Take a taxi or S74 bus from ferry terminal.

The Staten Island Ferry is worth taking just for the breathtaking views it affords. But if an additional excuse is required, this museum might head the list. It did for the Dalai Lama, who visited it in 1991 during a tour of the United States. Within the relatively accurate replica of a Buddhist temple (1947) are exquisite examples of Tibetan and Himalayan art, including bronzes, scrolls, paintings, masks, and ritual objects.

Japan Society Gallery

333 E. 47th St. (1st Ave.). ☎ 212/832-1155. Open Tues–Sun 11am–5pm during exhibitions. Closed Mon. $3 adults. Subway: 6 to 51st St.

In a tranquil setting near the United Nations, the Japan Society stages about 3 loan exhibitions a year of such diverse treasures as noh masks and umbrellas, lacquer boxes and folk art, modern ceramics and woodblock prints, religious sculpture, and traditional dolls. Founded in 1907, the society hosts a range of cultural activities, including film series, performing arts, lectures, and language classes.

Jewish Museum

1109 5th Ave. (92nd St.). ☎ 212/423-3200. Open Mon, Wed, Thurs noon–5pm; Tues noon–8pm; Sun 11am–6pm. Closed Fri, Sat. $7 adults; $5 seniors and students; free for children under 12 and on Tues 5–8pm. Subway: 4, 5, 6 to 86th St.

Within this conventional 1908 château, with its bland 1963 wing, is an important collection of Judaica that is of interest to people of all faiths. On view are a variety of ceremonial objects, both intricately wrought and stunningly simple: wedding rings, Torah headpieces and crowns, circumcision instruments, spice boxes, and amulets.

Lever House

390 Park Ave. (53rd St.). Subway: 6 to 51st St.

In its way as difficult to miss as **St. Bartholomew's Church** 2 blocks south, Lever House was in the forefront of the Bauhaus-influenced third phase of skyscraper fever that seized the imagination of developers in the post–World War II years. Its builders embraced the new glass-and-steel curtain wall technology, but with important variations. For one, they broke the unvarying high-rise canyon of Park Avenue by the astonishing decision not to use every bit of available air space. The wide side of the unadorned slab tower is turned south, at a right angle to the avenue, permitting air and sun to

Lever House

Lincoln Center

circulate. For another, the color is an unusual blue-emerald. In its totality, Lever House fulfills the promise of the International Style that was to be denied its descendants. Even architects Skidmore, Owings, and Merrill infrequently matched their achievement in subsequent efforts.

Liberty Island (See Statue of Liberty)

Lincoln Center
Broadway and Amsterdam bet. 62nd and 65th sts. Theaters: various times and prices. Subway: 1, 9 to 66th St.

An ambitious conglomeration of 6 concert halls and theaters, the Lincoln Center for the Performing Arts is the home of the Metropolitan Opera, New York Philharmonic, New York City Opera and Ballet, School of Amerian Ballet, Chamber Music Society, Juilliard School, and Lincoln Center Theater. It also hosts a variety of visiting ballet and repertory companies, symphony orchestras, film festivals, and popular and classical performing artists and events. Designed by Philip Johnson and Eero Saarinen, the architectural whole is stunning, with the 3 main buildings forming a horse-shoe around the fountain that has become a meeting place for friends and lovers.

Among the 4 restaurants at the center are Panevino and Fountain Café (noon–midnight) in Avery Fisher Hall, and the Grand Tier (open to ticket holders 2 hrs. before performances) in the Opera House. Guided tours of the center last for approximately 1 hour (☎ 212/875-5370). Backstage tours of the Opera House are also available (☎ 212/769-7020). Box office telephones are listed by theater in "The Arts."

Lincoln Tunnel
The 3 tubes of the tunnel were completed in 1937, 1945, and 1957. The one in the middle is the longest, at more than $1^1/_2$ miles. The tunnel connects the city of Weehawken in New Jersey with West 38th Street in Manhattan, providing an additional Hudson River crossing.

Lipstick Building

885 3rd Ave. (53rd St.). Not open to public. Subway: E, F to Lexington Ave.; 6 to 51st St.

Architect Philip Johnson has had several large commissions in the city, virtually all of them controversial, at least when first unveiled. None, however, has been so widely scorned as this office tower, designed with John Burgee, with its oval floor plan and reddish-brown facing. Lipstick Building isn't its official name, but New Yorkers dubbed it that because it looks like (a) a telescoping lipstick, or (b) the lipstick's tube. The Lipstick Cafe is located in the lobby and the exceptional Vong (see "Dining"), in the annex.

Madison Square Garden

8th Ave. (33rd St.). ☎ 212/465-6741. Opening times vary according to events scheduled. Subway: 1, 9, A, C, E to 34th St./Penn Station.

The present complex is the fourth version on the third site. In all its manifestations, from 1871 to the present day, Madison Square Garden has been concerned with sports and popular entertainment. It has conventions, a circus, ice shows, hockey, basketball, horse and dog competitions, rodeo, wrestling, prizefighting, and rock concerts.

Merchant's House Museum

29 E. 4th St. (Broadway). ☎ 212/777-1089. Open Sun–Thurs 1–4pm. Closed Fri–Sat. Group tours by appointment. $3 adults; $2 seniors and students. Subway: 6 to Astor Pl.; N, R to 8th St.

The city's only family home preserved intact from the 19thC, the row house was built in 1832. In style, it falls somewhere between Federal and Greek Revival. Merchant Seabury Tredwell and his family lived here from 1835 to 1933. Shortly thereafter, the Historic Landmark Society opened it as a museum, preserving its original furniture, textiles, and decorative arts, which are indicative of the lifestyle of a typical upper-middle-class family of the time.

Metropolitan Life Building

200 Park Ave. (45th St.). Open 6am–2am. Subway: S, 4, 5, 6, 7 to 42nd St./Grand Central.

Built as the Pan Am Building in 1963, the structure now known as Met Life forms a visual octagonal wall across Park Avenue. The fact that Bauhaus doyen Walter Gropius had a hand in its design is little compensation. Aesthetically pleasing or not, this building still says New York. A fatal accident in 1977 ended the function of its rooftop heliport.

Metropolitan Museum of Art

★★ Metropolitan Museum of Art

5th Ave. (82nd St.). ☎ 212/570-3711 (general number) ☎ 212/
535-7710 (recorded information) ☎ 212/570-3949 (concerts,
lectures). Open Sun, Tues–Thurs 9:30am–5:15pm; Fri–Sat 9:30am–
8:45pm. Closed Mon and some holidays (check ahead) Photography
without flash permitted, except at special temporary exhibitions.
Suggested admission $7 adults; $3.50 seniors and students; free for
chidren under 12. Wheelchair accessible. Subway: 4, 5, 6 to 86th St.

Grand in concept and numbing in scope, the Met is
the largest single repository of art and antiquities in the
Western Hemisphere. It boasts 18 departments and 248
galleries, with well over 1 million prints, paintings,
sculptures, furnishings, costumes, ceramics, musical instruments, armor, and reassembled sections of ancient
temples and palaces. Barely 25% of the collection is on
view at any one time. Additionally, the museum houses
3 libraries, 2 auditoriums, an art and book store, a gift
store, a cafeteria, a restaurant with table service, and a
snack shop. It also stages concerts, films, and lectures
(☎ 212/570-3949).

It might all be intimidating, were it not for an
imaginative administration determined to enhance
accessibility. Huge, colorful banners billow from the
5th Avenue facade, touting the 2 or 3 special exhibitions always on offer. These shows nearly always tie in
with popular enthusiasms of the moment—Chinese costumes, the treasures of Tutankhamen, Viking artifacts—
the better to draw infrequent museum-goers who are
unfamiliar with the permanent exhibits. Galleries are
laid out in an orderly manner; attendants are gracious
and often speak other languages. You will not be able
to absorb the Met in 1 lightning tour. Sit down for a
moment and determine which departments are of greatest interest.

Among the museum's highlights: the Egyptian Wing,
acknowledged to be one of the major collections of its
kind; the 2-story Lila Acheson Wallace Wing, which
houses works by Picasso, Max Beckmann, Thomas Hart

Benton, Henri Matisse, Georgia O'Keeffe, and Jackson Pollack; and the Lehman Pavilion, a collection of early Italian and 19th and 20thC French art that includes drawings by Leonardo DaVinci and Botticelli.

Recorded cassette tours are available at moderate rentals, covering 21 subjects and galleries, some of them in languages other than English. The museum takes on a festive, romantic air Friday and Saturday evenings after 5pm, when the music of a string quartet fills the Great Hall, and cocktails are served on the candlelit balcony.

Morris-Jumel Mansion

65 Jumel Terrace (near W. 161st St.). ☎ 212/923-8008. Open Wed–Sun 10am–4pm. Closed Mon–Tues and major holidays. $3 adults; $2 seniors and students. Subway: B to 163rd St. weekdays, C to 163rd St. weekends.

Given its age (built in 1765, it is Manhattan's oldest remaining house), Georgian core, and Federal overlay (1810), the mansion warrants attention for its architecture alone, starting with its lordly Palladian portico. But great historical figures lived and loved and dined here, and as is only fitting, ghosts are reported to have materialized. Roger Morris was the builder. Although a friend of George Washington, he was a loyal subject of the King and left the country at the outbreak of the Revolution. Washington and the British general Henry Clinton took turns making the house their headquarters during the war. After a period of service as a tavern, it was bought by French wine merchant Stephen Jumel for his wife Eliza Bowen.

The Jumels held lavish parties and banquets, which encouraged New York Society to overlook the rumor that Eliza was the illegitimate child of a prostitute and had pursued that profession herself. She reportedly started an affair with Aaron Burr before Stephen died in 1832, surprising only in part because the former vice president was then in his 70s. The two married in the

Morris-Jumel
Mansion

front parlor after Stephen's death, but the marriage was not a happy match, ending in divorce in 1836. Two of Burr's desks remain, as does a portrait of Eliza in her 80th year. The ghosts? A Hessian soldier and Eliza herself. Perhaps they are aided by the secret passageways.

El Museo del Barrio
1230 5th Ave. (104th St.). ☎ 212/831-7272. Open Wed–Sun 11am–5pm. Closed Mon, Tues. Wheelchair accessible. Subway: 6 to 103rd St.

Just a mile up 5th Avenue from the **Metropolitan Museum of Art,** El Museo is dedicated to Latino art. Founded by Puerto Rican educators, artists, and community activists in Spanish Harlem (El Barrio) in 1969, El Museo's first home was a classroom in a public school. Now it has filled this building on the Museum Mile with almost 8,000 objects spanning the Latin American experience from pre-Columbian civilization to the contemporary era. The permanent collection features paintings, sculpture, drawings, prints, and photographs.

Museum of American Folk Art
2 Lincoln Square (Columbus Ave., bet. 65th and 66th sts.). ☎ 212/595-9533. Open Tues–Sun 11:30am–7:30pm. Closed Mon. Admission free. Subway: 1, 9 to 66th St.

Ensconced in a glass-enclosed plaza opposite Lincoln Center, this homage to American craftspeople displays works from Colonial times to the present day. An enchanting assortment of weather vanes, carved and painted saints, whirligigs, toys, kitchen implements, quilts, shop signs, bird decoys, and clean-lined furniture that predates the Danish Modern style by a century is on view. The popular gift store sells examples of contemporary folk art—dolls, rugs, crafts—and has an excellent book selection.

Museum of American Illustration
128 E. 63rd St. (Lexington Ave.). ☎ 212/838-2560. Open Tues 10am–8pm; Wed–Fri 10am–5pm; Sat noon–4pm. Closed Sun, Mon. Admission free. Subway: B, Q to Lexington Ave.

Rotating exhibitions of commercial art for books, magazines, and print advertising are mounted in this museum, under the sponsorship of the Society of Illustrators. Augmenting the permanent collection are theme shows and the eagerly-anticipated annual exhibition of award-winning works.

Museum of the American Indian
(See National Museum of the American Indian)

Museum of the City of New York

5th Ave. (103rd St.). ☎ 212/534-1672. Open Wed–Sat 10am–5pm;
Sun and holidays 1–5pm. Closed Mon and Tues. $5 adults; $3
seniors, students, and children; $8 families. Wheelchair accessible
(104th St. entrance). Subway: 6 to 103rd St.

A museum as lively as the city it celebrates, the 5 floors
of this neo-Georgian building are crammed with historical dioramas, antique playthings, model ships, and
decorative arts. Take the elevator to the top and work
your way down. An engrossing multimedia presentation that spins through 400 years of local history in
barely 20 minutes, employing light, sound, and 24 syn-
chronized projectors. Concerts and walking tours of
the city are presented some Sundays during warm
weather. After a visit, it may take a while to obtain a
taxi, but the streets immediately to the east of the museum do not invite exploration.

★ Museum of Modern Art

11 W. 53rd St. (6th Ave.). ☎ 212/708-9480 (current exhibitions);
☎ 212/708-9490 (films); ☎ 212/708-9500 (other info.). Open
Sat–Tues 11am–5:45pm; Thurs–Fri noon–8:20pm. Closed Wed.
$8 adults; $5 seniors and students; free for children under 16.
Wheelchair accessible. Subway: E, F to 5th Ave.

Known with affection by its acronym, "MOMA", this
daring and innovative museum first lobbied for the
validity of modern art at a time when that belief was by
no means conceded, then in later years assumed the
role of arbiter. An artist represented in the collection is
among the anointed, assured of at least a sliver of
immortality.

   MOMA defines the genre as commencing with the
Impressionists in the 1880s. Although the history of
the many movements that have evolved since favors
abstract and nonobjective modes, figurative options are
also shown. Magic Realist Andrew Wyeth's *Christina's
World,* for example, is one of the most popular canvases

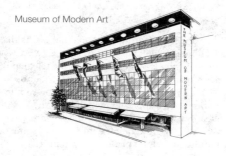

Museum of Modern Art

on view. The extensive film library and a collection of design triumphs of otherwise mundane objects, such as toasters and tableware, demonstrate the scope of the founders' intentions.

The glass wall bordering the main hall gives access to the outdoor Abby Aldrich Rockefeller sculpture garden, a delightful setting for lunch at one of the museum's 2 restaurants. Notable works among the permanent exhibitions inside are Van Gogh's *The Starry Night*, Picassso's celebrated *Girl Before a Mirror* and *Head of a Woman,* and Warhol's and Lichtenstein's Pop icons.

Museum of Natural History
(See American Museum of Natural History)

Museum of Television and Radio
25 W. 52nd St. (bet. 5th and 6th aves.). ☎ 212/621-6600. Open Tues–Sun noon–6pm; Thurs noon–8pm. Closed Mon, major holidays. Mornings reserved for groups, by appointment. $6 adults; $4 seniors and students; $3 children under 13. Wheelchair accessible. Subway: E, F to 53rd St./5th Ave.

The former Museum of Broadcasting moved to this impressive new 17-story building in 1991. With nearly 4 times more space than the old facility, the institution now has room to contain and display the 40,000-plus radio and television programs in the ever-growing collection. (About 3,000 new programs are added each year.) The entire inventory can be summoned via user-friendly computer terminals in the library, and they are available for transmission at 96 individual listening/ viewing consoles. Selected shows, changed daily, are presented on giant screens in 4 theaters, the largest with 200 seats. To contain the avid viewing habits of fans of "Star Trek" or "I Love Lucy," visitors are limited to 2 hours a day at the consoles.

National Academy of Design
1083 5th Ave. (89th St.). ☎ 212/369-4880. Open Wed–Thurs, Sat– Sun noon–5pm; Fri noon–8pm. Closed Mon–Tues. $5 adults; $3.50 seniors and students; pay as you wish Fri 5–8pm. Subway: 4, 5, 6 to 86th St.

Founded in 1825 by a group of American artists that included Thomas Cole and Samuel Morse (who was both a skilled painter and the inventor of the telegraph), the academy patterned itself after the art schools of Europe. A requirement of membership is the submission of works by each applicant, which form the 7,000-item collection. The academy's principal interest to casual visitors lies in its frequent exhibitions of some of these paintings, drawings, prints, and sculptures.

Upper West Side Sights

American Bible Society **13**
American Museum of
  Natural History **6**
Cathedral of
  St. John the Divine **2**
Central Park **10**
Children's Museum
  of Manhattan **5**
Columbia University **1**

Dakota Apartments **9**
Hayden Planetarium **7**
Lincoln Center **12**
Museum of American
  Folk Art **11**
New York
  Historical Society **8**
Pomander Walk **3**
Riverside Park **4**

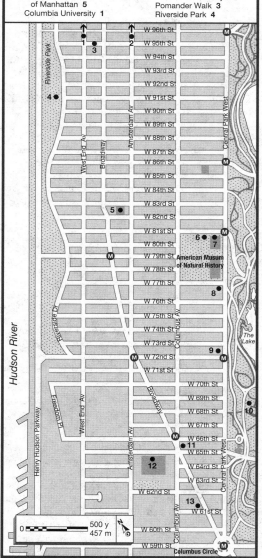

National Museum of the American Indian

1 Bowling Green (bet. State and Whitehall sts.). ☎ 212/825-6927.
Open daily 10am–5pm. Admission free. Subway: 4, 5 to Bowling
Green; N, R to Whitehall St., 1, 9 to South Ferry.

Years were lost in agonized discussion over various proposals for disposition of the much-coveted George
Gustave Heye Collection of Native American art and
artifacts. Largely ignored by the public and inadequately
housed for decades in what was the Museum of the
American Indian at **Audubon Terrace** in Harlem,
the fate of the 1-million-item collection became a
political, as well as scholarly issue. The Smithsonian
Institution won, dividing the collection between the
Washington, DC, area and this new museum in the
Alexander Hamilton US Custom House, near Battery
Park. (See "Walk 1" on page 170).

"American" here refers to the entire Western Hemisphere, with 1 million items ranging from Inuit carvings to Hopi kachina dolls, Chilean silverwork, and
costumes and fetishes from many Indian tribes and
empires. Free programs include American Indian dance
and music, storytelling, poetry readings, guided tours,
films, and lectures.

New Museum of Contemporary Art

583 Broadway (near Houston St.). ☎ 212/219-1222. Open Wed–Fri,
Sun noon–6pm; Sat noon–8. Closed Mon and Tues. $4 adults; $3
seniors, students and artists. Wheelchair accessible. Subway: B, D, F,
Q to Broadway/Lafayette St.

And they mean *new!* Young experimental artists have
always had difficulty finding spaces in which to show
the often outrageous results of their fertile creativity.
Here is one to rattle even SoHo's aesthetic perceptions.
The artists are virtually unknown, and most of their
works are no more than a few years old.

New York Aquarium

Surf Ave. (W. 8th St.), Coney Island, Brooklyn. ☎ 718/265-3474.
Open daily 10am–5pm; summer 10am–7pm. $6.75 adults; $3
children aged 2–12 and seniors. Wheelchair accessible. Subway:
F, D to W. 8th St. in Brooklyn.

While it may seem that every city in the United States—
even those that are landlocked—is building an aquarium,
this one dates back 100 years. From 1896 until 1941,
the aquarium was in Castle Clinton (see **Castle Clinton
National Monument**) in lower Manhattan. That
monument was threatened by proposed highway construction, so the fish were transported to this new
aquarium at **Coney Island,** on the southern rim of
Brooklyn. Predictably, popular exhibits are the sharks,

stingrays, 2-ton beluga whales, performing sea lions and dolphins (in the new 1,600-seat Aquatheater), walruses, and electric eels that light up bulbs.

New York Botanical Garden

Southern Blvd. (200th St.), Bronx. ☎ 718/220-8700; 718/220-8777. Grounds open Apr–Oct Tues–Sun and Mon holidays 10am–6pm; Nov–Mar 10am–5pm. Closed most Mon and major holidays. Conservatory open Tues–Sun 10am–4pm. Museum open Mon–Thurs 9:30am–6pm; Fri–Sat 9:30am-4pm. $3 adults; $1 seniors, students and children 6–16; free Wed all day and Sat 10am–noon. Subway: D, 4 to Bedford Park or 200th St. Bus: BX26 to the Botanical Garden stop.

Adjacent to the Bronx Zoo on its northern border, these 250 acres straddle the Bronx River. Here, the river is narrow and untamed, tumbling through a deep gorge. Its course is bordered by a 40-acre preserve of virgin oak and hemlock—the stately trees that covered much of the metropolitan region before the first Europeans arrived.

Among the specialty gardens are those devoted to roses, rocks, herbs, and native plants. The centerpiece of the preserve, the Enid A. Haupt Conservatory, is a grand rotunda of leaded glass that is the focus of a complex of 10 connecting greenhouses. The effect, inside and out, is of an enchanted crystal palace of the Victorian era. After years of deterioration, it was in danger of demolition. Reason and philanthropy finally prevailed in this glorious rejuvenation, and the rotunda now contains topiary, desert plants, and tropical flora.

Obviously the best time to go is between April and August, when the groves and gardens are ablaze with color, but special events, such as harvest celebrations, draw visitors at other times. Many also come for the bird-watching. Walking is the best way to experience the gardens, but a covered tram stops at choice locations. Hayrides are scheduled periodically from April to November.

New York City Fire Museum

278 Spring St. (bet. Hudson and Varick sts.). ☎ 212/691-1303. Open Tues–Sun 10am–4pm; open June–Aug Thurs until 9pm. Closed Mon and major holidays. $4 adults; $2 seniors and students; $1 children under 12. Subway: C, E to Spring St.; 1, 9 to Houston St.

New York bristles with quirky and beguiling specialized museums tucked in out-of-the-way corners. The Fire Museum is one of them. Housed in a renovated 1904 firehouse, the comprehensive collection of fire-related art and artifacts dates from the 18thC to the present. A lovingly polished nickel-plated steam engine highlights the assembly of hand- and horse-drawn vehicles from as early as the 1700s.

New York Historical Society

2 W. 77th St. (Central Park W.). ☎ 212/873-3400. Open Wed–Sun noon–5pm. Closed Mon–Tues. $3 adults; $1 seniors and children. Wheelchair accessible by prior arrangement. Subway: B, C to 81st St./ Museum of Natural History.

The name is misleading, for while the orientation is America as viewed from a New York perspective, the Historical Society casts its net widely. Although it lives in the shadow of the **American Museum of Natural History,** just across the street, the 2 floors of galleries are well worth perusal. The galleries have examples of folk art, works in silver, Colonial maps and prints, early American toys and carvings, and farm and household implements. The 2nd floor is devoted primarily to portraits and landscapes by painters of the Hudson River School. On the walls of the Audubon Gallery are the drawings and watercolors of birds by the naturalist John James Audubon. Paintings, maps, and drawings on the ground floor illustrate the city's growth from the days of Dutch rule.

★ New York Public Library

5th Ave. (42nd St.). ☎ 212/790-6161. Open Tues, Wed 11am–7:30pm; Thurs–Sat 10am–6pm. Closed Sun, Mon, holidays. Admission free. Subway: B, D, F, Q to 42nd St.; 7 to 5th Ave.

The citywide library system has more than 6 million volumes and 3 times as many related materials—much of it in this, the main branch. Their home is what many regard as the paradigm of the Beaux Arts style that was in vogue at the beginning of the 20thC. Beyond the famous pair of reclining lions (sometimes called Patience and Fortitude), long steps and a terrace lead up to the Roman portico. The majestically proportioned lobby

New York Public Library

beyond the entrance doors is impressive, but the palatial salons occupying the 3rd floor surpass it in grandeur.

First of these is the McGraw Rotunda, with an arched ceiling, carved and grooved paneling, and several large murals depicting what might be described as "great moments in literature" including Moses in a snit over his flock's bad behavior. Off the rotunda is the Public Catalog Room, with similarly effusive gilt and wood. The library is for reference, not for lending, but most of the volumes in the collection can be summoned from the stacks at the central desk here. Next is the grandest space of all, the Main Reading Room.

The library hosts frequent exhibitions of books, manuscripts, photographs, and prints in exhibition halls on this and the 1st floor. The library also has a noted telephone reference service, whose personnel can provide answers, with surprising alacrity, to questions ordinary and obscure (☎ 212/340-0849 Mon–Fri). Unfortunately, the line is often busy.

New York Stock Exchange

20 Broad St. (Wall St.). ☎ 212/656-3000. Open Mon–Fri 9:15am–4pm, but tickets must be obtained from the guards at the entrance by 1pm for a visit the same day. Tours free but compulsory. Subway: 4, 5 to Wall St.

A neoclassical "temple" a few steps away from Wall Street houses the oldest and most powerful stock exchange in the United States. Guards direct visitors to elevators that carry them to a gallery overlooking the main room. A number of interactive machines and displays attempt to explain, with varied success, what the seemingly anarchic hysteria down there attempts to accomplish.

New York University

Washington Sq. ☎ 212/598-3127. Open Mon–Sat 8am–9pm. Closed Sun. Subway: A, B, C, D, E, F, Q to W. 4th St./Washington Sq.; N, R to 8th St.

Founded in 1831, New York University is one of the largest private universities in the country, with more than 32,000 graduate and undergraduate students. Its first permanent home was a Gothic Revival pile at the northeast corner of **Washington Square** in Greenwich Village (see "Walk 2," on page 175). That was replaced by the present structure in 1894.

Over the last century, expansion has brought the additions of a postgraduate School of Business Administration in the **Financial District,** a medical-dental complex on the **East Side,** a respected Institute of Fine Arts on 5th Avenue, and a second campus in the Bronx.

Fiscal difficulties in the 1970s forced the sale of the Bronx campus and other smaller units, but the university retains ownership of most of the buildings on the east and south sides of Washington Square, as far over as 2nd Avenue and down to Houston Street. Purple-and-white banners proclaim its presence. Probably not your idea of a college "campus," NYU offers its students, quite literally, New York City as their playground.

News Building

220 E. 42nd St. (bet. 2nd and 3rd aves.). ☎ 212/210-2100. Open Mon–Fri 9am–5pm. Subway: S, 4, 5, 6, 7 to 42nd St./Grand Central.

Dating back to the Great Depression, this building was home to *The Daily News* until 1995, when modernization caught up to it, and it moved to 33rd Street. The building dates from the first wave of skyscraper fever, completed within months of **Rockefeller Center** and the **Empire State** and **Chrysler buildings.** Identified by its Art Deco detailing at ground level, the building is best known for the weather instruments and giant revolving globe in the lobby.

Numismatic Society
(See Audubon Terrace)

Oases

Walking the streets of Manhattan can come to feel like a mental and physical pummeling. Tranquil retreats abound when feet and legs are ready to give out. Here are some places to sit or plan or read awhile—and they are free. Churches and libraries are obvious choices, as are hotel lobbies and **Central Park.** Here are some others.

AT & T Building, 550 Madison Ave. (55th St.). Tables and chairs are available all around the street-level arcade, protected from rain and snow, but not the cold.

Chemcourt, 277 Park Ave. (47th St.). A bronze sculpture of a businessman hailing a taxi causes double-takes at the entrance to this lush greenhouse–atrium. There's a small art gallery, too.

Crystal Pavilion, 805 3rd Ave. (50th St.). A 3-level atrium offers tables and chairs, artificial waterfalls, plants, and several shops and restaurants.

Ford Foundation, 42nd St. (bet. 1st and 2nd aves.). One of the first enclosed atriums is a jungle of trees and plantings, with a pool. Open Mon–Fri 9am–5pm.

IBM Garden Plaza, 590 Madison Ave. (56th St.). Tall bamboo trees, chairs, a snack bar, occasional lunchtime concerts, and—scarcest of commodities—clean public rest rooms/lavatories. Open 8am–10pm.

New School for Social Research, 66 W. 12th St. (near 6th Ave.). Pass through the lobby, with chairs and telephones, to the terrace and sculpture garden beyond.

Olympic Tower, 645 5th Ave. (51st St.). Another office building atrium, with a waterfall and cafés.

Park Avenue Plaza, 55 E. 52nd St. (bet. Madison and Park aves.). Tables and chairs for playing chess and listening to frequent jazz concerts. Snack bar. Daily 8am–10pm.

Pierpont Morgan Library, 36th St. and Madison Ave. The new light-filled, glass-enclosed garden court is climate-controlled, with trees, tables and chairs, and a cafe. To avoid paying an entrance fee, enter through the bookstore in the building at the corner of Madison and 37th St.

World Financial Center, Battery Park City. The splendid Winter Garden of the **World Financial Center** is one of the city's great urban spaces, with benches and restaurants beneath towering palm trees.

Paley Park
3 E. 53rd St. (5th Ave.). Open Mon–Sat 8am–6pm. Closed Sun, Jan. Subway: E, F to 5th Ave.

The former chairman of CBS presented this chunk of valuable midtown real estate as a gift to the people of New York City. An enclosed "pocket park," the combination of trees, tables, chairs, snack wagon, and simulated waterfall are so popular that there is often a line to get in.

Pan Am Building (See Metropolitan Life Building)

Pierpont Morgan Library
29 E. 36th St. (Madison Ave.). ☎ 212/685-0008. Open Tues–Fri 10:30am–5pm; Sat 10:30am–6pm; Sun noon–6pm. Closed Mon. Guided tours Tues and Thurs 2:30pm. $5 adults; $3 seniors and students. Wheelchair accessible. Subway: 6 to 33rd St.

One of the quiet pleasures of subdued **Murray Hill,** the library was constructed for financier J. Pierpont Morgan in 1906 by the omnipresent firm of McKim, Mead & White. The neoclassical design reflects Pierpont Morgan's passion for the Italian renaissance. It contains, as would be expected, an excellent bookstore featuring fine art books and replicas of old manuscripts. In 1991, the library completed a climate-controlled glassed-roof garden court (now home of the Morgan Court Cafe), connecting the latter 2 buildings.

Consistent with its name, the library is primarily a repository of rare books, illuminated manuscripts, and other documents of the Middle Ages and the Renaissance, but it contains a great deal more that warrants attention: stained glass, sculpture, enamel and metal-work, and a number of somber Italian and Flemish paintings.

Planetarium, Hayden
(See American Museum of Natural History)

Police Academy Museum
235 E. 20th St. (2nd Ave.). ☎ 212/477-9753. Open Mon–Fri 9am–3pm. Closed Sat, Sun, holidays. Admission free. Subway: 6, N, R to 23rd St.

Installed on the 2nd floor of the city's police academy, the museum makes a forthright depiction of crime prevention and punishment in New York. Displays of the improvised weapons used by teenage street gangs are mixed with semihistorical lethal artifacts of the gangster era. Much of the material is unlabeled, and the collection is modest in scope, so don't make a special trip. It is an opportunity to eavesdrop on cop talk, however.

Pomander Walk
W. 95th St. (bet. West End Ave. and Broadway). Subway: 1, 2, 3, 9 to 96th St.

It looks older, but this private lane of 2-story houses wasn't built until 1922. The architect patterned it after the set of a popular play of the same name, with shuttered windows, flower boxes, brick facades, and Tudor gables here and there. Theater people were the original inhabitants, among them Rosalind Russell and Humphrey Bogart in his early "tennis, anyone?" years.

Prospect Park
West of Flatbush Ave., Brooklyn. Gateway from Grand Army Plaza. Subway: 2,3 to Grand Army Plaza, D to Prospect Park.

Frederick Law Olmsted and Calvert Vaux collaborated on this landscape design (1866–74), as they had on the larger **Central Park** in Manhattan. Many think this one the better of the two, with fewer roads and a more imaginative composition of wooded glades, water, and pathways. A small zoo established in 1935 along Flatbush Avenue houses elephants, zebras, monkeys, and bears (☎ 718/399-7339, open 10am–5pm). A 1912 carousel with charmingly carved horses functions Friday through Sunday.

In gentler times, this bucolic setting adjacent to the **Brooklyn Museum** and **Brooklyn Botanic Garden** would constitute a rare urban retreat. Sad to say, it is the victim of frequent acts of vandalism and lack of funds. The city has made a verbal commitment to overcome these problems. Until it does, go only during daylight.

Queens Museum of Art

Flushing Meadows Corona Park, Queens. ☎ 718/592-9700. Open Wed–Fri 10am–5pm; Sat–Sun noon–5pm; Tues groups by appointment only. Closed Mon. $3 adults; $1.50 seniors and children. Subway: 7 to Willets Point/Shea Stadium; follow yellow signs to museum, about a 10-minute walk.

For those enamored of maps and models, it can be worth the trek out here to see the remarkable scale model Panorama of the city of New York, replicating all 5 boroughs— more than 895,000 buildings, and every park, bridge, and roadway—in minute detail. The model takes up 9,335 square feet (867m²) of floor space and is billed as the largest of its kind in the world. In addition, the museum gives over gallery space to traveling art exhibitions, usually by 20thC artists and often incorporating video and mixed media. With so many other attractions in New York, getting out here may not be worth the time for most visitors. The museum isn't far from Shea Stadium, La Guardia Airport, and the U.S. Open Tennis Stadium, so a detour to the museum might fit in with a trip to those destinations.

Riverside Church

490 Riverside Dr. (122nd St.). ☎ 212/222-5900, ext. 265. Open 8am–10pm. Subway: 1, 9 to 166th St./Columbia University.

Despite the 74-bell carillon and the 20-ton bell at its top (both the largest of their kind anywhere in the world), the 392-foot (120m) tower of this interdenominational church looks vaguely like a Gothic 1930s' office building—and is, in part. It has an observation deck, which affords a sweeping panorama of the Hudson River from Wall Street to the **George Washington Bridge** (observation deck open Mon–Sat 11am–3pm; Sun 12:30–3pm; ☎ 212/749-7000 for times of carillon performances).

Riverside Park

New Yorkers owe an eternal debt to Frederick Law Olmsted and Calvert Vaux, the 19thC landscape architects who created **Central Park, Prospect Park**

Rockefeller Center

in Brooklyn, and this hilly, wooded strip bordering the Hudson River. It runs from West 72nd Street to West 125th Street, banked to the east by a wall of handsome apartment houses and blemished only by the Hudson Parkway, which was built along its length in the 1930s.

Rockefeller Center

47th to 52nd sts., just west of 5th Ave. Subway: B, D, F, Q to 47-50th sts./Rockefeller Center.

John D. Rockefeller Jr. put together the grand scheme for this 22-acre compound of office towers—"a city within the city." The heart of the complex is between 5th and 6th avenues and 49th and 50th streets. Here are the sights familiar from tourist literature and movies, most of them completed in the 1930s. Dominating is the **GE Building** (the former RCA Building), facing east. While it cannot compare in scale or inventiveness with the contemporary **Chrysler Building,** it bears a mantle of restrained elegance.

At the northwest corner of its base is the Art Deco Radio City Music Hall, with a breathtaking vaulted interior in which rock concerts and elaborate revues are staged. To the east, directly in front of the entrance, is a sunken plaza, which is an ice-skating rink in winter and an outdoor cafe in summer. A gold statue of Prometheus floats above. At the approach of Christmas, a tree more than 70 feet (21m) high rises behind him.

St. Bartholomew's Church

Park Ave. bet. 50th and 51st sts. ☎ 212/751-1616. Open Mon–Sat 8am–6pm; Sun 7am–3pm. Wheelchair accessible through 109 E. 50th St. entrance. Subway: E, F to Lexington Ave.; 6 to 51st St.

Providing a welcome antidote to the slabs of buildings of midtown Park Avenue, this pinkish pile of

Byzantine-Romanesque excess was designed by Bertram Goodhue and was completed in 1917. The front facade, salvaged from an earlier church, is the work of James Renwick. The Aoleian Skinner organ is the largest in New York and one of the largest in the country.

St. Mark's-in-the-Bowery

2nd Ave. (10th St.). ☎ 212/674-6377. Open 10:30am–4:30pm. Subway: 6 to Astor Pl.

One of the oldest houses of continuous worship in Manhattan, this church was built on farmland in 1799. The basic structure of the building is Federal, with a Greek Revival steeple added in 1828. The Dutch Director-General Peter Stuyvesant is buried here, in ground that he once owned.

St. Patrick's Cathedral

5th Ave. (51st St.). ☎ 212/753-2261. Open daily 7am–8pm. Subway: B, D, F, Q to 47–50th sts./Rockefeller Center.

When James Renwick submitted his drawings in 1850, the fashion for Gothic Revival was on the wane. By the time the cathedral was completed in 1888, it must have seemed dated. No matter, for the style returned to favor soon afterward, and by then St. Patrick's already ranked among the timeless. Echoing great cathedrals of Europe (for Renwick formulated his ideas after intense study of European examples), it is part lacy stonework, part soaring caprice, part massive pretense.

St. Patrick's Cathedral

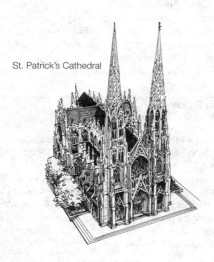

St. Paul's Chapel

St. Paul's Chapel
Broadway (Fulton St.). ☎ 212/285-0874. Open Mon–Fri 8am–4pm;
Sun 7am–3pm. Closed Sat, some holidays. Subway: 4, 5 to Fulton St.

The only existing nonresidential building in New York
that predates the Revolution (1766), St. Paul's holds its
own against the silvery glass curtain walls of the **World
Trade Center,** at least when viewed from street level.
Made of Manhattan schist quarried at the site, the
exterior facing is brownstone. Apart from the steeple,
added in 1794, it is authentic Georgian, inside and out.
Architect Thomas McBean is believed to have been a
pupil of James Gibbs, who designed the church of St.
Martin-in-the-Fields in London.

George Washington put in frequent appearances
during his first presidential term. His pew is marked.
The graveyard is a shaded resting place for footsore souls
still living, and the church sponsors frequent lunchtime
concerts of classical music on Mondays and Thursdays
(☎ 212/602-0760).

Seagram Building
375 Park Ave. (52nd St.). Subway: E, F to Lexington Ave.; 6 to
51st St.

First came **Lever House,** just across Park Avenue, then
Ludwig Mies van der Rohe's Seagram (1958). After
them, the glass-and-metal box International Style went
downhill. (For confirmation of that conclusion, simply
look south to the **Met-Life Building.**) The plaza in
front of the Seagram may appear banal but, considering the outrageous cost of midtown property, even this
much walking space seems generous. Landmark status
has been extended to the building and even to the

Sony Building

restaurant within, The Four Seasons (see "Dining"). By the way, Philip Johnson served as Mies van der Rohe's assistant on the project.

Seventh Regiment Armory

643 Park Ave. (bet. 66th and 67th sts.). ☎ 212/744-2008. Subway: 68th St./Hunter College.

This 1880 red-brick approximation of a fortress is the most prominent of several headquarters of military units in the city. While it retains that function, it also is home to 2 major antique shows each year, tennis courts, occasional theatrical productions, a shelter for the homeless, and a good restaurant, 7th Regiment Mess (☎ 212/744-4107). The interior, from the Park Avenue side, has wood paneling and stained glass by Tiffany.

Sony Building

550 Madison Ave. (56th St.). Subway: N, R to 5th Ave.

The monolithic American Telephone & Telegraph Company (AT&T) commissioned this building as their world headquarters in 1978; Sony leased it from them in 1993. Philip Johnson and John Burgee were responsible for the design, widely regarded as the first major reaction to the austerity of the long-dominant "International Style." It was heralded (or decried) as a postmodernist leap backwards to the use of decorative details inspired by the various architectural revivals of the last century. The principal departure from dogma was the broken pediment cap, said to resemble that atop a Chippendale secretary or chest of drawers.

South Street Seaport

Museum Visitor's Center: 12 Fulton St. (bet. South St. and Front St.). ☎ 212/748-8600. Museum buildings open 10am–5pm. Closed Christmas and New Year's Day. $6 adults; $5 seniors; $4 students; $3 children under 12. Subway: 2, 3, 4, 5 to Fulton St.

A living museum-in-progress, the Seaport has contributed to the resurrection of lower Manhattan as a place to live and stroll. More than 25 years ago a group of volunteers interested in preserving a segment of New York's maritime past forged an alliance with commercial interests to underwrite restoration of some of the last remaining blocks of early 19thC buildings and of a growing collection of antique sailing vessels. The largely salutary result is an expanding neighborhood of tasteful shops and restaurants that has proven immensely popular with both natives and visitors.

Standing just south of the Brooklyn Bridge, the Seaport has at its heart 7 ships of the early steam and clipper days, all docked in the East River. Visitors can board three of the ships: the 4-masted, metal-hulled 1911 bark *Peking,* the classic 1885 square-rigger *Wavertree,* and the 1906 light ship *Ambrose.* Cruises of the harbor can be taken aboard the century-old schooner *Pioneer* (May–Sept; ☎ 212/748-8590) and the 1930 wood tugboat *W.O. Decker.* They vary in length from 90 minutes to 3 hours. Weekend and week-long packages of an educational nature are available on the 1893 fishing schooner *Lettie G. Howard.*

Restoration is nearly complete on the 11-block official national historic district adjacent to the piers. More than $5 million has been spent on quayside rows of Greek Revival, Georgian, Federal, and Victorian warehouses and ships' suppliers. Venerable Schermerhorn Row and Front Street have undergone careful renovation, with much of their interior space given over to retail enterprises. A new 3-story structure dubbed the Fulton Market opened in 1983, filled mostly with specialty food stores and sidewalk cafés. Nearby is what remains of the old Fulton Fish Market, source of most of the fresh seafood served in Manhattan's better restaurants.

Strolling the historic district's 11 square blocks is free, assuming none of the shops and cafés prove too tempting. Combination museum and cruise tickets are also available. (See also "Walk 1," on page 170.)

Spanish Institute

684 Park Ave. (68th St.). ☎ 212/628-0420. Open Mon–Sat 11am–6pm. Closed Sun. Admission free. Subway: 6 to 68th St./Hunter College.

The home of the Center for American-Spanish Affairs is an architectural echo of the neighboring neo-Georgian structure, erected in 1926. Frequent lectures, recitals, and art exhibits showcase Spanish writers, poets, and artists. Native speakers hold classes in Spanish and Catalan.

Staten Island Zoo

614 Broadway (Forest Ave.), Staten Island. ☎ 718/442-3100. Open 10am– 4:45pm. $3 adults; $2 children. Wheelchair accessible. Ferry from Battery Park. Take a taxi or S-48 bus from the Staten Island Ferry terminal.

Specialization can make otherwise modest institutions rival grander establishments blessed with better resources. Although this zoo is of principal interest to residents of Staten Island, its reptile collection rivals any in the United States. It contains several types of pythons and specimens of almost every known type of rattlesnake. The aquarium has sharks and piranhas, just the thing for bloodthirsty little folk.

★ Statue of Liberty

Liberty Island, New York Harbor. ☎ 212/732-1236. Open daily 9am– 6pm. $7 adults; $5 seniors; $3 children aged 3–17. Tickets sold in Castle Clinton National Monument. Ferry from Battery Park every 30 min. 10am–4pm. Subway: 1, 9 to South Ferry.

French sculptor Auguste Bartholdi created Lady Liberty out of thin, beaten copper panels, with the engineering counsel of Gustave Eiffel, a man of recognized expertise in such matters. At 151 feet (46m), the statue dwarfs that wonder of the ancient world, the Colossus of Rhodes. The statue weighs 225 tons, each eye is 2 feet 6 inches (76cm) wide, and the tip of the upraised torch is 395 feet (120m) above sea level.

Inside, an elevator carries visitors halfway up, and 168 steps lead to the perforated crown, which presents a remarkable view of the bay, from the **Verrazano Narrows Bridge** to the spires of Manhattan. Visitors on ferries leaving after 2pm for the Statue of Liberty may not be able to get up to the crown because of long lines, which can last as long as 2 to 3 hours.

Studio Museum in Harlem

144 W. 125th St., (near Lenox Ave.). ☎ 212/864-4500. Open Wed–Fri 10am–5pm; Sat–Sun 1-6pm. Closed Mon, Tues. $5 adults; $3 seniors and students. Subway: 2, 3 to 125th St.

One of the most important cultural institutions in Harlem, especially since opening in these expanded and rehabilitated quarters, the museum concerns itself with the work of African-American artists. Most of the works on display are contemporary, some polemical in nature, some not. Every technique and medium is represented, along with insights into the African-American experience that larger, mainstream museums rarely pursue.

Temple Emanu-El

5th Ave. (65th St.). ☎ 212/744-1400. Open Sun–Thurs 10am–5pm; Fri 10am–4pm; Sat noon–5pm. Guided tour Sat noon; group tours by

Temple Emanu-El

appointment only. Services Sun–Thurs 5:30–6pm; Fri 5–6pm; Sat 10:30am–noon. For services, enter by 5th Ave. door; at other times, by E. 65th St. door. Wheelchair accessible. Subway: 6 to 68th St.

Founded in 1845 by 33 German-Jewish families, Temple Emanu-El was the first Reform congregation in New York City (the third in the nation). The current synagogue, the largest Jewish house of worship in the world, accommodating 2,500 congregants, was built in 1929. Stained-glass windows depict the tribes of Israel and historic synagogues from around the world. A Louis Comfort Tiffany stained glass representation of Jerusalem crowns the Ark, which holds the Torah, in the Beth-El Chapel.

Theodore Roosevelt Birthplace

28 E. 20th St. (bet. Park Ave. and Broadway). ☎ 212/260-1616. Open Wed–Sun 9am–5pm. Closed Mon, Tues. $2 adults; free for children under 17. Subway: 6 to 23rd St.; N or R to Broadway/23rd St.

The 26th president (1901–9) was born in 1858 and lived in a house at this site until 1873. The Roosevelts were a large and wealthy family even then, and this 4-story brownstone row house, a replica built to the original specifications, reflects that prosperity. In the 5 period rooms open to the public, careful attention has been paid to authenticity. The parlor is agleam with crystal chandeliers and gilt-framed mirrors. Plump horsehair sofas and chairs are arranged in inviting groups, and trophies reflect Roosevelt's roles of rancher, big-game hunter, explorer, and soldier. (See also "Gramercy Park" in "New York's Neighborhoods.")

Trinity Church

Broadway (Wall St.). ☎ 212/602-0700. Open 7am–6pm. Museum open Mon–Fri 9–11:45am, 1–3:45pm; Sat 10am–3:45pm; Sun 1–3:45pm. Subway: 4, 5 to Wall St.; N, R to Rector St.

The first Trinity Church was erected here in 1697, entirely of wood. That one burned down in 1776, in the first of the 2 great fires that decimated old New York. The second version was razed in 1839, and the present Gothic Revival manifestation (by Richard Upjohn) went up in 1846. The tower holds 10 bells, three of

Trinity Church

them dating from 1797. Decades of urban grime turned the red sandstone so black it nearly shone. Now it has been thoroughly cleaned, which some people complain has removed its distinctiveness. Noon concerts of classical music are held on most Mondays and Thursdays.

Trump Tower

725 5th Ave. (56th St.) ☎ 212/832-2000. Open Mon–Sat 8am–10pm. Closed Sun. Subway: B, Q to 57th St.

Only one of many monuments built by, and dedicated to, New York's most self-promoting multimillionaire, this office-residence-store tower characteristically falls on the glittery side of luxe. Donald Trump's sense of showmanship, revealed in this glossy structure, begins with exterior terraced stepbacks from the 3rd through the 8th floors, each planted with trees and ivy. Inside are an atrium aglint with brass and polished marble and a 3-story waterfall cascading into a sunken courtyard. A bistro-style café is down below, and a restaurant is on the 5th floor. The intervening floors are home to such pricey shops as Cartier, Blantre, and Abercrombie & Fitch.

Ukrainian Museum

203 2nd Ave. (12th St.) ☎ 212/228-0110. Open Wed–Sun 1–5pm. Closed Mon, Tues. $1 adults; 50¢ seniors and students. Wheelchair accessible. Subway: L to 3rd Ave.

Embroidery is the specialty—on garments, textiles, and ritual panels—but the intricately decorated Easter eggs shown during the Easter season are equally entrancing. Two galleries feature changing exhibitions. One is devoted to folk art; the other, to folk and fine art.

Union Square

In the 1930s, the 3.6-acre park was a vigorous if shabby version of Speakers' Corner in London's Hyde Park.

Anarchists, trade unionists, radicals, and simple eccentrics mounted soapboxes and endured hecklers. Its decline accelerated after World War II, and it eventually became the habitat of drug peddlers and prostitutes. An increased police presence and a major beautification project completed in 1985 encouraged families and office workers to return there—to lunch, to play, and to pass time. New restaurants and shops have opened around the perimeter. A very good farmer's market is held 3 times a week—usually Wednesday, Saturday, and Sunday.

United Nations

1st Ave. (45th St.). ☎ 212/754-1234. Open Mon–Fri 9am–5pm; Sat–Sun 9:15am–5pm; last tour at 4:45pm. Tours $6.50 adults; $4.50 seniors and students; $3.50 children. Wheelchair accessible. Subway: S, 4, 5, 6, 7 to 42nd St./Grand Central.

John D. Rockefeller, Jr. donated the East River site, and the first 3 buildings were ready for occupation in 1952. Despite the presence of a number of significant works of art by Marc Chagall, Henry Moore, and Barbara Hepworth, the overall visual effect of the complex is somewhat vapid, in the manner of quasi-governmental edifices.

Most offices and rooms are closed to the public but are of little general interest. The library is open to scholars and journalists. One-hour tours with multilingual guides leave about every 15 minutes from the Main Lobby of the General Assembly Building, which is the low structure with the concave roofline to the north of the simple slab of the Secretariat Building.

Obtain tickets to sessions of the General Assembly, the Security Council, and certain other meetings at the

United Nations

Information Desk shortly beforehand. (Admission is free, but on a first-come, first-served basis; starting times are usually 10:30am and 3pm.) The opening of the General Assembly, usually Monday of the 3rd week in September, is the most intriguing time to go.

Van Cortlandt Mansion and Museum

Van Cortlandt Park (246th St. and Broadway), Bronx. ☎ 718/543-3344. Open Tues–Fri 10am–3pm; Sat–Sun 11am–4pm. Closed Mon. $2 adults; $1.50 seniors and students; free for children under 14. Subway: 1 or 9 to 242nd St./Van Cortlandt Park.

This country house, with its deceptively modest field-stone exterior, served as one of George Washington's headquarters, as did the **Morris–Jumel Mansion** in Manhattan. Jacobus Van Cortlandt, destined to become a mayor of the city, bought the land in 1694 and made it a wheat farm and mill. His son built the existing mansion in 1748. The building has elements of the Dutch Colonial style but is essentially Georgian. Note the carved faces in the window keystones.

Verrazano Narrows Bridge

When opened in 1964, it became the longest suspension bridge in the world. England's Humber Bridge surpassed it in 1981. Two decks and 12 lanes link Staten Island and points west with the Belt Parkway in Brooklyn. The New York Marathon starts at the west end each November.

Villard Houses (Palace Hotel)

451 Madison Ave. (51st St.). Subway: E, F to 5th Ave.

This U-shaped Italian Renaissance palace, commissioned by German-born financier Henry Villard, was a departure for the firm of McKim, Mead & White. As the most popular architects of the late 19thC, they had dabbled in most revivalist styles except this one. In effect, the Villard Houses are 6 connected brownstones unified by a Roman aesthetic.

Villard Houses

After various changes of owner, Harry Helmsley purchased them. He was prevailed upon to restore, rather than raze them, and he erected his Palace Hotel to the east, incorporating the houses into the overall design.

Washington Square

Now it is the heart of **Greenwich Village**—playground, meeting place, open-air venue for street musicians, de facto campus of **New York University.** Brick row houses of the 1830s survive along the north side, east of 5th Avenue. Stanford White's Washington Arch (1892) marks the south end of 5th Avenue, while Philip Johnson's Bobst Library dominates the southeast corner. (See "Walk 2," on page 175.)

★ Wave Hill

675 W. 252nd St. (Independence Ave.), Bronx. ☎ 718/549-3200. Open Tues–Sun 10am–4:30pm; longer in summer; check ahead. Closed Mon. $4 adults; $2 seniors and students. Admission free in winter, and on Saturday mornings and Tuesdays in summer. Subway: 1 or 9 to 231st St., then bus 7 or 10 at the NW corner of 231st.

A formerly private estate with sweeping views of the Hudson River and the craggy cliffs called the Palisades, Wave Hill has been home to a British UN ambassador as well as Mark Twain and Theodore Roosevelt. Its 28 acres were bequeathed to the city of New York for use as a public garden that has been called the most beautiful place in the city, and as a cultural institution.

Programs range from horticulture to environmental education, visual and performing arts, landscape history, and forestry—more than enough to justify a visit, which might be coordinated with one to nearby **Van Cortlandt Mansion.**

Washington Square North

Whitney Museum

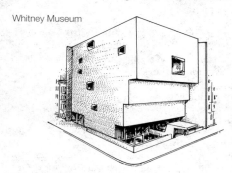

Whitney Museum of American Art

Madison Ave. (75th St.). ☎ 212/570-3676 (general information);
☎ 212/570-0537 (film information). Open Wed, Fri–Sun 11am–6pm;
Thurs 1–8pm. Closed Mon, Tues, holidays. $8 adults; $6 seniors and
students; free for children under 12; free for everyone Thurs 6–8pm.
Wheelchair accessible. Subway: 6 to 77th St.

The city's foremost repository of solely American
modern art is a perpetual whirlwind of controversy.
Depending upon whose interests are promoted—
or ignored—the show called the Whitney Biennial is
cited alternately as presumptuous, bland, stunning,
inept, and seminal. That ambitious survey of art by
currently active painters and sculptors rarely fails to out-
rage or to dismay the creative community, which many
observers take as evidence that the museum is doing
something right. As befits its basic premise—to survey
the growth of art in the preceding 2 years—the exhibition has ranged traditionally from unheralded talents to
such luminaries as James Rosenquist and Wayne
Thiebaud. The exhibition also endeavors to push conventions beyond their limits with avant-garde films, slide
and video presentations of "site works" by conceptual
artists, and dance programs and events. The Biennial
normally runs from mid-March to late June.

Virtually every major American talent since 1900
has a place in the permanent collection, examples of
which rotate into view as the limited space allows.
Among these works are pieces by Willem de Kooning,
Louise Nevelson, David Smith, Andy Warhol,
Hans Hofmann, Stuart Davis, Edward Hopper, George
Bellows, and Reginald Marsh. Some 50 Alexander
Calder mobiles and stabiles fill the courtyard and
are visible through the tall plate-glass windows of the
basement floor.

Sarabeth's at the Whitney serves lunch, snacks, and cocktails (see "Dining"). The Whitney has branches in the Philip Morris Building, which is opposite Grand Central Terminal (42nd St. and Park Ave.), and at Champion in Stamford, Connecticut.

Woolworth Building

233 Broadway (Barclay St.). Open Mon–Fri 9am–5pm. Closed Sat, Sun. Subway: N, R to City Hall.

Although best known as the consulting architect for the **George Washington Bridge,** Cass Gilbert was a favorite of tycoons and federal bureaucrats, largely on account of his unabashed enthusiasm for the power-inducing neoclassicism in vogue during the 50 years bracketing the turn of the century. His 1907 Beaux Arts U.S. Customs House (now housing the **National Museum of the American Indian**) bows only to the **Metropolitan Museum of Art** in effusive grandeur. Little question remains that the British Houses of Parliament played a role in his Woolworth commission. Replete with Gothic traceries and terra-cotta gargoyles, a blend of modern technology and stylistic nostalgia that so often fails, this "Cathedral of Commerce" is one of the most successful of the first generation of skyscrapers.

World Financial Center

Battery Park City (West St., bet. Vesey and Liberty sts.). ☎ 212/945-0505. Open 7am–1am. Subway: 1, 9 to Cortland St.

An ambitious cluster of buildings that contributes mightily to the resurgence of lower Manhattan as a place to live and play as well as work, this new complex is the centerpiece of the multiuse **Battery Park** landfill development. Included in its beguilements are a marina for those who can afford such extravagances, an unobstructed view of the **Statue of Liberty** and **Ellis Island,** 50 upmarket shops, and, at last count, 12 restaurants, including the already celebrated Hudson River Club (see "Dining").

At the center of the complex is the fabulous Winter Garden, a stunning urban space rivaling **Grand Central Terminal** and **Rockefeller Center.** Under its vaulted glass-and-steel roof is a grove of 16 palm trees, each at least 60 feet high, yet dwarfed by the soaring atrium. Cafés surround them, for a cappuccino or a full meal, and a gleaming marble staircase rises at the east end. Music, art exhibits, and other entertainments are staged frequently.

World Trade Center

Church St. (Liberty St.). ☎ 212/435-7377. Observation decks open Oct–May 9:30am–9:30pm; June–Sept 9:30am–11:30pm. $6 adults; $3 children. Wheelchair accessible. Subway: A, C to Chambers St.; E to World Trade Center; 1, 9 to Cortlandt St.

Long before their completion in 1974, the twin towers of the World Trade Center encountered censure. Critics charged they were visually banal and were displacing a thriving market district of little charm but much vitality. The terrorists responsible for the 1993 bombing had other objections.

Despite the complaints, businesses leased space, and shops and restaurants opened. The towers' vistas are stunning. At 1,350 feet (411m) they are 8 stories taller than the **Empire State Building,** but were surpassed within months by the Sears Tower in Chicago.

The observation decks are at 2 World Trade Center, and nearly 2 million visitors a year take the quarter-mile trip to the summit. An enclosed deck is on the 107th floor, and an open rooftop promenade is on the 110th. The latter is not for the vertiginous, nor is it open in blustery or otherwise inclement weather. On a clear day, you can see for 75 to 100 miles. Most of the 40 shops and 22 restaurants are at ground level or below, but the Windows on the World restaurant at 1 World Trade Center takes advantage of the views from the 107th floor.

Yeshiva University

187th St. (Amsterdam Ave.). ☎ 212/960-5400. Subway: 1 to 181st or 191st sts.

Both the largest and the oldest Jewish university in the Western Hemisphere, Yeshiva began in 1886 as a seminary called Yeshiva Eitz Chaim. Now a full-fledged university with more than 7,000 students, it maintains reverence for its origins while drawing wide respect for its courses in medicine and the mathematical sciences. The main building is a Moorish–Byzantine extravaganza of cupolas, minarets, and domes completed in 1928.

> If I live in New York, it is because I choose to live there. It is the city of total intensity, the city of the moment.
>
> —*Diana Vreeland*

New York Walks

New York is an island city, with four of its five administrative units, called boroughs, separated by water from the North American continent. Linking them together and to the mainland are 65 bridges and 19 tunnels. Every likely tourist destination is within reach of the extensive public transport system by subway, bus, or a combination of the two. Many out-of-town locations can be reached by rail or bus as well, although a car is often preferable.

Manhattan is at the heart of New York City. Even residents of the other boroughs refer to it as "The City," a reality made official by the postal service: all addresses in Manhattan are given as "New York, NY," while the others are designated Brooklyn, Queens, Bronx, and Staten Island. Nearly all visitors to New York stay in Manhattan. The major hotels are there, as are approximately 17,000 restaurants and most of the theaters, concert halls, art galleries, landmarks, corporation headquarters, libraries, universities and best-known churches and department stores.

The outer boroughs, although largely residential and industrial, are by no means bereft, however. The Bronx has its zoo and Yankee Stadium; Queens has Shea Stadium and the Aqueduct Racetrack; Brooklyn has its beaches and a fine museum; and Staten Island has golf courses, a zoo, and 2 complexes of restored architectural treasures.

Walk 1: Financial District

Allow 2–3 hours. Subway: World Trade Center.

From the day the first Dutch settlers crept into hastily constructed bark shelters, the foremost business of New York was commerce. Gradually, merchants became financiers, increasingly distant from the commodities they bartered, and as ever greater space was needed to contain the people who administered the system, so the present thicket of skyscrapers emerged, a 20thC metropolis built to the edges of a 17thC street plan.

By 1850, few people actually lived below Chambers Street and the **Brooklyn Bridge,** the approximate northern border of what was "Little Old New York" and is now the **Financial District.** From Monday to Friday, 8am to 6pm, the streets teemed with millions of workers, then at dusk and on weekends became dark, vacant canyons. That scenario is less true today, for New Yorkers have started to move back—albeit slowly—with restaurateurs and retailers following close behind them. So whether a Friday or a Saturday is chosen for a look around depends on the tastes of the visitor. Most buildings of note are open

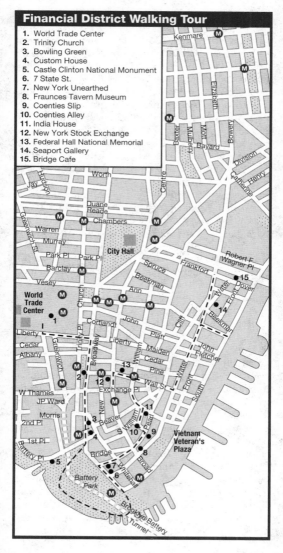

Financial District Walking Tour

1. World Trade Center
2. Trinity Church
3. Bowling Green
4. Custom House
5. Castle Clinton National Monument
6. 7 State St.
7. New York Unearthed
8. Fraunces Tavern Museum
9. Coenties Slip
10. Coenties Alley
11. India House
12. New York Stock Exchange
13. Federal Hall National Memorial
14. Seaport Gallery
15. Bridge Cafe

both days, but most eating places, except for those at **South Street Seaport,** lock up as soon as the last commuter has downed his or her martini and headed for home.

A walking tour logically begins with the observation deck of the south (no. 2) tower of the ① **World Trade Center,** the easiest structure to find in New York City. Exit onto Liberty Street. Turn left, to the

east, then right (south) on Broadway. Three blocks down
is ② **Trinity Church,** the Gothic Revival third version (1847) of a 1696 original. Once so black with grime
it almost glistened, it has now been scoured down to
the red sandstone. After a stroll through the surrounding graveyard, continue south on Broadway to
③ **Bowling Green,** a fenced pocket park guarded
by a large sculpture of a snorting bull. Directly beyond
the green is the ④ **Custom House,** often cited as
one of the city's best examples of the florid Beaux
Arts style popular at the turn of the century. The
4 "sculptures" in front are by Daniel Chester French,
best known for his monumental renderings of
Abraham Lincoln. They represent the continents of
Africa, America, Asia, and Europe. Across the 6th
floor cornice stand 12 "statues" symbolizing historical trading centers—from left to right, Greece,
Rome, Phoenicia, Genoa, Venice, Spain, Holland,
Portugal, Denmark, Germany, England, and France.
(The "Germany" designation was changed to "Belgium"
in 1917 in reflection of the anti-German sentiments
of the time.)

Bear right, southwest, into Battery Park, following
the main path to the semicircular ⑤ **Castle Clinton
National Monument.** An 1807 fortress that never fired
on an enemy ship, it served instead as a concert and
exposition hall, an immigrant processing center, and an
aquarium. There are historical exhibits inside, and booths
sell tickets for the Statue of Liberty and Ellis Island
ferries. Walk through the castle onto the promenade
at the water's edge, for a panorama that includes **Ellis
Island,** the **Statue of Liberty,** Governors Island
(a military base) and **Brooklyn Heights.**

Passing the ferry docks, turn inland opposite the
sign that reads "Gangway 1," keeping the park on the
left. A refreshment stand is on the right. Walk straight
ahead, to the opposite side of the park. Directly across
State Street is a ⑥ **Georgian–Federal mansion**
(no. 7), with an inset columned porch. Completed in

Ellis Island

1806, it is the last of a row of such homes that once bordered this avenue. Turn left (north) and cross over at the next intersection, Pearl Street. The narrow byway is now hemmed in by looming glass towers. After the first building is a grouping of benches and the entrance to ⑦ **New York Unearthed** (☎ *212/748-8600; open Mon–Sat noon–6pm),* a project of the **South Street Seaport Museum.** On display are objects discovered in archaeological digs around lower Manhattan, and explanations of their significance. Continue along Pearl Street. In 3 short blocks, at the corner of Broad Street, is the ⑧ **Fraunces Tavern Museum,** a re-creation of a Colonial Georgian residence. It has a museum of Revolutionary War artifacts upstairs, a pleasant restaurant downstairs. Breakfast is the best meal served, and there is afternoon tea.

Proceed along Pearl Street. The next corner is ⑨ **Coenties Slip,** so named because it was once a docking bay for merchant ships. Cross the street into what looks like a small plaza with herringbone brick paving, flanked by a block of convenience stores and the upstairs Grazio's Ristorante. The "plaza" is actually the refurbished ⑩ **Coenties Alley.** Pass the shops and turn right, onto narrow Stone Street, which was the first paved pathway in the Dutch colony. It isn't much to look at now, and it ends shortly in Hanover Square. To the right is the 1854 ⑪ **India House,** Italian Renaissance in style to serve the merchant princes who were its earliest occupants. It is now a private club, but members of the public are welcome to use the restaurant, Harry's at Hanover Square. Its food is fairly inexpensive, if unremarkable, and the bar is packed with brash young brokers and office workers at the end of the working day. Turn left, curving north along William Street, then left, to the west, into Exchange Place. Turning right (north) onto Broad Street, watch for the ⑫ **New York Stock Exchange** *(no. 8)* on the left. It is readily identified by the Greco-Roman facade. The seemingly inchoate frenzy in the pit of the main floor can be observed, if not necessarily understood, from the visitor's center (Mon–Fri 9:30am–4pm). You can get to the visitor's center through the building at 20 Broad St., taking the express elevator to the 3rd floor. At the next corner, glance left down Wall Street, its concrete canyon framing Trinity Church. The Greek Revival "temple" directly across the street is ⑬ **Federal Hall National Memorial** (both of these buildings are described in "Portraits"). On that site, in an earlier structure, George Washington took the oath of office as the first president of the United States.

Continue east down Wall Street, named for the wood stockade erected there in 1653 to protect the Dutch colonists from attack by Indians or the British. Turn left (north) on Water Street, crossing Maiden Lane, where young women once washed their laundry in a brook. At John Street, glance right for a startling view of the "four-masted bark *Peking*," one of the floating exhibits of an unusual maritime museum. Continue to Fulton Street, and turn right (east) to the heart of the South Street Seaport restoration district, a fetching amalgam of early 19thC architecture and artifacts and late 20thC merchandising and recycling techniques. From here to the East River, Fulton Street is a pedestrian mall, the buildings to either side filled with boutiques, fast food stalls, informal cafes and restaurants, and branches of such upmarket chains as Laura Ashley, Caswell-Massey, Ann Taylor, and Abercrombie & Fitch. On sunny days, every weekend, and most evenings, it is awash with locals and out-of-towners alike.

The row of buildings on the right, 1 block east, is Schermerhorn Row. Built around 1812 as a block of warehouses, it has been restored to its Federalist origins. At no. 12 is the museum's visitor center (open daily 10am–5pm). Upstairs at no. 2 is Sweet's seafood restaurant, opened in 1842 and, by some accounts, resting on its laurels since 1900. That doesn't stop the files of customers who dutifully line up for unadorned seafood lunches every weekday. At the end is the North Star, a persuasive imitation of a British pub, serving Guinness and Watney's brews. Just round the corner is the entrance to Sloppie Louie's, another historic spot that treats its patrons as cavalierly as its competitors but produces somewhat better fish. Sailing vessels of a more romantic era are moored at the piers of the **South Street Seaport** across the way. In good weather, the Seaport hosts concerts, puppet shows, and street musicians, and provides chairs in which to sit and admire the view of the Brooklyn Bridge.

Leave along the north side of Fulton Street, turning right (north) onto Water Street. A restored stationer's store is followed by the ⑭ **Seaport Gallery,** with maritime exhibits and helpful maps of the neighborhood. New shops open (and close) frequently with the ongoing development of the area. At the corner with Peck Slip, look toward the river at the amusing trompe l'oeil mural that covers the entire side wall of a brick building, complete with a reproduction of a bridge tower duplicating the real one just beyond. At the end of these last shabby blocks of Water Street is a forerunner of the bright new bar-restaurants that have sprung up in the district, the ⑮ **The Bridge Café.** It serves lunch, dinner, and Sunday brunch.

Walk 2: Greenwich Village

Allow 2–3 hours. Subway: Astor Pl. or 8th St.

"The Village isn't the same," say those who have prospered, matured, and moved away. They are correct, but it doesn't matter. The neighborhoods of New York are not static. They shrink, expand, divide, deteriorate, gentrify, adjust, or rally. Next year, or tomorrow, the Village will have changed again, but the past and provocative present remain.

Begin a tour at the University Place end of ① **Washington Mews,** one-half block north of the northeast corner of **Washington Square.** To the left is ② **La Maison Française,** to the right, ③ **Deutsches Haus.** Both are units of **New York University,** which owns much of the property in this area, as proclaimed by its ubiquitous purple-and-white banners. Proceed down the cobblestone Mews. Once servant quarters and stables for the grand houses on Washington Square North and 8th Street, most of the buildings are now private homes.

Turn left onto 5th Avenue, toward ④ **Washington Arch.** A wooden version of the monument was erected in 1886 to commemorate the centennial of George Washington's inauguration. It became an instant landmark, so the architect Stanford White designed this marble rendition, completed in 1892. ⑤ **Washington's statue** on the left was carved by A. Stirling Calder, father of Alexander Calder, the artist known for his mobiles.

Turn left along Washington Square North. This block of Greek Revival row houses was built in the 1830s, and ⑥ **no. 16** was the site of Henry James's novel, *Washington Square.* Note the bronze lions bracketing the steps of ⑦ **no. 6,** which now houses university offices and seminar rooms. Painter Edward Hopper maintained a studio at ⑧ **no. 3,** but the upper floors burned away in the early 1970s. Continue along as the street becomes Waverly Place, turning right onto Greene Street.

One block down, at the corner of Washington Place, is the site of the infamous Triangle Fire, which took the lives of 146 garment workers in 1911. The tragedy led to major legislation governing factory working conditions and fortified the then-weak labor movement. A plaque commemorates the event. At the foot of Greene Street is ⑨ **Tisch Hall,** with its flower- and tree-filled plaza. It is the second of Philip Johnson's commissions for the university, now being shouldered into the background by a cylindrical addition to the adjacent ⑩ **Shimkin Hall.** Turn right onto West 4th Street, which soon becomes Washington Square South.

The reddish building looming on the left is the ⑪ **Bobst Library,** Johnson's first design for NYU. You can step inside to see the 12-story balconied atrium. Outside, turn left, then left again on La Guardia Place, and walk south as far as Bleecker Street. Turn left (east) to see the 3 high-rise apartment houses on the right, the university-owned ⑫ **Silver Towers.** In the plaza at their base is a monumental rendering of Picasso's *Silvette,* one of only two exterior sculptures by the influential artist in North America. (The other is in Chicago.)

Return to Bleecker Street, now heading west, and continue to Sullivan Street. This intersection is the center of the long-established Italian community of the South Village. Walk north on Sullivan. Once a block of poultry stores and dim cafes, it is now undistinguished. Press on to the next intersection and turn left on West 3rd Street for a short block, then left again onto MacDougal Street. ⑬ **The Cafe Reggio** *(119 MacDougal St.)* is an authentic throwback to the legendary bohemian and beatnik days of the Village, as dark as always but less smoky than it used to be, with a well-used espresso machine hissing at one side. Continue south. At the next corner, across the street, is another famous old coffeehouse, ⑭ **Le Figaro.** Turn right onto Bleecker Street, crossing 6th Avenue and picking up Bleecker Street again on the other side.

Turn left onto Leroy Street, which becomes St. Luke's Place on the other side of 7th Avenue. The houses on the right-hand side of this peaceful tree-shaded block date from the 1860s. Turn right onto Hudson Street, right again onto Morton Street, then left onto Bedford Street ⑮ **(no. 75),** where Edna St. Vincent Millay, the poet and actress, resided for a time. Only 8 feet wide, it is the narrowest house in the Village. The oldest is probably ⑯ **no. 77,** next door, built in 1799.

Just beyond, turn left onto Commerce Street. At the end of the short block is the ⑰ **Cherry Lane Theater,** one of several in which the energetic

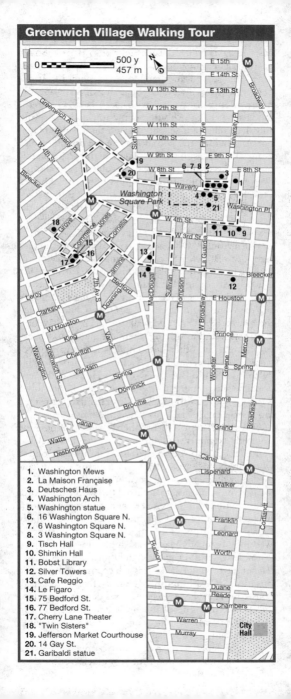

Greenwich Village Walking Tour

0 ———— 500 y
457 m

N

E 15th St
E 14th St
Broadway
W 13th St
W 12th St
Greenwich Av
W 11th St
Waverly Pl
Sixth Ave
Fifth Ave
University Pl
E 13th St
W 10th St
W 9th St
E 9th St
4th St
Bleecker
W 8th St
E 8th St
19
20
6 7 8 2
3
1
Waverly
4
5
21
*Washington
Square Park*
Washington Pl
Grove
Jones
Commerce
Cornelia
W 4th St
11
10
9
La Guardia
18
15
16
W 3rd St
13
17
Carmine
Bedford
Leroy
7th Av S
Downing
14
MacDougal
Sullivan
Thompson
12
Bleecker
E Houston
W Broadway
Clarkson
W Houston
Varick
King
Charlton
Vandam
Spring
Prince
Wooster
Greene
Mercer
Spring
Washington
Greenwich St
Dominick
Broome
Broome
Grand
Broadway
Canal
Watts
Desbrosses
Canal
Lispenard
Walker
Hudson
Franklin
Leonard
Worth
Cortlandt
Duane
Reade
Chambers
Warren
Murray
City Hall

1. Washington Mews
2. La Maison Française
3. Deutsches Haus
4. Washington Arch
5. Washington statue
6. 16 Washington Square N.
7. 6 Washington Square N.
8. 3 Washington Square N.
9. Tisch Hall
10. Shimkin Hall
11. Bobst Library
12. Silver Towers
13. Cafe Reggio
14. Le Figaro
15. 75 Bedford St.
16. 77 Bedford St.
17. Cherry Lane Theater
18. "Twin Sisters"
19. Jefferson Market Courthouse
20. 14 Gay St.
21. Garibaldi statue

Ms. Millay had a hand. Turn right onto Barrow Street, bearing right again until you are back on Bedford Street. Turn left and go another block on Bedford. At the corner of Grove Street, is a squarish wooden clapboard house of obvious age. It dates back to 1820, as does the much smaller frame house behind it, which was probably the kitchen and servant quarters for its larger neighbor. And behind the cookhouse are the double-gabled houses known as the ⑱ **"Twin Sisters,"** reputedly built by a seafaring father whose daughters would not live under the same roof. Turn left onto Grove Street. Proceed a few steps and look for the iron gate marked "private." Peer into the courtyard beyond. Among the bordering houses, built in the 1840s, are some of the few surviving wood houses in Manhattan.

Turn around, walk back along Grove Street and turn right onto Bleecker Street, a commercial artery dominated by abundant displays of foodstuffs. Turn left into Cornelia Street, and left again onto West 4th Street for more shops of even greater diversity. Make a right turn at 7th Avenue and continue as far as Charles Street, then turn right again and walk to Greenwich Avenue. Turn left, window-gazing, then cut across and backtrack down the other side. The triangular garden between 10th Street and 6th Avenue was made possible by the demolition of the Women's House of Detention. The adjacent structure with the fanciful brick tower is the ⑲ **Jefferson Market Courthouse Library,** a mouthful that describes its sequential uses.

Turn right onto Christopher Street, walking away from 6th Avenue, then left onto Gay Street, which was home (at ⑳ **no. 14**) to two sisters from Ohio, one of whom wrote *My Sister Eileen*. In a classic case of cultural recycling, her novel begat a play that was transformed into a musical that started the whole thing over again, complete with remakes and a television series. At the end of this crooked street, turn left onto Waverly Place and follow it to the northwest corner of Washington Square. Make one last detour—a half-block to the left. On the right is MacDougal Alley, a quaint relic of the privileged past. It is a deceptively ramshackle variation of Washington Mews, its former carriage houses now serving as expensive residences. Return to the square. It is one of the most frequented parks in Manhattan, both for innocent and "not-so-innocent" purposes and recently has experienced a pronounced police presence. At the northwest corner is a fenced section set aside as a dog run. Two blocks south, chess

and domino players and kibitzers form knots around
the cement games tables installed there. Cyclists,
joggers, skaters, and skateboarders swerve along the
paths. At and around the central fountain, which is intended more for splashing than beauty, and functions
on an unpredictable schedule, several musical groups
and individuals are bound to be performing, at least on
fine days.

Farther east is a statue of (21) **Garibaldi**. Consistent with campus legends everywhere, "Il Signore" is
said to unsheathe his sword whenever a virgin passes.
Finally, stroll over to the Grey Art Gallery on the
east side; this is another university facility, featuring
exhibitions more lively than the name suggests *(open
Tues, Thurs, Fri 11am–6:30pm; Wed 11am–8:30pm;
Sat 11am–5pm)*.

Walk 3: Central Park

Allow 2 hours. Subway: 77th St.

An amenity without which life in New York is un-
imaginable, the park is a product of mid-19thC vision
and expediency. At that time, the land north of 59th
Street was a place of mosquito-infested swamps, mal-
odorous meat-rendering factories, and the festering
hovels of thieves and the homeless. Prompted by poet-
journalist William Cullen Bryant and his supporters,
city authorities launched a design competition that was
won by landscape architect Frederick Law Olmsted and
the British architect Calvert Vaux. The project evicted
the squatters, drained the swamps or reshaped them into
lakes, planted 100,000 trees and pushed about tons of
rock and earth to supplement existing topographical
features and to create new ones. After 20 years it was
complete, with gravel carriageways, bridle paths, playing fields, secluded glades, and lakes for boating and
fishing. Most of these remain, despite the trampings of
generations of New Yorkers and periods of neglect,
vandalism, and intrusions both well-intentioned and
profane.

Olmsted and Vaux envisioned a people's park, a place
of refuge for poor and privileged citizens alike, not an
enclosed chunk of wilderness. To enhance circulation
and fantasy, they incorporated bridges, fountains, promenades, and even a castle. Ever since they completed
their commission, however, would-be benefactors and
entrepreneurs have proposed "improvements." Most are
turned away before the predictable firestorms of pro-
test, but over the decades a number of projects both

grand and irrelevant have squeezed through the screen. As a result, more structures and monuments stand within the park than even natives can enumerate, constituting an agreeable walking tour of surprising diversity.

One reluctant caveat, however: the stories about Central Park at night are overblown, but true enough to mandate caution. Apart from those frequent evening occasions—concerts and plays—that provide the security of large crowds, it is highly unwise to visit after dusk.

Enter the park at 79th Street and 5th Avenue, walking west along the path to the north of the Transverse Road. This hugs the south wing of the ① **Metropolitan Museum of Art,** continues over a low rise and heads down under an arched stone bridge. Go through, bearing right (north). A few steps farther on is ② **Cleopatra's Needle,** an Egyptian obelisk given to the city and erected in 1881. Turn around, taking the first footpath to the right. It soon bears left. The level green to the north called The Great Lawn was once a reservoir, drained and filled in the 1930s and now busy much of the year with softball and football players. Above the small lake on the left (south) is ③ **Belvedere Castle.**

At the end of the lake is the open-air ④ **Delacorte Theater** *(check newspapers for current performances or* ☎ *212/861-7277).* Bear left around the back of the theater and up the hill to the castle. Paths at the back cross over the Transverse Road. Take the one on the left, down the stone stairs, proceeding southwest, then southeast. Eventually, it winds past the ⑤ **Loeb Boat House** *(*☎ *212/517-2233, open Sat–Sun 11am–5pm).* Bicycles and rowboats are available for rent between April and October. A cafe with patio serves lunch and dinner on a seasonal schedule. Reservations are required for parties of 6 or more *(*☎ *212/517-3623).*

Follow the same pathway due east, crossing the nearby East Drive, until it soon reaches the concrete oval of Conservatory Pond. At its north end is a statue of ⑥ **Alice in Wonderland,** and on the west, one of ⑦ **Hans Christian Andersen.** Children clamber all over them, especially when stories are told at the Andersen monument on Saturday mornings (May–Sept).

Take the walkway that goes west from the south end of the pond, under the Park Drive, up the stairs, and along the bank of the lake. ⑧ **Bethesda Fountain** is just ahead, the most grandiose element

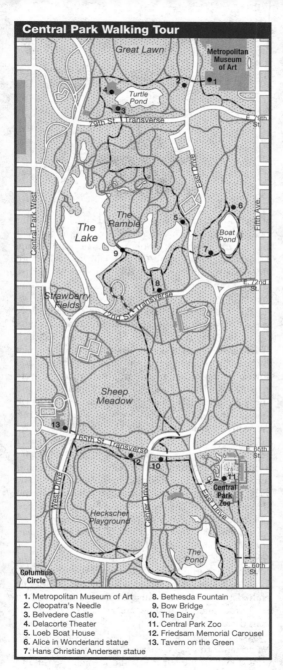

Central Park Walking Tour

Great Lawn

Metropolitan Museum of Art

Turtle Pond

79th St Transverse

E. 79th St.

The Ramble

The Lake

Boat Pond

Fifth Ave.

Central Park West

Strawberry Fields

72nd St. Transverse

E. 72nd St.

Sheep Meadow

65th St. Transverse

E. 65th St.

West Drive

Center Drive

East Drive

Heckscher Playground

Central Park Zoo

The Pond

E. 60th St.

Columbus Circle

1. Metropolitan Museum of Art
2. Cleopatra's Needle
3. Belvedere Castle
4. Delacorte Theater
5. Loeb Boat House
6. Alice in Wonderland statue
7. Hans Christian Andersen statue
8. Bethesda Fountain
9. Bow Bridge
10. The Dairy
11. Central Park Zoo
12. Friedsam Memorial Carousel
13. Tavern on the Green

Bethesda Fountain

of the Vaux contributions. A winged angel surmounts a gaggle of cherubim and, when New York is not having a water crisis, the pool at the base is splashing. The terrace surrounding the fountain has tables with umbrellas in summer. Peruvian instrumental groups, jugglers, and other performers often set up shop there.

Take the exit path leading west along the lake shore to the lovely cast-iron ⑨ **Bow Bridge.** Another Vaux design, it was restored in 1974. It crosses the lake into The Ramble, a cat's cradle of footpaths that curl through low trees, patches of grass, and plantings of bush and flower. Serious bird-watchers favor this section, for more than 200 species of birds reside in or visit the park and find these thickets hospitable. Return across the bridge to the Bethesda Fountain, go up the stairs, and cross the roadway. Walk south along The Mall.

Continue south on The Mall, a wide straight walk beneath a canopy of ancient trees. Off to the right, runners, skateboarders, picnickers, and musicians compete for space on a parallel road. At the end of the mall are bronze statues of Walter Scott, Robbie Burns, Shakespeare, and Christopher Columbus. Continue past Columbus, crossing the road. After about 20 yards, there is a walk on the right down to ⑩ **The Dairy** (*open Tues–Thurs and Sat–Sun 11am–5pm; Fri 1–5pm, until 4pm in winter; closed Mon*). Recent restoration of the building was faithful to its Victorian Gothic origins and recreated a loggia that was removed in the 1950s. The vaulted interior is now an information center, with exhibitions and a slide show, and walking tours depart from there.

Return to the nearby road and turn right (south). An entrance to ⑪ **Central Park Zoo** is about 100 yards down on the left (east), and it might be time to have a snack in one of its cafeterias, near the front gate. The zoo can be the end of a tour, but if energy and curiosity remain, leave the zoo through the south gate, emerging briefly from the park into Doris C. Freedman Plaza. Turn right (west), cross the road, turn right again, then go down the path on the left. Bear left at the lake encountered there. At the road that enters the park from Central Park South, head west, following the Park Drive as it curves north along the west side of the park. This stretch is the final leg of the New York Marathon in November, with the finish line at about 66th Street. A detour east along the Transverse Road soon arrives at the ⑫ **Friedsam Memorial Carousel** (*☎ 212/879-0244; open Mon–Fri 10:30am–5pm, Sat–Sun 10:30am–6pm, weather permitting*). The expanse of lawn to the north is **The Sheep Meadow.** To its west is the ⑬ **Tavern on the Green** restaurant (which until the 1930s was the barn for the sheep that grazed on the Meadow). The road in front of the restaurant exits on Central Park West.

Children's playgrounds, 22 of them, are located at intervals along the east and west borders of the park (see "Best Bets for Kids" on page 100). From May to October, park roads are closed to vehicular traffic Monday to Friday 10am to 3pm, Monday to Thursday 7 to 10pm, Friday 8pm until Monday 6am, holidays 7pm until 6am the next working day. From November to April only, weekend closing times apply. Horse-drawn carriages can be hired for rides through the park; they gather at stands near the ⑭ **The Plaza,** at the corner of Central Park South (59th St.) and 5th Avenue. For information on weekly events in the park call ☎ 212/427-4040.

STAYING ACTIVE

A FITNESS CENTER IS ALMOST OBLIGATORY AT Manhattan hotels these days. At a minimum, these rooms offer stairclimbers, stationary bicycles, treadmills, and some free-weights. At their most elaborate, they are full-scale health clubs with swimming pools and aerobics classes. In either case, they are within the confines of the hotel. This chapter offers some alternatives—activities that will provide both some exercise and a different view of New York. In addition, I'll cover various spectator sports you might want to attend.

Participant Sports A to Z

Baseball

The national game is played on fields all over New York. "Pick-up" teams come together for a few innings whenever a sufficient number of enthusiasts gather. If you are interested, contact the **Heckscher Ballfields** (Central Park, east of Central Park W. at about 64th St.; ☎ 212/408-0213).

Basketball

Manhattan has basketball courts within a few blocks of nearly every address, usually occupied by local youngsters or by aging executives who take the game very seriously (☎ 212/360-1311 for the closest court). Branches of the **YMCA** have gymnasiums (215 W. 23rd St., ☎ 212/741-9226; 224 E. 47th St., ☎ 212/756-9600; and 5 W. 63rd St., ☎ 212/787-4400), but they charge stiff fees for one-time use by nonmembers. Visitors who can present a membership card from a hometown "Y" usually can get in for smaller fees.

Beaches

See "Swimming" below.

Bicycling

Shops in most neighborhoods rent bicycles by the hour, day, or week. The Loeb Boathouse in Central Park (☎ 212/517-2233) rents bikes right where you'll most want to ride them. Don't go riding on the city streets; take to the park's roads, since some are closed to cars at midday, during weekday evenings, and throughout the weekends. Some other bike rental shops are: **Gene's,** 242 East 79th Street (2nd Ave.), ☎ 212/249-9218; **Metro Bicycles,** 9th Avenue and 47th Street, ☎ 212/581-4500; **Pedal Pushers,** 1306 2nd Avenue (near 69th St.), ☎ 212/288-5592; and **6th Ave. Bicycles,** 546 6th Avenue (15th St.), ☎ 212/255-5100.

Boating & Sailing

Rowboats can be rented by the hour in Central Park from the Loeb Boathouse (☎ 212/517-2233). The Boathouse also contains a cafeteria with a view of the lake. Rentals are made to anyone over 16. Children may go, if accompanied by an adult.

Sailing instruction is offered by the New York Sailing School (City Island, The Bronx; ☎ 718/885-3103).

Bowling

All the boroughs have bowling emporia, but only a few are still in business in Manhattan—you might try the 44-lane Bowlmor (110 University Pl.; ☎ 212/255-8188) in Greenwich Village. It's open every night until at least 1am. Time Bowling (625 8th Ave. at 41st St.; ☎ 212/268-6909) has 30 lanes with automatic scoring and is open Sunday to Thursday until 11pm; Friday and Saturday until 1am.

Chelsea Piers Sports & Entertainment Complex

On 30 acres along the Hudson River, developers have built this brand new ode to fitness and leisure. At the center is a 150,000-square-foot health club of cardio equipment and exercise classes. But this club goes well beyond the ordinary. It boasts the world's largest indoor running track (one-quarter mile), an enormous rock-climbing wall, a swimming pool, a gymnastics center, batting cages, basketball courts, and volleyball and sand-volleyball courts. Did I forget to mention the 2 indoor ice skating rinks, 2 outdoor roller rinks, the driving range, and the boxing ring? Other surprises await. A day pass costs $25 and provides access to most of the facilities. The complex charges reasonable fees for, say, just the ice rinks. The center is at Piers 59–62 between 17th and 23rd streets on the Hudson River; ☎ 212/336-6000.

Cricket

Immigrants from the former British West Indies keep the imperial heritage alive, on pitches in Flushing Meadows–Corona Park in Queens (☎ 718/520-5900), and in Van Cortlandt Park in The Bronx (W. 250th St. and Broadway; ☎ 718/430-1890).

Diving

Instruction in SCUBA is given by the Aqua-Lung School of New York (1089 2nd Ave.; ☎ 212/582-2800) and ITR (4 Park Ave.; ☎ 212/251-1706), both in Manhattan. They also arrange diving trips for qualified divers. A number of intriguing wrecks rest in offshore waters.

Fishing

Anglers over 16 must obtain a license to use the freshwater lakes and rivers of New York City and State. The permits are readily available for a small fee at many sporting goods stores. Lakes within Central Park, Prospect Park (Brooklyn), and Van Cortlandt Park (The Bronx) contain such gullible species as catfish, bluegills, and carp. Charters and party boats (each passenger pays a fare) are available year-round at City Island (The Bronx) and Sheepshead Bay (Brooklyn). Check the sports section of each Friday's *Daily News* for more information.

Golf

Manhattan does not have any golf courses, but the outlying boroughs have 13. For information in the various boroughs call: ☎ 718/822-4711 in The Bronx; ☎ 718/965-8912 in Brooklyn; ☎ 718/520-5311 in Queens; or ☎ 718/422-7640 in Staten Island. Expect to wait for a tee-off. (For a driving range, see "Chelsea Piers Sports and Entertainment Complex" above.)

Handball

New York City has more than 2,000 handball courts; call ☎ 212/397-3100 for the location of the nearest city-owned court in Manhattan.

Horseback Riding

Instruction and rent-by-the-hour are available at: Claremont Riding Academy (175 W. 89th St.;

☎ 212/724-5100), including classes for children; Clove Lake Stables (1025 Clove Rd., Staten Island; ☎ 718/448-1414); Van Cortlandt Park Stables (Broadway and W. 254th St., The Bronx; ☎ 718/549-6200). The trails for the Claremont Riding Academy wind through Central Park and are quite beautiful; it has an indoor ring, as well.

Ice-Skating

The rink at the base of the GE Building in Rockefeller Center has a constant crowd of spectators and so is used primarily by skilled and/or exhibition skaters—but beginners are welcome too. Central Park has 2 outdoor rinks: Lasker (near 5th Ave. at 107th St.; ☎ 212/996-1184) and Wollman (near the zoo, 5th Ave at 61st St.; ☎ 212/517-4800). All are open from November to April. The Sky Rink (450 W. 33rd St.; ☎ 212/695-6555) is large, indoors, and on the 16th floor. Open all year, it has disco skating on Friday and Saturday nights. (See also "Chelsea Piers Sports and Entertainment Complex" above.)

Skating is also permitted on natural lakes and ponds when there is safe ice cover, but it is wise to stick to the artificial rinks.

Racquetball & Squash

The popular racquet sports are available primarily at membership clubs. Hotels often have arrangements with nearby clubs; check with the concierge. A few clubs are open to the public on a courts-available basis. Daily rates aren't too steep. Some to try are: Manhattan Plaza Racquet Club, 450 West 43rd Street, ☎ 212/594-0554; Squash & Racquet Club, 404 5th Avenue, ☎ 212/594-3120; Athletic Complex, 3 Park Avenue, ☎ 212/686-1085; and City Hall Squash, 25 Park Place, ☎ 212/964-2677. All are usually open 7 days a week, 7am to midnight. They sell or rent equipment and accept credit cards. Reserve well ahead. Hotels that have courts include the Parker Meridien and the New York Vista.

Running

New York runners are a hardy breed, seen on every street, at all hours, in any weather. A morning jog or a serious 10-mile effort can follow any route, but certain areas and pathways are favored because of their even road surfaces, lack of vehicles and crowds, and relative freedom from air pollution. **Central Park** has 30-plus miles of roads, providing substantial variety in distances and difficulty. *Do not* run (or walk, or bike, or anything) in the park after dark. In daylight, avoid isolated areas. Suggested routes: The Reservoir, slightly north of the midpoint of the park, has a 1.6-mile (2.6km) dirt track that's easier on runners' joints than pavement. The view is so bucolic (for Manhattan) you might have extra energy. Enter the park at Engineer's Gate, at 5th Avenue and East 90th Street, or at 86th Street and Central Park West. Slightly south of the Reservoir is The Great Lawn Oval, with a measured circumference of half a mile and markers at 220-yard (200m) intervals. A 6-mile loop follows the main drive around the perimeter of the park. Cut east or west for runs of 1, 2, or 4 miles. Enter at Engineer's Gate, or at West 66th St. near the Tavern on the Green restaurant, or just beyond the zoo. Less crowded parks are Fort Tryon and Riverside parks in Manhattan, Prospect Park in Brooklyn, and Van Cortlandt Park in The Bronx. The **New York Botanical Garden** (also in The Bronx) is an ideal place for runners, and is a worthy destination by itself.

For river vistas, try Riverside Park (between 72nd and 96th streets) and the promenades along the East River, with easy access south from Carl Schurz Park.

Road races of varying lengths are held every month in the city. For dates, times, and registration details, contact the New York Road Runners Club (9 E. 89th St.; ☎ 212/860-4455). For indoor tracks: McBurney YMCA (215 W. 23rd St.; ☎ 212/741-9226); 92nd St. YMHA (1395 Lexington Ave.; ☎ 212/427-6000); West Side YMCA (5 W. 63rd St.; ☎ 212/787-4400). (See also "Chelsea Piers Sports and Entertainment Complex" above.)

Skiing

Cross-country skiing, on rolling terrain with gentle slopes, is available in Prospect Park (Brooklyn, ☎ 718/965-6511) and at Van Cortlandt Park (The Bronx, ☎ 718/430-1890). Equipment rental, instruction, tours to upstate and New England ski centers are all available from Scandinavian Ski Shop (40 W. 57th St.; ☎ 212/757-8524).

Swimming

Municipally-owned pools in the 5 boroughs are open from late May to early September. They tend to be shabby, crowded, and rowdy. Visitors are likely to prefer the indoor pools at the following hotels, some of which are open to outsiders as well as guests: Crowne

Plaza, Marriott Financial Center, Millenium, Parker Meridien, UN Plaza-Park Hyatt, Ramada Inn, New York Vista, and the Peninsula (see "Accommodations").

There are several fine area beaches as well. During the warm months, Jones Beach State Park (on the south side of Long Island) has the finest public beach and related facilities in the region, and is less than an hour by car (via Southern State Pkwy., exiting south on Wantagh State Pkwy.) or by special bus from the Port Authority Bus Terminal. Municipal beaches are nearly always crowded, and the color of the water is often suspect, even when certified safe for swimming, but most are within reach by public transportation. **Coney Island** beach (south Brooklyn) is best known, but Rockaway Beach, to the east, is 3 times as long, with a tenth of the humanity. Orchard Beach (near City Island in The Bronx), and Great Kills Park (Staten Island) are also popular.

Tennis

Commercial tennis clubs usually have equipment shops, lounges, instructors, and lockers available. Many also have saunas, air-conditioning, swimming pools, weekend brunches, and evening parties. Indoor courts are at: Crosstown Tennis, 14 West 31st Street (☎ 212/947-5780); Columbus Racquet Club, 795 Columbus Avenue (☎ 212/662-8367); HRC Tennis, East River piers 13 and 14 at the end of Wall Street (☎ 212/422-9300); Manhattan Plaza Racquet Club, 450 West 43rd Street (☎ 212/594-0554); Sutton East Tennis Club, 488 East 60th Street (☎ 212/751-3452); Tower Tennis Courts, 1725 York Avenue (☎ 212/860-2464); Turtle Bay Tennis & Swim Club, 1 United Nations Plaza (☎ 212/758-1234); USTA National Tennis Center, Flushing, Queens (☎ 718/760-6200); and Village Courts, 110 University Place (☎ 212/989-2300). These courts are normally open 7 days a week from 7am to midnight; always call ahead to reserve a court.

All boroughs have municipal courts, with more than 100 in Manhattan alone, but permits are usually required, and red tape slows the process. Most accessible is the 26-court Central Park Tennis Center (near Central Park W., between 94th and 96th streets; ☎ 212/280-0206), which has a country-club appearance with its public "clubhouse" overlooking the courts (it serves snacks, coffee and soda). Visitors can purchase a "same-day play" ticket for $5 for 1 hour of play; courts are often available during the week from 9am to 5pm. It's not too hard to pick up a partner if you don't already have one. Fanatics should take note of the Stadium Tennis Center (11 E. 162nd St. in The Bronx; ☎ 718/293-2386 or 718/884-1922; open Oct–May, 24 hrs. a day).

Spectator Sports A to Z
Arenas & Stadiums

Continental Airlines Arena (Meadowlands Sports Complex, E. Rutherford, NJ). The venue for the professional basketball team the Nets (☎ 201/935-3900) and the Devils hockey squad (☎ 201/935-6050), as well as rock concerts, circuses, college basketball, and other events. You can get there by bus from the Port Authority Bus Terminal on 8th Ave.

Giants Stadium (Meadowlands Sports Complex, E. Rutherford, NJ). Crowds fill the superb arena on Sunday afternoons from late August to December to watch professional football with the Jets (☎ 516/538-7200) and the Giants (☎ 201/935-8111); tickets for regular-season games are nearly impossible to obtain.

Madison Square Garden (8th Ave. and 33rd St.; ☎ 212/465-6741). Among its many guises, it is the home of New York Rangers ice hockey (Oct–Apr), Knicks basketball (Oct–Apr), and college basketball (Nov–Apr). Also boxing and wrestling matches and such special events as the circus, the Ice Capades, track and field, dog and cat and horse shows, women's tennis, and rock concerts.

Nassau Coliseum (Uniondale, Long Island; ☎ 516/794-9300). Special musical and entertainment events are presented at the Coliseum, as are the ice hockey games of the once highly successful Islanders (☎ 516/794-4100).

National Tennis Center (Flushing Meadows–Corona Park, Queens; ☎ 718/760-6200); site of the U.S. Open Championships (early Sept).

Shea Stadium (126th St. and Roosevelt Ave., Queens). The New York Mets (☎ 718/507-8499) play here (Apr–Sept), a park in which, inexplicably, almost all the seats seem to have bad views.

Yankee Stadium (River Ave. and W. 161st St., The Bronx; ☎ 718/293-6000). Home base (Apr–Oct) of the New York Yankees, who have often been champions and are one of the oldest teams in professional baseball.

Racetracks

For horse-racing results call ☎ 212/976-2121. Bets can be placed at nearly 100 Off-Track-Betting parlors (OTB) throughout the city. One of the most convenient is on the main floor of **Grand Central Terminal.** A list of racetracks in New York City follows.

Aqueduct (109th St. and Rockaway Blvd., Queens; ☎ 718/641-4700). The "Big A" features thoroughbred flat racing (Jan–May and Oct–Dec). The Pope visited in 1995. Think what you will. It can be reached by subway (☎ 718/330-1234).

Belmont Park (Belmont, Long Island; ☎ 718/641-4700). Thoroughbred racing (May–July, Sept–Oct). The Long Island Railroad, departing from Penn Station, has special trains and fare-admission packages (☎ 516/822-5477 for information).

Meadowlands (Meadowlands Sports Complex, E. Rutherford, NJ; ☎ 201/935-8500). Most of the grandstands are enclosed at this relatively new track, permitting comfortable viewing of thoroughbreds (Sept–Dec) and of trotters (Jan–Aug). Evening races can be watched from the Pegasus dining room.

Roosevelt Raceway (Westbury, Long Island; ☎ 516/222-2000). Evening trotters go through their paces (June–Aug, Oct–Mar). Package fares on the Long Island Railroad from Penn Station (see above) include bus transfers and track admission.

Yonkers Raceway (Yonkers, NY; ☎ 914/968-4200). Easily accessible off the Gov. Thomas E. Dewey Thruway, north of The Bronx. The track is devoted to trotting races (Mar–Apr, June–July, Sept–Oct and Dec). Special buses leave from the Port Authority Bus Terminal on 8th Avenue.

SHOPPING

To MANY VISITORS, NEW YORK'S MYSTIQUE IS inextricably linked to its great merchants. Bloomingdale's, Macy's, Tiffany, and FAO Schwarz all have branches in other cities, but symbolize New York as much as its less commercial monuments.

The center of American fashion, New York boasts a boutique from just about every major designer—French, Italian, Japanese, you name it. Photographic and home electronics equipment is consistently sold below list price. High volume permits this practice, and heavy competition requires it. Many camera dealers bypass the U.S. distributors, for example, to purchase directly from Japanese manufacturers, thereby eliminating intermediate price rises.

With more than 90% of the nation's publishers headquartered here, discounting of new books is widespread. All languages are represented, and rare and out-of-print volumes are quickly located. To survive today, bookstores take one of two routes: specialization or superstoredom. The first peppers the city with shops concentrating on everything from Marxism to travel.

Sales personnel can be brusque or helpful, irritable or patient. Department stores, understaffed from cutbacks, typically provide the worst service and sometimes have long lines at payment counters. Salespeople in camera and luxury clothing stores might also seem testy and/or indifferent. Many boutiques cultivate a higher standard of service however, employing salespeople who actually know how to put an outfit together.

Name almost any quirky item and New York probably has at least 1 shop, however tiny and out of the way, devoted to it. Small shop owners, fearing crime, often keep their doors locked, buzzing them open only after making snap judgments of potential clients. On the subject of crime, incidentally, take care of your hand-bag or wallet while shopping; stores can be a favorite hangout of pickpockets. Be wary, too, of shops that proclaim in foot-high letters that they are going out of business: Some of them have had those signs up for years. Check labels and identifications carefully, especially on watches and electronic equipment. Unknown brands aren't worth the risk, and some are made to look like products of reputable companies, right down to names with only 1 letter changed. Street vendors peddle scarves, umbrellas, belts, almost anything portable. Their prices are low, but remember that they move about and might not be at the same site tomorrow, and the "brand-name" products they hawk are almost certainly counterfeit. Canal Street, near SoHo, has a strip of stores selling fake and over-priced "designer" handbags and watches—don't waste your time.

For **specialized items,** here are some tips. For art galleries, see the tours listed under "Galleries." For discount designer clothing, make the popular pilgrimage to Orchard Street on the Lower East Side, but go there only on Sunday. For photographic equipment, head for 34th Street near Herald Square or for Lexington Avenue between 42nd and 52nd streets. Crafts and offbeat articles of clothing can be found on a gallery tour of SoHo and along the blocks of West 4th Street and Greenwich Avenue, just west of 7th Avenue, in Greenwich Village. Wander at will: The compilation that follows does no more than sketch the highlights.

As for the best times to shop, weekday mornings are the least crowded, lunch hours and Saturdays the most. The only days on which virtually everything is closed are Thanksgiving (last Thurs in Nov), Christmas, and New Year's Day. Many retailers use other holidays as the perfect excuse for sales. Although some stores still close on Sundays, more and more are opening their doors from noon until 5 or 6pm. As a rule, Midtown shops are open from 9:30am or 10am until 6pm, Monday to Saturday, with late closing 8pm or 9pm on Thursday evening and during the holiday season.

Elsewhere, the hours reflect the religious convictions or lifestyles of the communities. In Greenwich Village and SoHo, doors may not open until noon, but they won't close until midnight or later. Businesses owned by Orthodox Jews on the Lower East Side and elsewhere are closed on Friday afternoons and Saturdays but are open on Sundays. In the 9-to-5 world of the Wall Street area, many shops close on Saturdays as well as Sundays. Some establishments on the Upper East Side keep shorter weekend hours in the summer, a reflection of their clientele's exodus to the Hamptons.

Credit cards are widely accepted, even in the smallest shops, although a minimum purchase price might be stipulated. If you prefer to pay with **travelers checks,** retailers often require supplementary identification. Personal checks from out-of-town banks are not welcomed, but individual managers can sometimes be persuaded to take them, with 2 or more types of identification, if the customer appears trustworthy. Stores invariably refuse checks drawn in another currency.

Shopping Districts

While diversity prevails, certain streets and neighborhoods have taken on distinct commercial identities, with regard to either cost or types of merchandise. **Fifth Avenue,** roughly from 47th Street to 57th Street, is still home to the city's most famed jewelers, such as Tiffany and Cartier, and several legendary stores, including Saks Fifth Avenue and Bergdorf Goodman. But of late, 5th Avenue also has seen the opening of the Warner Bros. theme store, which is far from ritzy, and soon it will welcome Nike Town.

With the opening in 1993 of Barneys New York's uptown store, **Madison Avenue** had its semiofficial christening as the city's preeminent designer drive. From Valentino to Versace, Armani to Miyake, almost every Parisian, Milanese, and American designer of note now has a flagship on Madison from about 57th Street to 80th Street. Antique hunters and art lovers also will want to explore Madison Avenue.

A funkier shopper might prefer the eclectic boutiques of **SoHo.** Although not cheap, the SoHo shops tend to be more accessibly priced, and the styles more cutting edge. Up-and-coming designers' storefronts, such as Cynthia Rowley's and Todd Oldham's, are mixed in with coffeehouses and the likes of Origins Natural Resources, an emporium of good-smelling lotions and potions for the bath and body. The neighborhood is also host to scores of galleries.

On the **Upper West Side,** mainly north of Lincoln Center up to 84th Street, you'll find shops geared to the young working singles and families who live nearby. Not as trendy as downtown, not as snooty as the Upper East Side, Columbus Avenue and Broadway invite casual shopping and strolling.

Before settling on Tiffany or Cartier, stroll both sides of 47th Street between 5th and 6th avenues, known as the **Diamond District,** for a shimmering display of jewelry and precious stones of every description and price.

New York Shopping A to Z

Antiques

If rarity and beauty, not cost, are your criteria, you'll have a blast cruising the dozens of exclusive dealers along 57th Street, and north along Madison Avenue and the adjoining blocks. For antique porcelain, silver, jewelry, and accessories, look at:

A La Vieille Russie, 781 5th Ave. (59th St.), ☎ 212/752-1727.

Chinese Porcelain Company, 475 Park Ave. (58th St.), ☎ 212/838-7744.

Cobblestones, 314 E. 9th St. (2nd Ave.), ☎ 212/673-5372.

Gem Antiques, 1088 Madison Ave. (85th St.), ☎ 212/535-7399.

J&P Timepieces, 1057 2nd Ave. (56th St.), ☎ 212/249-2600.

James Robinson, 480 Park Ave. (58th St.), ☎ 212/752-6166.

Jean Hoffman/Jane Starr Antiques, 236 E. 80th St., ☎ 212/861-8256.

Maya Schaper Antiques, 106 W. 69th St. (Lexington Ave.), ☎ 212/873-2100.

Fine European and American furniture can be viewed at:

Better Times Antiques, 201 W. 84th St. (Broadway), ☎ 212/496-9001.

French & Co., 17 E. 65th St. (near 5th Ave.), ☎ 212/535-3330.

Old Versailles, 315 E. 62nd St. (near Lexington Ave.), ☎ 212/421-3663.

Overseas visitors may be more interested in American furnishings, quilts, and folk arts. Among shops focusing on these:

American Hurrah, 766 Madison Ave. (67th St.), ☎ 212/535-1930.

The Gazebo, 114 E. 57th St. (near Park Ave.),
☎ 212/832-7077.

Laura Fisher, 1050 2nd Ave. (near 56th St.),
☎ 212/838-2596.

Oldies Goldies & Moldies, 1609 2nd Ave.
(near 83rd St.), ☎ 212/737-3935.

Somethin' Else, 182 9th Ave. (in Chelsea),
☎ 212/924-0006.

The multifloored antique galleries of London and Paris
have their counterparts in New York. There can be good
buys, somewhat below the stratospheric price ranges
of the shops already mentioned. Dealers in silver,
enamel, crystal, music boxes, vintage clothing, china,
paperweights, brassware, and every category of bric-a-
brac lease space at Manhattan Art and Antiques Center,
1050 2nd Avenue (56th St.), ☎ 212/355-4400. There
are 85 stalls.

Antique shows large and small are frequently staged
around the city. The most prestigious is the Winter
Antiques Show at the 7th Regiment Armory (Park Ave.
and 67th St.; ☎ 212/452-3067) in January. The furniture and objets d'art on display are often unique, but
rarely cost less than several thousand dollars.

No collector, serious or casual, should miss Newel
Galleries (425 E. 53rd St.; ☎ 212/758-1970). Its 6 floors
of antiques of every type and period constitute a virtual
museum.

Auction Houses

Auctions are a source of enlightenment and great
entertainment even for those who have no intention of
bidding. But don't be scared off; not everything costs a
fortune.

Christie's
502 Park Ave. (near 59th St.). ☎ 212/546-1000.
'Christie's is a British house comprehensive in its
offerings. It has another branch, Christie's East, at
219 E 67th St. (☎ 212/606-0400).

Sotheby's
1334 York Ave. (72nd St.). ☎ 212/606-7000.
This result of a merger of British and American firms
continues to hold center stage. It deals in snuff boxes,
folk arts, antiquities, Oriental carpets, Impressionist
paintings, toys, Judaica, Art Nouveau—just about
everything.

Beauty Parlors & Hairdressers

Once the exclusive province of women, both skin-care centers and hairstylists now cater to men as well.

Facial treatments typically take 1 to 1½ hours. Inevitably, there are soft-sell efforts by attendants to sign you up for repeat sessions and to buy the whole skin-care regimen. Other services, such as massage and body wraps, are now widely available in "day spa" settings. Advance reservations are essential.

Elizabeth Arden, 691 5th Ave. (54th St.), ☎ 212/546-0200. Obnoxious staff, long waits, but still the Red Door salon is something of a New York institution. Book at least a week in advance for all sorts of services.

Borja and Paul, 712 Madison Ave. (58th St.), ☎ 212/308-3232 or 212/734-0477.

Frederic Fekkai, 745 5th Ave. (57th St., in Bergdorf Goodman), ☎ 212/753-9500. One of the leading salons in town.

Kenneth, 301 Park Ave. (49th St., in Waldorf-Astoria), ☎ 212/752-1800.

Georgette Klinger, 501 Madison Ave. (52nd St.), ☎ 212/838-3200; and 978 Madison Ave. (76th St.), ☎ 212/744-6900. Perhaps the best facials in town. Also amazing scalp treatments.

Let's Face It, 568 Broadway (Prince St.), ☎ 212/219-8970. A relaxed, cozy alternative to the sterile salons uptown. Come for a facial; stay and chat.

Lia Schorr, 686 Lexington Ave., ☎ 212/486-9670, open Sunday. Half the clients are men.

Christine Valmy, 767 5th Ave. (58th St.), ☎ 212/752-0303.

At the following hair salons, appointments are not always required, but call ahead for hours and rates.

Larry Matthews, 536 Madison Ave. (54th St.), ☎ 212/355-1900.

Nardi, 143 E. 57th St. (3rd Ave.), ☎ 212/421-4810.

Vidal Sassoon, 767 5th Ave. (near 58th St.),
☎ 212/535-9200.

In a category all its own is **Astor Place Hair Designers** (2 Astor Pl., near Broadway; ☎ 212/475-9854).
It's a haircutting assembly line, with 100 barbers on 3
floors. They'll do anything for anyone's hair, male or
female, including, but not restricted to, shaving a Batman
or a Mercedes-Benz logo on the back of your head, all
for a moderate price.

Books & Magazines

At the center of publishing in North America, the city
has bookstores to suit every taste and a newsstand at
virtually every alternate corner. Book lovers may want
to coordinate a trip with the "Book Country" street
fair in mid-September, when publishers set up open-
air booths along 5th Avenue from 48th Street to 57th
Street.

B. Dalton Bookseller
666 5th Ave. (52nd St.). ☎ 212/247-1740. Open daily.
The substantial stocks include more than 300,000 titles
on every imaginable subject at this flagship store of a
chain of 800 outlets nationwide. B. Dalton also carries
computer software programs. There's an even larger
branch at 396 6th Avenue, in Greenwich Village
(☎ 212/674-8780).

Barnes & Noble
105 5th Ave. (18th St.). ☎ 212/675-5500. Open daily.
One of a chain concentrating on recent books at
substantial discounts. The stores also sell tapes, records,
and magazines. The principal uptown branch is at 5th
Avenue and 48th Street. The Superstore at 2289 Broadway (82nd St.) has a sociable coffee bar, as well as
author readings several times a week.

Books & Company
939 Madison Ave. (75th St.). ☎ 212/737-1450. Open daily.
Classic bookstore, with creaking floors, piles of books
sitting about in organized disorder, and hardly a best-
seller in sight. Occasional poetry readings are another
attraction.

Doubleday
724 5th Ave. (57th St.). ☎ 212/397-0550. Open until 11pm
Mon–Sat.
Large 3-level shop. Every category is covered, with
a marked emphasis on the performing arts. It sells
records, too.

Gotham Book Mart

41 W. 47th St. (near 6th Ave.). ☎ 212/719-4448. Closed Sun (usually).

The founder of this revered bookstore was working in the shop on her 100th birthday, 68 years after she first opened these doors. Frances Steloff has passed on, but the stock remains comprehensive and iconoclastic, with particular strength in poetry and classic and experimental fiction.

Hotaling's News Agency

142 W. 42nd St. (bet. 6th and 7th aves.). ☎ 212/840-1868. Open daily.

This newsstand, near Times Square and an X-rated peep show, has been here for 90 years. It sells hundreds of newspapers and periodicals from other American cities and foreign countries in uncounted numbers of languages.

Murder Ink

2486 Broadway (bet. 92nd and 93rd sts.). ☎ 212/362-8905. Open daily.

Deals exclusively in crime mysteries.

New York Bound Bookshop

50 Rockefeller Plaza (near 5th Ave.). ☎ 212/245-8503. Closed Sun.

Specializing in out-of-print books and recent titles about New York, it also attracts clients for its old prints and for axonometric maps of midtown Manhattan, on which buildings are reproduced right down to the stairs and construction cranes.

Rand McNally

150 E. 52nd St. (near Lexington Ave.). ☎ 212/758-7488. Open daily.

Maps and atlases, of course, as well as language books, travel guides and videos, and children's games.

Rizzoli

31 W. 57th St. (near 5th Ave.). ☎ 212/759-2424. Open daily.

The New York outlet of the prestigious Italian publisher, with books in several European languages, and classical background music in keeping with its studied elegance. Another branch is in SoHo, at 454 West Broadway.

Shakespeare & Co.

2259 Broadway (81st St.). ☎ 212/580-7800. Open daily.

For literature lovers. Although it can't meet the heavily discounted prices at its neighbor Barnes & Noble, Shakespeare offers a more intimate setting and a well-edited selection. A branch is downtown at 716 Broadway (☎ 212/529-1330).

Strand
828 Broadway (12th St.). ☎ 212/473-1452. Open daily.

Shelf after shelf of mostly used books, in a gratifying clutter that can ensnare book lovers for hours. Reviewers sell off their advance copies here at discounted prices. An upstairs section (elevator is next door) sells rare books.

Cameras & Electronic Equipment

Manhattan stores trading in electronic and photographic equipment have been the target of some pretty bad publicity—and in many cases deservedly so. Beware of Midtown stores with enormous sale signs in the windows offering deals that are too good to be true; they may be inflating prices and selling merchandise that bears the name of an unknown company, without warranties. Below I have tried to list reputable stores where actual New Yorkers shop for camcorders, cellular phones, computers, stereos, televisions, calculators, fax machines, and the like. Sales and discounts are the rule in this enormously competitive field. Check the full-page ads in the Sunday *New York Times* before setting out. Profit margins are slashed to the bone, which makes some floor managers irritable when you inquire if they will match the lower price for the same lens or projector at a shop down the street. Ask anyway. When making a purchase, be certain you get it in a sealed factory carton.

Most shops listed below are open 7 days a week, and accept major credit cards.

47th Street Photo
115 W. 45th St. (bet. 6th Ave. and Broadway). ☎ 212/398-1530.

Having survived bankruptcy, 47th Street Photo's famed selection is still substantial. Arrive knowing exactly what make and model you want, since you'll get little advice, just low prices. The Orthodox Jewish owners close from 3pm Friday until 10am Sunday.

Grand Central Camera & Computer
420 Lexington Ave. (near 44th St.). ☎ 212/986-2270.

The personnel here have proved consistently helpful, and prices are good for laptops, cameras, and personal stereos.

J & R Music World
23 Park Row (Broadway). ☎ 212/238-9000.

A large, reputable dealer in computers, audio equipment, VCRs, etc. The staff is both knowledgeable and professional, and the prices are very competitive.

Nobody Beats the Wiz
12 W. 45th St. (near 5th Ave.). ☎ 212/302-2000.

With dozens of branches in the metropolitan area, Nobody Beats the Wiz guarantees to undercut competitors' advertised prices—but don't expect any deals unless you ask. The inventory of both office and home electronics is substantial.

Willoughby's
110 W. 32nd St. (near 7th Ave.). ☎ 212/564-1600.

Although known primarily as a camera shop, Willoughby's has substantial inventories of computers and other electronic appliances. The store even takes trade-ins. Members of the staff speak several languages and accept telephone orders.

Crafts

A city of immigrants and compulsive travelers is compelled to gather and display the treasures of its homelands and voyages. Folk arts of many countries are for sale, with an emphasis on goods from Africa and Latin America. Here's a short list:

Craft Caravan
63 Greene St. (near Spring St.). ☎ 212/431-6669.

African masks, baskets, artifacts, fabrics, stools.

Luna d'Oro
66 Greene St. (near Spring St.). ☎ 212/925-8225.

Molas from Panama, milagros from Mexico, crafts from 15 countries.

Objects of Bright Pride
455A Columbus Ave. (near 81st St.). ☎ 212/721-4579.

Carvings and jewelry of Inuits and Native Americans of the Pacific Northwest. Closed Wednesday.

Pan American Phoenix
857 Lexington Ave. (64th St.). ☎ 212/535-3383.

A wealth of Mexican handicrafts, especially fabrics and garments.

Sidewalk merchants display their wares on the north side of 53rd Street, near 6th Avenue, not far from the **American Craft Museum.** While there is no guarantee of authenticity, many of their African tribal masks and carvings are quite handsome.

Department Stores

They're often crowded with shoppers and have not a salesperson in sight, but New York's department stores still possess a certain mystique, whether by virtue of their size (Macy's still claims to be the world's largest store) or their fashion authority, with Bergdorf's, Saks, and Barneys foremost in that category today. The traditional department stores, particularly Bloomingdale's, Macy's, and Lord & Taylor, are good places to look for sales, as these stores tend to mark down merchandise that has been on the floor for more than 30 days.

Barneys New York

660 Madison Ave. (61st St.). ☎ 212/826-8900.

The third generation of the Pressman family now runs the operation, almost unrecognizable from the men's discount house Barney Pressman opened circa World War I. Today Barneys is one of the premier women's and men's fashion stores in the city, with prices to prove it. Don't expect glitz; Barneys specializes in New York black and other similarly subdued hues, sans adornment. The fabrics are rich, and the designers are primarily foreign. In addition to apparel, Barneys is known for Mad 61, the happening restaurant in its uptown store, which opened amid much fanfare in 1993 (see "Dining"). Not for the faint of heart, the annual warehouse sale takes place every summer from the last week in August through Labor Day at 255 W. 17th St.

Bergdorf Goodman

754 5th Ave. (57th St.). ☎ 212/752-3000.

At what may be the most glamorous intersection in New York, Bergdorf's reigns as one of the world's preeminent fashion stores. International designers, such as Yves Saint Laurent and Givenchy, are well represented here, and the lingerie, fragrances, and linens are of the highest order.

Bloomingdale's

1000 3rd Ave. (59th St.). ☎ 212/355-5900.

Always in touch with the trends, from miniskirts to polo shirts, Bloomingdale's continues to thrive. It is an immense emporium of merchandise, from clothes to cookware, food to furniture. Bloomie's is a department store of the old style. Service is not the greatest. Human traffic inside can be intense, but it's all part of the spectacle. A welcome innovation for foreign visitors is the currency exchange booth, next to the American Express office on the Metro level.

Century 21

22 Cortlandt St. (bet. Broadway and Church St.). ☎ 212/227-9092.
Closed Sun.

The discount department store across the street from
the World Trade Center has a broad selection of
apparel, cosmetics, and home goods. Wall Street men
favor the store for its discounted shirts by Hugo Boss,
Joseph Abboud and the like, and women like to stock
up on the low-price hosiery (Calvin Klein's for less
than $5, Wolford for about $15). Shopping for sports-
wear here requires some patience, but there are finds,
from Prada dresses to Versace jackets.

Curacao Export

20 W. 57th St. (near 5th Ave.). ☎ 212/581-6970.

Curacao Export is the first stop for in-the-know Europeans seeking a variety of products that are far more
expensive back in Milan or Munich. In fact, only shoppers with non-U.S. passports can buy here. They are
after Levi's jeans, Ray Ban sunglasses, Nike athletic
shoes, Sony radios, and Timberland shoes.

Henri Bendel

712 5th Ave. (55th St.). ☎ 212/247-1100.

Henri Bendel is more accurately described as a women's
specialty store; the store calls itself a "lady's paradise."
Although the store (pronounced Henry BENdle) stocks
plenty of designer merchandise from Claude Montana,
Todd Oldham, and the like, it also has a more reasonably priced selection of private label goods. The store
also tends to stock cute dresses from young designers,
including Nicole Miller and Cynthia Rowley. Bendel's
cosmetics department has been one of the first stores to
recognize the potential of such upstart makeup lines as
MAC, Trish McEvoy and Bobbi Brown Essentials. Try
a makeover followed by afternoon tea in the cafe.

Lord & Taylor

424 5th Ave. (39th St.). ☎ 212/391-3344.

Although not as expansive as Macy's or Bloomingdale's,
Lord & Taylor still fits in the mold of the traditional
department store, stocking everything from clothes to
housewares. Owned by a St. Louis company, L&T can
be a little dull these days, particularly for New York,
but every once in a while it shines.

Macy's

Broadway and 34th St. ☎ 212/971-6000.

Macy's occupies the area between the bland middle
ground of Lord & Taylor and the snappy upper-middle

ground represented by Bloomingdale's. One of its most admired departments is the basement repository of kitchenware and gourmet foods called The Cellar. The largest store in the world occupies an entire city block and is actually 2 buildings rather awkwardly joined. Macy's carries pretty much everything. The service, however, is maddening. It will take a while to peruse the store; if you get hungry, there are 7 places where you can eat a snack or a full meal.

Saks Fifth Avenue
611 5th Ave. (50th St.). ☎ 212/753-4000.

Scrupulously choreographed and relentlessly edited, Saks is a wonderland of luxury goods. Clothes are its particular strength, from sports to formal wear, as delineated by Bill Blass, Oscar de la Renta, Donna Karan, and their colleagues. Although still appealing to the Upper East Side matrons, Saks has made efforts to spice up its image in order to attract a younger, hipper customer. A delightful diversion: lunch in the cafe overlooking 5th Avenue.

Fashion

Befitting the fashion design and manufacturing capital of the country, New York's retail scene is vast, almost overwhelming. In general, the most upscale fashion houses—Chanel, Armani, and the like—have their boutiques along 57th Street or Madison Avenue on the Upper East Side, while many of the younger, kickier designers, including Cynthia Rowley and Todd Oldham, have their digs down in SoHo. Virtually every neighborhood has its share of boutiques. Try Columbus Avenue from Lincoln Center into the low 80s for wearable clothes with a sophisticated flare, and the Village, East and West, for of-the-moment fashion.

Clothing & Shoes for Women
Here are the trendsetters:

Calvin Klein
654 Madison Ave. (60th St.). ☎ 212/292-9000. Closed Sun.

Although he's been stirring controversy since the 1970s, Klein still is at the forefront of hip, defining it each season with either the New Length or the skinny belt or whatever else his atelier dreams up or picks up in Europe. The shop carries both his men's and women's top-tier collections and accessories but not his less expensive CK Calvin Klein line, which is available in the major department stores.

Chanel

5 E. 57th St. (bet. 5th and Madison aves.). ☎ 212/355-5050. Closed Sun..

Designed by Karl Lagerfeld, Chanel has never been hotter. Come for those cute little suits, those smashing jackets, those drop-dead evening gowns, and all those authentic quilted handbags.

Charivari

18 W. 57th St. (bet. 5th and 6th aves.). ☎ 212/333-4040. Open Sun.

No, the color tube didn't just break. That is all black you're seeing. Charivari carries little else. But what else would any self-respecting New Yorker want to wear? Taking into account the owner's partiality to Belgian designers known for deconstructionist fashion, the clothes are stark, somber, and sophisticated. Charivari has 2 other locations: on the Upper West Side at 257 Columbus Avenue (72nd St.; ☎ 212/787-7272) and on the Upper East Side at 1001 Madison Avenue (78th St.; ☎ 212/650-0078).

Cynthia Rowley

112 Wooster St. (bet. Prince and Spring sts.). ☎ 212/334-1144. Open Sun.

The young designer, more and more in the limelight of late, is best known for her fun little dresses, many priced under $300.

Gianni Versace

816 Madison Ave. (68th St.). ☎ 212/744-5572. Closed Sun.

The Italian designer who tends toward the bawdy. (That dress that made Hugh Grant's girlfriend, Elizabeth Hurley, a name was a Versace.) He makes no bones about designing for the well-aerobicized woman who has cash to spare.

Giorgio Armani

815 Madison Ave. (bet. 68th and 69th sts.). ☎ 212/988-9191. Closed Sun.

Versace's arch nemesis, Armani changed the way women dress. His clothes are fluid and graceful, elegant and timeless. The Madison Avenue boutique carries his top-line designer collection for men and women, but downtown at **Emporio Armani** are clothes for both sexes—and children—at slightly lower prices. It's at 110 5th Avenue (16th St.; ☎ 212/727-3240) and is open Sunday. His lowest price line, kind of the Milanese designer's version of the Gap, is at the A/X

store in SoHo, 568 Broadway (Prince St.; ☎ 212/
431-6000).

Gucci
683 5th Ave. (54th St.). ☎ 212/826-2600. Closed Sun.

Despite the (sadly, not-unwarranted) reputation of
the sales staff for sullenness, flocks of moneyed patrons
storm these 4 exclusive floors. They are men and women
who admire fine Italian craftsmanship in leather goods—
shoes, belts, handbags and luggage—and don't mind
wearing someone else's initials: the famed double G.

Issey Miyake
992 Madison Ave. (77th St.). ☎ 212/439-7822. Closed Sun.

The Japanese designer's creations are almost architectural in construction. Known for his intricate pleating,
many of Miyake's designs require a self-assured woman
to pull off, but in that category he has few equals.

Norma Kamali
11 W. 56th St. (5th Ave.). ☎ 212/957-9797. Open Sun.

After an exclusive deal with Bloomingdale's obscured
her star somewhat, Kamali is back selling her line of
comfortable yet body-conscious clothes to a variety of
stores. Here, in a grandly refurbished old building
just off 5th Avenue, you can see her whole concept,
beach to club, office to dinner party.

Origins Natural Resources
402 West Broadway (bet. Prince and Spring sts.). ☎ 212/219-9764.
Open Sun.

The cosmetics in this SoHo boutique have names like
Starting Over (an exfoliator) and Summer Vacation
(a self-tanner). The shop also has aromatherapy products and massage devices.

Polo/Ralph Lauren
867 Madison Ave. (72nd St.). ☎ 212/606-2100. Open Sun.

Make an excuse to visit this stunning 4-floor specialty
shop. The 1895 mansion captures every ounce, every
inch, of the designer's style. Antique furnishings and
accessories are arranged in rooms authentic to the last
detail, almost like movie sets for his women's, men's,
and children's clothing. Stop in the Polo Sport store
directly across the street for a glimpse of Ralph's vision
of the sporting life.

Screaming Mimi's
382 Lafayette St. (bet. 3rd and 4th sts.). ☎ 212/677-6464.

Why settle for the retro look when you can have the
real thing? Whichever decade is in, Screaming Mimi's

seems able to acquire authentic merchandise from it: platform shoes and flared pants from the seventies, or more ladylike fare from the forties and fifties.

Susan Bennis/Warren Edwards
22 W. 57th St. (near 5th Ave.). ☎ 212/755-4197. Open Sun.
High quality pumps and low heels of impeccable craftsmanship and exquisite materials, mostly imported, with prices to match.

Todd Oldham
123 Wooster St. (bet. Prince and Spring sts.). ☎ 212/226-4668 or 212/219-3531. Open Sun.
He's done MTV, and now he's done his own store. The clothes are multicolored, multipatterned, offbeat.

Valentino
825 Madison Ave. (68th St.). ☎ 212/744-0200. Closed Sun.
The Chic, as he is known, stocks his store with dresses, sweaters, and separates. Come marvel at the delicate fabrics and sartorial details that can be had only at very high prices. Saleswomen speak several languages.

Yves Saint Laurent/Rive Gauche
855 Madison Ave. (near 70th St.). ☎ 212/988-3821. Closed Sun.
From the striking front to the metal-and-leather interior, this boutique sizzles with the products of the restless mind of the celebrated French designer. Shirts, trousers, shoes, dresses, suits, belts are at the leading edge of fashion. One pays dearly to participate.

Clothing for Men
Men's fashion has come a long way, and this city, not surprisingly, is the best place to find it. In addition to the shops mentioned below, I recommend men with a taste for fashion visit Giorgio Armani and Ralph Lauren, both listed in the women's category above, and Barneys New York and the other department stores listed in that section.

Bergdorf Goodman Men
5th Ave. & 58th St. ☎ 212/753-7300. Open Sun.
Essentially an annex to the main store across the street, this store features the major names in the biz: Armani, Hermès, Turnbull & Asser, and their exclusive compeers.

Brooks Brothers
346 Madison Ave. (44th St.). ☎ 212/682-8800. Open Sun.
In an aberrant world, it is comforting to know that there is still Brooks Brothers. This is the 170-year-old home of the natural-shoulder suit that long has been

the preferred wear of American business leaders and those who aspire to succeed them. The conservative detailing has been updated somewhat in recent years.

Custom Shop Shirtmakers

555 Lexington Ave. (50th St.). ☎ 212/759-7480. Closed Sun.

Men of proportions that don't quite fit off-the-shelf shirts can stop here for made-to-measure cottons and cotton blends that cost not much more than readymades, depending on fabric and collar style. The Custom Shop has a minimum order of four, but first-time customers get a substantial discount. Custommade suits are also available. There are 5 branches.

The Gap

657 3rd Ave. (42nd St.). ☎ 212/697-3590. Open daily.

This and a multitude of other branches throughout Manhattan purvey jeans and khakis in every style and size for about $30 a pair. Truly a unisex store.

Harry Rothman

200 Park Ave. S. (near Union Sq.). ☎ 212/777-7400.

Discounts up to 50% on midlevel suits and furnishings. The shop has a better selection of large, tall, and unusual sizes than is the rule.

Paul Stuart

Madison Ave. and 45th St. ☎ 212/682-0320. Open Sun.

For the mid-Atlantic look, Paul Stuart has suits and sports jackets in a subdued palette of checks and herringbones and conservative fabrics of flannels and twills. The arm-holes are higher than those of the equally traditional Brooks Brothers, the shoulders are squared, the waists ever-so-slightly more suppressed. Most are of natural fibers, but there are some blends. The prices are high, but not out of sight.

Sulka

430 Park Ave. (57th St.). ☎ 212/832-1100.

Made-to-measure silk shirts are the ultimate luxury in this exclusive shop, which celebrated its centennial in 1995. The suits, coats, and accessories in cashmere, shearling, linen, and leather, among other luxury fabrics, are also of a high standard.

Sym's

42 Trinity Pl. (near Rector St.). ☎ 212/797-1199.

Attention all travelers with lost luggage: Sym's boasts same-day alterations. The original list price is followed on the tag with Sym's price, generally a 40% to 60% reduction. Those willing to examine carefully 5 floors of racks and counters can emerge with twice as much clothing as the same expenditure would obtain in Midtown. Sym's also carries women's and children's clothing.

Victory: The Shirt Experts
125 Maiden Lane (Water St.). ☎ 212/480-1366. Closed most Sat and Sun.

This shop is a real boon to the odd-sized man or woman who doesn't care to pay for custom tailoring. Victory makes 100% cotton shirts of made-to-measure quality at ready-made prices. The shop also stocks shirts in sizes 14 to 32 through 18^1/2 to 36 and a variety of ties and accessories. Telephone orders are accepted.

Food & Kitchenware

Food shopping in New York can take on a European flair, with stops at several different outposts to acquire the very finest produce, fish, bread, cheese, and coffee. Zabar's is probably the best known, but the city has several other worthy markets. Thanks to the stew of ethnic groups, unusual spices and other ingredients from far-flung lands are readily available. Unless you like crazed crowds, try to avoid Saturdays. These stores are all open 7 days a week, unless otherwise noted.

Balducci's
424 6th Ave. (9th St.). ☎ 212/673-2600.

Some wise soul once said, "Never go shopping when you're hungry." That guy must have been to Balducci's, a market where throngs compete for the tempting cheeses, pastries, thick slabs of prime meats, ringlets of homemade sausages, smoked fish, and lobsters.

Bridge Kitchenware
214 E. 52nd St. (near 2nd Ave.). ☎ 212/688-4220. Closed Sun.

The shelves are packed with quality utensils for the serious cook. Pick through stainless carbon knives, food processors, graters, coffee grinders, bowls of steel and ceramic, copper molds, crystal. The prices are fair, which helps make up for the grumpy sales staff.

Caviarteria
502 Park Ave. (59th St.). ☎ 212/759-7410. Closed Sun.

Unprepossessing inside and out, this small shop is easy to dismiss. The caviar is Iranian, Russian, and American. The last is an increasingly successful undertaking, and at half the price of the imports. The shop also stocks smoked salmon and related delicacies and enjoys a substantial mail-order trade.

Citarella

2135 Broadway (75th St.). ☎ 212/874-0383.

Who says fish can't be art? Window-shop at Citarella on the Upper West Side and you'll look at sea creatures in a whole new way. Each day in its large front window, Citarella designs a new, satisfyingly symmetrical sculpture with pieces of fish. After building its sterling reputation on fish and seafood, Citarella expanded into meats and, most recently in fresh pasta.

Dean & Deluca

560 Broadway (Prince St.). ☎ 212/431-1691.

Expensive, yes, but not unconscionably so. To some loyal customers, the mark-up is justified merely by the aroma encountered at the front door: coffee, freshly baked bread, cheeses, fresh produce. White walls and marble floors are the minimalist setting for 10,000 square feet of exotic mushrooms, pâtés, terrines, produce, cheeses, smoked fish, pastas, an extraordinary selection of spices, herbs, honeys and jams, plus racks of kitchen utensils. Drink it all in with a cappuccino at the handsome coffee bar near the front door, perhaps with a fresh muffin or pastry.

E.A.T.

1064 Madison Ave. (81st St.). ☎ 212/772-0022.

Prepared dishes and baked goods are made on the premises, from sourdough and raisin bread to pâtés and complete meals. Teas, jams, salmon, and cheeses are imported. Prices are as eye-popping as the food.

Fairway

2127 Broadway (74th St.). ☎ 212/595-1888. No credit cards.

Unlike most of the shops on this list, the prices are low at Fairway, a mecca for New Yorkers from every neighborhood. Crimson rhubarb is heaped next to indigo Japanese eggplants, next to stacks of Portobello and shiitake mushrooms. Cheeses, pastas, and sausages are excellent. It is open from 7am until 11pm or midnight and is usually packed.

Grace's Marketplace

1237 3rd Ave. (71st St.). ☎ 212/737-0600.

Upper Eastsiders needn't journey across Central Park for their approximation of Zabar's. At Grace's, the pastries are special, and the air is filled with seductive

aromas from prepared dishes, fresh produce, and cheeses.
Breads come in bewildering variety.

Zabar's

2245 Broadway (80th St.). ☎ 212/787-2000.

Balducci's and Zabar's are the perennial contenders for
the throne of gourmet stores, but Zabar's may have
pulled ahead by virtue of its 2nd-floor expansion for
kitchenware. On the crowded 1st floor, cheese, coffee,
caviar, smoked fish, prepared terrines and entrees,
pumpernickel bread, ice cream, coffeecake, chopped
liver, herring, and other intoxicating sights and aromas
battle for attention.

Galleries

Although galleries are in the business of selling art,
browsers are welcome. Most galleries are open from
Tuesday to Saturday, usually from 10am to 5 or 6pm,
and a few are open on Monday as well. Summer, a
time when wealthy New Yorkers flee to the Hamptons,
is the slow season, with various closing periods, often
July or August, or both. The galleries cluster in 3 principal areas—Soho, 57th Street, and Madison Avenue
on the Upper East Side. Cheap, spacious industrial
lofts have made Chelsea the new hub of several major
galleries.

Walking tours, as those laid out below, are the prac-
tical way to get to know the galleries. Since they move
and close with the unpredictability of dance clubs,
however, the ones mentioned here are only samplings.
Most art houses offer a free citywide gallery guide with
complete listings. They often gather in substantial numbers under single roofs, forming de facto minimuseums,
and those locations are emphasized below.

Caveat emptor: The galleries' pricing policies bear
striking resemblances to those of Middle Eastern rug
merchants, relying on artists' reputations, market
factors, overhead costs, and informed and/or wishful
thinking. Bargaining is expected, even on very expensive artworks, but don't expect to negotiate reductions
akin to those in the Casbah.

57th Street

Start on the west side of 5th Avenue, walking north
toward 57th Street to 724 5th Ave.

Grace Borgenicht (☎ 212/247-2111). The
New York School and movements that followed.

Holly Solomon (☎ 212/941-5777). Moderns.

Krausharr (☎ 212/307-5730). Recent sculpture. At 752 5th Ave.:

Mary Boone (☎ 212/752-2929). Contemporary giants.

Turn west (left) on 57th St., walking along the south side to 24 West 57th St. Among many are:

Arras (☎ 212/751-0080). Multimedia works by living artists.

Jack Tilton (☎ 212/941-1775). New paintings and sculpture.

Marian Goodman (☎ 212/977-7160). Living Americans.

Reece (☎ 212/333-5830). Contemporary sculptures and paintings.

Suzuki Graphics (☎ 212/582-0373).

At 40 W. 57th St.:

Frumpkin/Adams (☎ 212/757-6655). Figurative artists.

Kennedy (☎ 212/541-9600). American graphics and figurative paintings since 18thC.

Marlborough (☎ 212/541-4900). 19th and 20thC works in many styles and media.

At 50 W. 57th St.:

Lillian Heidenberg (☎ 212/628-6110). Impressionists and Postimpressionists.

Luise Ross (☎ 212/307-0400). Recent paintings and sculpture.

Tatistcheff (☎ 212/664-0907). Young Americans.

Terry Dintenfass (☎ 212/581-2268). Recent representational work.

Cross to the north side of 57th Street and walk east to 41 W. 57th St.:

Brewster (☎ 212/980-1975). Modern masters, American, European, and Mexican.

Sherry French (☎ 212/247-2457). Recent landscapes and figurative paintings.

Schmidt-Bingham (☎ 212/888-1122). Landscapes and representational images.

Tibor de Nagy (☎ 212/421-3780). A range of modern paintings and sculpture.

At 41 E. 57th St. The Fuller Building has 25 galleries, including:

ACA (☎ 212/644-8300). Contemporary American and European painting and sculpture.

Andre Emmerich (☎ 212/752-0124). Paintings and sculpture since the 1950s.

James Goodman (☎ 212/593-3737). Calder, Hepworth, and other 20thC masters.

Jan Krugier (☎ 212/755-7288). Specializes in Picasso and other 20th-century European masters.

Marisa del Re (☎ 212/688-1843). Postwar Europeans.

Madison Avenue

Many of these galleries are on side streets, but near Madison Avenue. Start at 63rd Street and walk north.

Wildenstein (19 E. 64th St., ☎ 212/879-0500). 17th–20thC paintings, sculpture, and furniture.

Knoedler (19 E. 70th St., ☎ 212/794-0550). Prominent dealer in American vanguardists.

Hirschl & Adler (21 E. 70th St., ☎ 212/535-8810). British and American 20thC art, including folk and modern artists.

Avanti (22 E. 72nd St., ☎ 212/628-3377). Contemporary Americans from 1960s forward.

Mary-Anne Martin (23 E. 73rd St., ☎ 212/288-2213). Latin American painters.

Jane Kahan (922 Madison Ave., ☎ 212/744-1490). Important 20thC Americans and Europeans.

Sindin (956 Madison Ave., ☎ 212/288-7902). European, Latin, and North American masters since 1900.

Solomon & Co. (959 Madison Ave., ☎ 212/737-8200). 19th and 20thC sculptors and painters.

David Findlay (984 Madison Ave., ☎ 212/249-2909). Primarily figurative paintings.

Weintraub (988 Madison Ave., ☎ 212/ 879-1195). Mostly sculpture, by Henry Moore, Calder, Giacometti, et al.

Graham (1014 Madison Ave., ☎ 212/ 535-5767). 19th and 20thC Americans.

Acquavella (18 E. 79th St., ☎ 212/734-6300). French postimpressionists and American abstractionists.

SoHo

SoHo was once the only place in the city where avant-garde artists could afford to defy accepted boundaries—and commercial viability. But the artists attracted dealers, galleries drew big spenders, and pricey boutiques quickly followed, to compete for rents that have become some of the city's highest. SoHo is consequently a commercial mecca now, rather than a hotbed of creativity. Nevertheless, it is still—however tenuously—the principal art marketplace in New York.

The galleries are concentrated in the area bounded by Houston Street on the north, Grand Street on the south, West Broadway, and Broadway (4 blocks apart in downtown's scrambled geography.) Those mentioned here are a sampling, largely of buildings with 3 or more galleries. Keep in mind that even prominent dealers move to new quarters without warning.

Walk south on West Broadway from Houston Street.

Nancy Hoffman (429 W. Broadway, ☎ 212/ 966-6676).

Sonnabend (420 W. Broadway, ☎ 212/ 966-6160).

Charles Cowles (☎ 212/925-3500).

Leo Castelli (☎ 212/431-5160).

Gimpel/Weitzenhoffer (415 W. Broadway, ☎ 212/925-6090).

Witkin (☎ 212/925-5510).

Turn east on Spring St.:

Stux (155 Spring St., ☎ 212/219-0010).

Turn north on Broadway, to 548 Broadway:

Exit Art/The First World (☎ 212/966-7745).

At 560 Broadway, among many:

Wolff (☎ 212/431-7833).

Jack Shainman (☎ 212/966-3866).

Max Protetch (☎ 212/966-5454).

David Nolan (☎ 212/925-6190).

Perlow (☎ 212/941-1220).

Stephen Haller (☎ 212/219-2500).

Julie Saul (☎ 212/431-0747).

At 583 Broadway:

New Museum of Contemporary Art (☎ 212/219-1355). Multiple simultaneous exhibitions. Turn west on Houston Street, then south on Mercer Street to 164 Mercer St.

Pleiades (☎ 212/274-8825).

John Szoke Graphics (☎ 212/219-8300).

Blom & Dorn (☎ 212/606-4254).

Turn west on Prince Street, then north on Greene Street to 142 Greene St.

Sperone Westwater (☎ 212/431-3685).

John Weber (☎ 212/966-6115).

Pace (☎ 212/421-3292).

A few other don't-miss galleries in the neighborhood:

The Drawing Center (35 Wooster, ☎ 212/431-7833).

The Earth Room (141 Wooster, ☎ 212/473-8072).

Sean Kelly (43 Mercer, ☎ 212/343-2405).

West Chelsea

Many wonder whether this remote warehouse district, in the low 20s between 10th and 11th avenues, can become "the next SoHo." Rents are cheap, but the subway is far away, the neighborhood is deserted by day and can be dangerous by night, and art shoppers will find few amenities like restaurants. By fall 1996, however, several prominent galleries will have relocated here and are expected to inspire mass migration to Chelsea on the Hudson.

Metro Pictures (513–523 W. 24th St., ☎ 212/206-7100).

Barbara Gladstone (513–523 W. 24th St., ☎ 212/431-3334). American, English, and German conceptual work.

DIA Center for the Arts (548 W. 22nd St., ☎ 212/989-5912). Extended exhibitions of major contemporaries.

Matthew Marks Gallery (522 W. 22nd St., ☎ 212/243-1650).

Paula Cooper (534 W. 21st St., ☎ 212/674-0766). Works by established artists.

Home Furnishings

Sure a four-poster bed is large, but no one's expecting you to pack it in your suitcase or store it in the overhead bin. These places do ship, and they also have small decorative items that can make all the difference in a room. Here are a very few of the city's home decor stores, most of them open on Sunday afternoons.

ABC Carpet & Home

888 Broadway (19th St.). ☎ 212/473-3000. Open Sun.

As the name implies, this downtown store has all manner of carpets, rugs, and other floor coverings. Plus it has an attractive assortment of other merchandise for the home, from antiques to bed linens, that has made the store one of New Yorkers' favorites.

Ceramica

59 Thompson St. (Spring St.). ☎ 212/941-1307. Open Sun.

Colorful Mediterranean ceramics in profusion— hand-painted and glazed terra-cotta jugs, vases, amphoras, and bowls—are on display at good prices. Italian, Portuguese, and Moroccan products dominate.

Crate & Barrel

650 Madison Ave. (59th St.). ☎ 212/308-0004. Open Sun.

The legendary Chicago store has landed in Manhattan—finally. The store has comfortable, if somewhat pricey, furniture, but where it really shines is in the extensive and creative selection of everything imaginable for cooking and entertaining. Prices for the kitchen items and housewares tend to be in the "that's worth it" category.

The Gazebo

114 E. 57th St. (near Park Ave.). ☎ 212/832-7077. Open Sun.

Quilts, handmade and bountiful, are the focus, with braided rag rugs and appliquéd curtains and pillow covers adding accents.

Maxilla & Mandible

451–5 Columbus Ave. (bet. 81st and 82nd sts.). ☎ 212/724-6173. Open Sun.

This little shop doesn't quite belong under this heading, but then, it's difficult to fit anywhere. Why? Because what we have on sale here are bones. Skulls, animal and human. Skewered butterflies and beetles. Hippo teeth. Antlers. It sounds grisly, but it is, in fact, fascinating. Appropriately, it's only steps away from the American Museum of Natural History.

Pavillon Christofle
680 Madison Ave. (62nd St.). ☎ 212/308-9390. Open Sun.

Silver and crystal are the raison d'être of this Parisian firm, founded in 1830. The designs it sells are exquisite and often highly contemporary, without being at all stuffy. A range of porcelain is also available.

Portico Home
379 W. Broadway (bet. Spring and Broom sts.). ☎ 212/941-7800. Open Sun.

A tasteful collection of finely crafted furniture, some antique and some newly constructed, together with unusual decorative pieces. A nearby offshoot, Portico Bed & Bath (139 Spring St.; ☎ 212/941-7722), has iron beds and the like.

Ségriès A Solanée
866 Lexington Ave. (65th St.). ☎ 212/439-6109. Closed Sat in summer.

Glassware, pottery, linens in the style of haute Provence. Full dinner services, platters and tureens, quilts, and even a selection of Provençal furniture are on hand.

Takashimaya New York
693 5th Ave. (bet. 54th and 55th sts.). Closed Sun.

Despite the Japanese moniker, Takashimaya bills itself as an international store. The Asian and French influences, though, are probably the strongest in this exquisite array of furniture, articles, and art. On the lower level is a jewel box of a cafe, and on the 1st floor is one of the best florists in town, Christian Tortu.

Jewelry
From the waiting limousines to the understated window displays and the hushed, almost ecclesiastical interiors, Cartier, Harry Winston, Tiffany & Co., and Van Cleef & Arpels, the Titans of the retail trade in gold, gems, silver, and watches, breathe an ever-tasteful opulence. Dress for the occasion. All of them have a well-crafted trinket or two at relatively modest cost for those who take pleasure in doing business in fine establishments.

Department-store marketing techniques are used by Fortunoff, and its stock consists of fine jewelry and watches, antique silver, and flatware. There are 4 floors, and prices are reasonable, as these things go.

While all these shops are within a few steps of each other, true comparison shopping is best undertaken along 47th Street, between 5th and 6th avenues, known as the Diamond District. Every imaginable sort of jewelry is on hand in shoulder-to-shoulder (and floor-upon-floor) shops that sell nothing else. Start at the International Jewelers Exchange, with its dealers installed in 84 cubicles, then work west along 47th Street, crossing to the opposite side and returning east. Prices are often negotiable, so it's best to delay purchase until several trays of the desired object have been examined.

Bulgari, 730 5th Ave. (57th St.), ☎ 212/ 315-9000; with a branch at 2 E. 61st St. (5th Ave.), ☎ 212/486-0326.

Cartier, 5th Ave. and 52nd St., ☎ 212/ 753-0111.

Michael C. Fina, 580 5th Ave. (78th St.), ☎ 212/869-5050.

Fortunoff, 681 5th Ave. (near 54th St.), ☎ 212/758-6660.

International Jewelers Exchange, 5th Ave. and 47th St., ☎ 212/869-1528.

Tiffany & Co., 5th Ave. and 57th St., ☎ 212/ 755-8000.

Van Cleef & Arpels, 5th Ave. and 57th St., ☎ 212/644-9500.

Harry Winston, 718 5th Ave. (56th St.), ☎ 212/245-2000.

Museum Stores

See individual entries in "Sights and Attractions" for addresses and telephone numbers.

Predictably, the shop in the Metropolitan Museum of Art is largest, with excellent reproductions of many items in the collections, notably jewelry and carvings, as well as art books and illustrated catalogs. The National Museum of the American Indian has handcrafted "squash-blossom" necklaces, silver belt buckles, "concha" belts, and Navajo rugs. Reproductions of Egyptian jewelry and authentic Latin

American ceramics and dolls are the specialty of the Brooklyn Museum.

Books and posters once dominated at the Museum of Modern Art, but its new design shop, on the opposite side of the street from the museum, has a greatly expanded inventory of exquisite glassware, pottery, flatware, garden shears, and clocks.

The Jewish Museum has brass candlesticks and menorahs, mezuzah boxes, and jewelry. At the Cooper-Hewitt Museum, Christmastime brings out the tree ornaments and toys. The shop at the Museum of American Folk Art stocks quilts and crafts, antique and contemporary. Garments of Latin American Indian textiles, exotic jewelry, and stuffed toy animals fill the 2 shops of the American Museum of Natural History.

Pharmacies

The typical New York pharmacy, whether part of a large chain or a small, independently-owned store, offers a selection of personal-care items and toiletries, cosmetics and fragrances, and, of course, prescription and nonprescription medicines. Be sure to bring along your doctor's prescription. Foreign visitors should also bear in mind that certain drugs that can be bought without prescription at home require one here. Two of the oldest pharmacies in New York are Caswell-Massey (established 1752) and Bigelow Pharmacy (established 1838). The Duane Reade chain, with locations all over town, is noted for its discounts.

Bigelow Pharmacy
414 6th Ave. (near 8th St.). ☎ 212/533-2700.
Still in its original quarters, and open every day.

Caswell-Massey
518 Lexington Ave. (near 48th St.). ☎ 212/755-2254. Closed Sunday.
Caswell-Massey blended soaps and colognes for George Washington and Sarah Bernhardt, and its products are good both for gifts and for souvenirs.

Kaufman Pharmacy
Lexington Ave. and 50th St. ☎ 212/755-2266.
Open 24 hours a day, 7 days a week.

Zitome
969 Madison Ave. (between 75th and 76th streets).
☎ 212/737-2037 or 212/737-5560.
An upscale pharmacy, complete with a prestige cosmetics department, toys, and a delivery service.

Records, CDs & Tapes

All genres can be had (yes, even country). Although the vernacular is still "record store," most of these music emporia concentrate on CDs. Some shops manage to eke out a living dealing in used LPs.

Bleecker Bob's Golden Oldies

118 W. 3rd St. (near 6th Ave.). ☎ 212/475-9677. Open daily.

This Village institution has enough endearing quirks to amuse any audiophile. It doesn't open until noon, but doesn't close until 1am (3am Sat, Sun). The huge inventory concentrates on rock in its many forms, but has recordings of other musical persuasions, too.

HMV Music

72nd & Broadway. ☎ 212/721-5900. Open daily until midnight.

A new and large music chain, with 3 floors of CDs and audio and video cassettes, as well as a Ticketmaster booth for the purchase of tickets to Broadway shows.

Sam Goody

666 3rd Ave. (E. 43rd St.). ☎ 212/986-8480. Open Sun also, noon–5pm.

Records and tapes in all categories. Audio equipment, musical instruments, and sheet music are also on sale. Additional branches at 51 West 51st Street; 901 6th Avenue; 575 5th Avenue; and 42nd Street and 2nd Avenue.

Tower Records

4th St. and Broadway. ☎ 212/505-1505. Open daily.

A chain with several locations in Manhattan, Tower encourages hanging out. With as many as 50,000 different recordings in all formats, plus videos and books, browsing for hours is easy. The discounted prices are good to excellent.

Virgin Megastore

Broadway at 45th St. ☎ 212/921-1020. Open daily.

Another recent entry in the music-superstore category. CD and tapes are here by the boatload—though the selection is not as extensive as you'd expect. The store also sells videotapes, laser discs, and books. A cafe is in the basement, as well as a multiplex theater.

Sports & Camping Equipment

Ever-competitive New Yorkers relieve stress and relive their youth on dozens of tracks, courts, playing fields, and StairMasters around the city. No enthusiasm is denied, and discounting of list prices is widely practiced.

Athlete's Foot
390 5th Ave. (36th St.). ☎ 212/947-6972.

Runners stop here, or at one of its six branches, for its full line of footwear and warm-up suits.

Eastern Mountain Sports
20 W. 61st (Broadway). ☎ 212/397-4860.

Camping and hiking are emphasized.

Paragon
867 Broadway (near E. 18th St.). ☎ 212/255-8036. Open daily.

Huge stock of general sporting goods.

Spiegels
Nassau and Ann streets. ☎ 212/227-8400. Closed Saturday in summer.

For all sports in lower Manhattan, at discounted prices.

Toys

Many visitors begin and end with FAO Schwarz, but other shops stock their own brand of fantasy equally compelling to children and those who love them. All of them will wrap and ship.

FAO Schwarz
767 5th Ave. (58th St.). ☎ 212/644-9400. Open Sun.

Ten-foot-high stuffed giraffes, child-sized cars, marionettes, electric trains, and baby dolls only begin to fill the 3 floors of a child's heaven. Standing at the center is an elevator disguised as a giant robot.

Penny Whistle
1283 Madison Ave. (near 91st St.). ☎ 212/369-3868.

A designated soap bubble-blowing bear guarding the front door, Penny Whistle is a charming toy store that actually encourages its young patrons to test the wares. The West Side has a branch at 448 Columbus Ave.

Toy Park
112 E. 86th St. (bet. Lexington and Park aves.). ☎ 212/427-6611. Also at 626 Columbus Ave. (near 90th St.), NY 10024. ☎ 212/769-3880.

Extra-large toy emporia, with play areas for children so grownups can shop.

Toys "Я" Us
1293 Broadway (Herald Square). ☎ 212/594-8697.

Another outpost of the highly successful chain, this one has 45,000 square feet of heavily advertised Barbie dolls, Tonka trucks, and Nintendos.

Wines & Liquor

Special sales are frequent, sometimes of wine from unexpected countries—Lebanon, Chile, Yugoslavia. Their advantage is price, of course. Choices can be bewildering, but the salespeople at the following shops are generally helpful. All liquor stores are closed on Sunday; most accept credit cards and make deliveries.

Astor Wines & Spirits, 12 Astor Pl. (near Lafayette St.), ☎ 212/674-7500.

Embassy Liquors, 796 Lexington Ave. (near 61st St.), ☎ 212/838-6551.

Morrell & Co., 535 Madison Ave. (54th St.), ☎ 212/688-9370.

Sherry-Lehmann, 679 Madison Ave. (E. 61st St.), ☎ 212/838-7500.

67 Wines & Spirits, 179 Columbus Ave. (W. 67th St.), ☎ 212/724-6767.

SoHo Wines & Spirits, 461 West Broadway (Prince St.), ☎ 212/777-4332.

THE ARTS

With the possible exception of Rome and, in a different way, New Orleans, few cities come alive at night the way New York does. What's as amazing as the density of people prowling the streets after dark is their diversity. It's not just club kids and partiers hitting the dance and rock clubs, but people in their 30s, 40s, 50s, and older, hearing their favorite style of music, taking in a Broadway show, having a drink at a cabaret, enjoying their season tickets at the opera or the ballet, having a laugh at a comedy club, or trying to appreciate some experimental form of performing arts. Many haunts stay open until 4am, which might explain why New Yorkers are so fond of starting work as late as 10am. There's always a predawn breakfast at a 24-hour diner or a box of Entenmann's from the corner deli.

Presented with such a banquet of choices, some people can be paralyzed with indecision. My advice: Spend one evening doing something you've always imagined to be the real New York, whether it's a big, splashy musical on Broadway, a night at the opera, or a concert at Carnegie Hall. Then spend another evening trying something totally different, be it a jazz club, a piano bar, or an experimental dance performance.

On the topic of dress code, the middle-aged establishment has fewer rules than today's supposedly rebellious youth. Trendy dance clubs, for example, are known to turn away people at the door if they are clad in sneakers and jeans. Broadway theaters, on the other hand, are full of underdressed enthusiasts. My advice, though, is to leave the jeans in the hotel room unless you're planning a night of rock clubs, stand-up comedy, Off-Off-Broadway, or barhopping. While certainly not required, a jacket (and maybe even a tie)—and similarly festive women's dress—may contribute to the special experience of seeing a ballet or an opera

Discount Tickets, Etc.

If money is a consideration, remember that discounts are available for many Broadway shows. Good seats at a hit musical can run as high as $75 a pop (at last count); seats are not cheap even at the back of the theater. You do, however, have ways of reducing the bite. Productions nearing the end of their runs often issue coupons to shops, hotels, and other businesses. Take the coupons to the box office of the appropriate theater and receive 2 tickets at a 33% discount. Or, visit the TKTS booth at the north end of Times Square (at 47th St.) on the day you wish to attend (Mon–Sat 3–8pm for evening performances; Sun noon–8pm, Wed, Sat 10am–2pm for matinees). In a very orderly fashion, the outpost sells unsold seats at substantial discounts, although not for all plays, of course. The line begins forming about 45 minutes to an hour before the booth opens. The blockbuster musicals are usually the first to go.

Additional TKTS booths are on the mezzanine at 2 World Trade Center (open Mon–Fri 11am–5:30pm, Sat 11am–1pm), and at Court and Montague streets in downtown Brooklyn (Tues–Thurs 11am–2pm and 2:30–5:30pm; Fri 11am–5:30pm; Sat 11am–3:30pm).

Many theaters accept telephone or mail orders for tickets to their current productions. Their numbers are listed in the daily "Theater Directory" of the *New York Times.* Have a credit card ready when calling. If there is time, theaters can mail the tickets; otherwise pick them up at the box office, usually on the day of performance. You also can buy tickets in person at the theater box offices, but the hours are typically limited.

The other common means of obtaining tickets is through independent tickets-by-telephone agencies, which represent most theaters and sports arenas. The major ones are Ticketmaster (☎ 212/307-7171) and Telecharge (☎ 212/239-6200 or 800/233-3123). They take orders 24 hours a day, 7 days a week. A surcharge is added to credit card purchases. Ticketron has outlets throughout the city and suburbs selling tickets for most Broadway and Off-Broadway productions (and concerts and sports events, too). Ticket brokers and hotel concierges can handle requests, but be sure that their handling fee will not exceed the going rate.

at the stunning **Lincoln Center.** As for the proper attire at a Broadway show, I recommend dressy casual, unless it's opening night, in which case you'll see plenty of folks in black tie. And for an evening at an old-fashioned supper club, go ahead and glam it up.

Not even the most avid of culture seekers, blessed with unlimited funds and few encumbrances, could exhaust the music, dance, and theater options the city spreads before us for 12 months of the year. If you have your heart set on a particular play or performance, you may want to arrange for tickets well before arriving in town. But if you're up for anything, you can take advantage of same-day discounts and of staying flexible, deciding at the last minute, say, to hit that jazz bar or a foreign flick.

For arts and entertainment **listings,** check the weekly newspaper the *Village Voice* (especially for off-beat, avant-garde fare), or the *New York Times* (particularly Friday's "Weekend" and Sunday's "Arts & Leisure" sections). The weekly *New York* magazine, *Time Out New York,* and the *New Yorker,* offer comprehensive listings, as well.

New York Arts A to Z
Cinema

Films are of profound concern to many New Yorkers, often to the point of reverence. In strong-mindedly rejecting the foolishness of the notorious Cannes event, for example, the New York Film Festival (Alice Tully Hall, Lincoln Center, mid-Sept to early Oct) over-compensates on the side of solemnity. No prizes are awarded, no starlets reveal their bras, and few outsiders notice that anything happened.

Worthwhile films are introduced, nonetheless, some of which go on to limited release. "Art" films—often foreign-made and of slim domestic appeal—are showcased by managers who no doubt pray for the rare hit. Many are subtitled. Theaters specializing in such films have been known to switch to commercial releases, so check the newspapers or call ahead. Among them:

Angelika Film Center, Houston and Mercer streets, ☎ 212/995-2000.

Cineplex Odeon Art Greenwich, Greenwich Ave. and 12th St., ☎ 212/929-3350.

Cineplex Odeon Carnegie Hall, 7th Ave. and 57th St., ☎ 212/265-2520.

Cineplex Odeon Cinema 3, 59th St. (near 5th Ave.), ☎ 212/752-5959.

Lincoln Plaza, Broadway (near 63rd St.), ☎ 212/757-2280.

Sony Paris Fine Arts, 4 W. 58th St. (near 5th Ave.), ☎ 212/980-5656.

The Public Theater, 425 Lafayette St. (near E. 4th St.), ☎ 212/598-7171.

Quad Cinema, 13th St. (between 5th and 6th avenues), ☎ 212/255-8800.

In addition, several movie theaters specialize in revivals, often in "festival" or retrospective form. They can be high-minded or high camp, composed of movies foreign or domestic, from silents and early talkies to relatively modern films. Such theaters include:

Anthology Film Archives, 32-34 2nd Ave. (2nd St.), ☎ 212/505-5181.

Cinema Village, 22 E. 12th St. (near University Pl.), ☎ 212/924-3363.

Cineplex Odeon Waverly Twin, 323 Ave. of the Americas (W. 3rd St.) ☎ 212/929-8037.

Film Forum, 209 W. Houston St. (near 6th Ave.), ☎ 212/727-8110.

Walter Reade, 165 W. 65th St. (Lincoln Center), ☎ 212/875-5600.

Several museums have regular film programs. The most comprehensive is at the Museum of Modern Art (11 W. 53rd St. at 6th Ave.; ☎ 212/708-9480). Also try the American Museum of the Moving Image (35th Ave. and 36th St., Queens; ☎ 718/784-4520) and the Museum of Television and Radio (25 W. 52nd St.; ☎ 212/621-6600).

For first-run Hollywood movies, check the *Village Voice,* the *New York Times,* or another daily.

Classical Music

Avery Fisher Hall (Lincoln Center; ☎ 212/875-5020) is home for the New York Philharmonic and its German conductor, Kurt Masur. When the orchestra is not in residence, all manner of visiting organizations fill the seats, as diverse as the Bulgarian State Female Choir and the Royal Liverpool Philharmonic. Chamber orchestras, string quartets, and instrumentalists perform at Alice Tully Hall (Lincoln Center; ☎ 212/875-5050). The National Orchestra of New York and such large out-of-town organizations as the Philadelphia and Cleveland orchestras play at Carnegie Hall (57th St. and 7th Ave.; ☎ 212/247-7800), while smaller groups and individual artists use the attached Weill Recital Hall.

Venues used by classical artists as well as by pop, dance, jazz, and/or rock ensembles include Merkin Concert Hall (129 W. 67th St.; ☎ 212/362-8719), Town Hall (123 W. 43rd St.; ☎ 212/840-2824), the Tisch Center for the Arts of the 92nd Street Y (Lexington Ave.; ☎ 212/415-5440), the Brooklyn Academy of Music (30 Lafayette Ave.; ☎ 718/636-4100), and Symphony Space (Broadway and 95th St.; ☎ 212/864-5400). Florence Gould Hall (55 E. 59th St.; ☎ 212/355-6160 or 212/355-6100) often showcases French chamber groups and instrumentalists as well as dance. Also, check the Metropolitan Museum of Art (5th Ave. and 82nd St.; ☎ 212/570-3949) for recitals by individuals and small groups. As is to be expected, the renowned Juilliard School for the performing arts has its own theater for music, opera, and dance, at 60 Lincoln Center Plaza (☎ 212/799-5000). Tickets must be obtained but are usually free. The same is true at the Manhattan School of Music (120 Claremont Ave.; ☎ 212/749-2802). New music has a regular outlet at The Kitchen (512 W. 19th St.; ☎ 212/255-5793).

A service similar to TKTS (see page 224) offers half-price day-of-performance tickets for opera, classical music, and dance events. A modest service charge is added. Look for the booth in Bryant Park on 42nd Street, near 6th Avenue (☎ 212/382-2323 after 12:30pm; open Tues, Thurs, Fri noon–2pm and 3–7pm; Wed, Sat 11am–2pm and 3–7pm; Sun noon–6pm). It also sells full-price tickets for future performances. To charge tickets by phone for events at **Lincoln Center,** call Centercharge at ☎ 212/721-6500.

Dance

No other city enjoys ballet in such abundance and variety. In addition to a dozen or more locally-based companies, the troupes of other cities and nations are regular visitors. The best-known companies are American Ballet Theater (at the Metropolitan Opera House, Lincoln Center; ☎ 212/769-7000,) and New York City Ballet (at the New York State Theater, Lincoln Center; ☎ 212/870-5570). The ABT, which long had Mikhail

Baryshnikov as its artistic director and has seen performances by most of the other famous Russian emigrés, now has Kevin McKenzie at the creative helm. To be honest, both troupes have had their problems of late, but both also can turn in soaring performances.

Numerous other venues frequently host dance performances. The Brooklyn Academy of Music (30 Lafayette Ave. in downtown Brooklyn; ☎ 718/636-4100) makes room for experimental works in its annual Next Wave festival and also presents such companies as the Martha Graham troupe, the Dance Theatre of Harlem, and the Pennsylvania Dance Company, in addition to music, theater, and opera productions. City Center (131 W. 55th St., between 6th and 7th avenues; ☎ 212/581-1212) has a modern inclination, with such troupes as the Merce Cunningham Dance Company, the Alvin Ailey American Dance Theater, and the Paul Taylor Dance Company all making appearances in recent seasons.

The avant-garde, including combined experimental dance and poetry readings, are the focus of the DIA Center for the Arts (155 Mercer St.; ☎ 212/431-9233), which gives weekday performances in SoHo. The Joyce Theater (175 8th Ave. at 19th St.; ☎ 212/242-0800) also provides a space for avant-garde efforts, often by skilled troupes from abroad. It's also the permanent home of the Feld Ballets/NY.

Some other spaces that regularly book dance performances are: Manhattan Center Studios, 311 West 34th Street, ☎ 212/279-7740, which has featured the innovative Mark Morris Dance Group; Symphony Space, 2537 Broadway, ☎ 212/864-5400; Bessie Schönberg Theater, 219 West 19th Street, ☎ 212/924-0077; Florence Gould Hall, 55 East 59th Street, ☎ 212/355-6160; Performance Space, 150 1st Avenue, ☎ 212/477-5288; St. Mark's-in-the-Bowery, 2nd Avenue and 10th Street, ☎ 212/924-0077; Soundance Studio, 385 Broadway, ☎ 212/340-8043; and Theatre for the New City, 155 1st Avenue, ☎ 212/254-1109.

Jazz

It can be argued that America's purest music should be listed among the smoky cellar clubs and grungy bars in which it is so often heard, not here among the divas and corps de ballet. But jazz is probably this continent's most original art form, its practitioners as profoundly skilled as any who work the operatic and symphonic genres. From Benny Goodman to Wynton Marsalis, they cross over to the shores of classical music as readily as to those of pop and rock. Lincoln Center for the Performing Arts has belatedly recognized its importance, in 1991 establishing a jazz department charged with producing year-round concerts.

Jazz was born in New Orleans and journeyed up the Mississippi to Kansas City and Chicago, ultimately destined for New York, where it thrives today. Jazz musicians were not—are not—certain of recognition until they were accepted here. One of their number was credited with the invention of that celebrated nickname for the metropolis: "I made it, brother, I'm going to the Big Apple."

Jazz flourished and grew in New York from World War I into the 1950s. It persists, as vital as ever, available in all its permutations—Dixieland, swing, fusion, mainstream, bop, progressive, and wildly experimental. It is performed in old-line clubs that have been on the scene for 50 years and in 5th-floor lofts that are no more settled than Bedouins. Concerts are also held in the halls of colleges and churches all over town, and jazz brunches are often mounted Sundays at restaurants that have no other regular live entertainment.

In June, a citywide jazz festival brings in the biggest names in the business. They perform indoors and out, in clubs and concert halls, and often for free.

Call Jazzline (☎ 212/479-7888) for a daily recorded announcement on jazz events. The clubs listed below are a good place to start. Cover charges vary, but as a general rule, listening from the bar is less expensive than sitting at a table. All accept major credit cards unless otherwise noted.

The Blue Note (131 W. 3rd St. at Ave. of the Americas; ☎ 212/475-8592; open nightly) should be at the top of jazz-lovers' must lists. New York's premier jazz showcase boasts a long roster of performers that includes just about every notable artist, past and present, from Nancy Wilson and Joe Williams to Illinois Jacquet and Tito Puente. Naturally, it's packed with fans nearly every night. Headliners have two shows during the week, three on Friday and Saturday, and afterwards, a house trio jams on until 4am. On weekends, the Blue Note offers matinees with late brunch. Minimum and cover charges vary but are never small. To lessen the bite, listen from the bar.

The Knitting Factory is quickly becoming an essential stop (74 Leonard St., between Broadway and Church St.; ☎ 212/219-3006 or 212/219-3055; open nightly). Owner Michael Dorf books mainstream jazz musicians alongside more avant-garde ones in an attempt to broaden the genre. Patrons drink Rolling Rock and are an attentive lot, treating the music as the centerpiece, not as a backdrop. From time to time, acoustical folkies, and people who don't fit into pigeonholes, take one of the three TriBeCa stages. The first of two nightly sets usually begins between 8 and 9pm.

If you're more interested in music as background to good conversation, try **Bradley's** (70 University Pl. at 11th St.; ☎ 212/473-9700; open daily), a bright, bubbling spot with good burgers and even better "straight-ahead" mainstream duos and trios. They tune up three times nightly, somewhere around 10pm, midnight, and 2am. Not infrequently, but always late, name musicians drop by to jam. The $12 to $15 cover charge is often reduced for later sets.

Village Vanguard (178 7th Ave. S., near 11th St.; ☎ 212/255-4037; open nightly) delivers mainstream jazz nightly in the landmark cellar club that has been on the scene for over 50 years. The bands, often with 20 musicians or more, include the likes of Milt Jackson and Terence Blanchard. Two sets nightly Monday to Thursday, three Friday to Sunday. No food, just booze and music.

Sweet Basil (88 7th Ave. S. at Bleecker St.; ☎ 212/242-1785; open daily) is another jazz club, housed in an attractive brick-and-wood setting and visited by such artists as Nat Adderley and Chris Conner. Music starts at 10pm; or show up for Saturday and Sunday afternoon sessions and avoid the cover charge. Meals from lunch through late supper are served, with jazz brunches on Saturday and Sunday.

At the jumping **Red Blazer Too** (349 W. 46th St., between 8th and 9th Avenues; ☎ 212/262-3112; open daily), the riffs and rumbles date back to the epoch between the Volstead Act and V-E Day. From the dawn of the Roaring Twenties, that is, when New Orleans checked into Prohibition Chicago with ragtime and Dixie, up to a few years after Goodman and Krupa had them dancing in the aisles at the old Paramount. Le jazz hot hadn't learned to be cool yet. Big bands often take the stand, and jazz brunches swing on Sunday.

A trouble-free Dixieland jazz is the sound of **The Cajun** (129 8th Ave. at 16th St.; ☎ 212/691-6174; open daily), which serves Creole-Cajun food, more or less, and occasionally leavens the mood serious blues.

As attractive as any club in the Village, the **Knickerbocker Bar & Grill** (33 University Pl. at 8th St.; ☎ 212/228-8490; closed Mon, Tues) features piano and bass duos and sometimes singers, all with no crowding, no cover, and a reasonable minimum at tables (none at the bar).

For a jolly, celebratory ambiance where patrons routinely show up in tuxedos and evening gowns, **B. Smith's Rooftop Cafe** (771 8th Ave. at 47th St.; ☎ 212/247-2222; open daily; music on Fri and Sat only) is right in the theater district. Upstairs, on a stage wrapped in glass, is the combo of the week. As a general rule, it is as cool and contained as its audience.

The far upper west side offers **Birdland** (2745 Broadway at 105th St.; ☎ 212/749-2228; open nightly). It's not the fabled Birdland of the 1940s and 1950s that hosted jazz greats Charlie Parker and Dave Brubeck and others of their prominence. This namesake is far from the midtown original and infrequently signs up stars of that luminosity. Buffs still think it worth the trek. Lesser-known practitioners such as the capable Jimmy Heath and Paul Ostermayer quartets are the rule, with occasional appearances by such legends as Milt Jackson. Management believes in a synergy of the senses: The menu is soul food.

Several establishments have managed to provide both good music and good food. **Andiamo** (312 5th Ave. at 32nd St.; ☎ 212/564-8498; open daily) is one. Mostly mainstream jazz complements the Italian food (and vice versa). On Sunday, there is an all-you-can-eat brunch with live blues groups. **Visiones** (125 MacDougal St. at Bleecker St.; ☎ 212/673-5576; open nightly) specializes in Spanish cuisine, perhaps an unlikely venue for jazz, but here it is, in the middle of the Village entertainment district. The groups on stage aren't marquee names, the reason a cover charge is zero much of the time. But don't think the performers don't give full measure every night at 9 and 11pm. Late third shows on Friday and Saturday, with jam sessions Monday night and Saturday afternoon. At **Zinno** (126 W. 13th St., near 7th Ave.; ☎ 212/924-5182; open daily), duos and trios (there isn't room for more) split their time between the bar and dining room nightly to tender immaculate versions of blues and mainstream jazz. It's not unlike a party at a friend's house. The bonus is the delicious, not too overpriced, Italian fare, which makes the minimum charge easy to meet. A cover is levied, too. Sets usually start at 8 or 9pm. Reservations are essential if you intend to eat.

Other Options

Those are just some of about 50 possibilities where jazz is the centerpiece. For a night (or brunch) out in which music is primarily a pleasant backdrop or a filler of gaps in conversation, choices include: **Tavern on the Green** (Central Park W. at W. 67th St.; ☎ 212/873-3200), which, though the definitive tourist restaurant, has made a valiant effort at attracting youngish New Yorkers with a respectable jazz scene in its Chestnut Room; **Café de la Paix** (Hotel St. Moritz, 50 Central Park S.; ☎ 212/755-5800), and **Hors d'Oeuvrerie** (1 World Trade Center; ☎ 212/938-1111).

Opera

Few forms of entertainment can match the drama, the spectacle, and the artistic accomplishments of opera. In New York, fans not only have 2 world-class companies, but they also can choose from a crop of smaller, locally based ones and touring companies. Full-scale productions are mounted during extended seasons of the Metropolitan Opera Company and the New York City Opera at the **Metropolitan Opera House** (Lincoln Center; ☎ 212/769-7000) and the **New York State Theater** (Lincoln Center; ☎ 212/870-5570), respectively. The Met has introduced subtitles, a controversial move intended to make the art form less intimidating and more accessible. Both theaters also host visiting companies.

City Center (131 W. 55th St.; ☎ 212/581-7907) is an important site for smaller touring and regional companies, while Gilbert and Sullivan and Victor Herbert fans support a year-long season at the **Light Opera of Manhattan** (Playhouse, (316 E. 91st St.; ☎ 212/831-2000).

Singing principals of these and other companies perform in concerts in other venues around the city, including:

Alice Tully Hall, Lincoln Center, ☎ 212/875-5050.

Brooklyn Academy of Music, 30 Lafayette Ave. (downtown Brooklyn), ☎ 718/636-4100.

Carnegie Hall, 57th St. and 7th Ave., ☎ 212/247-7800.

Town Hall, 123 W. 43rd St., ☎ 212/840-2824.

Amateurs and young professionals form the companies of the **Amato Opera Theater** (319 Bowery; ☎ 212/228-8200). A source for small-scale contemporary opera (veering over the edge into performance art) is **La Mamma** (74A E. 4th St.; ☎ 212/475-7710). **The Juilliard Opera Center,** tapping its talent from the eponymous performing arts school, mounts skilled productions (155 W. 65th St.; ☎ 212/799-5000).

Theater

Doomsayers have been predicting the death of the New York theater since the invention of talking movies. As recently as 1990, it looked as if the final curtains might have fallen. Then the 1991–1992 season arrived and theatergoers spent more money on tickets than ever before in Broadway history, over $292 million. That result was due in large measure to higher prices—the musical *Miss Saigon* hit the $100-per-ticket plateau. But attendance figures were higher, too, provoked substantially by the resuscitation of the American musical, both original and in revival. But one has to question the health of the art form: Andrew Lloyd Webber's *Sunset Boulevard* won the Tony Award for best original musical by default. It was the only Broadway show mounted during that season with an original score.

Broadway, the avenue, long ago gave its name to Broadway, the theater district. Few of the 36 theaters actually front onto that thoroughfare, however. Rather, they cluster on the side streets around Times Square. Here are the lavish musicals, popular intimate comedies, and, against heavy odds, the occasional serious drama.

Economics mitigated against experimentation, so that role traditionally has been assumed by what came to be known as Off-Broadway—smaller houses with lower overheads and greater daring. Many of these theaters are found in and near Greenwich Village, but they are also located throughout Manhattan. Alternative theater, often raw and wildly avant-garde, is known as Off-Off-Broadway. These productions might be mounted in garages, churches, lofts, backrooms of restaurants, galleries, anywhere.

For information on obtaining discounted tickets, see "Discount Tickets, Etc." at the beginning of this chapter.

NEW YORK
AFTER DARK

INTENSE, STRESSFUL DAYS IN THE BIG CITY BEGET
electrified nights. All that energy has to go somewhere. New Yorkers—and those who stop over here—
channel it into pursuits of the physical kind, such
as dancing, and of the more emotional variety, such as
listening to music or seeing a stand-up comic. The
nightly catharsis enables them to face the subway and
work in the morning.

As they do with restaurants, New Yorkers tend to
tire easily of their after-dark playgrounds. Not for nothing has the phrase "faster than a New York minute"
shouldered its way into the American lexicon. The rec-
ommendations below scratch the surface, and I guarantee some of them will have sunk into oblivion by the
time you arrive in town. Many of these bars and clubs,
such as CBGB's and Cafe Carlyle, are hardy perennials,
though, and nearly always, younger, brasher competitors surround them, so seeking out one is bound to
expose others.

Liquor laws are relatively liberal. Establishments serving alcoholic beverages are required to close at 4am
and may not reopen until 8am (noon on Sunday),
although most do not open before 11am, and lock up
whenever business is slow. Anyone 21 and over can
purchase liquor. Some bars and clubs set higher age
limits and require 2 forms of positive identification.

Bars and clubs offering live entertainment often fix
a cover charge (basically an admission fee); and the range
can be considerable, depending on the standard or elabo-
rateness of the show. In dance clubs it tends to rise with
the chicness of the place. It might be collected at the
door or simply added to the check. Many establishments, particularly those with table service, also levy a

minimum charge for consumption of beverages and/or food, per person.

Fine food and good music infrequently appear in combination, although the city has seen some improvement on that score. Getting something to eat—a hamburger, a bowl of chili—is nearly always possible, but in general expect no more than alleviation of hunger pangs. So if your schedule and wallet allow, eat first, then do the night-crawling thing.

To learn who is appearing where, consult the entertainment listings of the Friday and Sunday editions of the *New York Times,* the weekly magazines *New York, Time Out New York,* and the *New Yorker,* and, for more offbeat diversions, the weekly newspaper the *Village Voice.* Even then, call ahead for reservations and to inquire about last-minute changes in hours and performers. And, for that matter, to find out if the place still exists.

New York Nightlife A to Z
Bars & Lounges

Passing the night in a bar (or several) is a common diversion and, except when it becomes an addiction, not as decadent as it sounds. I've tried to compile a group that are a bit more interesting, in terms of either the people who patronize them or the mood they stir. Of course, to some devotees, a bar is like a poem; those that speak to some will leave others unimpressed. Unless otherwise noted, all bars are open 7 days a week, usually from 11am or noon until at least 2am.

If you prefer to take your spirits in an atmosphere of history, among the ghosts of drunks past—be they literary or working-class—several such downtown establishments survive. **Fanelli's** (94 Prince St. in SoHo; ☎ 212/226-9412; closed Sat, Sun) predates the Civil War—and looks it. Neighborhood working men share it with recent artistic immigrants. **McSorley's Old Ale House** (15 E. 7th St.; ☎ 212/473-9148) is even older and did not miss a working day during the 13-year experiment called Prohibition. Only about 25 years ago did it grudgingly allow women inside the door.

Still no sign marks **Chumley's** (86 Bedford St. in Greenwich Village; ☎ 212/675-4449), and it retains the Bohemian aura of Edna St. Vincent Millay and Eugene O'Neill. Yellowing book jackets of former clients line the walls, and a working fireplace keeps the place warm in winter. Good burgers, too. O. Henry was a regular patron of **Pete's Tavern** (129 E. 18th St.;

☎ 212/473-7676), which opened in 1864. Sidewalk tables allow for warm-weather dining, with mostly Italian food.

Not far away is the 1890s' **Old Town Bar** (45 E. 18th St.; ☎ 212/529-6732), which retains its tile floor and molded tin ceiling. The venerable **P.J. Clarke's** (915 3rd Ave. at 55th St.; ☎ 212/759-1650) remains dark and cobwebby in the corners, with sawdust beneath the feet; an archetypal Irish saloon, but the clientele wears 3-piece suits now and chatters of media campaigns and TV audience shares. **The White Horse Tavern** (W. Hudson St. at 11th St.; ☎ 212/243-9260) was established in Greenwich Village in 1880. Dylan Thomas, Norman Mailer, poet Delmore Schwartz, and Brendan Behan gathered there. British pub grub—shepherd's pie, steak-and-mushroom pie—is on the menu of the 1868 **Landmark Tavern** (626 11th Ave. at 46th St.; ☎ 212/757-8595). Drop in after the theater, but before midnight, or for Sunday brunch.

Joe Allen (326 W. 46th St.; ☎ 212/581-6464) looks older than it is, perhaps because of the photos of Leslie Howard, W. C. Fields, and Billie Holliday. The battered bar frequently supports the tailored elbows of stars of the New York–based soap operas. Serious students of hops and barley malt have a home at the **Peculier Pub** (145 Bleecker St.; ☎ 212/353-1327), which claims to stock over 250 different brands of beer.

Wine bars, where the titular tipple is the only one available, never quite caught on. Some conventional bars have installed Cruvinets and have more and better selections than the usual jug wines. Among these are **I Tre Merli** (463 Broadway; ☎ 212/254-8699) and the **SoHo Kitchen and Bar** (103 Greene St.; ☎ 212/925-1866).

Desperate loneliness often pervades hotel bars, and the occupants seem to exude their disinclination to venture more than 100 feet from their bedrooms. Among the exceptions, so engaging that even New Yorkers stop in, is **Bemelman's Bar** in the plush Carlyle (Madison Ave. and 76th St.; ☎ 212/744-1600). Jazz piano, often played by luminary Barbara Carroll, is the backdrop, and the justification for the cover charge.

The bar of the **Algonquin Hotel** (59 W. 44th St., near 5th Ave.; ☎ 212/840-6800) is still a charmer, burbling with talk of book packages and theatrical contretemps. Bankers' pinstripes dominate at the handsome **Oak Bar** of the Plaza (5th Ave. and 59th St.;

☎ 212/546-5330), where the principal diversion is the sound of egos colliding.

Very different indeed is **The Whiskey** (235 W. 46th St.; ☎ 212/819-0404), the lounge of the Philippe Starck–designed **Paramount.** Many people, mostly hip, usually pretty, often famous, sidle up to the mahogany bar and sink into the asymmetrical velvet chairs. Similar in their aggressively postmodernist appeal are the bar of **Charlotte,** the restaurant of the Millenium Broadway (145 W. 44th St.; ☎ 212/789-7508), and **44,** at the Royalton Hotel (44 W. 44th St.; ☎ 212/944-8844), where visitors can choose between the very public lobby and a hidden, jewel box of a bar.

For a most civilized cocktail, try the **King Cole Bar** at the St. Regis (2 E. 55th St.; ☎ 212/753-4500) or the hushed sophistication of the lounge at the **Michelangelo** (152 W. 51st St.; ☎ 212/765-1900).

Strictly for tourists is **The View,** the rotating bar-restaurant of the Marriott Marquis (1535 Broadway; ☎ 212/704-8900); the free hors d'oeuvres during happy hour are some compensation for the mob scene and steep prices. Quieter, with gentle piano background and less restricted overlooks is **Top of the Tower,** on the 26th floor of the refurbished Beekman Tower (3 Mitchell Pl. at 49th St.; ☎ 212/355-7300).

The hope of human contact, of conversation, however brief, is a primary motive for barhopping. Patrons of the modern era's "social" bars are more flirtatious than heavy hitting.

Allegiances shift, sometimes rapidly, but try:

All State, 250 W. 72nd St. (between Broadway and West End Ave.), ☎ 212/874-1883. A neighborhood bar a few steps down from the street, with a laid-back atmosphere and pretty good food.

Bowery Bar, 40 E. 4th St. (Bowery), ☎ 212/475-2200. The latest hangout for supermodels, actors in town from Los Angeles, and assorted hangers on.

Jim McMullen's, 1341 3rd Ave. (77th St.), ☎ 212/861-4700.

Live Bait, 14 E. 23rd St. (near Broadway), ☎ 212/353-2400.

Lucky Strike, 59 Grand St. (W. Broadway), ☎ 212/941-0479. Though a bit older (and therefore not quite as "in") than Bowery Bar, still a trendy downtown place.

Polly Esther's, 186 W. 4th St. (between 6th and 7th avenues), ☎ 212/924-5707. Anybody who survived the seventies, particularly those of us whose childhoods were deeply affected by the "Brady Bunch" and the "Love Boat," will get a kick out of the ironic decor and disco beat.

Tortilla Flats, 366 W. 12th St. (Hudson St.), ☎ 212/627-1250.

Clusters of highly social bars pop up overnight like toadstools, for no discernible reasons, along previously dank and dreary avenues and in quarters once shuttered by nightfall. Try the stretch of Amsterdam Avenue in the high 70s and 80s or on the Upper East Side along 1st and 2nd avenues. Both areas are magnets for what used to be called yuppies.

Cabarets & Supper Clubs

While the cabaret scene never went out of style in New York, its sister, the supper club, suffered through decades of neglect before dance-club ennui or nostalgia for the breed of glamor personified by Astaire and Rogers forced a comeback. The city was never entirely without them, but usually in leaner versions of those of the World War II era. Back then, gorgeous chorines, over-plumed and under-dressed, descended staircases to the strains of Cole Porter, attended by top-hatted, tap-dancing young men. Between shows, patrons in black tie or sequins dined and danced to swing bands. Although those days are gone forever, several new establishments do a respectable job of approximating them. You can have a better meal at dozens of places, but these clubs are about fantasy and play, not gastronomy.

The current resurgence in the genre had as its instigation the reopening of the fabulous **Rainbow!** complex at the top of the **GE Building** (30 Rockefeller Plaza; ☎ 212/632-5000; closed Mon). Here the glamor has returned with a vengeance to what was once the premier supper club in Manhattan. The famous Art Deco extravaganza once again conjures images of Fred Astaire and Ginger Rogers whirling across the revolving dance floor, beneath hundreds of pinlights. From 7:30pm onward, a 12-piece dance band alternates with a similar group that swings to a Latin beat. Even the food is good, if expensive. (A Sunday prix-fixe meal, available noon–9pm, takes out some of the sting.) The cover charge is $20 daily. Another new feature is the transformation of the once ordinary bar-lounge. Called the **Rainbow Promenade,** its floor was raised 16 inches (41cm) and the walls opened in banks of glass to take maximum advantage of the most stunning vista in New York. As a bonus, it serves delectable "little meals" that are the ideal pretheater snack: Grilled shrimp, Cajun sausage, and 3 types of caviar are some of the dishes likely to be encountered.

In another part of the complex is a small supper club with slightly lower tariffs—**Rainbow & Stars**—which offers intimate cabaret entertainment. American standards, popular once again thanks to Tony Bennett, are the guiding factor here, with the likes of the McGuire Sisters and Rosemary Clooney figuring highly on the bill. The cabaret is closed both Sunday and Monday. Men are required to wear a jacket and tie in all areas of the club. Reservations are essential in the main room and in the cabaret.

The **Rainbow Room** may be the most grand, but so is it probably the most expensive supper club. Other options abound. **Tatou** (51 E. 50th St., between Lexington and 3rd avenues; ☎ 212/753-1144; closed Sun.) provides plush decadence with velvet swags, carved moldings, and spinning mirrored balls, though the patrons are not always so stylish. On stage, starting about 8:30pm, easy-on-the-ear jazz combos and Ella Fitzgerald clones perform through the dinner hour. The food is quite respectable, the main courses in servings large enough to make appetizers unnecessary. At 11pm, tables are pushed aside and a deejay plays records for dancing.

The Supper Club (240 W. 47th St.; ☎ 212/921-1940; open Thurs–Sat) seats 400 in a sea of cobalt-blue and crimson velvet. With the look of old-time Los Angeles (i.e., the Coconut Grove before the fire), the place is loud thanks to a 10-piece band and singer, and the food is passable. **The Elixir Restaurant and Lounge** (492 Broome St.; ☎ 212/966-3371; open daily) is SoHo's answer to the supper club, offering mediocre Italian fare to thirties and forties music. At the **37th Street Hideaway** (32 W. 37th St., at 6th Ave.; ☎ 212/947-8940; closed Sun), patrons stop for pre- or post-theater suppers and dance to live music beside glowing fireplaces.

Not every supper club is an ode to America's golden era. **Le Bar Bat** (311 W. 57th St., between 8th and 9th avenues; ☎ 212/307-7228; open daily) is a goofy mixture of Polynesia and Indonesia before the French left. The quality of the food—with a pan-Asian flair—varies, but the crowd is jovial, and the dance floor is packed. **S.O.B.'s** (204 Varick St., at Houston St.; ☎ 212/243-4940; closed Mon–Tues)—the moniker comes from "Sounds of Brazil"—features calypso, mambo, samba, and salsa, as well as other strains of Latin American and African dance music. Colorful and lively, the club's decor is mainly gourds, drums, and other musical instruments. Dinner, served from 7pm, is reminiscent of the tropics with a Latin American flavor. Shows are at 8 and 11pm, and the admission charge is lower if you eat there. **Blue Angel** (323 W. 44th St., bet. 8th and 9th avenues; ☎ 212/262-3333; closed Mon) hosts an even wackier evening. The entertainment is typically a musical comedy and sometimes calls for audience participation. In addition to evening shows, the club runs Saturday and Sunday matinees. Next door at **The Nile** (327 W. 44th St.; ☎ 212/262-1111), belly dancers do their thing while diners risk the Middle Eastern food.

The cabarets typically serve food but feature a more intimate form of entertainment than the supper clubs and tend to stay away from dancing. Singers, backed by a pianist or as many as 5 musicians, have a penchant for Broadway tunes and torch songs. Expect a lot of Gershwin and a good dose of Cole Porter.

Cafe Carlyle (in the Carlyle Hotel at 76th St. and Madison Ave.; ☎ 212/744-1600; closed Sun–Mon) is the granddaddy of cabarets. Bobby Short has reigned in this warm room for 3 decades. Short used to be at the piano and in full silky voice about 8 months a year. These days, he's usually around only in May, June, November, and December. An eternal favorite with society types, his métier is the show tunes of Cole Porter, Rodgers and Hart, and George Gershwin. You will pay dearly to hear them. When he is away, performers of similar stature sit in, among them, the modern Jazz Quartet, pianist George Shearing, and singers Eartha Kitt and Dixie Carter.

Woody Allen fans will recall Cafe Carlyle as the sight of his first, miserable date with Dianne Wiest in *Hannah and Her Sisters.* They also will likely know that he can be found Monday nights at **Michael's Pub** (211 E. 55th St., at 3rd Ave.; ☎ 212/758-2272; closed most Sun), not relaxing at a cozy table, but playing the clarinet. Early in the week the program focuses on traditional jazz—Dixie, blues, ragtime—but later in the week, the offerings vary to singers like Anita O'Day and Vic Damone, comics like Joan Rivers, and swing combos. Sets begin at 9:30pm and carry a stiff $35 minimum.

A classic cabaret where you can't go wrong is the **Oak Room** (in the Algonquin Hotel, 59 W. 44th St., near 6th Ave.; ☎ 212/840-6800; closed Sun–Mon). In this venerable hotel favored by British actors and Manhattan literati, the Oak Room features singers who have built impressive careers by focusing on the cabaret venue. Usually accompanied only by a piano, performers include the ageless Julie Wilson, newcomer Nancy LaMott, and the widely acclaimed Andrea Marcovicci, who construct eclectic programs by Sondheim, Kern, Berlin, and other Broadway composers. Nightly shows are usually at 9pm Tuesday to Thursday and 9 and 11:30pm Friday and Saturday.

A downtown, sometimes bawdy version of the cabaret entertains at the **Duplex** (61 Christopher St. at 7th Ave.; ☎ 212/255-5438). In business since 1949, the Duplex served as a testing ground for Woody Allen and Rodney Dangerfield and continues to host a range of comics, magicians, jazz combos, and singers nightly. The cover dips as low as $3 for the Friday midnight show featuring comics from the other New York clubs. Downstairs in the popular piano bar, servers double as performers, and there's no cover.

Another 2-level facility is **Eighty Eights** (228 W. 10th St., between Bleecker and Hudson streets; ☎ 212/924-0088; open nightly; no credit cards), with a downstairs piano bar and an upstairs cabaret showcasing a different comic, singer, or revue nightly. Show times are 8 and 10:30pm Sunday to Thursday, 8:30 and 11pm Friday and Saturday. Also in Greenwich Village, **55 Grove Street** (55 Grove St., at Bleecker St.; ☎ 212/366-5438; open daily; no credit cards) rotates parodists, singers, comics, and musical revues. On the Upper West Side, **Steve McGraw's** (158 W. 72nd St., at Amsterdam Ave.; ☎ 212/595-7400; open daily) is home to the long-running cabaret play, *Forever Plaid,* and also makes room for short-term revues and musical groups.

Comedy Clubs

As an alternative to cabaret or a show, try stand-up comedy. Its most typical manifestation is in the form of showcase clubs, in which parades of would-be comics hoping to be the next Jerry Seinfeld or Robin Williams test their material before live audiences. Should you attend, don't sit near the stage unless you are prepared to be the object of the performers' jibes. Their language, furthermore, is often scatological. Non-Americans and even non–New Yorkers may find many references obscure.

The first of the showcase (read: tryout) clubs and therefore the one able to boast the longest list of alumni who've made it is **The Improvisation** (433 W. 34th St., between 9th and 10th avenues; ☎ 212/279-3446; open nightly). Most of the comics here are seasoned professionals, some of them familiar from TV gigs, others who've been on the national club circuit. The by-play between performers and hecklers can get vicious at times.

Caroline's Comedy Club (1626 Broadway, at 49th St.; ☎ 212/757-4100; open daily) also draws the big names to its 275-seat emporium. Since the club's policy is to have just 1 opening act followed by a headliner, the comics have the luxury of time to develop their material without the pressure of lines of novices anxiously awaiting their turns at the mike. The surroundings are downright opulent by comparison with others of the breed.

The Comic Strip (1568 2nd Ave., at 81st St.; ☎ 212/861-9386; open nightly) is one of those clubs that can feel almost like a cattle call, as fledgling comics—up to 14 a night—take the stage in 10-minute intervals. More hits than misses, but that's the nature of the game. No cover Monday nights, known as Audition Night. Shows begin at 8:30pm Monday through Friday, with an additional 10:30pm set Friday; Saturday shows are at 8pm, 10:15pm, and 12:30am, and a Sunday performance begins at 8pm. Greenwich Village's **The Comedy Cellar** (117 MacDougal St., near Bleecker St.; ☎ 212/254-3480; open nightly) also puts the spotlight on young comics looking for a big break. Still, these performers are far from being amateurs. Shows begin nightly at 9pm, with an additional 11pm set Friday and 10:45pm and 12:30am shows Saturday.

Three other showcase clubs are:

Dangerfield's (1118 1st Ave., near 61st St.; ☎ 212/593-1650; open nightly), owned by the perennially dissed Rodney Dangerfield for the past 25 years and still featuring up to 8 comics a night. Many are middlebrow, but big names occasionally pop by.

New York Comedy Club (241 E. 24th St., between 2nd and 3rd avenues; ☎ 212/696-5233; open nightly), booking the unknown and the moderate name-recognition comics. Prices are relatively low.

Stand Up New York (236 W. 78th St., near Broadway; ☎ 212/595-0850; open daily), a bare-bones operation, with packed tables, exposed pipes, and a brick wall as backdrop for the performers. But it's the only comedy club on the Upper West Side, and it occasionally hits upon a winner. The 3 or 4 comics who perform each night often return as a group to engage in improvisations based on code words solicited from the audience.

For more comedy of an improvisational nature, try **Chicago City Limits** (1105 1st Ave., at 61st St.; ☎ 212/888-LAFF; closed Sun and Tues). The troupe takes suggestions from the audience and improvises sketches à la Chicago's famed Second City. Some are hysterical; some fall flat. Shows begin at 8:30pm weeknights, 8 and 10:30pm Friday and Saturday.

Country & Western

New Yorkers, who prefer to think of themselves as worldly, were among the last to adopt this otherwise popular American genre. Responding some years back to a fad fueled by such movies as *Urban Cowboy,* some briefly took to wearing snakeskin boots and pearl-button shirts, and to supporting radio stations and clubs that specialized in the heartfelt plaints of Waylon Jennings and Willie Nelson. That fixation faded to a flicker, but another resurgence in national interest has even uptight Manhattanites learning to line dance. I'm not placing any bets on how long this renewed interest will last.

The key spot where otherwise sophisticated types go is **Denim and Diamonds** (511 Lexington Ave., between 47th and 48th streets; ☎ 212/371-1600; open daily). If you don't know the steps, they'll teach you. No cover Sunday through Wednesday, $5 Thursday, and $8 Friday and Saturday. Foot-stompin' and hootin' by transplanted Texans from Houston and Brooklyn set the walls trembling from 10pm on at the **Rodeo Bar** (375 3rd Ave.; ☎ 212/683-6500). It's open every night with no cover charge. Business is booming and twanging as well at the **Cowgirl Hall of Fame** (519 Hudson St.; ☎ 212/633-1133). The margaritas and serviceable Tex-Mex food attract at least as many customers as the music.

    The Cottonwood Café (415 Bleecker St.; ☎ 212/924-6271) is a little ol' chunk of Texas plunked down in Greenwich Village, but it's so friendly and relaxed (if sometimes a little rowdy) that even native New Yorkers fit right in. When the **Lone Star Café** was down in Greenwich Village, it billed itself as "the biggest and best honky-tonk north of Abilene." Now, as the **Lone Star Roadhouse** (240 W. 52nd St.; ☎ 212/245-2950), and moved to larger quarters in the theater district, it has broader tastes in music. Different bands are on every night, playing just about anything that will get toes tapping—blues, gospel, 1950s rock 'n' roll, and, of course, country. Many of the accouterments of the old Lone Star have been salvaged, along with the better-than-average Texas vittles and brews for which it was known. Loyalties of country purists have transferred to **O'Lunney's** (12 W. 44th St.; ☎ 212/840-6688), still a fair approximation of a Waco beer hall, with music every night. See also "Pop/Folk/Rock."

Dance Clubs

Discotheques nearly disappeared after their 1960s' heyday, revived and faded in each of the next 2 decades, and now, in their 1990s' incarnations as "clubs," seem reasonably healthy. Just take a late-night stroll around what has been called the Chelsea Discoland and see.

    Dedicated club kids at times seem to have the attention spans of toddlers, standing in line and striking their best poses to gain admission to a new dance club one week and completely shunning it in favor of an even newer one—or an old flavor—the next. Hence the difficulty in committing to print which are hot and which are not. Some that survive well beyond the average life expectancy, such as Palladium and Limelight, are cavernous spaces ablaze with multimillion-dollar special effects that would do credit to *Star Wars*. Others are little more than cafes that shove aside a few tables after the dishes are cleared away.

    Today's clubs pulse with various forms of "house" music, a rhythmic, monotonous beat that keeps some dancing for hours and leaves others begging for musical relief. Club-goers' garb, on the other hand, seems to change weekly, thanks to cheaply made throw-away fashion. If you want to costume yourself like the natives, try the East Village or vintage-clothing shops for inspiration. At the least, skip your jeans and sneakers; they will only give the bouncer a reason to ban your entrance automatically.

It's still difficult to get into the clubs-of-the-moment, with entrance denied or permitted by hard-eyed centurions at the door. Wearing an extra trendy or outrageous outfit, being rich or famous, or arriving in the company of a comely young woman may help your case. Or not. It is safest to approach with a firm grip on your ego.

If you do meet with approval, be prepared to lay out some change. Most of the dance clubs charge rather stiff prices for both admission—up to $20—and drinks. Almost all of these places are cash-only, and most are open until 4 or 5am.

The granddaddy of the club scene, **Palladium** (126 E. 14th St., between 3rd and 4th avenues; ☎ 212/473-7171; open Thurs–Sun) is no longer the exclusive disco it once was, but it still, amazingly enough, attracts quite a crowd; both New Yorkers and bridge-and-tunnel types willing to fork over the $20 cover. The creators of the notorious **Studio 54** are responsible for this 7-story former rococo theater, now a visual phantasmagoria. The other venerable club (if that's not an oxymoron) is **Limelight** (660 6th Ave., at 20th St.; ☎ 212/807-7850) in what was once a church.

Looking for something a little more current? **System** (76 E. 13th St., between Broadway and 4th Ave.; ☎ 212/388-1060; open Wed–Sat) is a chic East Village spot that at last check still was attracting A-list-type models, fashion folk, and the like. More sophisticated and upscale than the traditional disco, System has a large, modern lounge area gently separated from the dance floor. **Bob** (235 Eldridge St., between Houston and Stanton streets; ☎ 212/777-0588) attracts a slightly older, 30-something, crowd to its basic bar-with-a-dance-floor operation.

Roxy (515 W. 18th St., at 10th Ave.; ☎ 212/645-5156; closed Sun, Mon, Thurs) gives club kids a chance to enjoy their other favorite hobby—in-line skating. The immense, loud space in Chelsea has skating Tuesday and Wednesday nights and dancing Friday and Saturday, all to house music. At last check, Tuesday and Saturday were gay nights.

Somewhere between a supper club and a disco is **Au Bar** (41 E. 58th St., at Madison Ave.; ☎ 212/ 308-9455; open nightly), once a magnet for Euro-lemmings and celebrities but of late more democratic. Au Bar may cut its cover charge, which hits $20 on weekends, if you arrive before 10:30pm and order dinner. That deal may not be such a bargain, though, as menu prices are high.

If you prefer live bands to the monotonous beat of spinning house music, **China Club** (2130 Broadway, at 75th St.; ☎ 212/877-1166; closed Sun) books bands every night but Monday. Most fit solidly in the rock category, and big-name musicians are known to drop by unexpectedly after a concert (or just because they feel like it) and to join in the jam. For an alternative dance beat, **Roseland** (239 W. 52nd St., near Broadway; ☎ 212/247-0200; open Mon–Sat) plays thirties swing and forties Latin rhythms from 2:30 to 11pm. All ages waltz or samba or whatever to 2 orchestras in this grand old ballroom, which has been around for 7 decades. It also has a huge buffet-style restaurant. **Copacabana** (617 W. 57th St.; ☎ 212/582-2672; open Fri, Sat, Tues) is known for a torrid salsa beat.

Gay & Lesbian Bars

The gay scene traditionally has flourished downtown, specifically in Greenwich Village and Chelsea. But this is New York, and the gay community is no longer confined within any neighborhood's borders. One popular lesbian hangout is **Cafe Tabac** (232 E. 9th St., between 2nd and 3rd avenues; ☎ 212/674-7072), which attracts a chic lipstick crowd. A crunchier, more subdued atmosphere permeates **Julie's** (204 E. 58th St., at 3rd Ave.; ☎ 212/688-1294). **Crazy Nanny's** (21 7th Ave. S., at Leroy St.; ☎ 212/366-6312) has a pool table downstairs and a dance floor upstairs, where women groove to house music every night but Thursday, which is two-stepping country and western night.

For men, **The Boiler Room** (86 E. 4th St., between 1st and 2nd avenues; ☎ 212/254-7536) serves a diverse crowd in the East Village. Sick of the usual scene? Try **Champs,** a gay sports-bar in Chelsea (17 W. 19th St., between 5th and 6th avenues; ☎ 212/ 633-1717). Or venture up to the seemingly straight Upper West Side, where **The Works** attracts a clean-cut crew (428 Columbus Ave., at 81st St.; ☎ 212/799-7365). In addition, many of the dance clubs, such as Roxy, have gay nights. Call for schedules.

Pop/Folk/Rock

While most performers in these categories appear in dance clubs and bars of one kind or another, check the publications suggested above, particularly the *Village Voice*, for other venues. Or, call any of the following for schedule information:

Alice Tully Hall, Lincoln Center, Columbus and Amsterdam avenues, ☎ 212/875-5050.

Apollo Theater, 253 W. 125th St., ☎ 212/864-0372.

Avery Fisher Hall, Lincoln Center, Columbus and Amsterdam avenues, ☎ 212/875-5020.

Beacon Theater, Broadway and 75th St., ☎ 212/496-7070.

Carnegie Hall, and its annex Weill Recital Hall, 7th Ave. and 57th St., ☎ 212/247-7800.

Joyce Theater, 175 8th Ave., ☎ 212/242-0800.

Merkin Concert Hall, 129 W. 67th St., ☎ 212/362-8719.

92nd St. Y, 92nd St. and Lexington Ave., ☎ 212/996-1100.

Paramount, at Madison Square Garden, 7th Ave. and 33rd St., ☎ 212/465-6741.

Radio City Music Hall, 6th Ave. and 50th St., ☎ 212/247-4777.

Symphony Space, Broadway and 95th St., ☎ 212/864-5400.

Town Hall, 123 W. 43rd St., ☎ 212/840-2824.

Some of the clubs suggested below have survived decades of changing fashions, but many opened yesterday and will close tomorrow. Always call ahead to learn of scheduled performers, prices, dress code, and present policies. And don't bother rushing through dinner to make the 9pm start time—I've never been to a club where the band started less than a half hour late. See also "Country & Western," "Dance Clubs," and "Cabarets & Supper Clubs."

CBGB's (315 Bowery at Bleecker St.; ☎ 212/982-4052; open nightly), once a haven for punk, now books a steady stream of "mainstream" alternative rock bands, some with indie record deals, others struggling to get signed. Numerous bands that made it, including the Talking Heads, got their start here. The atmosphere of the club, a garage in a former life, is grungy but unintimidating. Next door is CB's Gallery, a forum for acoustic acts.

History also permeates **Bottom Line** (15 W. 4th St., near Washington Sq.; ☎ 212/228-7880 or 212/228-6300; open nightly), where Bruce Springsteen and Stevie Wonder played in their salad days. Tickets go in advance for the name bands that do 1-night gigs here. Eclectic musical tastes are served with blues, jazz, rock, folk, blue-grass, and pop—and good sound.

Variation is also the rule at **Wetlands** (161 Hudson St., at Vestry St.; ☎ 212/966-4225; open nightly and Sun matinee; major credit cards), where the politics are green and the spotlight veers from rock to reggae, soul, funk, folk, industrial, hip-hop, punk, or ska, on any given night. For all you Dead Heads still mourning Jerry Garcia, Tuesday is Grateful Dead Night. Admission ranges from free to $12, depending on the band.

Aging boomers as well as younger types will get into the updated nostalgia of **The Bitter End** (147 Bleecker St., near La Guardia Pl.; ☎ 212/673-7030; open daily). Bob Dylan and Joni Mitchell performed their folk ballads here in the sixties, and the cozy room still lends its good sound system and acoustics to talented folk, rock, and jazz artists. Live music lasts from 8pm until closing.

Those who think that no good songs have been written since 1970 will feel right at home at **The Back Fence** (155 Bleecker St., at Thompson St.; ☎ 212/475-9221; open daily). The casual bar, has been a Greenwich Village mainstay since 1945. The format is heavy on the classic rock, with some blues, country, and folk tossed in. Minimal cover on weekends, and inexpensive drink prices.

Tributes to the old are at the core of the scruffy **Rock 'n' Roll Cafe** (149 Bleecker St., at Thompson St.; ☎ 212/677-7630; open nightly; major credit cards). Bands play covers of rock hits from the sixties through the eighties, including Springsteen, Led Zeppelin, AC/DC, and Van Halen.

Current stuff is more the rule at **Brownie's** (169 Ave. A, at 11th St.; ☎ 212/420-8392; open nightly). Kind of a dive, Brownie's pulls in that post-college crowd for indie rock. Two other gritty bars with live music nightly are **Continental Divide**

(25 3rd Ave., at St. Marks Pl.; ☎ 212/529-6924), showcasing rock, and **Mercury Lounge** (217 E. Houston, at Essex St.; ☎ 212/260-4700), offering a mix of folk, rock, and blues.

For good-to-excellent blues, try **Manny's Car Wash** (1558 3rd Ave., between 87th and 88th streets; ☎ 212/369-2583; open nightly; major credit cards). The crowd stands shoulder-to-shoulder, both on the postage-stamp dance floor and at the bar. Music begins about 9pm, and covers range from free to $12. Blues is also the staple at **Tramps** (45 W. 21st St., between 5th and 6th avenues; ☎ 212/727-7788; open nightly), although the Flatiron District spot occasionally throws in some jazz, country, zydeco, and experimental rock.

XXX

Where my male friends planning bachelor parties who don't want strippers entering their apartments go: **Stringfellows** (35 E. 21st St.; ☎ 212/254-2444), which likes to bill itself as a classy strip club, if such a thing exists. Men in suits and ties dine on prime rib, while a dozen or so women dance in G-strings and high heels. Bars of the more lewd variety still dot the environs of Times Square. I'm sure I needn't remind you that prostitution is illegal.

For women who enjoy ogling men removing their clothes, there's **Man Alive** (20 W. 20th St.; ☎ 212/288-5190). Call ahead for show schedules.

Only in New York

The possibilities are limitless in the city that never sleeps. Something as simple as eating ice cream or drinking a cup of coffee while sitting on the fountain at Lincoln Center, can be exciting, romantic, amusing. So can ice-skating at Rockefeller Center.

For a very civilized evening, try a cabaret; if you're really lucky, Bobby Short will be playing at the Carlyle. For a different take on civilization, I recommend heading downtown to CBGB's (or another rock club of choice) to catch an up-and-coming band. A night hanging out in Greenwich Village or SoHo will teach you much about the energy coursing through this city, but perhaps nothing is as quintessential New York as Broadway. Get tickets for a big, splashy musical and walk through the Theater District at 7:45pm or so, and with thousands of others, take in the thrill.

THE BASICS

Before You Go

Tourist Offices

The New York Convention and Visitors Bureau (2 Columbus Circle, near 59th St. and Broadway, New York, NY 10019; ☎ 212/397-8200 or 800/NYC-VISIT), will answer questions and mail out information on hotels, dining, theater, shopping, and sights, plus maps and coupons. There's another visitors' center in the Harris Theater, 226 West 42nd Street (between 7th and 8th avenues). Both are open Monday to Friday, 9am to 6pm; Saturday to Sunday, 10am to 3pm.

Money

ATMs

Most American banks belong to the CIRRUS, PLUS, or NYCE networks, which have 24-hour automatic teller machines throughout the city: call your network for locations: CIRRUS (☎ 800/424-7787); PLUS (☎ 800/843-7587); and NYCE (no central number, but you can get network locations from your local bank). Be careful using the machines late at night, when you're an obvious target for criminals.

Getting Money from Home

American Express MoneyGrams (☎ 800/543-4080) can be wired around the world in just minutes from any American Express Travel Service Office, but you must go to an agent in person. Up to $1,000 can be charged on a credit card (only Discover, MasterCard, or Visa—you can't use American Express). Amounts over $1,000 must be paid in cash; the maximum amount for a single transaction is $10,000. Recipients must present a reference number (phoned in from sender) and identification to pick up the cash.

   Western Union (☎ 800/325-6000), works in a similar fashion, except that they also allow customers to wire money over the phone by using their credit cards (MasterCard and Visa only). Fees for both of the above companies range from 5% to 10%, depending on the amount sent and method of payment (see "Useful Numbers & Addresses," below).

Traveler's Checks/Credit Cards

Travelers checks issued by American Express, Bank of America, Barclays, Citibank, and Thomas Cook are widely recognized; MasterCard and Visa also have introduced them. American Express provides extensive local refund facilities through its local offices. Credit cards are welcomed by nearly all hotels, airlines, and car rental agencies, as well as most restaurants, garages, and shops. While personal checks drawn on out-of-town banks are not normally accepted, many hotels will cash small amounts in conjunction with a credit card.

When to Go

Not long ago, the conventional advice was to avoid New York in its relentlessly humid summer. Indeed, New Yorkers who can afford it flee the city to summer cottages in the Hamptons or the Berkshires. But the widespread availability of air-conditioning makes July bearable, and it's a refreshing change of pace not to have to endure endless waits at the trendy restaurants.

   Some of the deluxe restaurants lock up for 2 to 3 weeks in August, but most remain open for business, as do the museums and landmark buildings. A glance at the "Calendar of Events" will attest to the full schedule of established cultural events in the summer. Many of these events feature front-rank performing groups at little or no cost—which is decidedly not the case from October to May. One downside, though, is that many art galleries close in July and August.

   Shoppers should prepare for large crowds and frayed tempers in the weeks between Thanksgiving and Christmas. The biggest sales are in January through February. Sports enthusiasts find that the seasons of the 8 major professional teams overlap in early fall.

Climate

May, June, September, and October tend to be the most agreeable months. Extended periods of oppressive humidity and temperatures of 90°F (32°C) and more are characteristic in July and August. December through March you can expect cold rains, occasional snow, and readings at or near freezing. True extremes are rare, however. Temperatures infrequently drop far below freezing point or exceed 100°F (38°C), and a snowfall of more than 4 inches is unusual.

To receive up-to-the-minute weather forecasts, dial 1-900/WEATHER anywhere in the United States (it costs 95¢ per minute).

Calendar of Events

January

Early January: One-day *Winter Festival.* Central Park, on the Great Lawn, near 81st St. Festivities include snow sculpture contest, cross-country skiing demonstrations, and winter fashions. Snow is provided by machine if nature is uncooperative (☎ 212/360-3456 for exact date and information).

Mid-January for 2 weeks: *Boat Show.* Jacob K. Javits Convention Center (☎ 212/216-2000). Same motives and same lavish display as the Auto Show, but the subject is pleasure craft, both power and sail.

Mid-January–early February: *Chinese New Year.* Chinatown, lower Manhattan. Ten days of fireworks and celebrations feature silk lions and a fearsome dragon that snakes and dances along Mott St. to frighten evil spirits away (☎ 212/397-8222 for details).

Late January: *Winter Antiques Show.* 7th Regiment Armory, Park Ave. and E. 67th St. (☎ 212/452-3067). This exhibit of serious antiques is also an excuse to see the grand interiors by Stanford White and Louis Comfort Tiffany, usually closed to the public.

February

February is *Black History month:* Libraries, schools, universities, TV stations, and neighborhood associations sponsor a wide range of events highlighting the contributions of African-Americans to American history and culture. Newspapers carry specifics (☎ 212/397-8222 for information).

Mid-February: *Westminster Dog Show.* Madison Square Garden, 7th Ave. and 33rd St. (☎ 212/465-6741). Two days of intense competition.

Mid-February for 1 week: *National Antiques Show.* Madison Square Garden, 8th Ave. and 32nd St. Perhaps the largest show of antiques and related objects in the world (☎ 212/465-6741 for dates).

Late February: *Lantern Day.* Chinatown and City Hall, lower Manhattan. On the night of the 15th day of the Chinese Lunar New Year, children form a parade to present paper lanterns to the mayor. There are martial arts demonstrations, dancing, and singing (☎ 212/397-8222 for details).

March

For **Easter** events, see "April."

Early March: *International Cat Show.* Madison Square Garden (☎ 212/465-6741).

March 17: *St. Patrick's Day Parade.* 5th Ave. from 44th St. to 86th St. All New Yorkers are Irish on this day. Beer is green, clothing is green, even the line down the middle of 5th Ave. is green. Irish taverns and St. Patrick's Cathedral are the centers of activity.

Mid-March for 1 week: *New York Flower Show* (☎ 800/553-2121) or call the Horticultural Society of New York (☎ 212/757-0915). New York Coliseum (59th St. and Broadway). More than 15,000 square yards of gardens and landscapes; free lectures.

Late March for 2 months: *Ringling Brothers and Barnum & Bailey Circus.* Madison Square Garden, 7th Ave. and 33rd St. (☎ 212/465-6741). A small parade of elephants and wagons heralds the opening.

April

2 weeks preceding Easter: *Easter Egg Exhibition.* Ukrainian Museum, 2nd Ave. (12th St.). A specially mounted display of hand-painted eggs, a staple of this small museum (☎ 212/228-0110 for details).

Mid-April: *International Auto Show* (☎ 718/746-5300). Jacob K. Javits Convention Center (☎ 212/216-2000). A vast, glittery exhibition of foreign- and American-made cars: antique, classic, custom, and brand new.

Week before Easter: *Easter Flower Show.* Macy's Department Store, Herald Square (☎ 212/695-4400). The largest department store in the world blooms on several floors.

Week before Easter: *Easter Lilies display.* Channel Gardens, Rockefeller Center.

Easter Sunday: *Easter Parade.* 5th Ave., from 49th St. to 59th St. Not an organized parade at all, but a promenade of celebrants showing off their spring finery, some of it extraordinary.

May

Weekend in mid–May: *Ninth Avenue International Festival.* 9th Ave., from 36th St. to 59th St. Once known as "Paddy's Market," this stretch of 9th Ave. specializes in prosaic and exotic foods. The festival is a gustatory orgy of kielbasa, quiche, falafel, knishes, tacos, Belgian waffles, zeppoli, baklava, souvlaki, and every fast food conceived by humans. Crafts, merchandise, and entertainment.

May 20: *Martin Luther King, Jr., Memorial Parade.* 5th Ave. above 59th St.

Around mid–May: *Greek Independence Day Parade.* 5th Ave. above 59th St. Less widely celebrated than St. Patrick's Day, but a growing Greek population provides a substantial parade each year, with floats and bands.

Late May–early June: *Washington Square Outdoor Art Exhibition.* Washington Square and adjacent streets. Artists, amateur and otherwise, fill walls and fences with paintings (landscapes, tigers and Elvis on velvet, sedate nudes), metalwork, tooled leather, and wire jewelry. Everything is for sale, and bargaining is expected. Repeated in early September.

June

All month: *Music and other cultural events,* many of them free. Dance, Shakespeare, opera, jazz, and pop and folk music. Leading groups and companies perform outdoors, in Central Park, at Rockefeller Center, in the Sculpture Garden of the Museum of Modern Art, at the South Street Seaport, and at the World Trade Center. For information call the Parks and Recreation Info Hotline ☎ 212/360-3456 or ☎ 800/201-PARK.

Sunday in mid–June: *Puerto Rican Day Parade.* 5th Ave. above 59th St. Colorful, well-attended, sprightly celebration associated with the patron saint of the Puerto Rican capital, San Juan.

Early June for 10 days: *Festival of St. Anthony.* Little Italy, lower Manhattan. Sullivan St. below Houston St. is lined with booths selling games of chance, sizzling sausages, calzone, pizza, and flavored ices. Religious observances dominate during the day; secular entertainments take over after dusk. Go hungry, for the aromas are irresistible.

Early June: *Rose Day Weekend.* New York Botanical Garden, The Bronx (☎ 718/220-8700 or 718/

220-8777). Stunning demonstration of the horti-
culturist's craft, with tours and lectures.

Mid–June: *Salute to Israel Parade.* 5th Ave. above 59th St.

Late June–early July: *JVC Jazz Festival.* Concert halls
and outdoor locations around Manhattan. Jazz in all its
permutations, from Dixieland to atonal, takes over from
noon to midnight. Some events are free. Check newspapers for details.

Also late June: *Lesbian and Gay Pride Day.* Parade down
5th Ave. to Greenwich Village.

July

July 4th: *Independence Day Festivities.* Battery Park, lower
Manhattan. Old New York Harbor Festival takes place
in the afternoon and evening, with patriotic ceremo-
nies, food, music, and performers. South Street Seaport, downtown Manhattan, is one of the best vantages
for the spectacular fireworks over the East River, sponsored by Macy's. The display starts around 9:30pm, but
check newspapers. Tall ships and sailing vessels from
other nations and ports often visit. The street festival
features music, crafts, and food.

Mid–July through August: *Mostly Mozart Festival.*
Lincoln Center, West Side Manhattan. This treasured
event commences with a free outdoor concert, then
carries on through the rest of the summer indoors,
primarily in Avery Fisher Hall. Tickets are unusually
inexpensive (☎ 212/875-5030 for details) or call
CenterCharge (☎ 212/721-6500).

Late July to mid–August: *New York Philharmonic Parks
Concerts.* Park locations in all boroughs. The famed
symphony orchestra performs beneath the stars, free
(☎ 212/875-5000).

Also July–August: *Summergarden Concerts.* Free performances in the Museum of Modern Art sculpture
garden by students of the famed Juilliard School.

August

August: *Greenwich Village Jazz Festival.*

Mid–August–early September: *Lincoln Center Out-
of-Doors.* Lincoln Center, West Side Manhattan. Free
live entertainment on the plaza from noon to sunset
(☎ 212/875-5400 for details).

Late August–September: *U.S. Open Tennis Championships.* National Tennis Center, Flushing Meadows,
Queens (☎ 718/760-6200).

September

Early September for 2 weeks: *Washington Square Outdoor Art Exhibition.* Washington Square and adjacent streets. A duplicate of the spring event (see "May").

Sunday in mid-September: *"New York is Book Country" street fair.* 5th Ave. from 48th St. to 57th St. and adjacent blocks. More than 160 publishers and booksellers set up booths.

Mid-September: *Steuben Day Parade.* 5th Ave. from 59th St. to Yorkville. Exuberant small-scale commemoration of the German officer who aided the Revolutionary cause.

Late September: *Festa di San Gennaro.* Little Italy, lower Manhattan. Blocks of gaming- and eating-booths tantalize with prizes and great greasy food. It is becoming an increasingly intercultural event, Sicilian sausages being augmented by Cantonese egg rolls.

Mid-September to early October: *New York Film Festival.* Alice Tully Hall, Lincoln Center. Serious film buffs revel in 3 weeks of afternoon and evening showings, with no questionable awards or overheated publicity. For information call (☎ 212/875-5610).

October

On or about October 5: *Pulaski Day Parade.* 5th Ave. The Polish community takes its turn.

Weekend in early October: *Brooklyn Heights Art Show.* The Promenade. Arts and crafts from scores of local artists compete with spectacular vistas of lower Manhattan. From about noon–6pm.

Early October: *Columbus Day Parade.* 5th Ave. Second only to the St. Patrick's Day Parade in intensity and numbers, and along the same route.

Late October for 1 week: *Fall Antiques Show.* W. 52nd St. and Pier 92 (☎ 212/777-5218). Come here for Americana; for worldwide antiques try the more important International Antique Dealers Show, 7th Regiment Armory, Park Ave. and 66th St.

October 31: *Halloween Parade.* Greenwich Village, lower Manhattan. Villagers in outlandish costumes wind through the streets of their district, with ghoulish happenings along the route, and a party at Washington Square.

November

Early Sunday in November: *New York City Marathon.* From Staten Island to Central Park. Not the oldest, but the biggest marathon, with more than 24,000 runners following a route from the west end of the Verrazano Narrows Bridge through all 5 boroughs.

Early November for 6 days: *National Horse Show.* Madison Square Garden (☎ 212/465-6741). Equestrian competition of jumping and dressage.

Last Thursday in November: *Macy's Thanksgiving Day Parade.* Broadway, 77th St. to 34th St. Traditional 3-hour morning event with bands, celebrities, and huge helium-filled balloons in the shapes of such folk as Bugs Bunny, Snoopy, Superman, and Mickey Mouse.

November 26–January 6: *Star of Wonder Show.* Hayden Planetarium. The night sky of Bethlehem is vividly reproduced, with music and commentary (☎ 212/769-5100).

Thanksgiving–New Year's Day: *Lord & Taylor Christmas Windows.* 424 5th Ave. (39th St.). All the big stores vie with one another in Christmas decorations, but this one is the perennial champion, managing to outdo itself every year.

December

Late afternoon in early December: *Rockefeller Center Tree-Lighting Ceremony.* 5th Ave. between 50th St. and 51st St. The huge tree that rises above the ice-skating rink and the gilded statue of Prometheus is illuminated by dignitaries and celebrities, to the accompaniment of Christmas carols. Extravagantly decorated trees are also set up in the American Museum of Natural History and the Metropolitan Museum of Art.

First night of Chanukah: *Lighting of Chanukah Candles.* City Hall, lower Manhattan, and 92nd St. YM–YWCA, 1395 Lexington Ave.

All month: *Nutcracker Ballet.* Lincoln Center. Traditional performance by the New York City Ballet (☎ 212/870-5570).

The 2 Sundays before Christmas: 11am–3pm. *Fifth Avenue Holiday Mall.* 5th Ave., 34th St. to 57th St. The Avenue is closed to traffic, and public entertainments draw shoppers past windows gaudy and sublime.

December 31: *New Year's Eve.* Celebrated all over the city. A "Big Apple" slides down a flag pole above Times Square, reaching the bottom at the 1st second of the New Year to the inebriated cheers of thousands. Cars honk, boats in the harbor blow their whistles, and celebrants kiss each other in the ballrooms of dozens of hotels. There's also a 5-mile run in Central Park, beginning at midnight and accompanied by fireworks.

What to Pack

A raincoat with a warm zip-out lining is a good investment for visits between October and April, as are collapsible rubber boots and a waterproof hat. The winds that accompany rain often turn umbrellas inside-out. High settings of interior heating and air-conditioning make layering of clothes advisable.

New Yorkers have grown less formal in dress in recent years. Men are comfortable with a jacket at most medium-priced and luxury restaurants; a tie is mandatory at only a very few establishments. It's wise to bring along extra eyeglasses and medications, in the event of lost or stolen baggage.

Reservations

Advance tickets for the theater and many special events are available through Ticketmaster (☎ 212/307-7171) or Telecharge (☎ 212/239-6200 or 800/233-8123). You can also call ahead to your hotel concierge and offer a "reward" for help. Major events are listed in the *New York Times, New York* magazine, *Time Out New York,* or the *New Yorker.* If you're willing to pay high commissions, call the ticket brokerages Edwards and Edwards (☎ 212/944-0290 or 212/775-1150; 800/223-6108) or Keith Prowse (☎ 212/398-1430).

For Travelers with Disabilities

Federal regulations have brought about some improvements in recent years. Many public lavatories/rest rooms have accessible facilities, and about 90% of buses are now equipped with motorized platforms to lift wheelchairs. Most hotels have some accessible rooms. Subways offer reduced fares for passengers with disabilities, but only about 20 stations have elevators or ramps, and the stairs are difficult to negotiate. Seeing-eye dogs are permitted everywhere in New York. For further information, contact Rehabilitation International USA (25 E. 21st St., 4th floor, New York, NY 10010; ☎ 212/420-1500). For information about special events and programs, contact The Lighthouse, Inc. (111 E. 59th St., New York, NY 10017; ☎ 800/334-5497), which serves people with impaired vision; or the New York Society for the Deaf (817 Broadway, 7th floor, New York, NY 10003; ☎ 212/777-3900). *Access for All,* a guide to the city's cultural institutions, is available free from Hospital Audiences, Inc. (220 W. 42nd St., New York, NY 10036; ☎ 212/575-7676).

Arriving by Plane

Most international flights are served by John F. Kennedy Airport, a 30- to 60-minute trip from midtown, depending on traffic. Most national and some international airlines fly in and out of La Guardia Airport (25 to 45 min.), and Newark Airport, across the Hudson River in New Jersey (40 to 60 min.).

Getting In & Out of Town

Carey Airport Express (☎ 718/632-0500) buses depart Kennedy and La Guardia every 20-30 minutes between early morning and midnight, less frequently at other times. They stop at the Carey Ticket Office, across from Grand Central Terminal, Port Authority Bus Terminal, and at the New York Hilton, the Sheraton Manhattan, and the Marriott Marquis hotels. The fare from Kennedy is slightly higher than that from La Guardia, but each is around $10. A similar service is provided by the Olympia Trails Airport Express buses (☎ 212/964-6233), which travel between Newark Airport and Penn Station, the World Trade Center, and Grand Central Terminal. They leave Newark about every 20 minutes between 6:15am and midnight.

Gray Line Air Shuttle operates 11-seat vans and 21-seat coaches from 52 midtown hotels to all 3 airports. The service operates daily from 7am to 11pm: rates are $13.50 to La Guardia, $16.50 to Kennedy, and $18.50 to Newark. Information is available at the ground transport desks at the airline terminals, or ☎ 212/757-6840. Some hotels provide their own transport to and from airports, if advance arrangements are made.

Taxis from La Guardia to destinations within the city are metered. Expect to pay $18 to $22 from La Guardia to mid-Manhattan. Taxi service to and from Kennedy is a flat rate of $30. From Newark, the taxi fare is twice the amount shown on the meter. From New York to Newark, the fare is the amount on the meter plus $10. Bridge and tunnel tolls are extra, and traveling in the rush hour can double the fare. Licensed yellow taxis from New York are not allowed to charge per passenger or for luggage. Don't accept rides with unlicensed "gypsy" cabs. Nonmetered car services provide transport to the airports at somewhat lower rates than regular taxis, but generally charge an additional $5 for airport pick-ups. Two that have proved themselves to be reliable are Aviv (☎ 212/505-0555), $28 (plus tips and tolls) to JFK and Newark, $18 to La Guardia; and Allstate (☎ 212/741-7440) $29 to Newark, $28 to JFK, and $18 to La Guardia.

Helicopters fly among the 3 airports and between Kennedy and the Heliport at 34th St. and the East River. The flights between Kennedy and the Heliport take 10 minutes and leave every 30 minutes between 1:30 and 7:30pm, but cost twice as much as a taxi. Operations are sometimes suspended due to bad weather.

Private limousines are clean, comfortable, and often cost little more than taxis, as they charge a flat rate and can be shared. You can arrange in advance to have one waiting for you (see "By Other Transport").

Arriving by Train or Bus

Long-distance trains and commuter trains from Long Island and New Jersey arrive at Pennsylvania Station (7th Ave. and 32nd St.); Grand Central Terminal (Park Ave. and 42nd St.) is for commuter trains that run along the northeast corridor. All buses, both long-distance and commuter, arrive at the Port Authority Bus Terminal (8th Ave. and 41st St.).

Arriving by Car

From the west and south, Interstate Highways I-78, I-80, and I-95 connect with Manhattan via the George Washington Bridge (for upper Manhattan), the Lincoln Tunnel (for mid-Manhattan), and the Holland Tunnel (for lower Manhattan). From the north, I-87 (Governor Thomas E. Dewey Thruway) and I-95 (New England Thruway) lead to the Triborough Bridge and other Harlem River and East River crossings. Most of these funnel into the FDR Drive, which parallels the East River.

Tolls across the Hudson River are paid when entering the city, but not when leaving. There is a hefty toll charged on the Verrazano Bridge going from Brooklyn to Staten Island, however. Automobile clubs can suggest the best route from your point of departure.

Staying in New York
Getting Around

Strange as it may sound to those who spend the better part of their days in their cars, I find New York a relatively easy city to get around. Granted, the slightest precipitation can create gridlock from Wall Street to Harlem and can make hailing a taxi more difficult than finding a good man. Taxis can be especially frustrating in Midtown at lunchtime and during rush hours.

In such circumstances, the subway is generally the easiest and quickest mode of transportation. Tragic stories of violence in the city's underground train system understandably have created fear among many non–New Yorkers, but crime has decreased in the subway. Most New Yorkers rely on it as a primary means of getting around. Take a few basic precautions: Don't flaunt flashy jewelry; don't stand too close to the platform edge; and don't ride the subway late at night.

Some New Yorkers prefer buses, which tend to be very clean and which they consider safer. Bus routes are particularly convenient for going across town (east–west), as most of the subway lines run primarily the length of Manhattan (north–south). Of course, buses are hostage to traffic jams and to red lights.

And for the truly ambitious, nothing beats walking for soaking up the city and all it has to offer.

By Subway

The subway system has improved a bit in recent years, but maddening delays and dilapidated stations are still part of reality. Although they have been banned, panhandlers regularly work their way through the trains, and many stations are still dirty, littered, and populated by homeless people. For information on subways and buses, call 718/330-1234 between 6am and 9pm. Free maps are theoretically available at most token booths.

Trains operate 24 hours a day, with substantially reduced frequency between midnight and 6am. A single fare lets you journey as far as you like along any 1 line and on connecting lines. Peak rush hours, to be avoided if possible, are 8 to 9am and 5 to 7pm. A criticized recent decision to reduce the number of rush-hour trains has, inevitably, caused more crowding.

To use the subway, buy a token at the booth near the entrance, or, if you want at least 4 tokens, you can use the vending machines that require a minimum of a $5 bill. A token costs $1.50. Free transfers can be made at 25 intersections with other lines.

In order to get on the right train going in the right direction, first note whether you must go uptown, downtown, or across town, and whether your final station is a local or express stop (see the subway map at

the end of the book). Insert the token into the turn-
stile, then follow directional signs to the correct platform. Once there, look for signs to indicate whether
express and local trains stop on the same or on opposite
sides of the platform. The front and sides of a train have
signs indicating the route number, whether the train is
express or local, and the last station on the route.

Platform loudspeakers give information about
delays and rerouting of trains, but more often than not
the announcements blare out as indecipherable noise.

By Bus

Many New Yorkers prefer the modern, very clean,
and well air-conditioned buses to the subway
system, despite the fact that they are hostage to traffic
and usually much slower. Upon boarding, deposit
a subway token or the equivalent in coins in the box
next to the driver. The driver cannot give change,
but can provide free transfers to intersecting lines.
Routes roughly follow the major north–south avenues.
East–west cross-town routes serve as connections
between subway lines. Buses operate on a 24-hour basis, but very infrequently between midnight and 6am.
Route maps are sometimes available at subway token
booths, but rarely on buses themselves. A better source
is the New York Convention and Visitors Bureau at
Columbus Circle (near 59th St. and Broadway).

By Taxi

There are only 11,787 taxicabs in operation. That total
has been frozen since 1937, the reason an official me-
dallion costs a new owner nearly $140,000. Licensed
taxis are painted yellow. They can be hailed anywhere if
the sign on the roof is illuminated. Taxi stands are also
found outside major hotels.

Within the 5 boroughs there is a set rate for the first
ninth of a mile and for every additional ninth. Bridge
and tunnel tolls are extra. Drivers are required by the
Taxi & Limousine Commission to take passengers to
any destination in the city. This law doesn't necessarily
mean they actually will, particularly if a prospective
passenger looks as if he or she might want to go to a
dangerous or out-of-the-way neighborhood. Get in the
cab before announcing where you wish to go.

The 40-hour training course for drivers falls well
short of its objectives, especially when compared to
London's demanding 2-year program. Its inadequacy is
hardly surprising, considering that nearly 90% of the

students are immigrants, most of them from countries where English is not the primary language. For that reason, it is wise to know the full address of your destination and the nearest cross street. Simply asking for a particular hotel, restaurant, or museum, no matter how well-known, may draw a blank stare from the driver. Even so, he (and it is nearly always a "he") will expect a tip that is 20% of the total fare. Taxis have electronic digital meters that print out receipts if requested.

For articles lost in taxis, call ☎ 212/825-0416.

By Car

Using a car in New York is not an entirely rational act. Street parking is often nonexistent, and garage parking is very expensive. Most large hotels have garages, but these are often expensive and a fee is usually charged every time a car is taken out and returned. If you must bring a car to New York, at least try to confine its use to evenings after 9pm and weekends, to get to such out-of-the way sights as **The Cloisters** or Staten Island, or for touring the outskirts. When parking, do not exceed the posted time limit, or your car could be towed away to a pound. If that happens, it costs a great deal of money and much time untangling red tape.

Most cross streets and avenues are one-way, the direction alternating from one street or avenue to the next. In New York City, unlike the rest of the state, right turns are not permitted at red lights unless stated.

For further details and information, contact the American Automobile Association (Broadway and 62nd St.; ☎ 212/586-1166), or seek advice from your own automobile club.

By Foot

The best, and most agreeable, way to cover short distances in Manhattan is on foot. Above 14th Street, it is difficult to lose your way. Streets are laid out in a straight grid. Named and numbered avenues run north to south, from 1st Avenue on the East Side to 11th Avenue on the West Side. Fifth Avenue is the dividing line between east and west. Cross streets run east to west from 14th Street in the south to 225th Street in the north. Building numbers increase from one to the mid-hundreds to the east, and in the same way to the west. On the avenues, numbers increase as they proceed north.

Because the avenues and Broadway are so long (and because each avenue has its own unique numbering system), the nearest cross street is often mentioned when

asking for a main avenue address. Avenue of the Americas is always spoken of as 6th Avenue, although the grander name is still used for addresses.

The Manhattan grid is not perfect, of course. Broadway cuts diagonally across the island from Park Avenue and 14th Street to the west of Central Park. Below 14th Street, in the older part of the city, the grid goes awry. Down there, a good street map is essential. With some exceptions, odd street numbers are on the west side of avenues and on the north side of cross streets.

By Ferry

America's favorite boat ride—the Staten Island ferry— is still the biggest bargain in town (50¢ round-trip), serving up spectacular views and bracing breezes. It departs from the Whitehall Street pier at downtown Battery Park every 20 to 30 minutes, 24 hours a day, 7 days a week.

The Statue of Liberty ferry also leaves from Battery Park and follows a route stopping at **Ellis Island.** The price of the ride includes a guided tour of the museum (for more information, see "Sights and Attractions"). Tickets for the Statue of Liberty and Ellis Island are sold inside the **Castle Clinton National Monument,** near the piers. Still another ferry operates between La Guardia Airport and piers at 34th Street and Wall Street on the East River.

By Other Transport

Hourly rates for private limousines are high, but there are special airport and theater/dinner flat rates that can total little more than taxi fares. Dozens of companies are listed in the Yellow Pages. Some are 1- or 2-car operations, others have entire fleets. These are a few of the reputable firms:

Allstate Car & Limo, 163 8th Ave.; ☎ 212/741-7440.

Dave-El, 4205 10th St., Long Island City; ☎ 718/645-4242.

London Towncars, 40-14 23rd St., Long Island City; ☎ 718/988-9700.

Manhattan International, 13-05 43rd Ave., Long Island City; ☎ 718/729-4200.

Sabra, 326 2nd Ave.; ☎ 212/777-7171.

Silver Screen Limo, P.O. Box 4283, Sunnyside, NY 11104; ☎ 718/937-3808, 718/937-3321, or 718/937-5466.

Tel-Aviv, 139 1st Ave.; ☎ 212/777-7777.

Rent a rowboat or bicycle at the 72nd St. boathouse in Central Park. Bicycles and mopeds can be rented from the following:

Bicycle & Exercise Equipment Store, 242 E. 79th St. (2nd Ave.), ☎ 212/249-9218.

Metro Bicycles, 9th Ave. and W. 47th St., ☎ 212/581-4500. Five other branches around Manhattan. Open 7 days.

Pedal Pusher, 1306 2nd Ave. (near 69th St.), ☎ 212/288-5592.

6th Ave. Bicycles, 546 6th Ave. (15th St.), ☎ 212/255-5100.

Rides in horse-drawn hansom cabs begin from near the 5th Avenue and 59th Street corner of Central Park, day or night. Most of the rides take 30 minutes. It is advisable to establish the rate in advance.

Getting Out of the City

The Harlem, Hudson, and New Haven commuter lines of the Metro North **railroad** system snake up to 100 miles north of New York City; they all depart from Grand Central Terminal (Park Ave. and 42nd St.). Pennsylvania (Penn) Station (7th Ave. and 32nd St.) is the gateway for train service to Long Island (The Long Island Railroad) and New Jersey (New Jersey Transit), as well as the departure point for Amtrak trains to Canada, Boston, Chicago, Washington, Florida, and intermediate points. The Port Authority Bus Terminal (42nd St. and 8th Ave.) is the major departure point for buses to all parts of the country.

Amtrak, ☎ 800/523-8720 (Metroliners).

Long Island Railroad (LIRR), ☎ 718/ 217-LIRR (trains); 516/766-6722 (buses).

Metro North, ☎ 212/532-4900 (commuter; Westchester County and Connecticut).

New Jersey Transit (NJT), ☎ 201/762-5100.

Port Authority Bus Terminal, ☎ 212/ 564-8484.

Domestic airlines operate from all 3 airports. The USAir Shuttle and the Delta Shuttle to Washington and Boston have separate terminals at La Guardia. These 2 services have hourly flights during the day and early evening. The addresses below are for Manhattan ticket offices, while the telephone numbers are for central reservation networks. The offices listed at 100 East 42nd Street are on the 2nd floor of a building opposite Grand Central Terminal (entrance on 41st St.).

Air Canada, 488 Madison Ave., ☎ 800/ 776-3000.

American, 100 E. 42nd St., ☎ 800/433-7300.

Continental, 100 E. 42nd St., ☎ 212/ 319-9494.

Delta, 100 E. 42nd St., ☎ 212/239-0700.

Northwest, 299 Park Ave., at 49th St., ☎ 800/225-2525.

TWA, 100 E. 42nd St., ☎ 212/290-2121.

United, 100 E. 42nd St., ☎ 800/241-6522.

US Air, 100 E. 42nd St., ☎ 800/428-4322.

Local Publications

Special arts and leisure sections appear on Friday and Sunday in the *New York Times* and in the weekly magazines *New York, Time Out New York,* and the *New Yorker*. They provide useful reviews and listings of current plays, concerts, films, performances, exhibitions, ballets, and operas; The *New York Times* includes ticket availability. The *Village Voice* is a weekly that emphasizes the cutting-edge arts and presentations. The *Daily News* and *New York Post* have extensive sports coverage.

Opening & Closing Hours

Department stores, and clothing and sports equipment shops usually open between 9 and 10am and close at 6pm. Late-night shopping is on Monday and Thursday, usually until 9pm. Many department and electronics stores are open Sunday afternoon.

Although many fast-food stands, coffee shops, and delicatessens open by 8am and don't close until 10pm or later, more formal restaurants tend to confine themselves to noon to 3pm and 6 to 11pm, with slight variations. Bars and dance clubs do not have to close until 4am. In sections of the city where merchants are predominantly Jewish, shops often close from midafternoon Friday through Saturday and are open on Sunday. In Greenwich Village and SoHo, boutiques and galleries often do not get going until noon and may stay open well into the late evening hours.

Postal, Telephone & Business Services

Post offices are open Monday through Friday 8am to 5pm and Saturday 8am to noon. The main post office at 8th Avenue and 33rd Street is open 24 hours.

A letter marked General Delivery, addressed to a specific post office, will be held there until collected. Identification is usually required when you collect your mail, and a fee may be charged. Some commercial firms also provide this service for their customers. The following are centrally located: American Express (150 E. 42nd St., New York, NY 10017), Central Post Office (42 8th Ave., New York, NY 10001), and Thomas Cook (18 E. 48th St., New York, NY 10017).

Telephones are everywhere. Try to use those in shops or public buildings—the ones installed on street corners are sometimes out of order. Manhattan has its own area code: 212. A local call within the 212 area needs only its 7-digit number. The Bronx, Brooklyn, Queens, and Staten Island use area code 718. When calling an out-of-town number, or one of the other 4 boroughs from Manhattan, dial 1, then the area code, and finally the 7-digit number. Remember that hotels typically add surcharges. Cheaper rates apply after 5pm and on weekends.

Scores of independent shops specialize in photocopy, fax, telex, and postal services; larger hotels also offer these services. Money can be wired from one Western Union office to another, and a mailgram might arrive sooner than a letter (see also "Getting Money From Home," above).

Public Holidays

New Year's Day, January 1; Martin Luther King Day, 3rd Monday in January; President's Day, celebrated on a 3-day weekend in mid-February; Memorial Day, a 3-day weekend at the end of May; Independence Day, July 4; Labor Day, 1st Monday in September; Columbus Day, 2nd Monday in October; Election Day, 1st Tuesday in November; Veterans Day, November 11; Thanksgiving, last Thursday in November; Christmas, December 25.

As in the rest of the country, schools, banks, post offices, and most public services are usually closed on the above days, although some shops stay open on the 3-day weekends. Shops generally close on the major holidays only—usually Thanksgiving, Christmas, and New Year's Day.

A number of other special days are observed with religious services, parades, gift-giving, or other celebrations. These include: Chinese New Year, January/February; St. Patrick's Day, March 17; Easter and Passover, March/April; Puerto Rican Day, June; Rosh Hashanah, September; Halloween, October 31; Chanukah, December.

Rest Rooms

Avoid the ones in subway stations. Those in museums, public buildings, and department stores are usually satisfactory. In extremes, duck into the nearest hotel or do what New Yorkers do—buy a beverage from a coffee shop in order to use the rest room. A promising experiment in self-cleaning public toilets has been conducted, and might someday result in widespread installation.

Rush Hours

Driving, or using subways or buses, between 8 and 9am and 5 to 6:30pm could be considered an exercise in masochism, and the situation is almost as bad for an hour before and after these times. Without reservations, you may have long waits for lunch between noon and 2pm and for dinner between 7:30 and 9pm, but it depends on the place.

Safety

Most visitors to this city have some apprehensions. It may be comforting to know that violent crime is on the decrease here. But taking precautions is still advisable. My strongest warning is to stay out of Central

Park after dark. Also at night, some side streets, particularly in Chelsea, around Wall Street, on the fringes of SoHo and TriBeCa, and in parts of Midtown, can be fairly deserted, making them less desirable routes, so you may want to stick to the busier, well-lit thoroughfares. Although the subway is busy all day, the crowds thin out dramatically after 8pm or so. You will probably feel more comfortable taking a bus or a taxi.

Taxes
New York sales tax is 8.25%; hotel tax is 13.25%, plus occupancy tax of $2 per person per night

Tipping
In restaurants, tip the waiter at least 15% of the check before tax; 20% is more usual in luxury establishments, or if the service warrants it. An easy way to compute the minimum is to double the 8.25% sales tax. Some restaurants have taken to adding a service charge, so don't tip twice. Bellmen expect at least $1 per bag. Doormen get 50¢ to $1 for hailing a taxi; tip chambermaids a similar amount for each night of a stay, too. Rest room/lavatory attendants should be given 50¢, to be left on the conspicuous plate. When there is a stated fee for checking coats and parcels, that will be sufficient. Otherwise give $1 per item. Tour guides expect $2 to $5, depending upon the length of the tour.

Useful Phone Numbers & Addresses

American Express Travel Service, 150 E. 42nd St., ☎ 212/687-3700 a valuable source of information for any traveler in need of help, advice or emergency services. Nine other locations in Manhattan, including Macy's and Bloomingdale's.

Dentists Emergency Service, ☎ 212/679-3966; 9am–8pm; ☎ 212/679-4172; 8pm–9am.

Late Night Pharmacy: Kaufman, 557 Lexington Ave. (at 50th St.), ☎ 212/755-2266.

Main Post Office, 8th Ave. (33rd St.), or Lexington Ave. (45th St.).

Medical Emergencies Ambulances called on 911 carry patients to the nearest municipal hospital. Private hospitals are preferable, however, so if possible take a taxi to one of these:

Financial District: Beekman Downtown Hospital, 170 William St., ☎ 212/312-5000.

Greenwich Village: St. Vincent's Hospital, 7th Ave. (11th St.), ☎ 212/604-7000.

Midtown West: Roosevelt-St. Luke's Hospital, 9th Ave. (58th St.), ☎ 212/263-7300.

Upper East Side: New York Hospital, York Ave. (68th St.), ☎ 212/746-5454.

West Harlem: Columbia Presbyterian Medical Center, 622 W. 168th St., ☎ 212/305-2500.

NY Convention and Visitors Bureau, 2 Columbus Circle, ☎ 212/397-8222. Open Monday to Friday 9am to 6pm; Saturday and Sunday 10am to 3pm.

Police, Fire, Ambulances, ☎ 911—You will need a coin or phone card if using a phone booth.

Sportsphone, (for scores and highlights) ☎ 212/976-1313 or ☎ 212/976-2525.

Telephone information, ☎ 411; for long-distance information, dial 1, the area code, then 555-1212.

Time, ☎ 212/976-6000.

Times Square Business Improvement Center, 226 W. 42nd St. (between 7th and 8th avenues), ☎ 212/869-5453.

Traffic report, (during rush hours) ☎ 212/976-2323.

Wake-up call, ☎ 212/540-WAKE (9253).

Weather, ☎ 212/976-1122.

PORTRAITS

A Brief History

The broad, protected harbor was discovered in 1524, but permanent settlement did not take place until a century later. The English took New Amsterdam from the Dutch in 1664 and renamed the city New York. Resentment against British rule culminated in the War of Independence in 1776, and New York was for a time the capital of the infant nation before the Southern states forced its move to the newly carved District of Columbia.

The city's population was then slightly more than 30,000. It increased dramatically with the mass immigrations of the 19thC. In the 40 years following the Civil War (1861–5), Central Park was finished and the first skyscrapers erected. In 1898, the 4 outer boroughs were annexed to Manhattan, instantly fashioning the largest city in the world. The population totaled more than 3 million.

Despite the Wall Street Crash of 1929, construction of the Empire State Building began. Twenty years later, following the end of World War II, the city's population hit 8 million, and the United Nations moved into its new headquarters on the East River. The city was at its zenith—the capital of the world, untouched by war, a model of progress and modernity.

Since then, the pattern has been one of decline followed by resurgence, punctured in turn by sharp descents into fiscal crises, deteriorating public services, accelerating crime rates, and loss of industry and workers. Despair continues to mount over the seemingly unbreakable cycle of poverty, gangs, drugs, homelessness, and AIDS. But violent crime actually has declined in recent years. Reaction and proposals for remedies to the city's many problems have been slow in coming, partly because New York in the mid–1980s enjoyed renewed prosperity after a brush with near-bankruptcy only a few years before. That euphoria evaporated when the stock market crashed in October 1987, signaling the end of the free-spending decade and the start of a recession that rippled across the country. The crippled economy and consecutive administrations in Washington (and now Albany) that have proved indifferent to the plight of the cities, especially New York, have stalled efforts to deal with the city's apocalyptic problems. Still, some have taken tentative steps; controversial campaigns have distributed condoms among school children and have created shelters for the homeless that are smaller and less dangerous than the virtual warehouses so many of them refuse to use.

Visitors who condemn New York seem to ignore that London has an estimated 75,000 illegal squatters and homeless people, and that Paris, with a core population of 2.2 million, has 15,000 to 20,000.

Flip the coin and realize that tourism continues to grow, as new generations of Americans and foreigners rediscover the pleasures that never left New York. The demise of Broadway has been proclaimed with tedious regularity since the Great Depression, yet it continues to flourish, attracting stars like Glenn Close, Julie Andrews, and Carol Burnett, playwrights like Tom Stoppard and Steve Martin, and hordes of eager theatergoers. Despite 2 decades of unprecedented construction, hotels fill up as soon as they open their doors. Every time a restaurant closes down one seems to spring up in its place. New York remains the white-hot center of activity for those intent on careers in publishing, finance, advertising, fashion, ballet, opera, and the visual arts. There are still free concerts and Shakespeare in the Park. And vigorous new neighborhoods. And jazz in the subway. And hawkers selling their wares on street corners. And Miss Liberty in her rightful place in the harbor, as inviting as ever.

Safety First

To avoid New York because of stories of crime is akin to denying oneself Venice because of rubbish in the canals. Several U.S. cities are statistically more dangerous, but New York's status as a world media capital focuses international attention here.

Still, prudence is in order. First and foremost, always be aware of what is going on around you. At airports and railroad stations, carry your own luggage and don't surrender it until well inside your hotel. Avoid making direct eye contact with suspicious-looking people. Carry only the amount of money and the credit cards needed for each excursion. Pickpockets are most often at work in crowded areas, including elevators and revolving doors. Those called "spitters" use diversions—accidentally spilling something on a victim and helping clean it up while an accomplice lifts cash and credit cards. Don't carry a wallet in the obvious places; put it in the left or right front trouser pocket. In crowded places, hold handbags like footballs, rather than letting them dangle from shoulders. You might want to leave expensive-looking jewelry at home.

After dark, avoid the parks. Stick to the main thoroughfares, preferably in groups. Don't be embarrassed to make a commotion or a detour into a hotel lobby or shop if feeling threatened. When in the subway at night, wait in the designated section near the token booth and ride in the crowded central cars, not the empty ones in the front and back. Or take a taxi.

All that said, don't jump at every sound and don't think that reading this book or looking up at a building will brand you as a tourist. Most New Yorkers already know you're from out of town.

Landmarks in New York's History

Discovery to Revolution

1524: Italian explorer Giovanni da Verrazano discovered New York Bay while searching for a northwest passage.

1609: Henry Hudson sailed his *Half Moon* up the river that was eventually given his name.

1623: New Netherland became a province of the Dutch West India Company, and the cluster of huts at the south tip of Manhattan was called New Amsterdam.

1626: Provincial Director, General Peter Minuit bought the island from the Algonquin Indians.

1643: Population grew to about 500 people, speaking 18 different languages. During the tenure of Governor Peter Stuyvesant, settlements were established in the areas eventually known as The Bronx, Queens, Brooklyn, and Staten Island.

1664: The Duke of York sent a fleet into the harbor. Abandoned by the burgomasters who chafed under his authoritarian rule, Stuyvesant surrendered the city to the English. It was renamed New York.

1674: After extended hostilities between the English and Dutch—and one brief reoccupation by the Dutch—the city and province were ceded by treaty to the English.

1689: A German merchant, Jacob Leisler, led a revolt against oligarchic trade monopolies when he learned of the overthrow of James II. He was hanged for treason.

1712: Slaves now constituted a substantial segment of the population. Despite ordinances denying them weapons and the right of assembly, a number of blacks set fire to a building near Maiden Lane and killed 9 whites who attempted to stop the blaze. When soldiers arrived, 6 of the Blacks committed suicide; 21 others were captured and executed.

1725: The *New York Gazette* was founded.

1734: John Peter Zenger, publisher of the *New York Weekly Journal,* was charged with libeling the government. He was acquitted in the first test of the principle of press freedom in the colonies.

1754–63: Population now 16,000. King's College founded. Benjamin Franklin proposed union of the colonies for common defense during the French and Indian War, but was rejected. A force led by George Washington was defeated by the French at Fort Necessity in Pennsylvania. The conflict, which was part of the worldwide Seven Years War, ended with the Treaty of Paris. English sovereignty over the major part of explored North America was thereby conceded.

1764–70: Colonial grumblings over British rule escalated into sporadic demonstrations and protests. At the Stamp Act Congress held in Manhattan, delegates of the 9 colonies passed a Declaration of Rights and Liberties. Skirmishes between soldiers and the insurrectionist Sons of Liberty culminated in January 1770 in the killing of a colonial and the wounding of a number of others. The Boston Massacre, in which British troops fired upon taunting protesters, occurred 7 weeks later.

1775–83: The American Revolution. The Continental Congress appointed Washington as Commander-in-Chief and, on July 4, 1776, adopted the Declaration of Independence. After early battles ranging from Manhattan to Long Island, most of which he lost, Washington withdrew. The British occupied New York for the remainder of the war. With the Treaty of Versailles in September 1783, the British troops left the city.

1789: Washington was sworn in as first president at Federal Hall in New York, the first capital of the federal government.

1790: An official census recorded the population at 33,000.

1807–9: Robert Fulton made a round-trip from New York to Albany in his steamboat *Clermont*. In reaction to British and French seizure of American ships at sea, Congress prohibited export of most goods. This act did more harm to New York and New England agriculture and commerce than to the other side, and was repealed.

1812: War declared against Britain. New York blockaded.

1814: Peace treaty signed at Ghent.

1825: Erie Canal opened, enhancing New York's role as a port.

1832: New York and Harlem railroad completed.

Immigration & Internationalism

1830–60: The influx of immigrants—largely German and Irish—rose to flood proportions. Epidemics of yellow fever and cholera followed, made worse by poor water supplies, lack of sanitation, and the poverty of most of the newcomers. Yet, on the eve of the Civil War, the population neared 740,000.

1861–5: Civil War, caused by growing differences between northern and southern states, notably over matters of slavery and economics.

1863: Draft Riots, following a conscription law that permitted the rich to buy deferment. New Yorkers set fire to buildings and looted shops and homes. More than 1,000 people died.

1868–98: The first waves of Italian and Eastern European immigrants arrived, many of them working on the new elevated railroad, the Brooklyn Bridge, and early skyscrapers. The Statue of Liberty, a Franco-American project, was inaugurated in 1886. At the culmination of a period of annexation and expansion, New York assumed its present boundaries. The city now had more than 3 million inhabitants, making it the world's largest city.

1900–29: Immigration continued unabated, despite growing pressure for its curtailment. The railroad system was extended, now underground as well as above. The decade after World War I brought Prohibition, women's suffrage, economic prosperity, and a federal act cutting immigration (1924).

1929–39: The Wall Street Crash and the start of the Great Depression. The worst of the depression was over by 1936, but it did not end until 1939, when the country began to prepare for war.

1941–5: Apart from rationing, blackouts, and shortages, the city itself was not greatly affected by World War II. It grew more prosperous, as did the rest of the country.

1948: Idlewild Airport opened in Queens (renamed after John F. Kennedy in 1963).

1952: United Nations headquarters complex opened.

1954: Ellis Island is closed.

1964: Original Pennsylvania Station demolished and construction of Madison Square Garden sports arenas begins.

1964–5: World's Fair in Flushing Meadow, Queens, attracts 50 million visitors within 2 years.

1968: Lincoln Center for the Performing Arts completed.

1973: World Trade Center opened.

1975–6: American Bicentennial celebration.

1989: World Financial Center opened at Battery Park City.

1990: Ellis Island transformed into a museum.

1992: The renovated Guggenheim Museum opened after a closure of almost 3 years, with a new annex.

1993: The World Trade Center bombed, killing 6 and injuring hundreds. Islamic extremists later were convicted of the terrorist act.

1994: Disney leases the New Amsterdam Theater, on 42nd St., with plans to convert it into a family-entertainment complex. The agreement is part of a long-term urban renewal project designed to clean up and revitalize seedy Times Square.

1996: The Chelsea Piers, a 30-acre sports center opens on the Hudson River waterfront.

Who's Who

One of the most cosmopolitan of cities, New York has a history rich in memorable characters. What follows is a small, but representative selection.

Allen, Woody (b. 1935).   The writer-actor-comedian-satirist-director is said to get the bends whenever he ventures beyond the city limits of New York. Nevertheless, by his own account, a Brooklyn childhood and an aborted career at New York University gave him little joy but much material for his *New Yorker* magazine essays and his many memorable movies, which include *Annie Hall, Hannah and Her Sisters,* and *Manhattan.*

Beecher, Henry Ward (1813–87).   A minister, lecturer, author, and firebrand abolitionist, he was also the older brother of Harriet Beecher Stowe, who wrote *Uncle Tom's Cabin.* His pulpit was the Plymouth Church on Orange Street, in Brooklyn Heights.

Booth, Edwin (1833–93).   Often cited as the first important American actor, Booth made his permanent home in New York. His career was blighted after his brother, John Wilkes, killed Abraham Lincoln.

Bryant, William Cullen (1794–1878).   Best known as a poet, Bryant made his living as a reform-minded editor of the *Evening Post* (1826–78). He is credited with prodding the city into the development of Central Park.

Burr, Aaron (1756–1836).   In a checkered political career that saw him lose as many elections as he won, Burr's highest position was as vice president to Thomas Jefferson. The image of Burr as an amoral schemer gained strength from his shooting of Alexander Hamilton in a duel (see below), and from the plan, attributed to him, to establish an independent republic in the southwest. He was tried for treason and acquitted, but never re-entered public life.

Dinkins, David N. (b. 1927).   The first African-American mayor of New York worked his way quietly and diligently up through the ranks of the powerful local Democratic party, finally assuming the city's highest office in 1990. He was defeated after 1 term by Rudolph Giuliani (see below), a liberal Republican.

Fulton, Robert (1765–1815).   Talented and energetic, Fulton's curiosity led him to careers in painting, gunsmithing, civil engineering, and inventing ambitious mechanical devices. Although he was not, as is widely believed, the creator of the steamboat, his *Clermont* (1807) was the first profitable version.

Giuliani, Rudolph W. (b. 1944). Elected in 1993, he was the city's first Republican mayor since John Lindsay. His pugnacious, law-and-order nature, coupled with a willingness to break party ranks in support of an issue, has made enemies, to be sure; but on the whole, he enjoys a certain grudging, bipartisan respect.

Greely, Horace (1811–72). After his arrival in New York at the age of 21, Greely worked as a printer, editor, and newspaper columnist. He founded the *New Yorker* (1834) and the *Tribune* (1841) and edited them, in various combinations, for more than 30 years. Although initially considered a conservative, he advocated women's suffrage, labor unions, experiments in communal living, and the abolition of slavery—all daring stands at that time.

Hamilton, Alexander (1755–1804). Born out of wedlock in the West Indies, Hamilton came to New York to study at King's College in 1773. His anonymous writings on behalf of the revolutionary cause drew much attention, as did his service on the battlefield and as General Washington's aide. An influential delegate to the Continental Congress at 25, he was one of the leading proponents of the Constitution drafted by Jefferson. Undeniably brilliant, he nevertheless made enemies. One of them, Aaron Burr (see above), mortally wounded him in a duel in 1804.

Henry, O. (1882–1910). The pen name of William S. Porter, a short-story writer noted for his tight plots and surprise endings, exemplified in *Gift of the Magi*. He began writing in prison, while serving time for embezzlement. Most of his literary production took place in the last 10 years of his life, spent in New York.

Hopper, Edward (1882–1973). Born in a small town on the Hudson River, Hopper moved in young adulthood to Greenwich Village. The muted, melancholy cityscapes of this realist painter began to gain favor in the 1920s, although they ran against modernist trends. In later years, his studio was at 3 Washington Square N.

Irving, Washington (1783–1859). Diplomat, biographer, satirist, and author—of *Rip Van Winkle* and the *Legend of Sleepy Hollow*, among other tales—Irving was born in New York. His estate in nearby Tarrytown is open to the public.

Koch, Edward (b. 1924).   Child of immigrant parents, Koch narrowly won election as mayor of New York in 1977. Known for speaking his mind, he established himself early on as the most popular mayor since La Guardia. He was elected to 3 terms, and although his later years in office were dogged by scandal, he managed to remain detached from it.

La Guardia, Fiorello Henry (1882–1947).   Probably the most beloved mayor in the city's history—serving from 1935 to 1945 for an until-then unprecedented 3 terms—the "Little Flower" gave luster and color to an office that had become celebrated for the flamboyance and corruptibility of its previous incumbents.

Lauder, Estee (c.1910).   The year of her birth is a secret as closely guarded as the formulas of her fragrances and skin care products. Born in Queens of Hungarian-Jewish descent, the undisputed queen of the beauty industry built a multibillion-dollar empire with her late husband, Joseph, that now commands roughly 40% of the US department store cosmetics market.

Millay, Edna St. Vincent (1892–1950).   The poet was a leader of the Greenwich Village bohemian group that founded the Provincetown Players.

Minuit, Peter (1580–1638).   The famous $24 purchase of Manhattan was negotiated by Minuit, who then was appointed Director General (1626–31) of the new colony by the Dutch West India Company.

Morgan, John Pierpont (1837–1913).   Beginning with the fortune accumulated by his father, J. P. built a financial empire that is said to have exceeded even that of the first Rockefeller. Along the way, he bought out industrialists Andrew Carnegie and Henry Frick. All three of them spent their declining years in New York, where they engaged in a variety of good works and acts of philanthropy, thereby forming New York's strong cultural foundation.

Morse, Samuel F. B. (1791–1872).   While a member of the faculty at New York University, Morse perfected his telegraph device and the code to be used with it. A demonstration was given at Castle Clinton in 1842. Morse was also a pioneer in the development of photography.

Olmsted, Frederick Law (1822–1903).   Travel writer and prolific landscape architect in the United States and Canada, Olmsted designed Central Park,

Prospect Park (Brooklyn), and Riverside Park, all in collaboration with Calvert Vaux.

O'Neill Eugene (1888–1953).   The work of the playwright who fashioned *The Iceman Cometh* and *Mourning Becomes Electra* is the standard against which all American dramatists must be measured. One of his finest plays, *Long Day's Journey into Night,* was discovered among his papers after his death. O'Neill was awarded the Nobel prize in 1936.

Parker, Dorothy (1893–1967).   Renowned for the razor-sharp wit she directed as readily at herself as at others, Parker employed that gift in verse, plays, movies, essays, and short stories. Much of her work appeared in the *New Yorker* magazine.

Perelman, S. J. (1904–79).   Brooklyn-born Perelman wrote for the *New Yorker* magazine from 1934 almost until his death. Essentially a humorist and satirist, his interests focused on the inanities of advertising and Hollywood. He also wrote movie scripts and plays in the 1930s and 1940s often in association with such luminaries as the Marx Brothers, Ogden Nash, and George S. Kaufman.

Poe, Edgar Allan (1809–49).   Poe moved to New York with his child bride in 1844. Their cottage in the Fordham section of the Bronx is now a museum. He achieved recognition for his poetry with "The Raven," which led to fame for such mystery stories as "The Gold Bug" and "The Murders in the Rue Morgue."

Pollack, Jackson (1912–56).   Although contemporaries were working in similar directions, the seminal work of this innovative artist heralded the explosion of postwar creativity known as the New York School.

Porter, Cole (1893–1964).   The enduring sophistication of Porter's lyrics is remarkable. He penned words and music of more than 400 songs, for such musicals as *Can-Can, Silk Stockings* and *Kiss Me Kate.*

Pulitzer, Joseph (1847–1911).   Hungarian-born Pulitzer immigrated to the United States in 1864 and became a journalist, editor, and publisher in short order. He bought the *New York World* in 1883, and in competition with William Randolf Hearst permitted it to plummet to the nadir of yellow journalism. After the Spanish-American War (1898), his newspapers altered course to become relatively dignified. His will

bequeathed money for the establishment of the
Columbia University School of Journalism, and his
name today is most associated with the annual prizes
so coveted by journalists.

Rauschenberg, Robert (b. 1925).   Rauschenberg
first attracted attention with an exhibition of entirely
black canvases, but then moved on to "combine-
paintings"—assemblages of pigment, collage, and such
3-dimensional objects as stuffed goats and rubber tires.
Born in Texas, he is nonetheless an exemplar of the
New York School of painting.

Rockefeller, John D. Jr. (1874–1960).   The son of
the incalculably wealthy oil magnate and financier was
granted control of his father's assets at the age of 37.
To a large extent, the estate involved philanthropic
activities, many of which benefited New York. Among
the projects he inspired or helped underwrite were
Riverside Church, the Cloisters of the Metropolitan
Museum of Art, and Rockefeller Center.

Rockefeller, Nelson Alrich (1908–79).   After able
participation in both Democrat and Republican federal administrations during World War II and after,
Nelson defeated W. Averell Harriman for the gover-
norship of the state of New York in 1958. His subsequent bids for the Republican presidential nomination
were unsuccessful, but he was re-elected governor
3 times and was appointed vice president for the brief
term of Gerald Ford (1974–7). He made substantial
contributions to New York's cultural and educational
institutions, as did his siblings.

Roosevelt, Theodore (1858–1919).   The 28th president passed the first 15 years of his extraordinarily
active life at 28 E. 20th St., near Gramercy Park. Hunter
and environmentalist, rancher and author, statesman and
chauvinist, peacemaker and militarist, explorer and
politician, he pursued these contradictory interests
vigorously until his death.

Runyon, Damon (1884–1946).   Born in Manhattan (the one in Kansas), this popular journalist came to
New York, where he quickly mastered the patois of the
criminal fringe and transferred that knowledge to a long
string of evocative and humorous short stories, which
provided the basis of the hit musical *Guys and Dolls*.

Ruth, George Herman (1895–1948).   A near-
legendary athlete, "Babe" Ruth played for the New

York Yankees from 1920 to 1935. Most of his pitching and batting records were unchallenged for decades, and some still stand.

Stuyvesant, Peter (1610–72). A harshly autocratic man intolerant of religious and political dissent, this Director General of New Amsterdam held power from 1647 to 1664. In 1664 he surrendered the colony to an English naval force and retired to his farm, near the present Lower East Side.

Tweed, William Marcy (1823–78). The undisputed leader of Tammany Hall, which controlled the city and state Democratic party, "Boss" Tweed ruled the city from 1857 until the early 1870s. He died in prison, having defrauded taxpayers and contractors of unaccounted millions in bribes, kickbacks, and related schemes.

Warhol, Andy (c.1930–1986). No one is certain when he was born (about 1930), or where (probably Philadelphia), but there is no question of his primacy in the Pop Art movement of the 1960s. Through repeated prints of commonplace objects—cows, soup cans, movie stars—he endeavored to elevate the mundane and overexposed into subjects worthy of serious consideration. He went on to found a "factory" that produced films of elusive intent, and *Interview,* a magazine of celebrity interviews.

White, Stanford (1853–1906). As the most celebrated partner of the architectural firm of McKim, Mead & White, he probably received more credit than his due for their collective achievements. Many of their buildings have been lost, but a rich heritage remains, including Washington Arch, the Villard Houses (pictured on page 165), the portico of St. Bartholomew's Church, 3 buildings at Columbia University, and 3 more at the former Bronx campus of New York University. White had a hand in all of these.

Whitman, Walt (1819–92). The innovative free verse of *Leaves of Grass* drew mostly negative reaction on its first appearance in 1855, but many 20thC scholars regard Whitman as America's finest poet.

Wolfe, Thomas Clayton (1900–38). The haunted author of *Look Homeward Angel* and *You Can't Go Home Again* joined the English faculty at New York University in 1924 and spent most of the last years of his life in the city.

Art & Architecture
Art

Creativity found a foothold as soon as the city emerged from the early settlement period. The first theater opened its doors on Maiden Lane in 1732, to be followed by dozens more. But New York was chiefly a commercial center, and artists who achieved prominence—painters Benjamin West and John Singleton Copley, for example—went off to Europe, setting a pattern that was to prevail for nearly 2 centuries.

Impressionism and the other "isms" that reverberated around Europe in the later 19thC had little influence across the Atlantic. The aesthetic ferment did not spill over to the United States until the New York Armory Show of 1913, when Duchamp's *Nude Descending a Staircase* scandalized public opinion. By then, however, most of the artists who were to form the first generation of post–World War II Radical Abstractionists were already alive. Encouraged by such artist-teachers as Hans Hofmann, who fled the festering European tragedy in the 1930s, these artists toiled under the restraints of the depression and war, exploding after 1945, into what seemed to be a movement already mature at the instant of birth.

The controlled "splash and dribble" canvases of Jackson Pollock were no less shocking than the earlier cubist fantasies, which now seemed sedate by comparison. Pollock died young, but compatriots Robert Motherwell, Clyfford Still, Mark Rothko, Willem de Kooning, Philip Guston, James Brooks, Jack Tworkov, Franz Kline, and Sam Francis all contributed to the importance of the abstract expressionist movement. All were associated with the city, and together they became known as the New York School. They gathered in the same bars, summered on Long Island, and inspired a new row of galleries along East 10th Street. It was a zesty era, enhanced, not inhibited, by its coexistence with the conformist Eisenhower-McCarthy period.

New York, which had long regarded itself as an oasis on the edge of a cultural wasteland, was the natural wellspring of what proved to be a surge to international preeminence in the arts. As the only major city to emerge unscathed from the global conflict of 1939 to 1945, it could indulge its artists with almost unlimited support. The Guggenheim Museum, Frank Lloyd Wright's only commission in the city (illustrated on page 136), was intended to serve as a repository for modern painting and sculpture. It was completed in 1959.

The Lincoln Center for the Performing Arts was conceived in 1955, and its 5 principal buildings were finished between 1962 and 1966. Additions to the Metropolitan Museum and the Museum of Modern Art, and the erection of a new home for the Whitney Museum of American Art, maintained the pace.

During the last couple of decades, creative endeavor in the visual arts has been highly experimental: conceptual, minimal, neo-Constructivist, Optical—all executed in wildly mixed media: neon, ferroconcrete, forged metal, shaped canvas, boxes, and heaps of earth. The descendants of Jackson Pollack are as unrestrained as he was, and every bit as provocative.

> **Art, like life, should be free, since both are experimental.**
>
> —*George Santayana*

Architecture

As in all matters, the architecture of New York both dismays and exalts, often in ways unexpected by those who have never walked these streets. The city has been a laboratory of sorts, giving succor to native-born architects and drawing virtually every major American architect of the last century into its thrall, at least for a commission or two. Few tycoons and corporations have been able to resist the temptation to erect monuments to themselves. From Carnegie to Morgan to Woolworth to Chrysler, they have enriched the city nearly as often as they have blighted it. No easy feat, that, given the impulse to make salable space out of every expensive cubic foot of ground and air.

Shelter was the first requirement of those who colonized Manhattan on behalf of Dutch traders. The Great Fires of 1776 and 1835 destroyed every last dwelling built in the 17thC. However, if the existing structures of the following century in New York were to be grouped together, they would constitute a sizable and quite handsome village. As it is, the buildings are scattered through the city, largely neglected survivors of the conflagrations. Most are made of wood, in the Georgian or Federal styles inspired by those that were prevalent in England during the successive reigns of the 4 Georges.

Although the Georgian style was itself imitative of classical Greco-Roman themes, the first half of the

19thC saw a heightened enthusiasm for Greek and Gothic Revival. These overlapping modes dominated from 1830 to 1855, manifest in the Athenian "temple" that is the **Federal Hall National Memorial** (1842), perhaps the purest example of Greek Revival architecture in New York, and that tribute to medieval workmanship, **Trinity Church** (1846). A landmark at the end of Wall Street, Richard Upjohn's church is the city's best known example of Gothic Revivalism. In the attached town houses that became increasingly popular at this time, Greek Revival was largely confined to decorative facades.

After the Civil War, an enthusiasm for European styles took hold. Motifs ranged from Venetian Renaissance to French Second Empire to Tudor to Romanesque, not infrequently all on the same building. The result was often called "Kitchen Sink." The fashionable architectural firm of the time was McKim, Mead & White, whose fondness for the Italian Renaissance is best seen in the **Villard Houses** (1886).

Technology prompted fresh looks at old design assumptions. **The Brooklyn Bridge** (1883) employed Gothic granite towers, but also spidery cables of woven steel. No longer limited by the weight of masonry, and able to use steel and reinforced concrete, architects capitalized on the presence of a sturdy bedrock known as "Manhattan schist." Skyscrapers rapidly became a reality. Fortunately, the hydraulic elevator was invented at the same time. By 1900, commercial buildings of 20 floors and higher were routine.

At first, architectural styles changed remarkably little, despite the new horizons that had been opened up by the introduction of caisson (steel pile) foundations. The **Flatiron Building** (1902), although constructed around a steel frame, was decked out with cornices reminiscent of the Florentine Renaissance style. **The Woolworth Building** (1913) has all the detail of a Gothic cathedral complete with gargoyles.

Row houses persisted as the favored residential mode, but they were now embellished with Italianate carving around arched doors and pediments. The wide use of red sandstone as a facing material gave this style the generic name *brownstone*. Blocks of brownstones remain throughout Manhattan and Brooklyn, lending a Parisian flavor to such neighborhoods as the West Village and Brooklyn Heights..

Luxury high-rise apartments made their appearances with the **Chelsea** and the **Dakota** (see "Sights and

Attractions") in 1884, but the wealthy resisted that innovation for decades. The turn of the century brought a flirtation with the voluptuous Beaux-Arts style and the related neochâteau fancies, which is best demonstrated in the **Metropolitan Museum of Art** (1902) and the **New York Public Library** on 5th Avenue.

A measure of reason prevailed in 1916, when newly formulated zoning laws created a regulation for the height of buildings in relation to the width of the street below. One side effect of this was the development of buildings that were tiered, and a number of "wedding cakes" emerged.

Meanwhile, commercial architecture was entering the modernist phase with the form-follows-function theories of Louis Sullivan, who proved to his successors that tall structures need not simulate stacked neo-Georgian or Romanesque tiers. Sullivan, sometimes described as the father of the skyscraper, was associated primarily with Chicago, and had only one commission in New York, the **Bayard Building** on Bleecker Street in Greenwich Village.

The next major influence was Art Deco, applied to spectacular effect in the steel arched tower of the **Chrysler Building** (1930), the world's tallest building until it was overtaken by the **Empire State Building** (1931). With the Empire State and the RCA Building (built in 1932 and now renamed the **GE Building**), the Chrysler is the apogee of the first phase of the skyscraper phenomenon. Many feel this period in New York's architecture has never been surpassed.

Further developments were delayed until the peacetime economic recovery of the late 1940s. Then a technique was developed in which walls of glass without a weight-bearing function were hung on the sides of steel skeletons. Among the first and most enduring realizations of this International Style were **Lever House** (1952) and the **Seagram Building** (1958).

More recently, sculptural planes and masses have shaped both small and large buildings, such as the **Whitney Museum** (1966) and the **Waterside Houses** (1974). Those departures from the austerities of Bauhaus convention prompted the emergence of the so-called postmodernist style. The label is misleading, at least to the degree that it suggests a new evolutionary stage beyond the modernism of Walter Gropius and Ludwig Mies van der Rohe.

On the contrary, the postmodernist trend of the 1980s in many ways represents a look back, a revival in decorative interest and borrowings from past eras as with the "Chippendale" cornice of Philip Johnson's **AT&T Building** (sold to the Sony firm in 1991).

A more successful product of this enthusiasm is the block-long **Equitable Center,** designed by Edward Larrabee Barnes and built from granite, limestone, and glass. About as tall as the AT & T Building, it manages not to loom quite as much.

On nearby Times Square, 2 hotels have taken a playful attitude, in keeping with the fun-seeking tone of the area. **The Holiday Inn Crowne Plaza** and **Embassy Suites** look like huge gaudy jukeboxes, striped with primary colors and neon. Their builders were required to do this, as ongoing testament to the hub's status as the animated Great White Way. If residents and visitors are fortunate, this riotously eyefilling subcategory of postmodernism will be confined to that gaudy venue.

> **New York is Gershwin's "Rhapsody in Blue"** . . . **Majestic, hot, spicy, vulgar, stately, exquisite and overwhelming.** . . .
> —*Marilyn Michaels, actress and*
> *impressionist*

INDEX

296 **Index**

NEW YORK

1-6 New York Street Atlas
7 Manhattan Subways

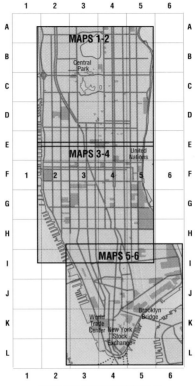

KEY TO MAP SYMBOLS

City Maps

Major Place of Interest	P Parking
Park	← One-way Street
Built-up Area	⋯⋯ Ferry
Military/Airport	■ Point of Interest

0   .25 Mile
0   .25 Kilometer

8 Adjoining Page No.

Metro Area

ROADS

- ═══ Freeway
- ═══ Tollway
- ▪▪▪ Road under construction
- ═══ Other divided highway
- ═══ Primary road
- ═══ Secondary road
- ═══ Other road

CITY

- New York City
- Other City
- Park
- Marsh
- Military/Airport
- ■ Point of Interest

0   1   2 miles
0   1   2 Kilometers

3

1 2

E

F

F

G

G

H

H

I

W 50TH ST
W 49TH ST
W 48TH ST
W 47TH ST
W 46TH ST
W 45TH ST
W 44TH ST
W 43RD ST
W 42ND ST
W 41ST ST
W 40TH ST
W 37TH ST
W 36TH ST
W 35TH ST
W 34TH ST
W 33RD ST
W 32ND ST
W 30TH ST
W 29TH ST
W 28TH ST
W 27TH ST
W 26TH ST
W 25TH ST
W 24TH ST
W 23RD ST
W 22ND ST
W 21ST ST
W 20TH ST
W 19TH ST
W 18TH ST
W 17TH ST
W 16TH ST
W 15TH ST
W 14TH ST
W 13TH ST
LITTLE W 12TH ST
GANSEVOORT ST
HORATIO ST
JANE ST
W 12TH ST
BETHUNE ST

50TH ST
W 49TH ST
W 48TH ST
W 47TH ST
W 46TH ST
W 45TH ST
W 44TH ST
W 43RD ST
W 42ND ST
W 41ST ST
W 40TH ST
W 39TH ST
W 38TH ST
W 37TH ST
W 36TH ST
W 35TH ST
W 34TH ST
W 31ST ST

W 33RD
W 31S
W 30
W 29
W 27
W 25
W 24

W 23RD

W 49TH S
W 48TH S
W 47TH S
W 46TH ST
W 45TH ST
W 44TH S

ELEVENTH AVENUE
TENTH AVENUE
NINTH AVENUE
EIGHTH AVENUE
SEVENTH AVENUE
BROADWAY
TWELFTH AVENUE

Times
Square

Port Authority
Bus Terminal

Jacob Javitz
Convention
Center

GARMENT
DISTRICT

General
Post Office

Pennsylvania
Station

Madison
Square
Garden

Penn Station
South Houses

Chelsea
Park
Elliot
Houses

Robert
Fulton
Houses

63
62
61
60
59
58
57
56
54
53
52
51
50
49
48
46

Hudson River

JACKSON
SQ
GREENWICH
GREENWICH AV
BLEECKER ST
GREENWIC
VILLAGE

ABINGDON
SQ

W 11TH
BANK ST
PERRY ST
CHARLES ST
W 10TH
CHRISTOPHER ST
BARROW ST

WEST ST
WASHINGTON ST
BEDFORD ST
GROVE ST
COMMERCE

WAVERLY
SEVENTH AVENUE
WASHIN

1 2 3

5

2 3

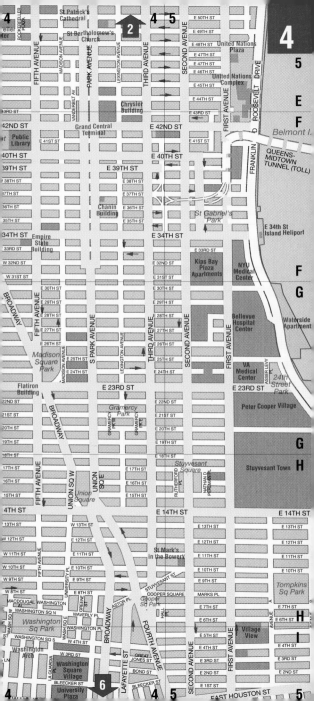